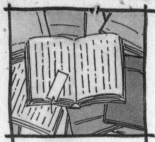

岸本斉史

Recently, the people around me tell me they have been reading books. I rarely read books, so I'm thinking about picking one up for the first time in a while. I'm considering either a mystery or a fantasy work.

—*Masashi Kishimoto, 2006*

Author/artist Masashi Kishimoto was born in 1974 in rural Okayama Prefecture, Japan. After spending time in art college, he won the Hop Step Award for new manga artists with his manga **Karakuri** (Mechanism). Kishimoto decided to base his next story on traditional Japanese culture. His first version of **Naruto**, drawn in 1997, was a one-shot story about fox spirits; his final version, which debuted in **Weekly Shonen Jump** in 1999, quickly became the most popular ninja manga in Japan.

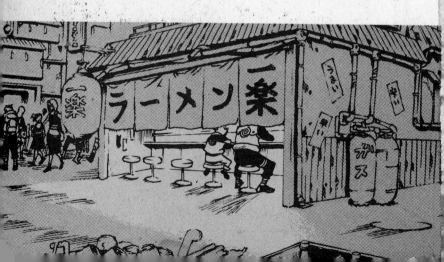

NARUTO VOL. 34
The SHONEN JUMP Manga Edition

This graphic novel contains material that was originally published in
English in **SHONEN JUMP** # 73-74. Artwork in the magazine may
have been slightly altered from that presented here.

STORY AND ART BY MASASHI KISHIMOTO

Translation/Mari Morimoto
English Adaptation/Deric A. Hughes & Benjamin Raab
Touch-up Art & Lettering/Gia Cam Luc
Design/Sean Lee
Editor/Joel Enos

Editor in Chief, Books/Alvin Lu
Editor in Chief, Magazines/Marc Weidenbaum
VP, Publishing Licensing/Rika Inouye
VP, Sales & Product Marketing/Gonzalo Ferreyra
VP, Creative/Linda Espinosa
Publisher/Hyoe Narita

Printed in the U.S.A.

Published by VIZ Media, LLC
P.O. Box 77010
San Francisco, CA 94107

SHONEN JUMP Manga Edition
10 9 8 7 6 5 4 3 2 1
First printing, February 2009

PARENTAL ADVISORY
NARUTO is rated T for Teen and is recommended
for ages 13 and up. This volume contains realistic
and fantasy violence.
ratings.viz.com

www.viz.com

THE WORLD'S
MOST POPULAR MANGA

SHONEN JUMP
www.shonenjump.com

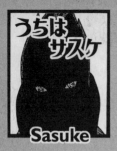

うちはサスケ
Sasuke
綱手
Tsunade
サイ
Sai
薬師カブト
Kabuto
大蛇丸
Orochimaru
ヤマト
Yamato

The Story So Far...

With the aftershocks of *Operation: Destroy Konoha* still reverberating throughout their elite shinobi corps, the new Team Kakashi, under the substitute leadership of Captain Yamato, and joined by the enigmatic, emotionless Sai, sets out on a mission to rescue Sasuke from Orochimaru.

But their mission is soon jeopardized. First, by Orochimaru and his henchman, Kabuto...Then, by Naruto himself as he succumbs to the power of the Nine-Tailed Fox demon hidden inside him and goes on a rampage...And finally by Sai who is secretly working for Danzo, leader of the military organization The Foundation.

But with Sai's private picture book now in their possession, Naruto, Sakura and Yamato regroup in an attempt to unravel the secrets of Sai's *real* mission...

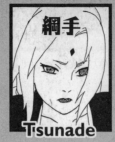

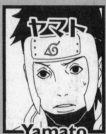

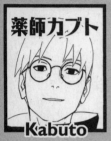

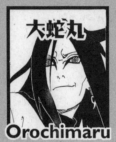

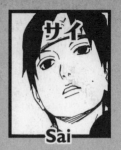

NARUTO

VOL. 34
THE REUNION

CONTENTS

Number 300: Sai's Picture Book!!

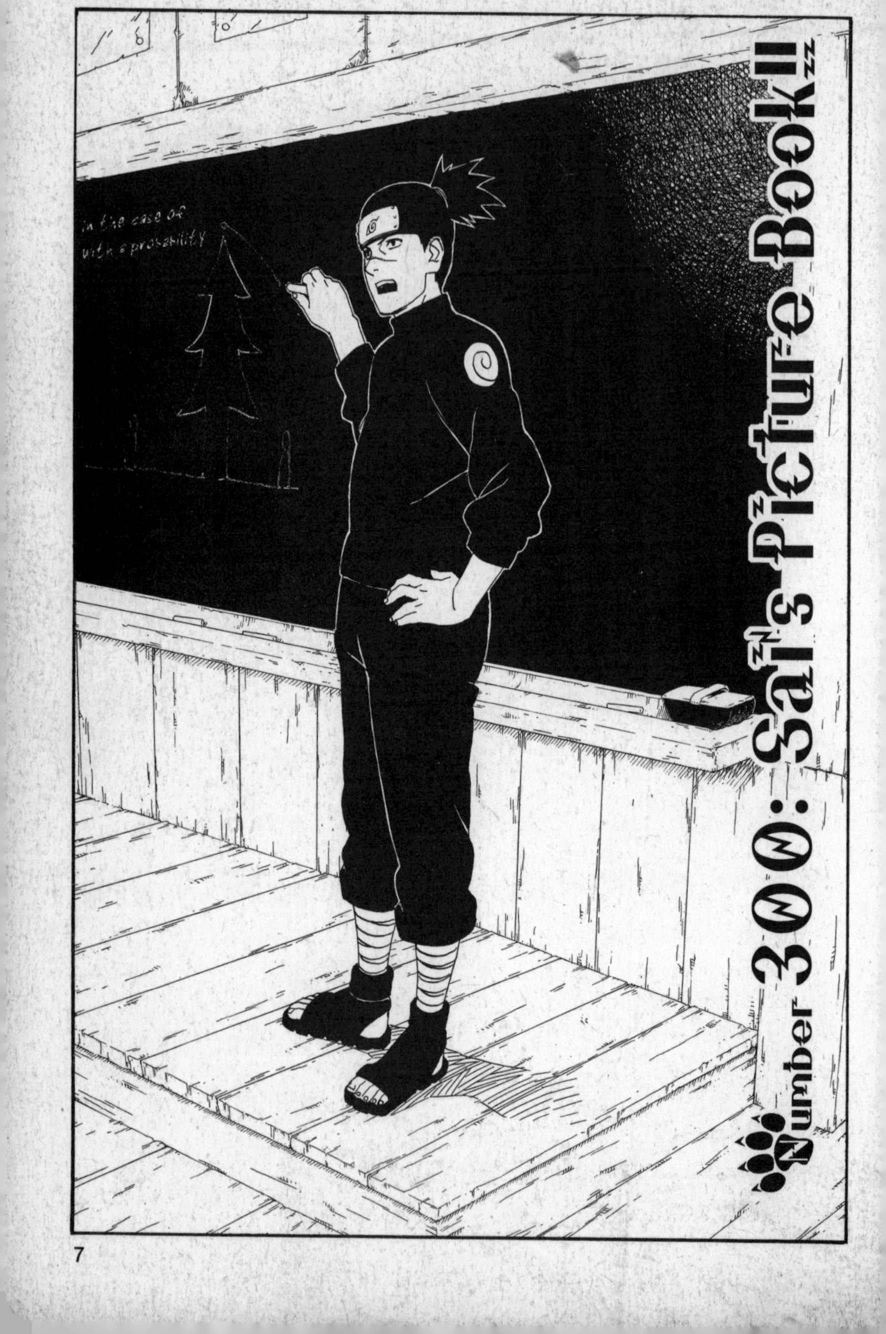
in the case of
with a probability

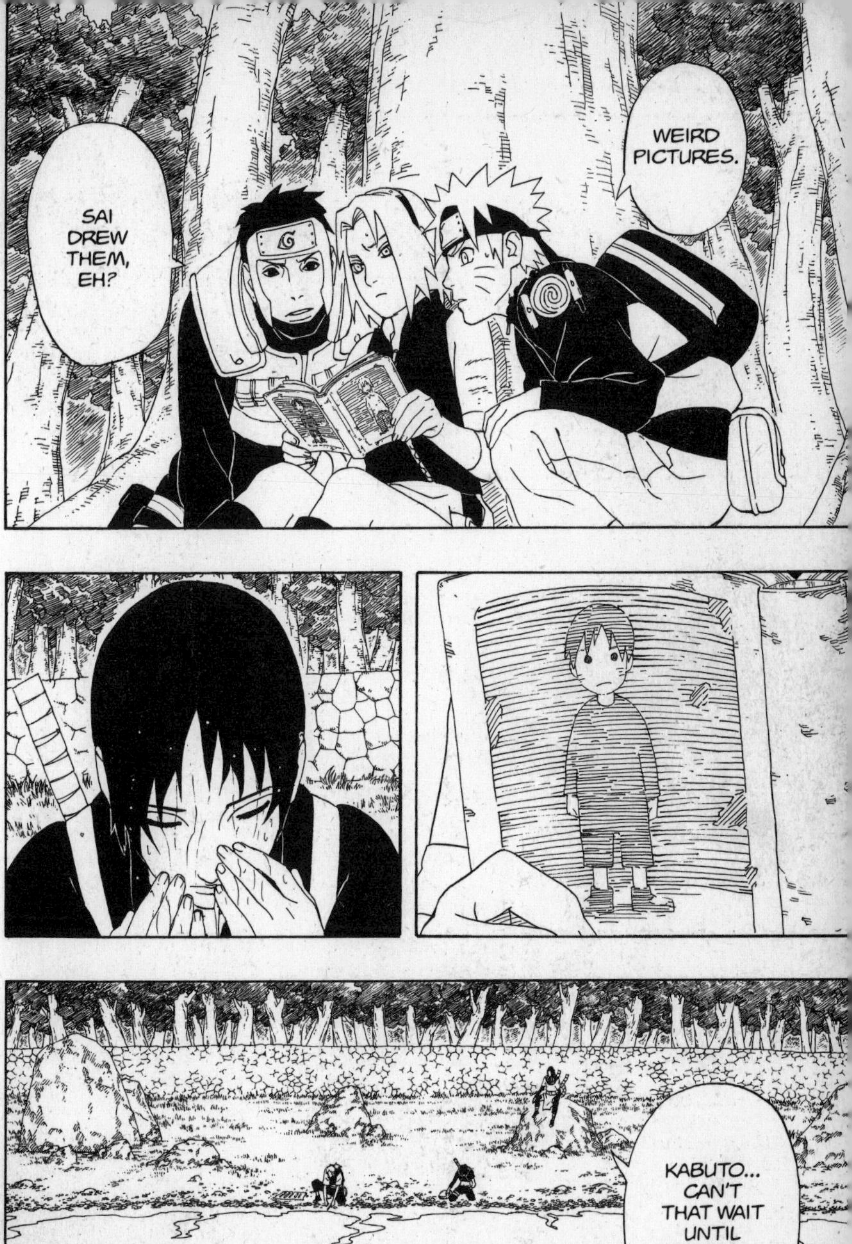
WEIRD PICTURES.
SAI DREW THEM, EH?
KABUTO... CAN'T THAT WAIT UNTIL WE GET HOME?

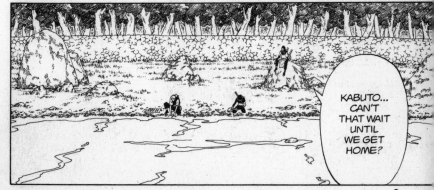

READ THIS WAY

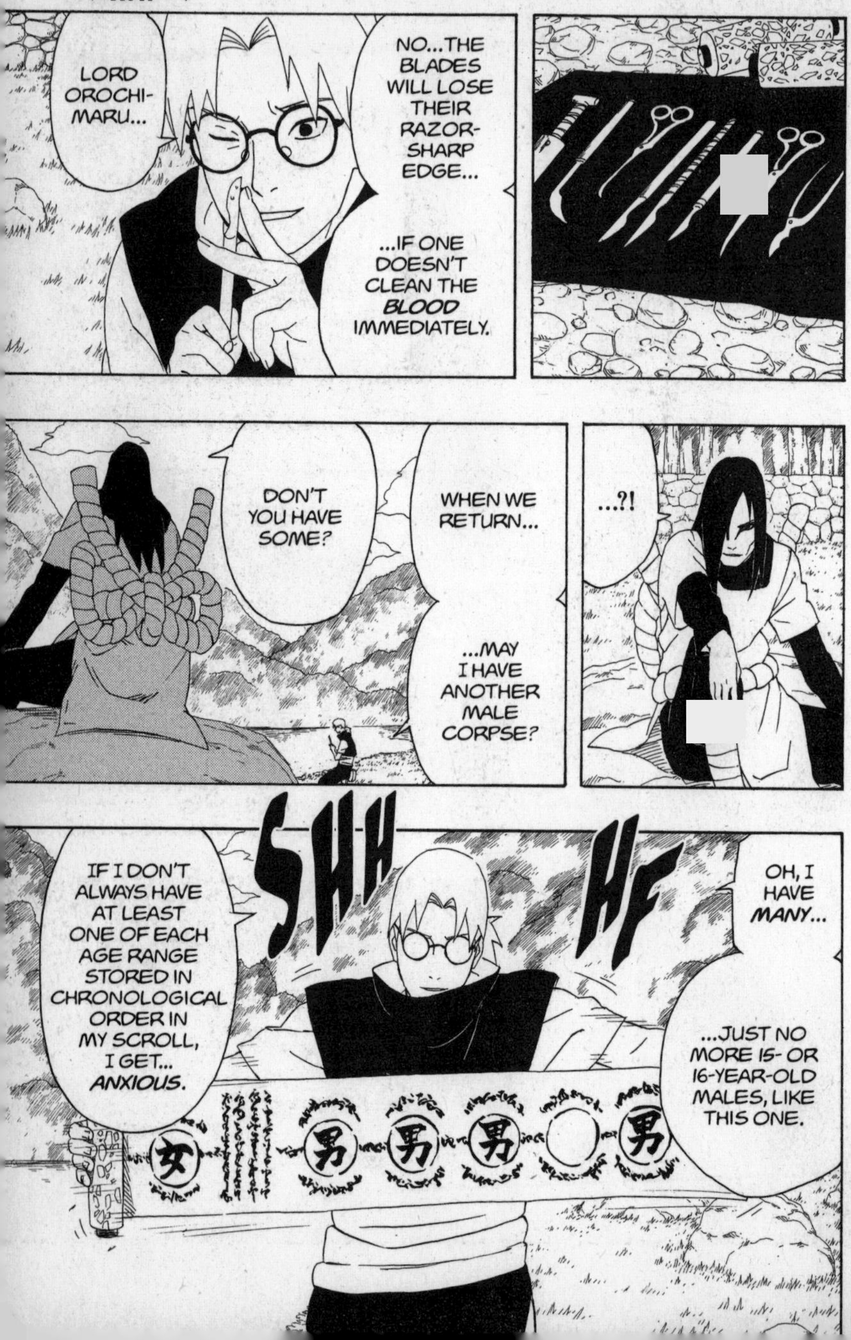
NO...THE BLADES WILL LOSE THEIR RAZOR-SHARP EDGE...
...IF ONE DOESN'T CLEAN THE BLOOD IMMEDIATELY.
LORD OROCHI-MARU...
...?!
WHEN WE RETURN...
...MAY I HAVE ANOTHER MALE CORPSE?
DON'T YOU HAVE SOME?
SHHHF
OH, I HAVE MANY...
...JUST NO MORE 15- OR 16-YEAR-OLD MALES, LIKE THIS ONE.
IF I DON'T ALWAYS HAVE AT LEAST ONE OF EACH AGE RANGE STORED IN CHRONOLOGICAL ORDER IN MY SCROLL, I GET... ANXIOUS.
女
男
男
男
男

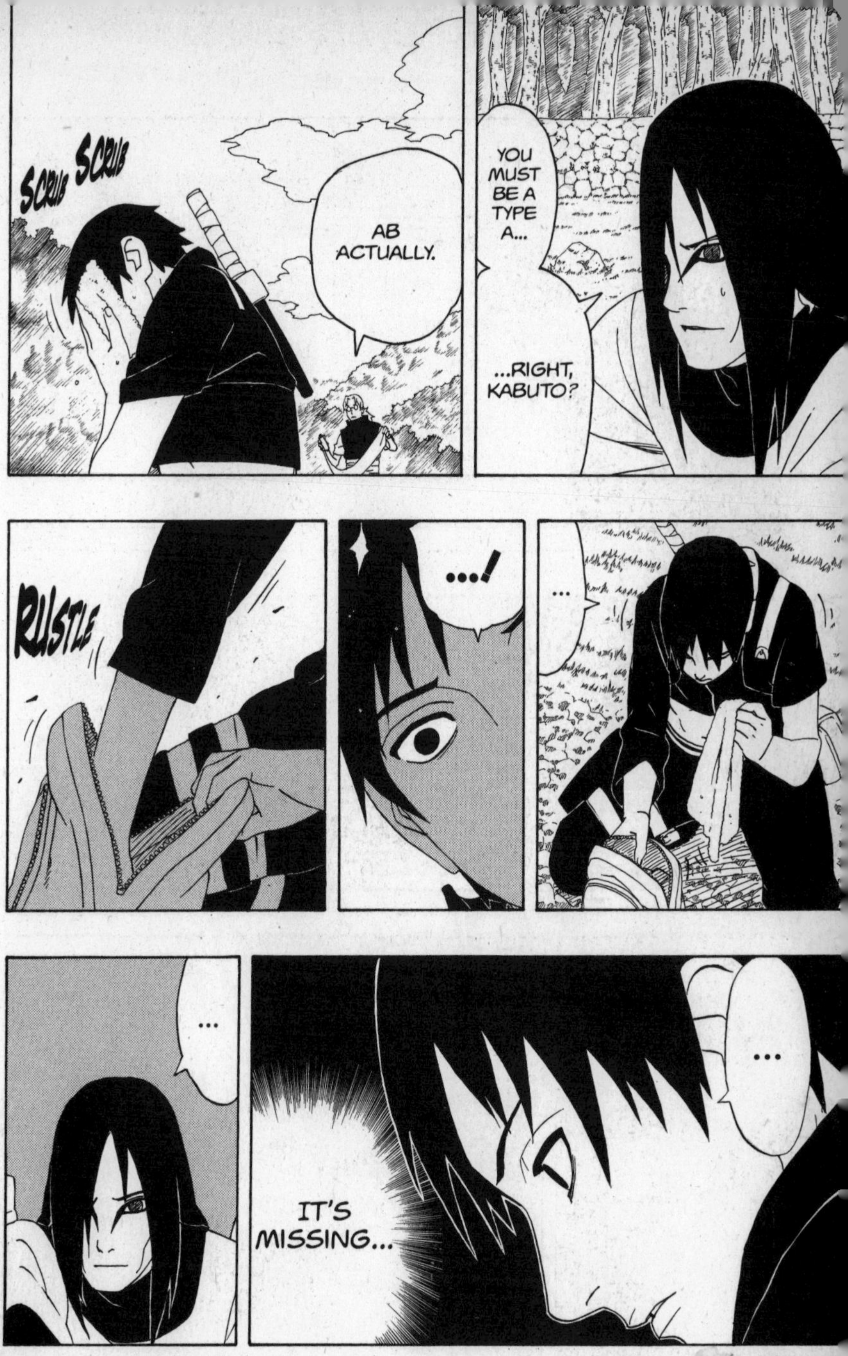
YOU MUST BE A TYPE A...
...RIGHT, KABUTO?
AB ACTUALLY.
SCRUB SCRUB
...
...!
RUSTLE
...
IT'S MISSING...
...

READ THIS WAY

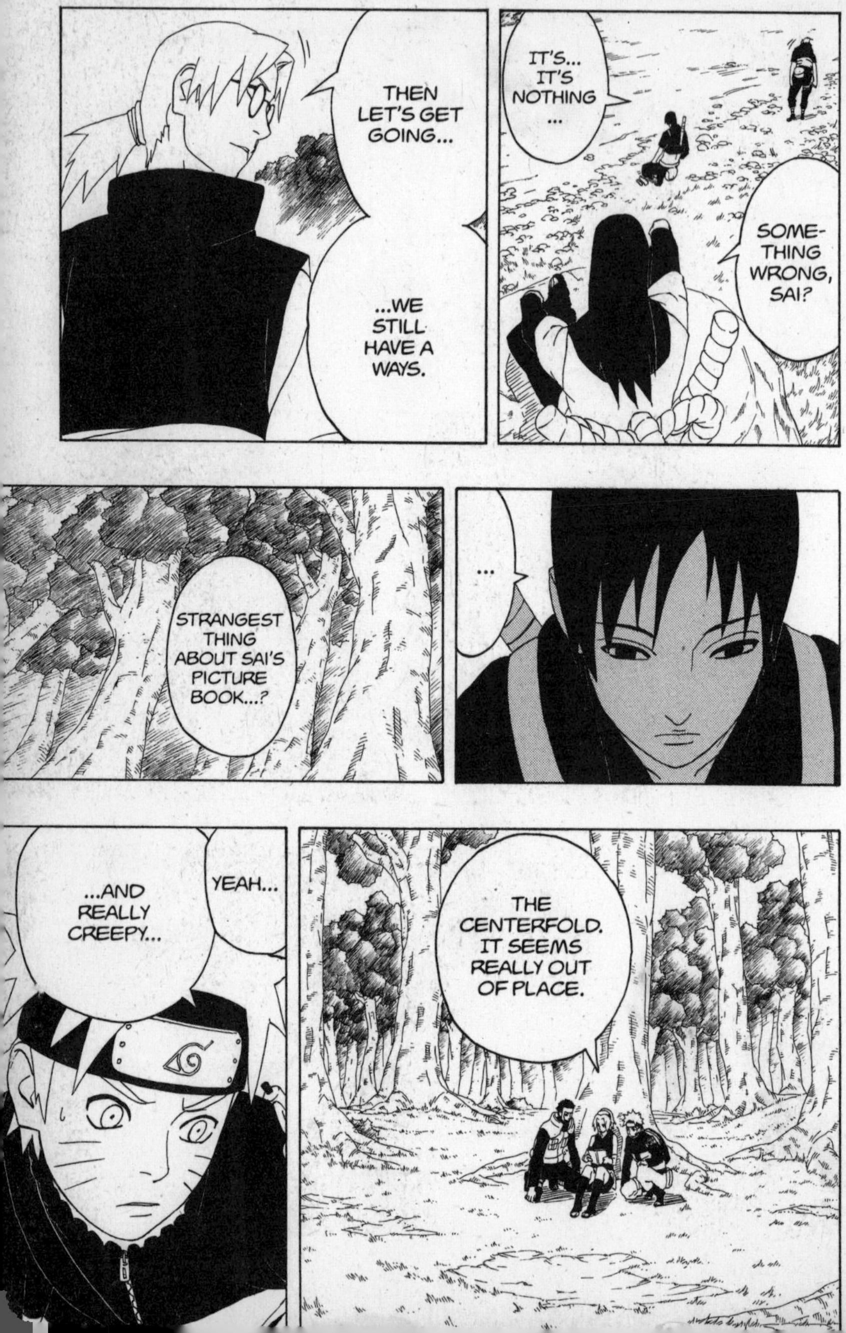
SOME-
THING
WRONG,
SAI?
IT'S...
IT'S
NOTHING
...
THEN
LET'S GET
GOING...
...WE
STILL
HAVE A
WAYS.
...
STRANGEST
THING
ABOUT SAI'S
PICTURE
BOOK...?
THE
CENTERFOLD.
IT SEEMS
REALLY OUT
OF PLACE.
YEAH...
...AND
REALLY
CREEPY...

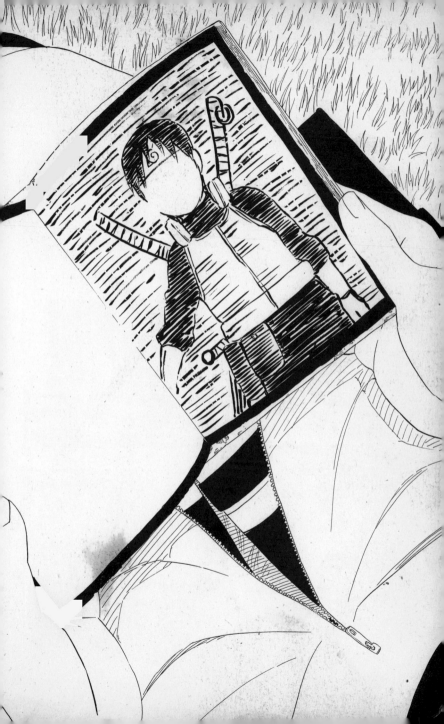

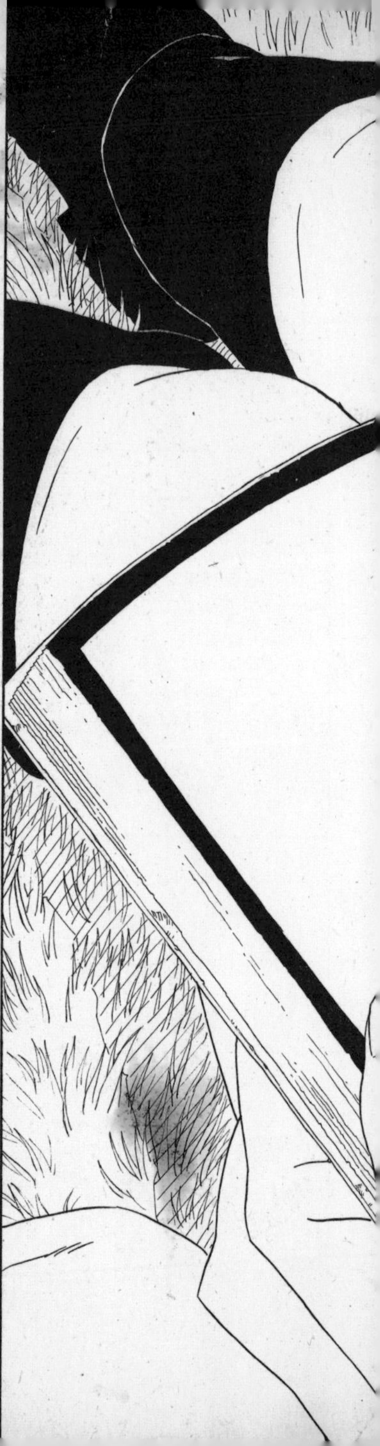

READ THIS WAY

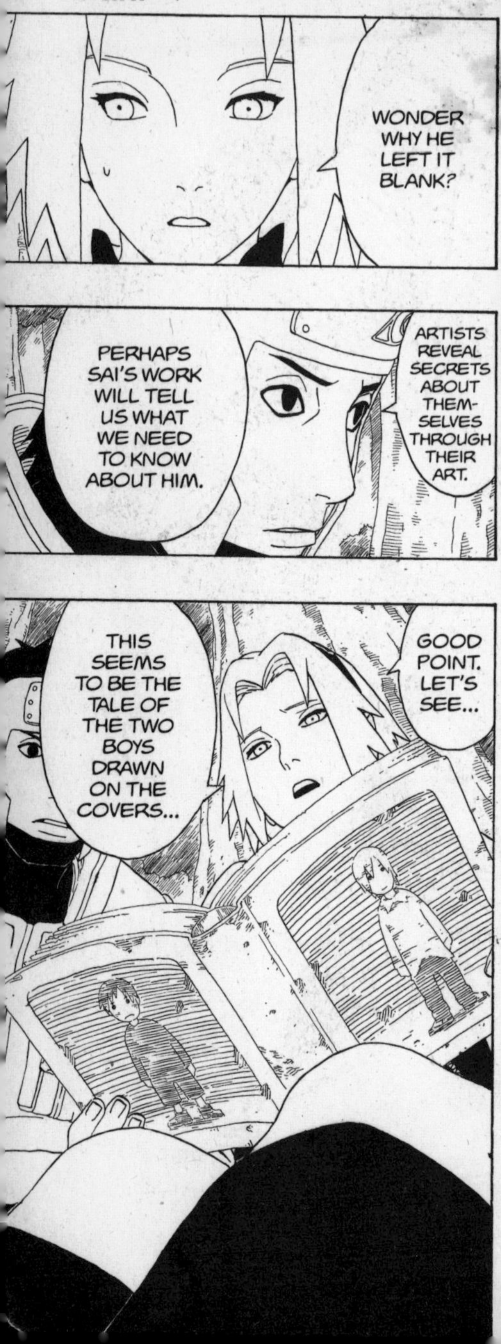
WONDER WHY HE LEFT IT BLANK?
ARTISTS REVEAL SECRETS ABOUT THEMSELVES THROUGH THEIR ART.
PERHAPS SAI'S WORK WILL TELL US WHAT WE NEED TO KNOW ABOUT HIM.
GOOD POINT. LET'S SEE...
THIS SEEMS TO BE THE TALE OF THE TWO BOYS DRAWN ON THE COVERS...

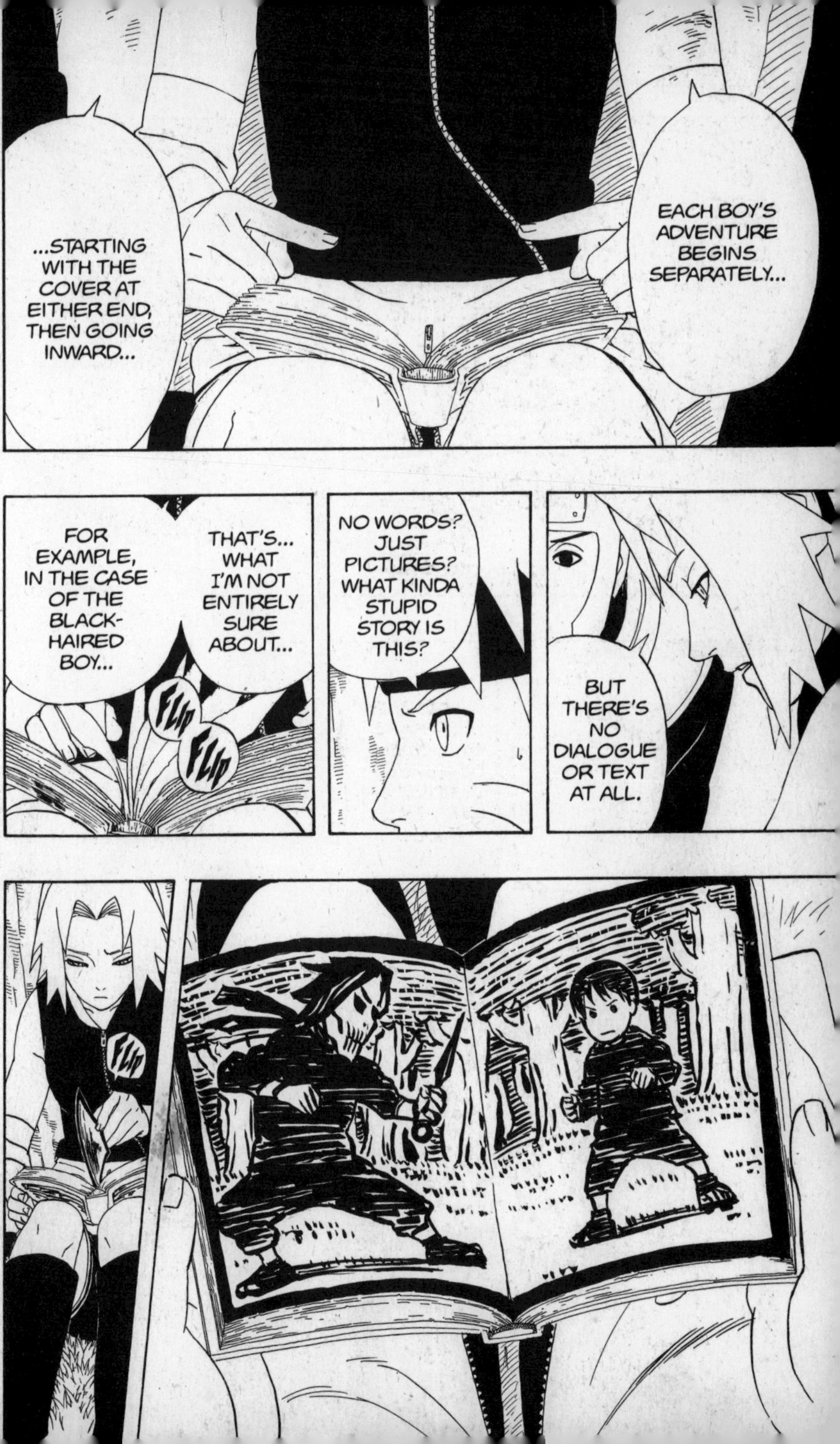
EACH BOY'S ADVENTURE BEGINS SEPARATELY...
...STARTING WITH THE COVER AT EITHER END, THEN GOING INWARD...
BUT THERE'S NO DIALOGUE OR TEXT AT ALL.
NO WORDS? JUST PICTURES? WHAT KINDA STUPID STORY IS THIS?
THAT'S... WHAT I'M NOT ENTIRELY SURE ABOUT...
FOR EXAMPLE, IN THE CASE OF THE BLACK-HAIRED BOY...
FLIP
FLIP
FLIP

READ THIS WAY

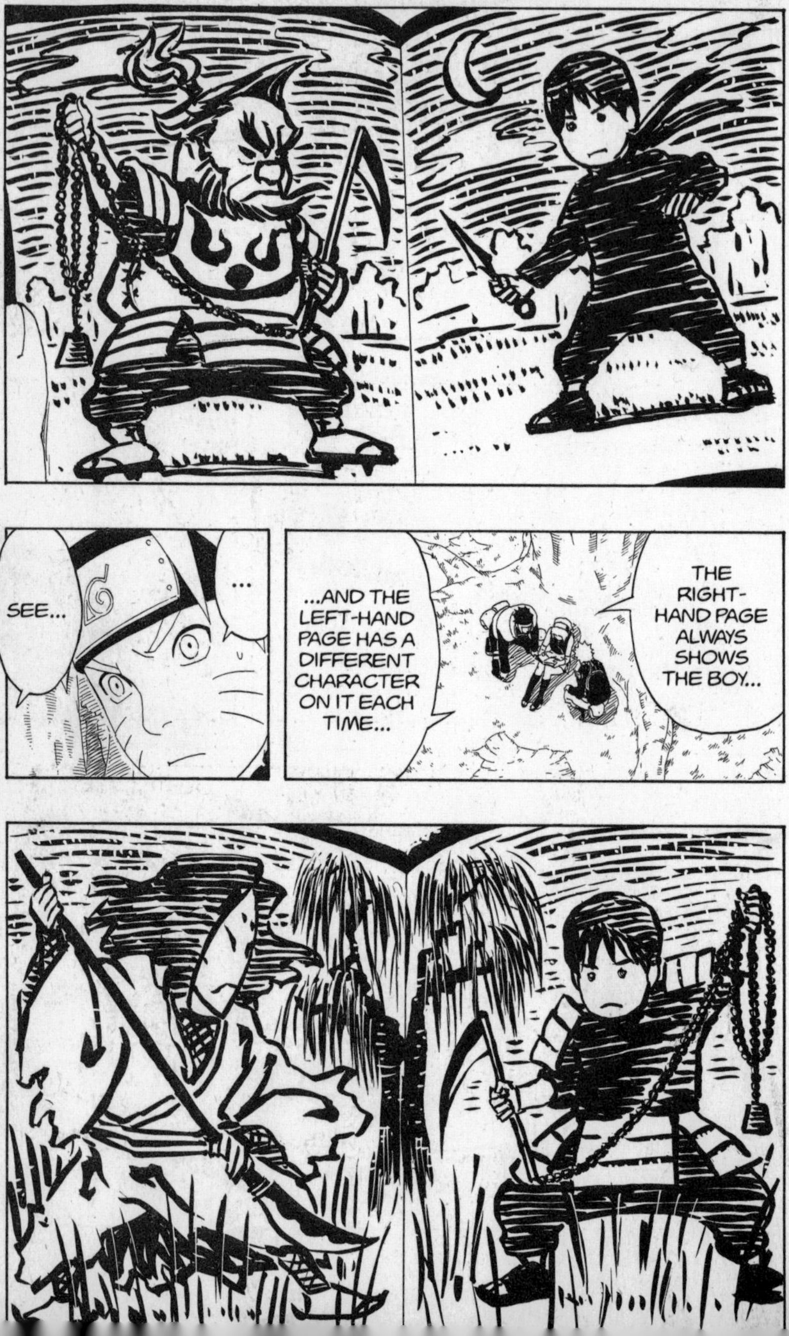
THE RIGHT-HAND PAGE ALWAYS SHOWS THE BOY...
...AND THE LEFT-HAND PAGE HAS A DIFFERENT CHARACTER ON IT EACH TIME...
...
SEE...

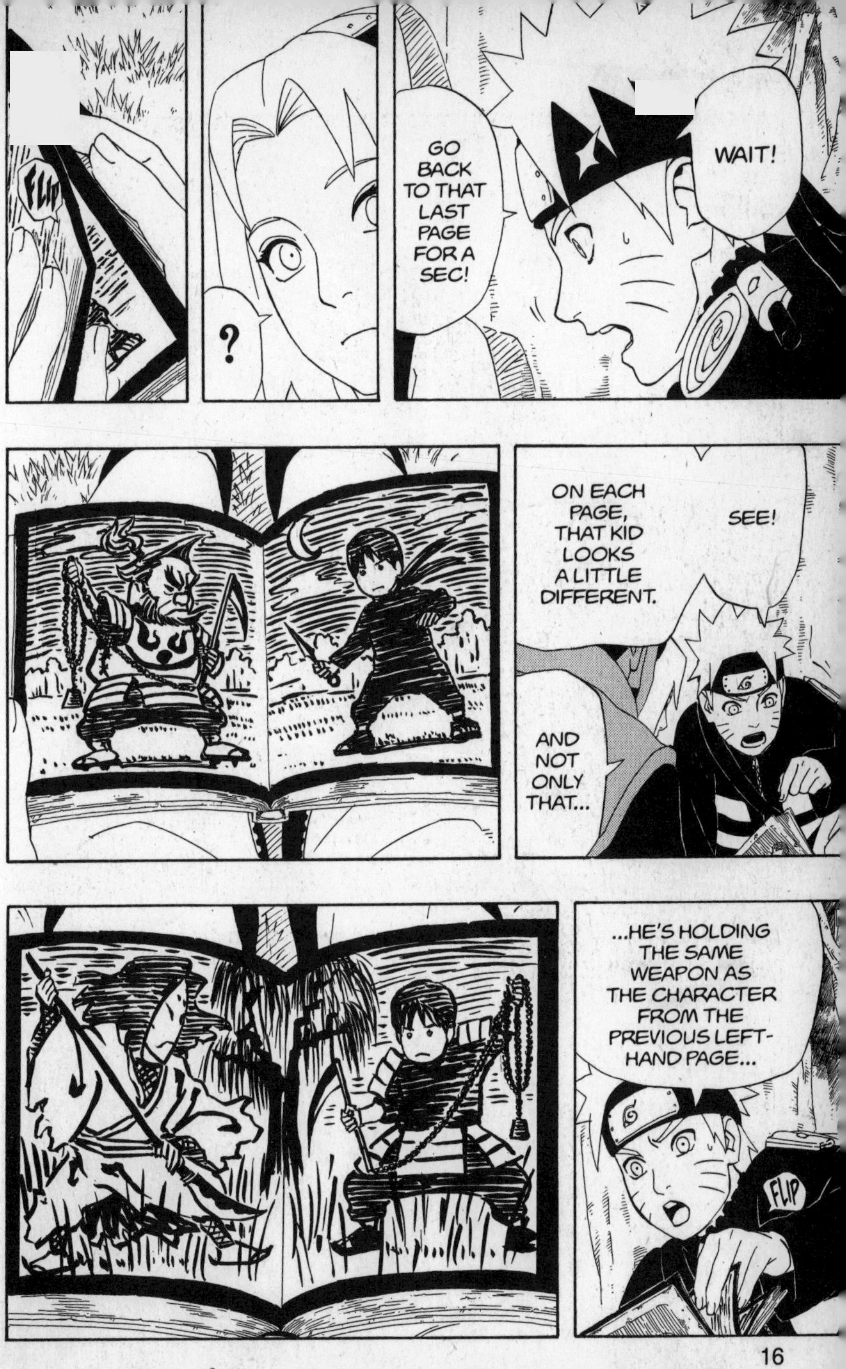
WAIT!
GO BACK TO THAT LAST PAGE FOR A SEC!
?
FLIP
SEE!
ON EACH PAGE, THAT KID LOOKS A LITTLE DIFFERENT.
AND NOT ONLY THAT...
...HE'S HOLDING THE SAME WEAPON AS THE CHARACTER FROM THE PREVIOUS LEFT-HAND PAGE...
FLIP

READ THIS WAY

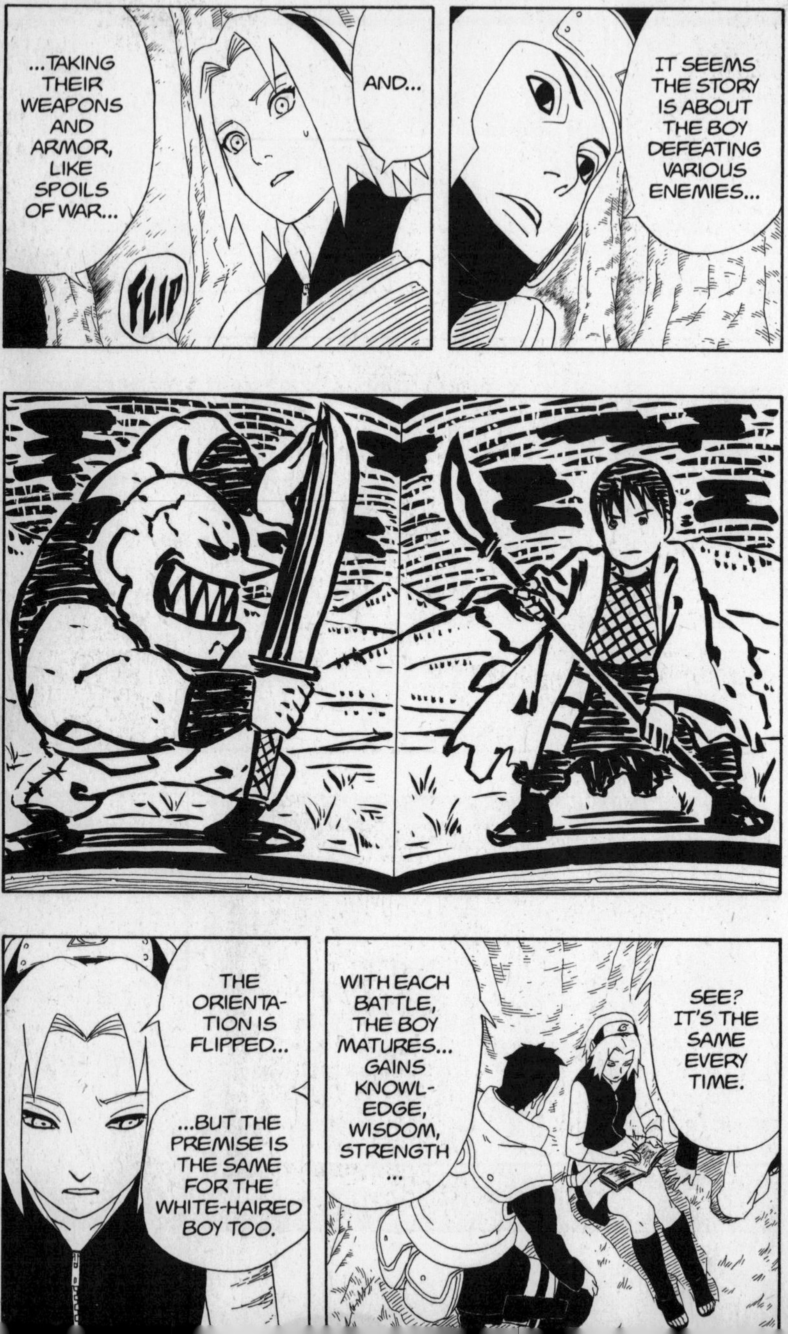
IT SEEMS THE STORY IS ABOUT THE BOY DEFEATING VARIOUS ENEMIES...
AND...
...TAKING THEIR WEAPONS AND ARMOR, LIKE SPOILS OF WAR...
FLIP
SEE? IT'S THE SAME EVERY TIME.
WITH EACH BATTLE, THE BOY MATURES... GAINS KNOWLEDGE, WISDOM, STRENGTH...
THE ORIENTATION IS FLIPPED...
...BUT THE PREMISE IS THE SAME FOR THE WHITE-HAIRED BOY TOO.

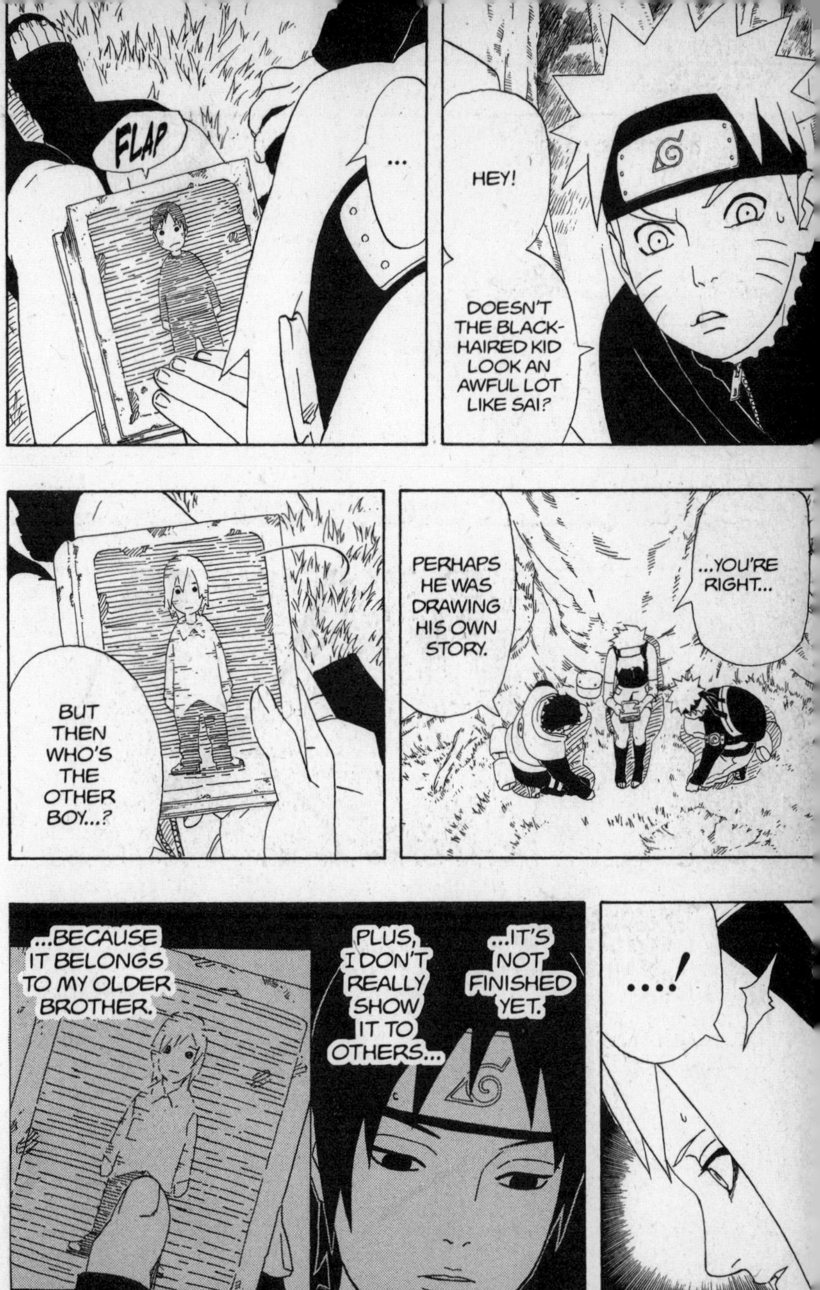
HEY!
DOESN'T THE BLACK-HAIRED KID LOOK AN AWFUL LOT LIKE SAI?
...
FLAP
...YOU'RE RIGHT...
PERHAPS HE WAS DRAWING HIS OWN STORY.
BUT THEN WHO'S THE OTHER BOY...?
....!
...IT'S NOT FINISHED YET.
PLUS, I DON'T REALLY SHOW IT TO OTHERS...
...BECAUSE IT BELONGS TO MY OLDER BROTHER.

READ THIS WAY

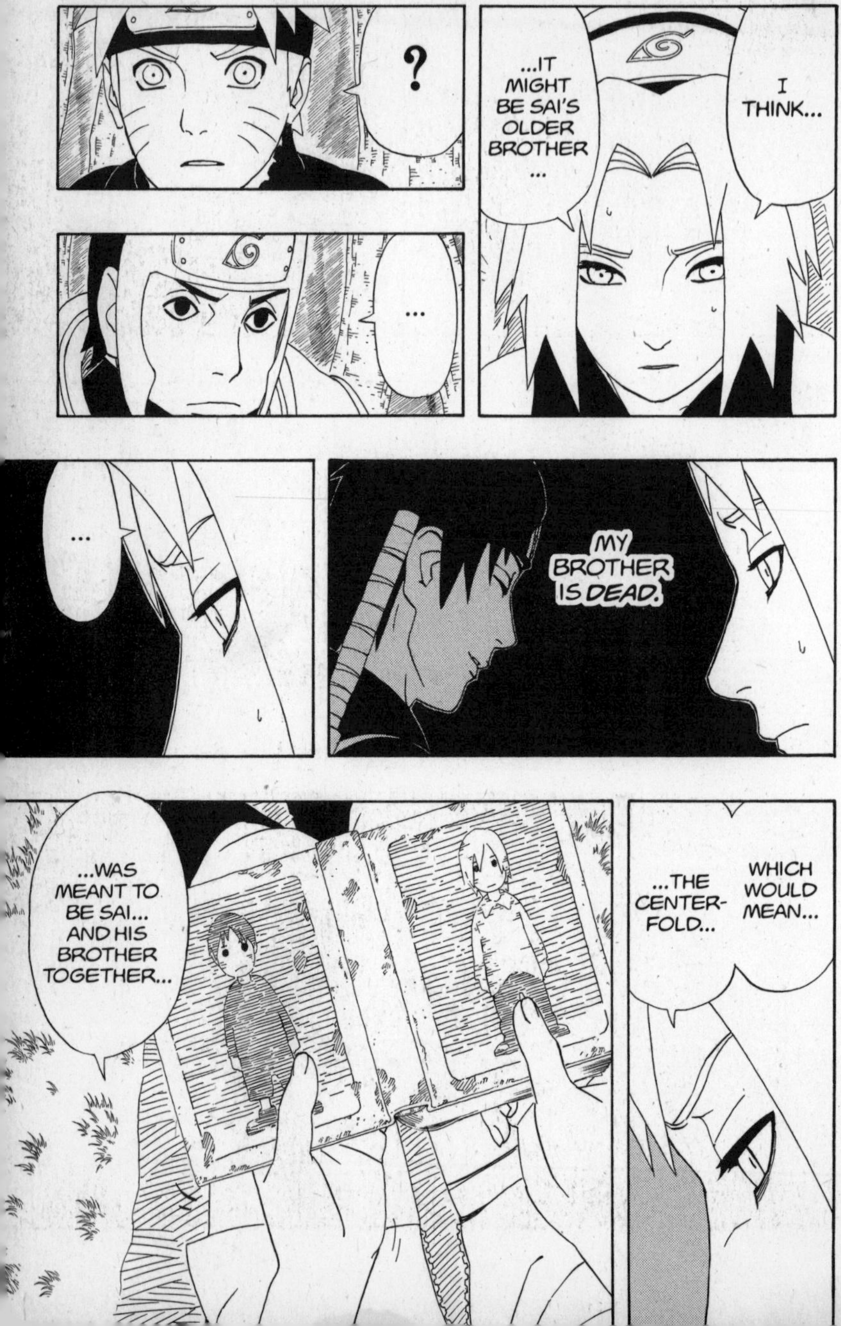
I THINK...
...IT MIGHT BE SAI'S OLDER BROTHER...
?
...
MY BROTHER IS DEAD.
...
WHICH WOULD MEAN...
...THE CENTER-FOLD...
...WAS MEANT TO BE SAI... AND HIS BROTHER TOGETHER...

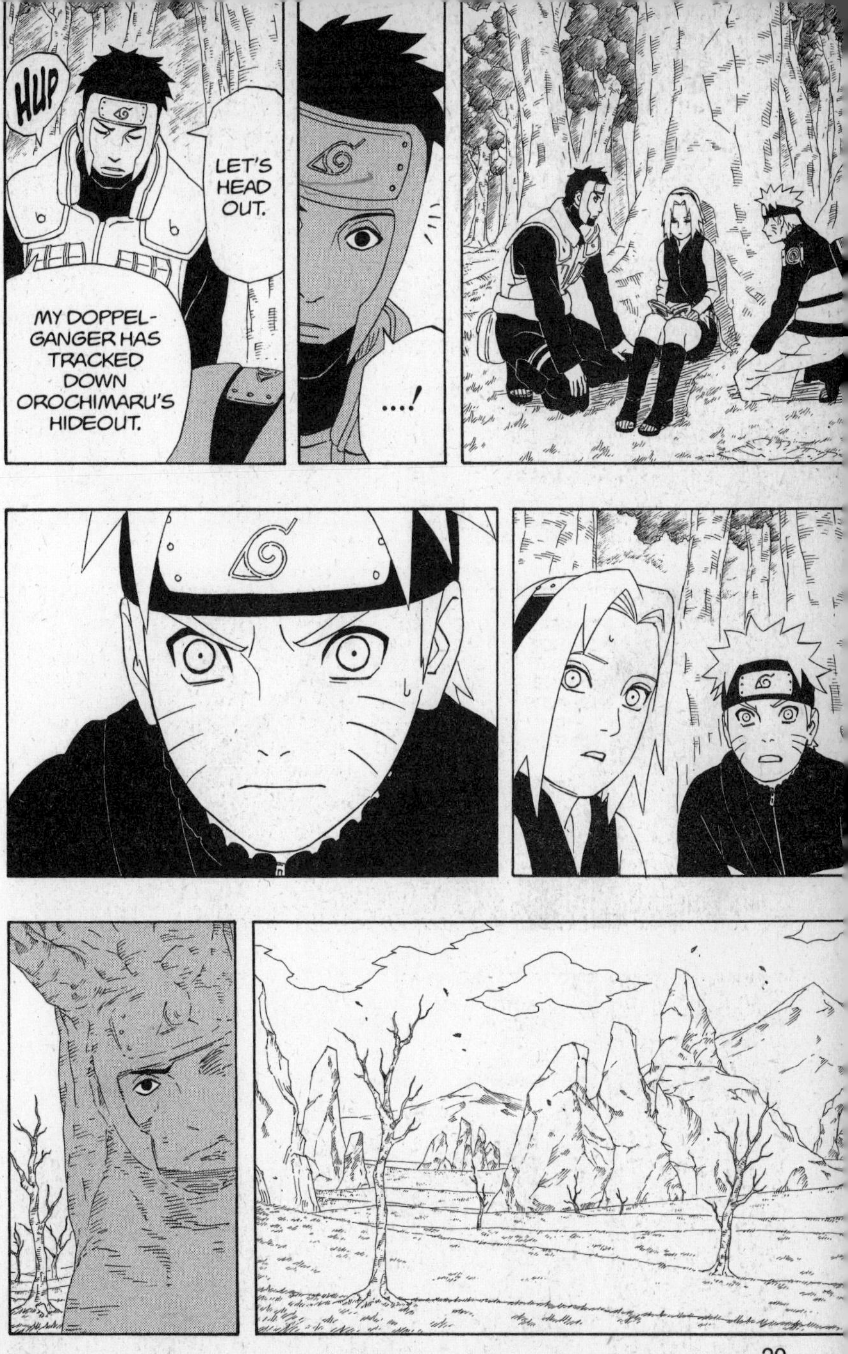
...!
HUP
LET'S HEAD OUT.
MY DOPPEL-GANGER HAS TRACKED DOWN OROCHIMARU'S HIDEOUT.

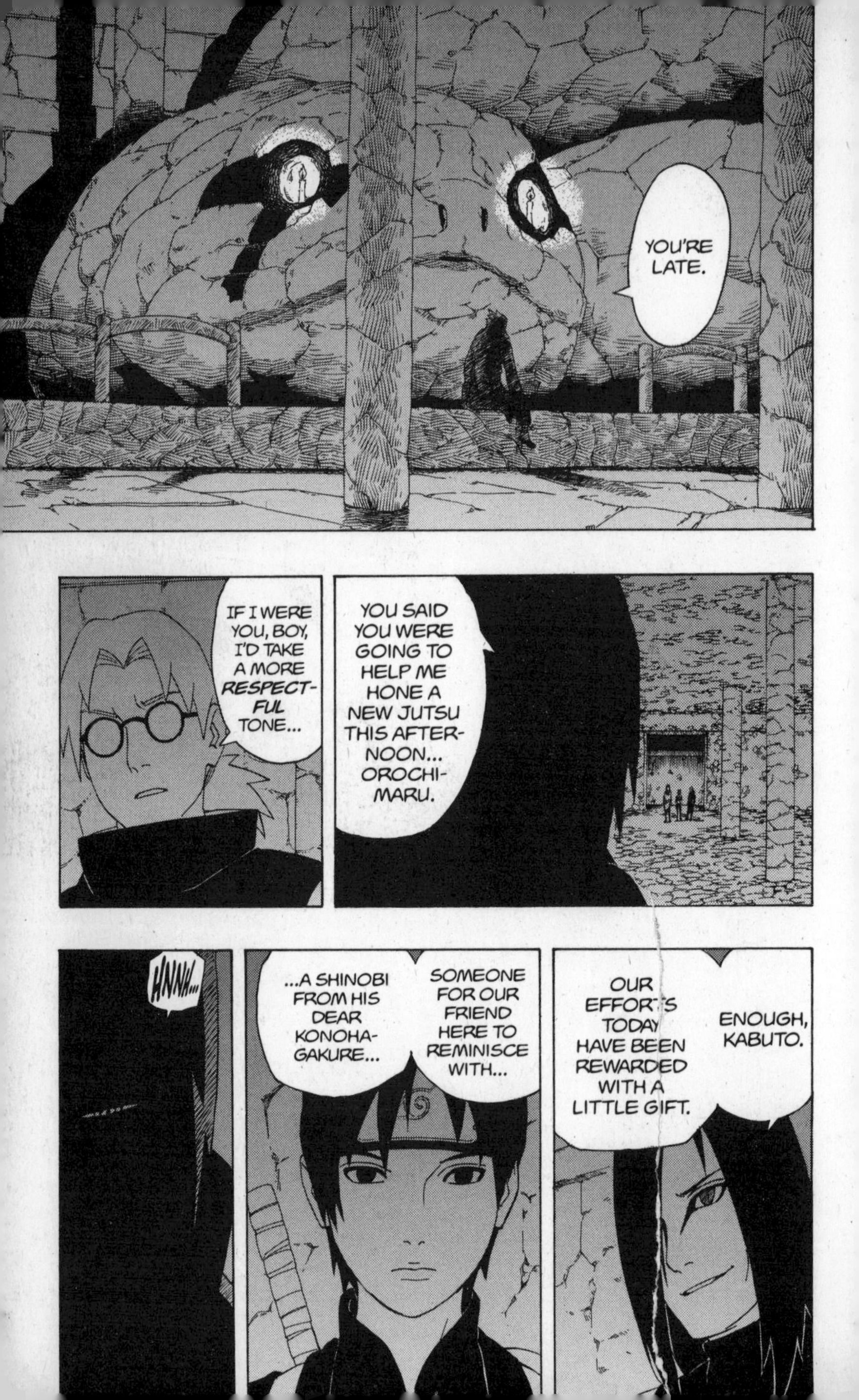
YOU'RE LATE.
YOU SAID YOU WERE GOING TO HELP ME HONE A NEW JUTSU THIS AFTERNOON... OROCHIMARU.
IF I WERE YOU, BOY, I'D TAKE A MORE *RESPECTFUL* TONE...
ENOUGH, KABUTO.
OUR EFFORTS TODAY HAVE BEEN REWARDED WITH A LITTLE GIFT.
SOMEONE FOR OUR FRIEND HERE TO REMINISCE WITH...
...A SHINOBI FROM HIS DEAR KONOHAGAKURE...
HNNH...

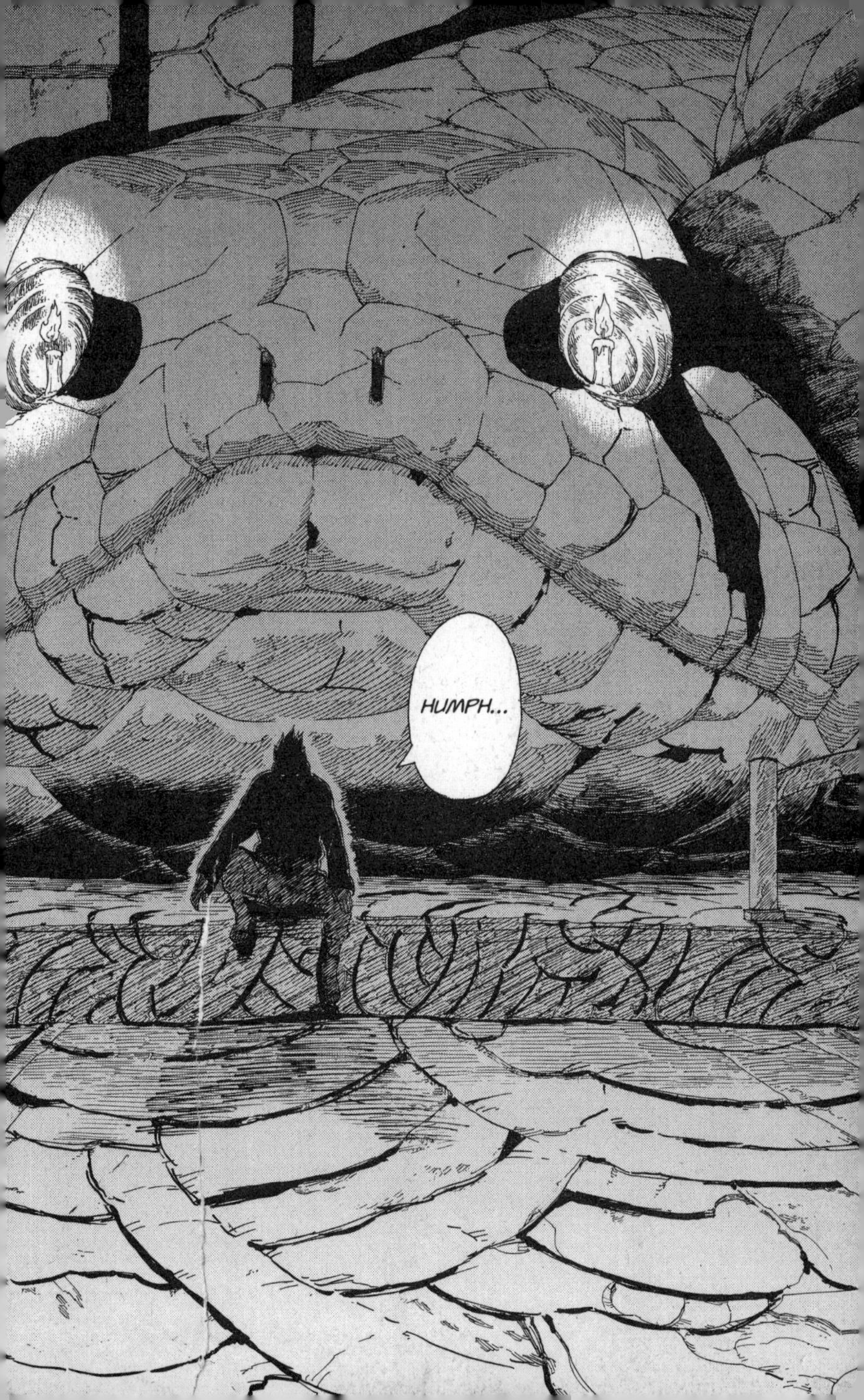
HUMPH...

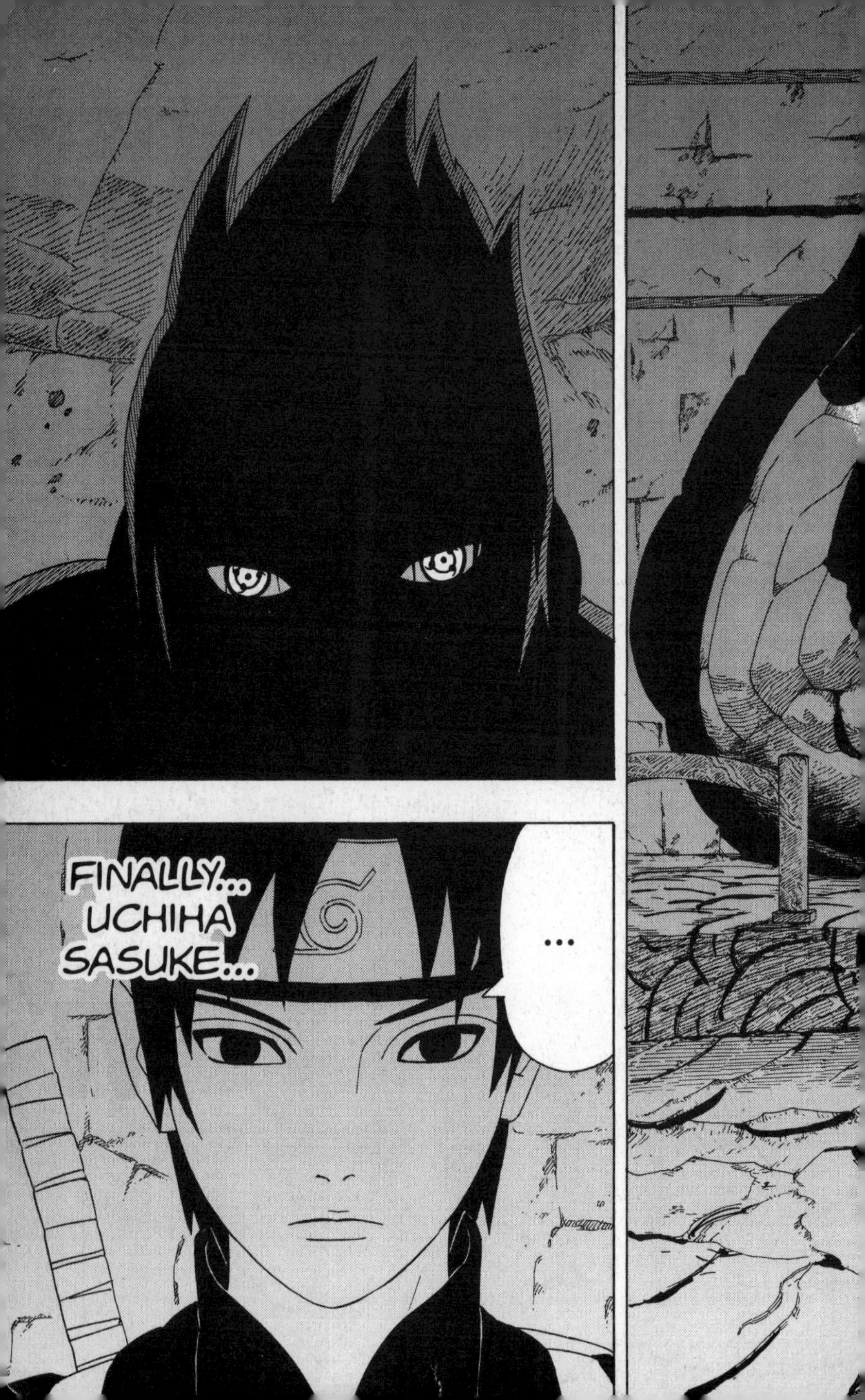
...
FINALLY... UCHIHA SASUKE...

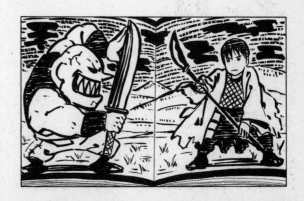

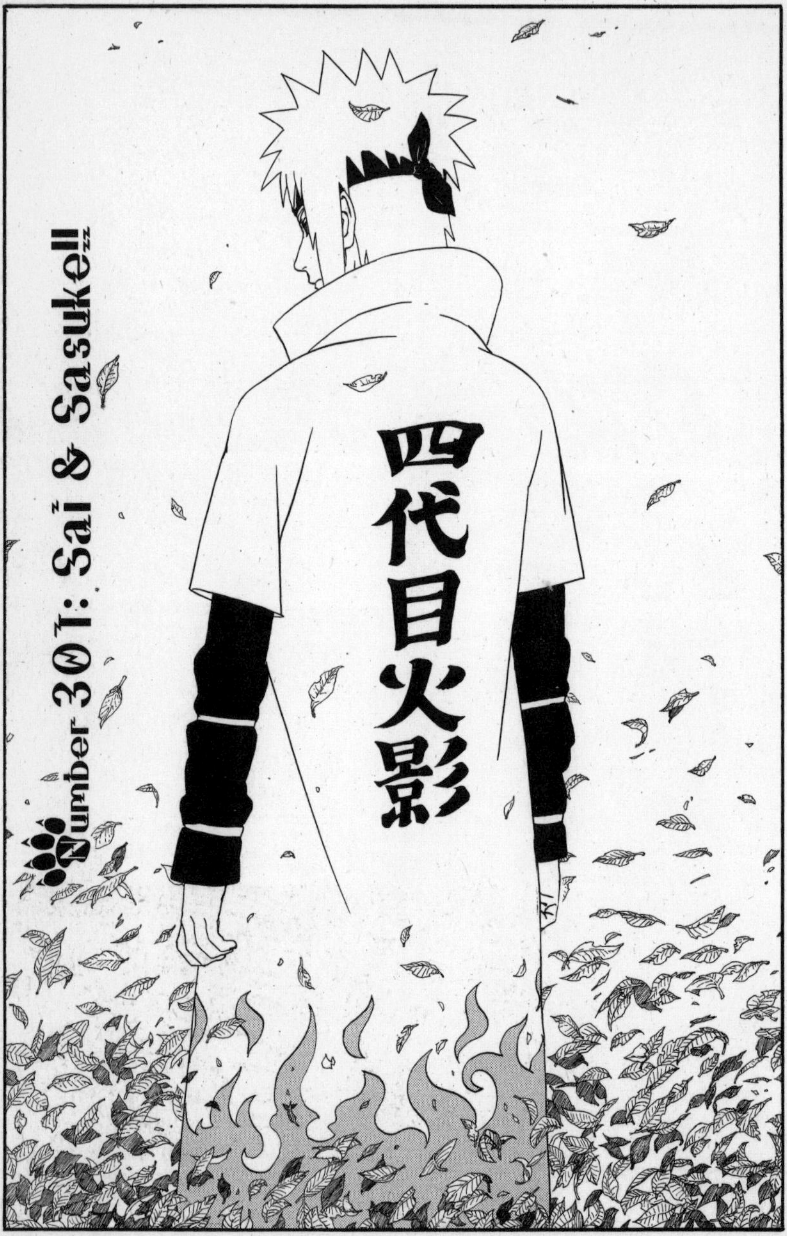
Number 301: Sai & Sasuke!!
四代目火影

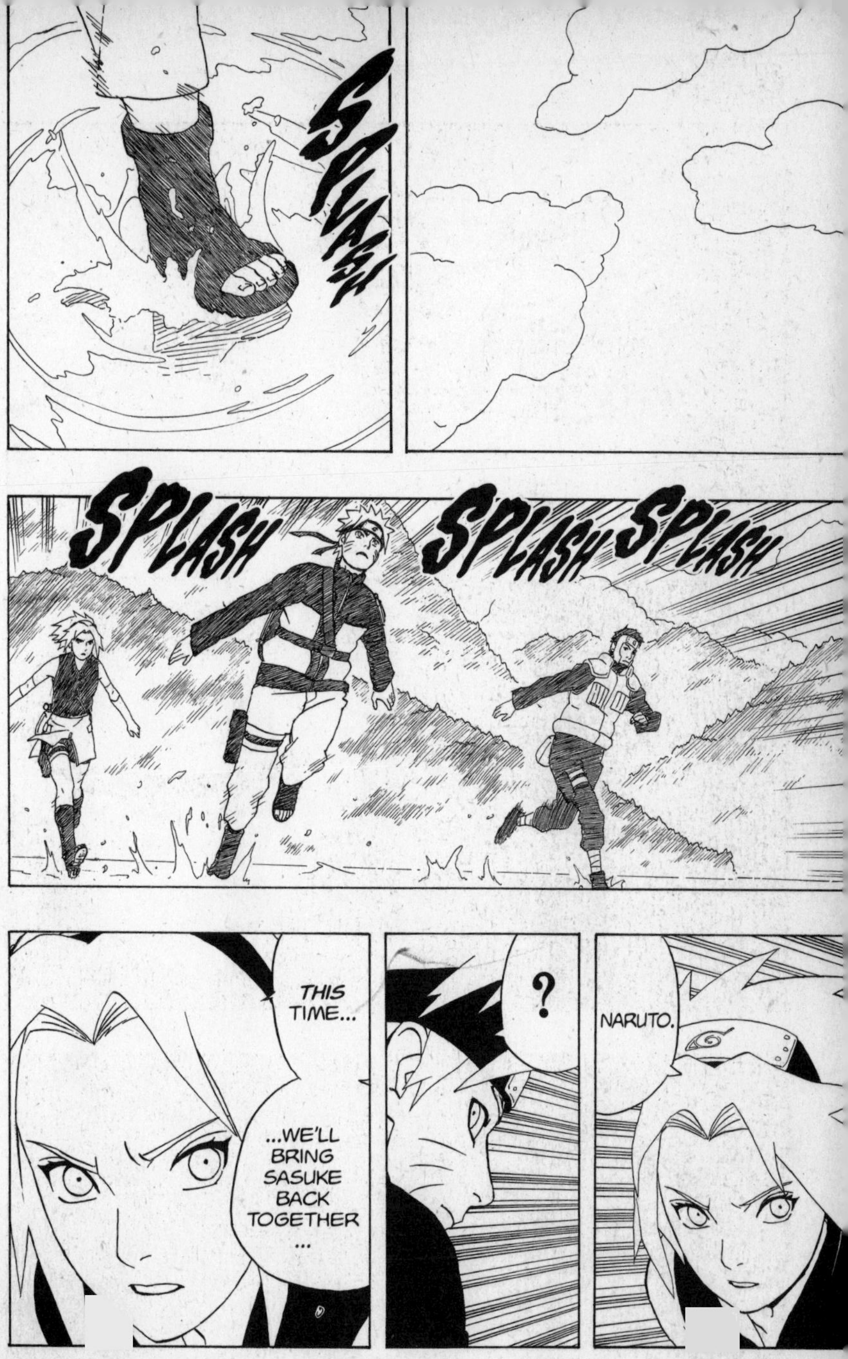
SPLASH
SPLASH SPLASH
SPLASH
NARUTO.
?
THIS TIME...
...WE'LL BRING SASUKE BACK TOGETHER ...

READ THIS WAY

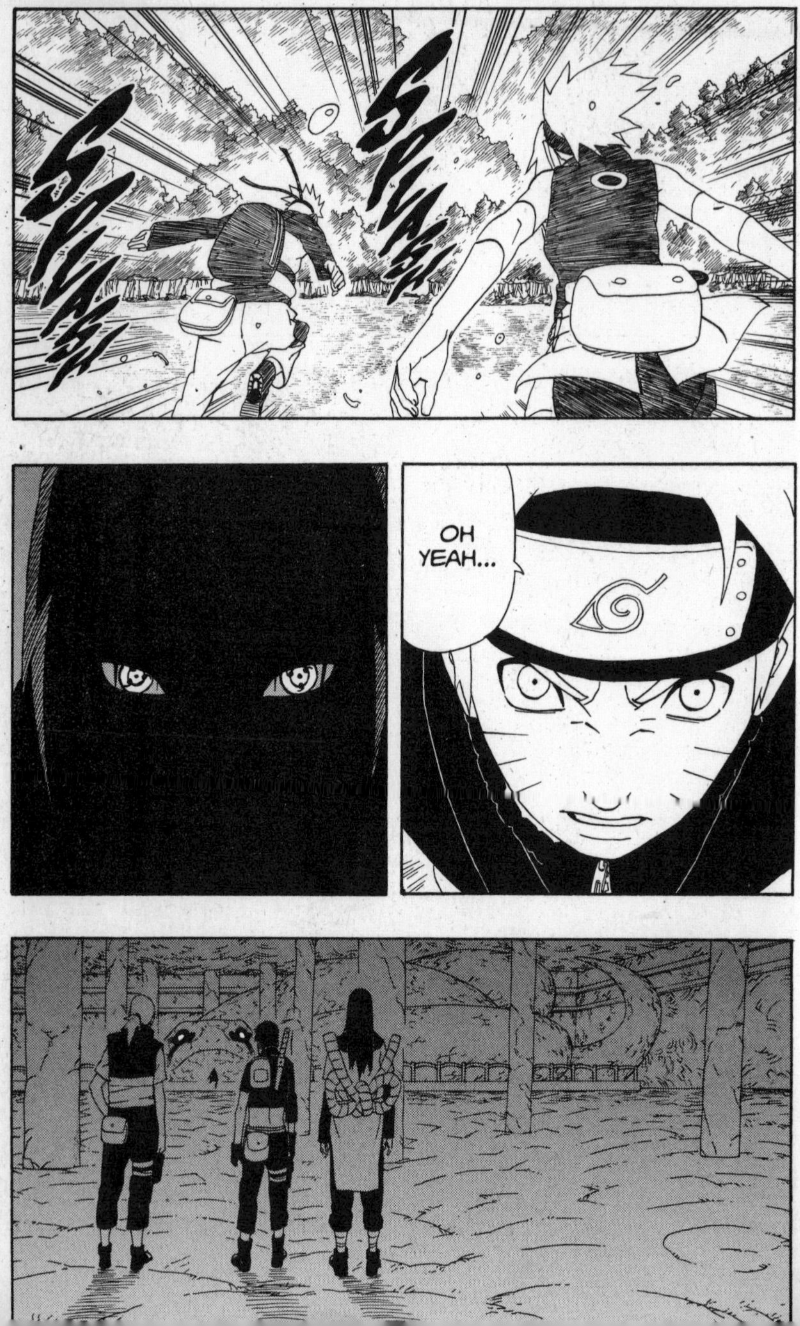
OH YEAH...

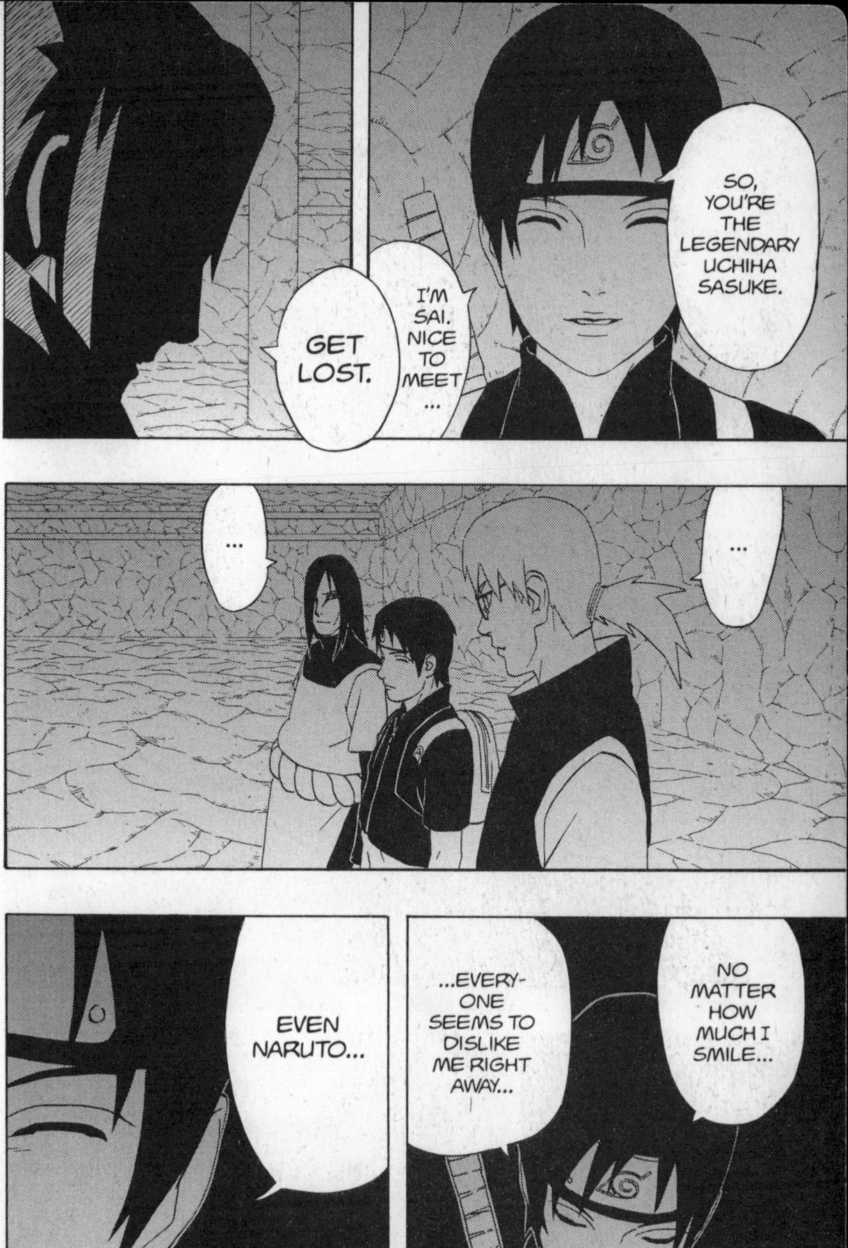
SO, YOU'RE THE LEGENDARY UCHIHA SASUKE.
I'M SAI. NICE TO MEET ...
GET LOST.
...
...
NO MATTER HOW MUCH I SMILE...
...EVERY-ONE SEEMS TO DISLIKE ME RIGHT AWAY...
EVEN NARUTO...

READ THIS WAY

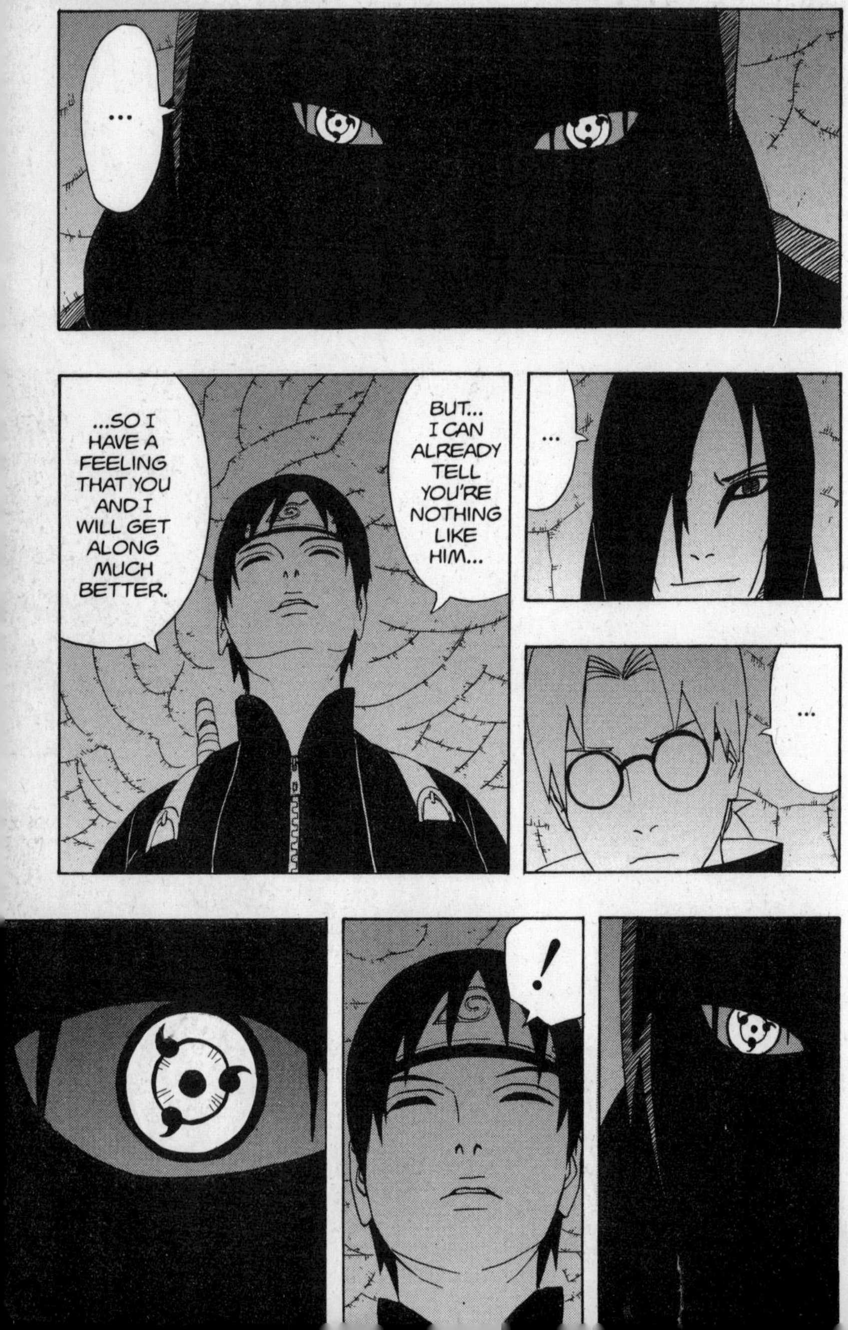
...
...
...
BUT... I CAN ALREADY TELL YOU'RE NOTHING LIKE HIM...
...SO I HAVE A FEELING THAT YOU AND I WILL GET ALONG MUCH BETTER.
!

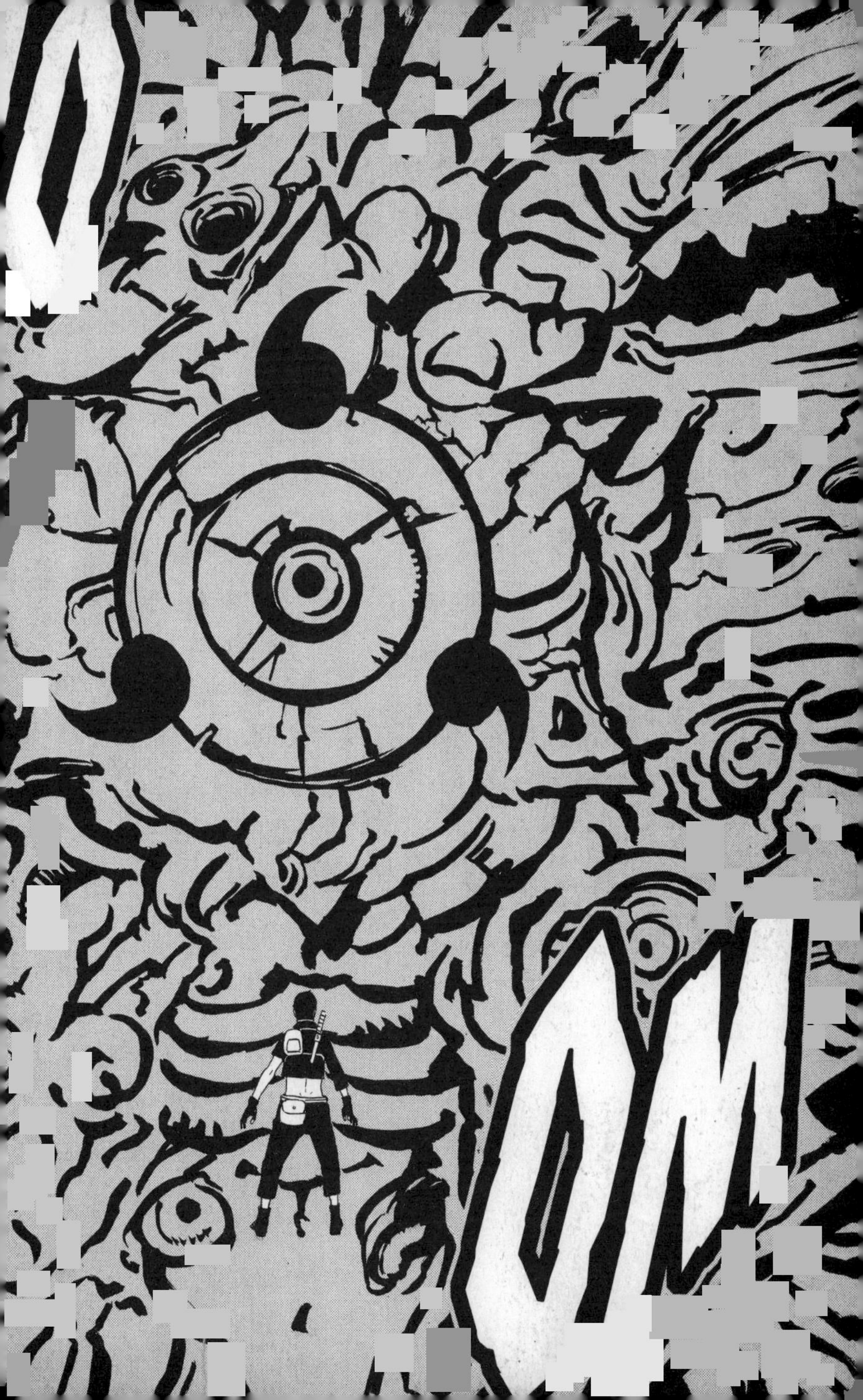
O
OM

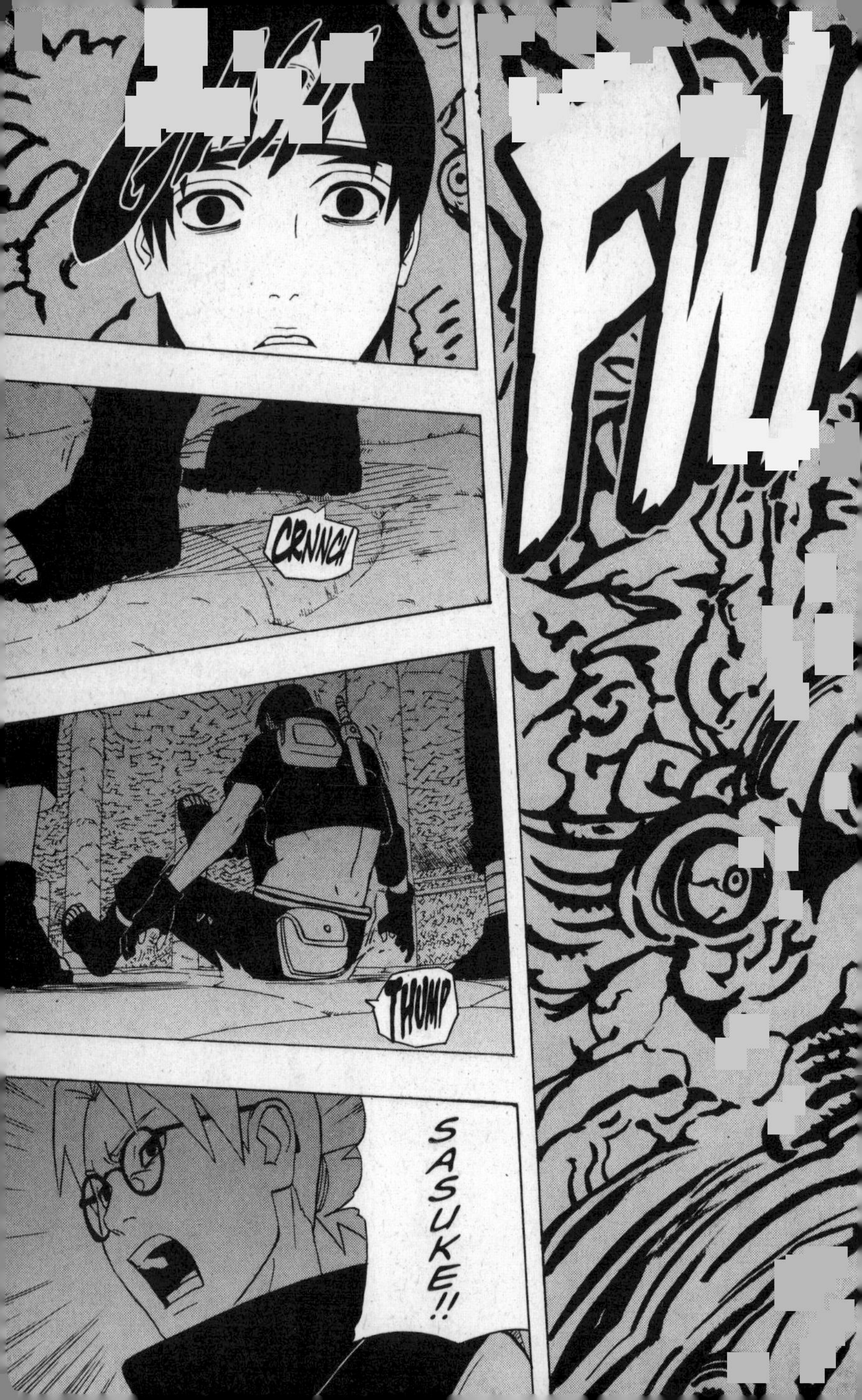
CRNNCH
THUMP
SASUKE!!

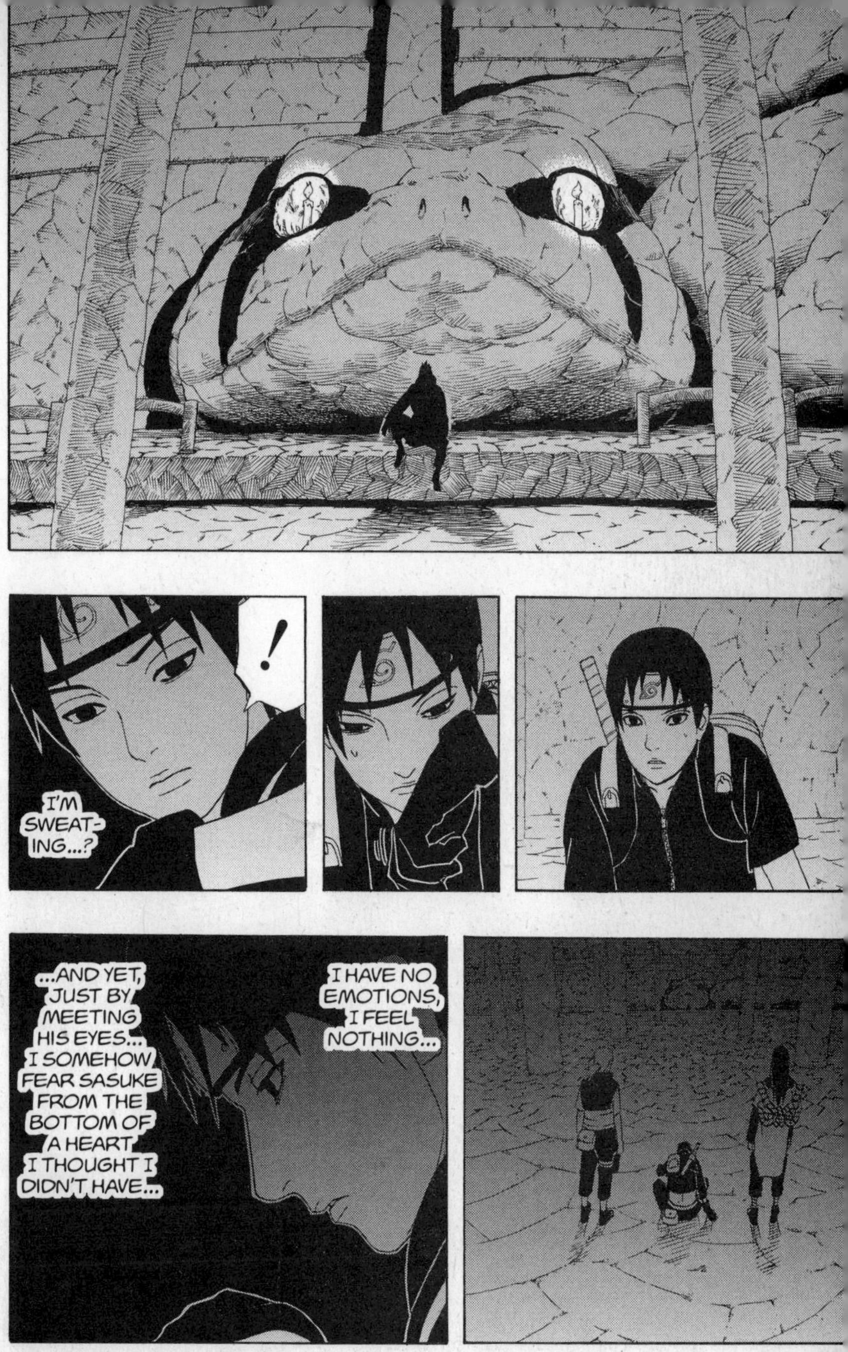
!
I'M SWEATING...?
I HAVE NO EMOTIONS, I FEEL NOTHING...
...AND YET, JUST BY MEETING HIS EYES... I SOMEHOW FEAR SASUKE FROM THE BOTTOM OF A HEART I THOUGHT I DIDN'T HAVE...

READ THIS WAY

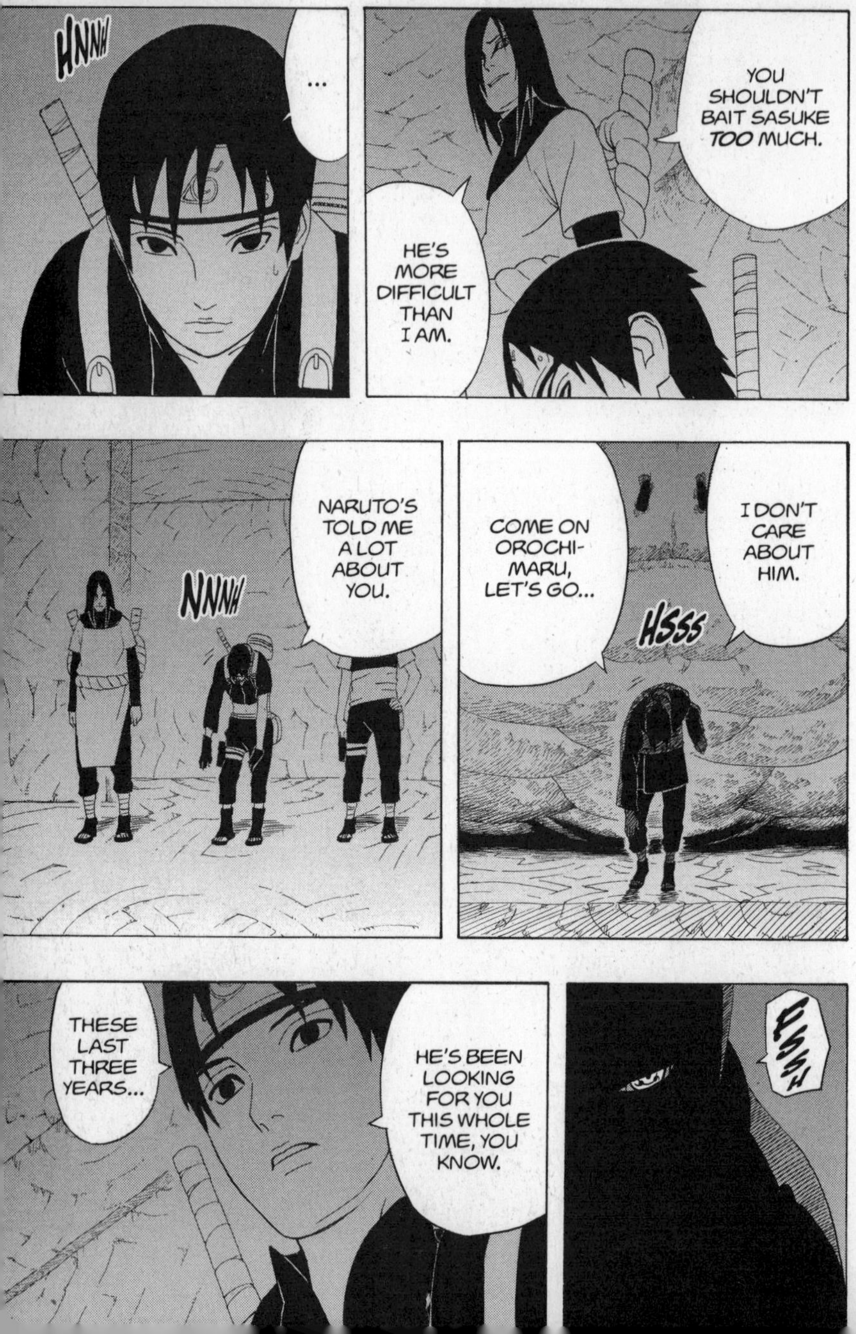
YOU SHOULDN'T BAIT SASUKE *TOO* MUCH.
HE'S MORE DIFFICULT THAN I AM.
HNNH
...
I DON'T CARE ABOUT HIM.
COME ON OROCHIMARU, LET'S GO...
HSSS
NARUTO'S TOLD ME A LOT ABOUT YOU.
NNNH
THESE LAST THREE YEARS...
HE'S BEEN LOOKING FOR YOU THIS WHOLE TIME, YOU KNOW.

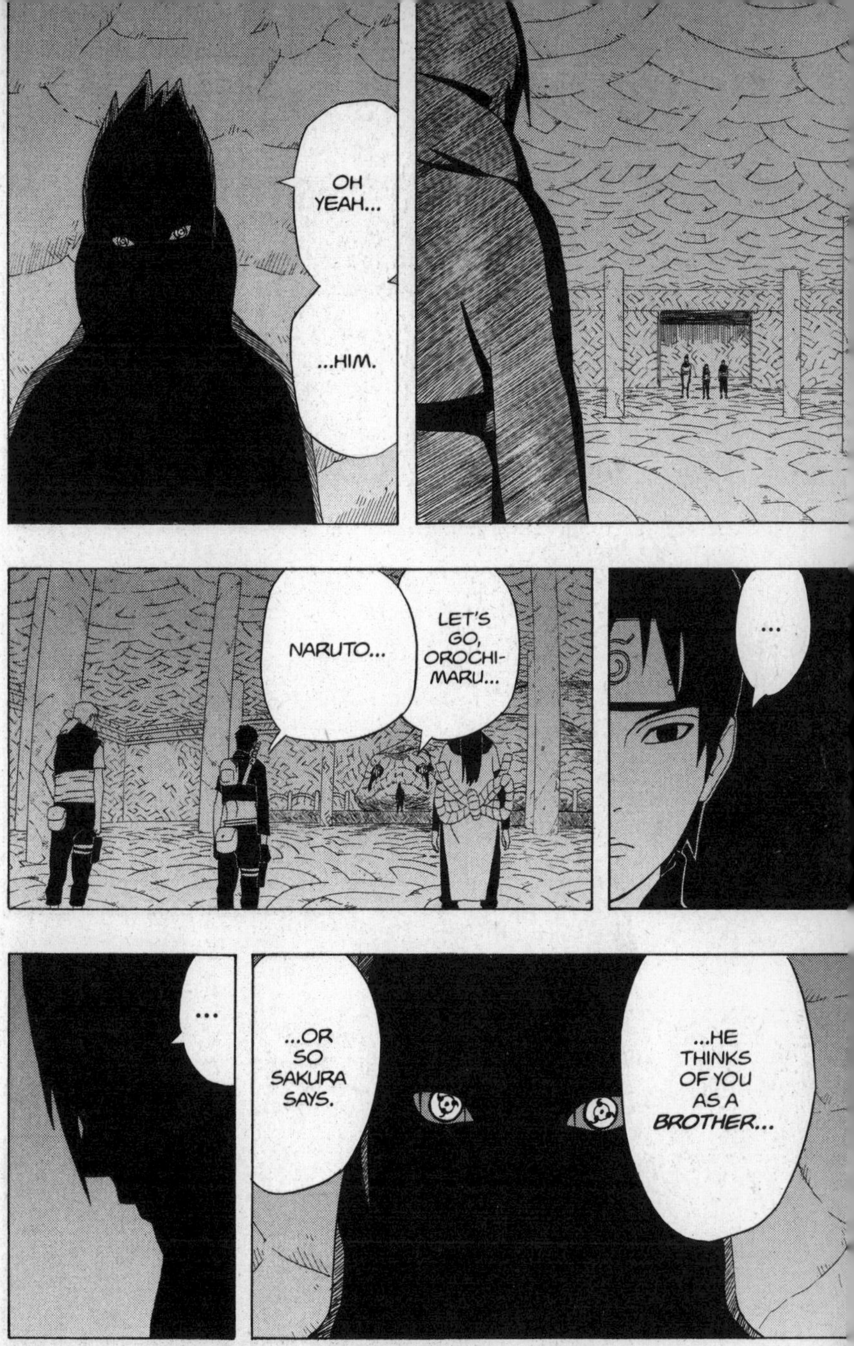
OH YEAH...
...HIM.
...
LET'S GO, OROCHI-MARU...
NARUTO...
...HE THINKS OF YOU AS A *BROTHER*...
...OR SO SAKURA SAYS.
...

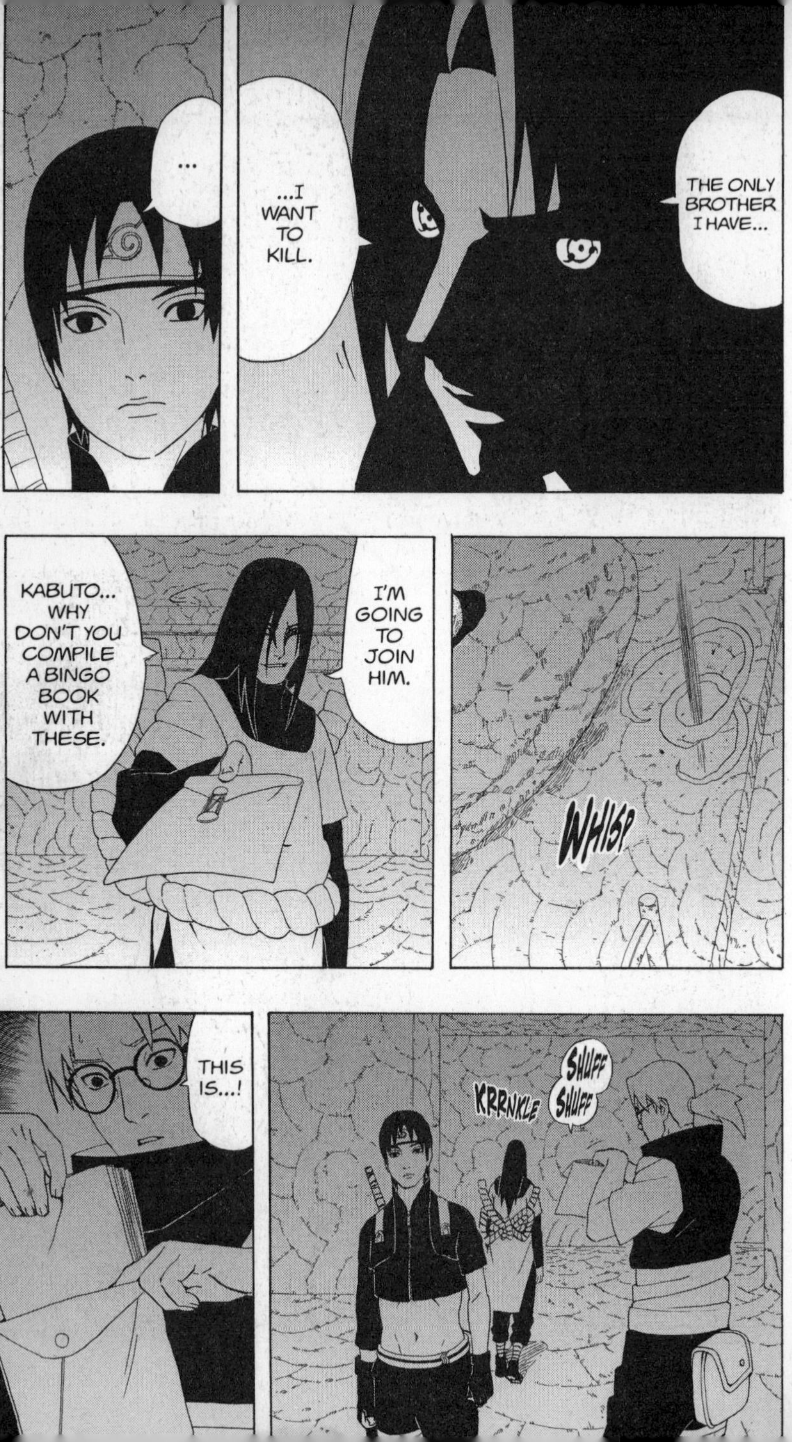
THE ONLY BROTHER I HAVE...
...I WANT TO KILL.
...
WHISP
I'M GOING TO JOIN HIM.
KABUTO... WHY DON'T YOU COMPILE A BINGO BOOK WITH THESE.
SHUFF SHUFF
KRRNKLE
THIS IS...!

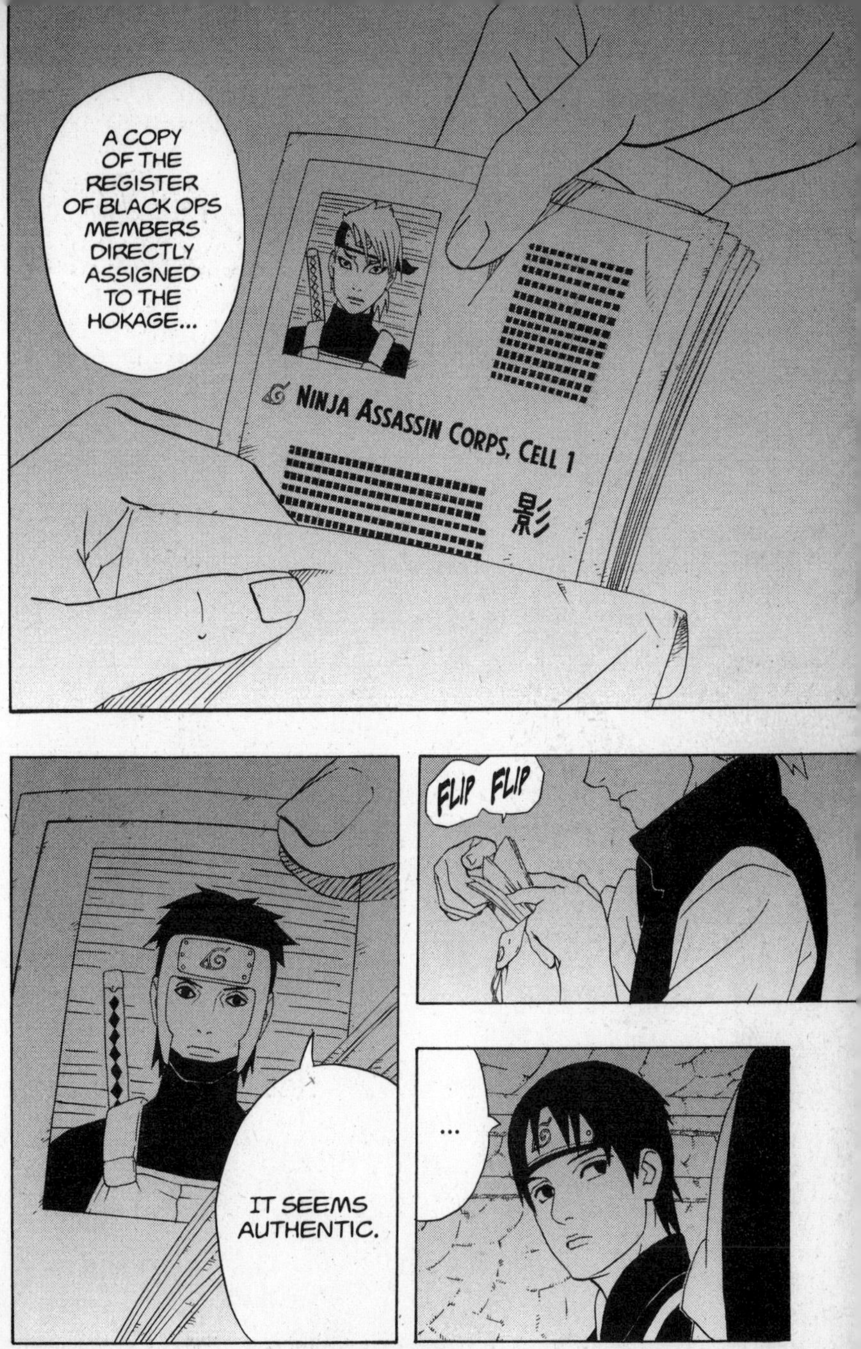
A COPY OF THE REGISTER OF BLACK OPS MEMBERS DIRECTLY ASSIGNED TO THE HOKAGE...
NINJA ASSASSIN CORPS, CELL 1
影
FLIP FLIP
...
IT SEEMS AUTHENTIC.

READ THIS WAY

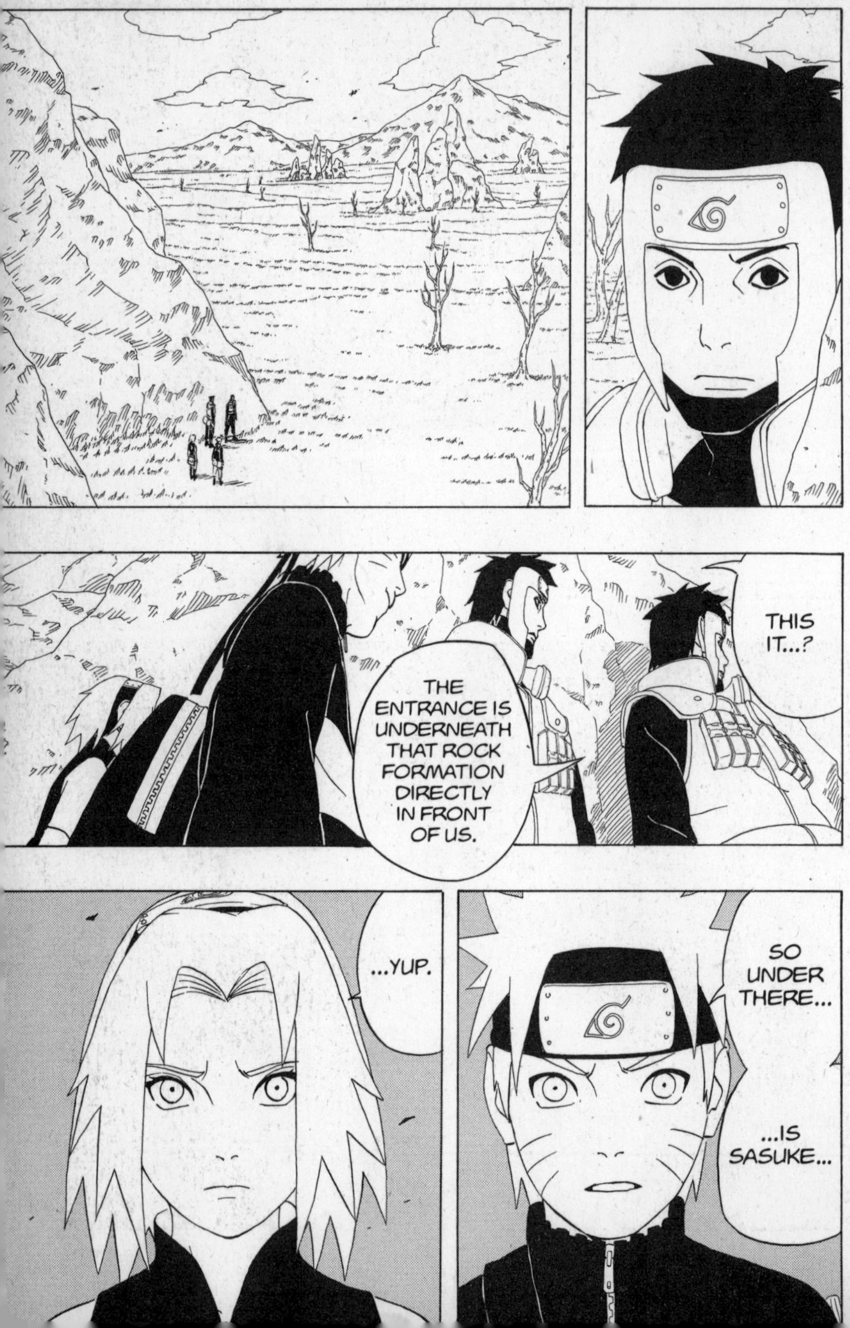
THIS IT...?
THE ENTRANCE IS UNDERNEATH THAT ROCK FORMATION DIRECTLY IN FRONT OF US.
SO UNDER THERE...
...IS SASUKE...
...YUP.

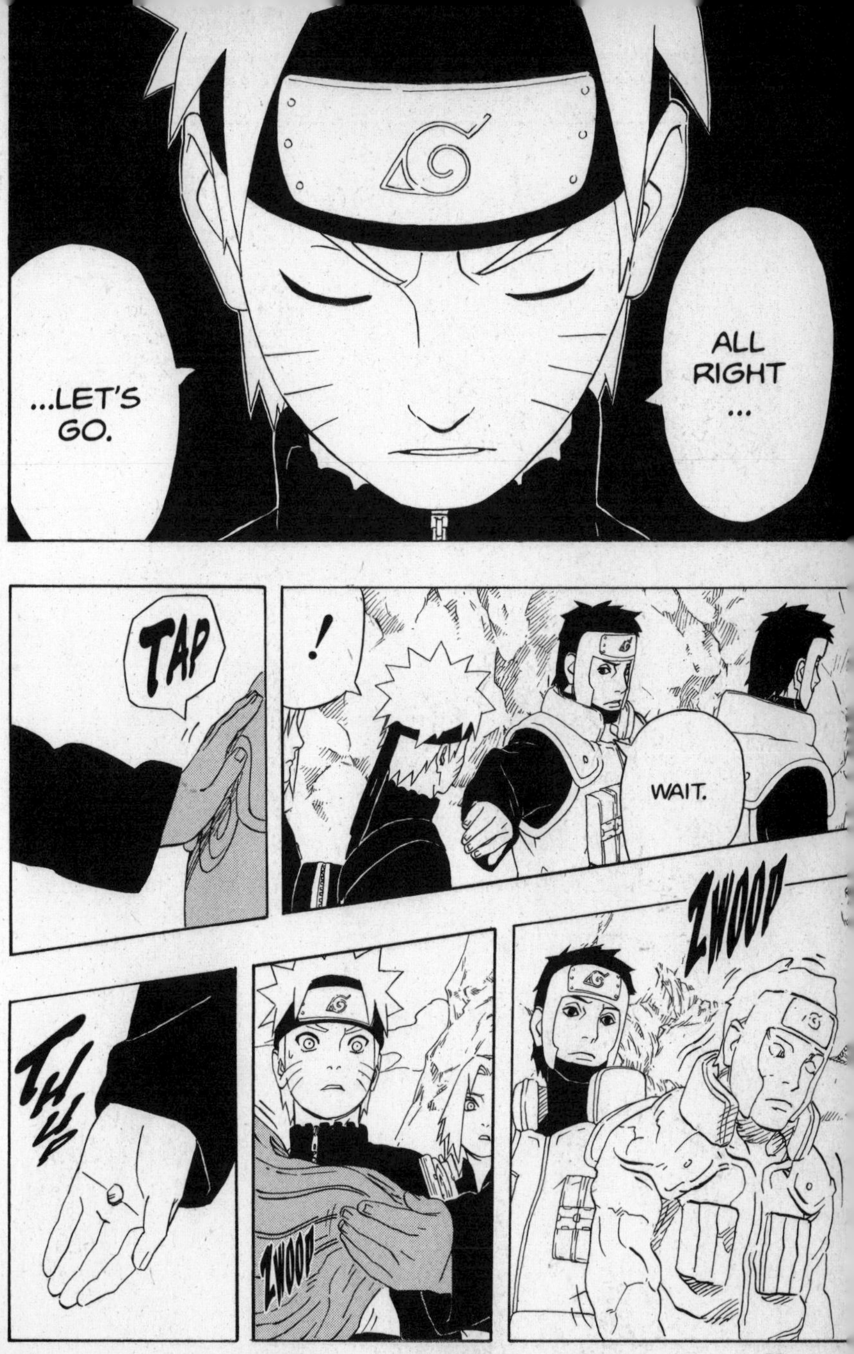
ALL RIGHT ...
...LET'S GO.
WAIT.
!
TAP
ZWOOP
ZWOOP
THUP

READ THIS WAY

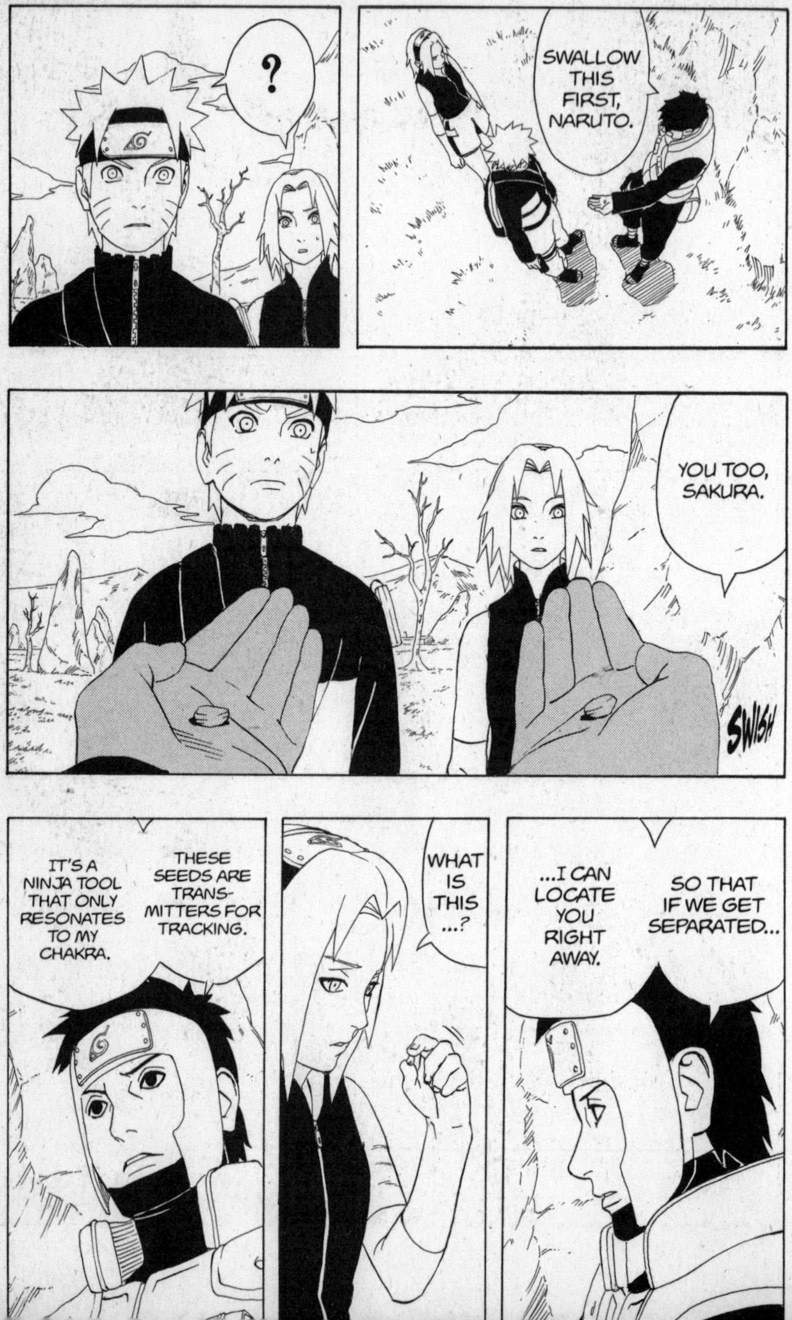
SWALLOW THIS FIRST, NARUTO.
?
YOU TOO, SAKURA.
SWISH
SO THAT IF WE GET SEPARATED...
...I CAN LOCATE YOU RIGHT AWAY.
WHAT IS THIS ...?
THESE SEEDS ARE TRANS-MITTERS FOR TRACKING.
IT'S A NINJA TOOL THAT ONLY RESONATES TO MY CHAKRA.

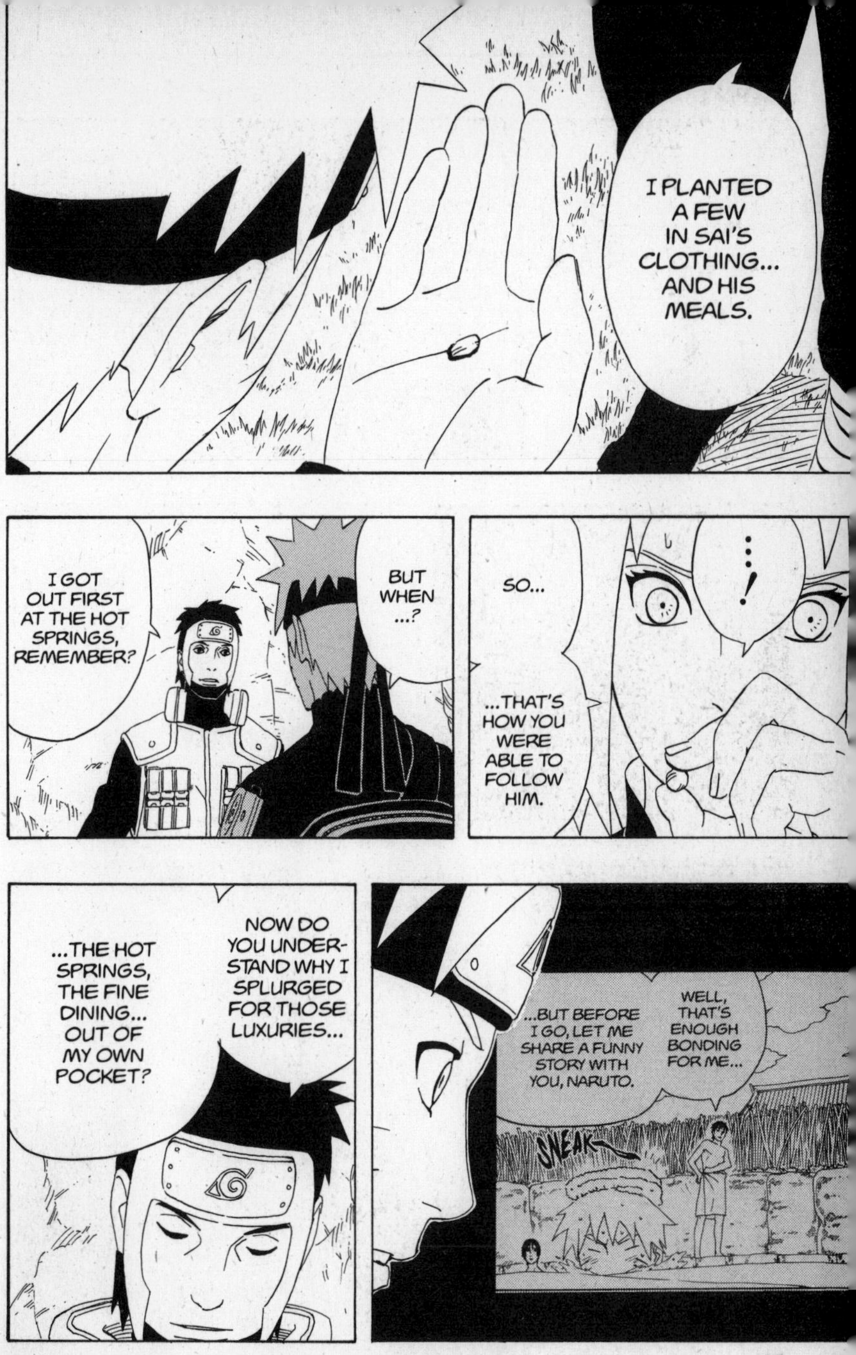
I PLANTED A FEW IN SAI'S CLOTHING... AND HIS MEALS.
...!
SO...
...THAT'S HOW YOU WERE ABLE TO FOLLOW HIM.
BUT WHEN ...?
I GOT OUT FIRST AT THE HOT SPRINGS, REMEMBER?
WELL, THAT'S ENOUGH BONDING FOR ME...
...BUT BEFORE I GO, LET ME SHARE A FUNNY STORY WITH YOU, NARUTO.
SNEAK
NOW DO YOU UNDERSTAND WHY I SPLURGED FOR THOSE LUXURIES...
...THE HOT SPRINGS, THE FINE DINING... OUT OF MY OWN POCKET?

READ THIS WAY

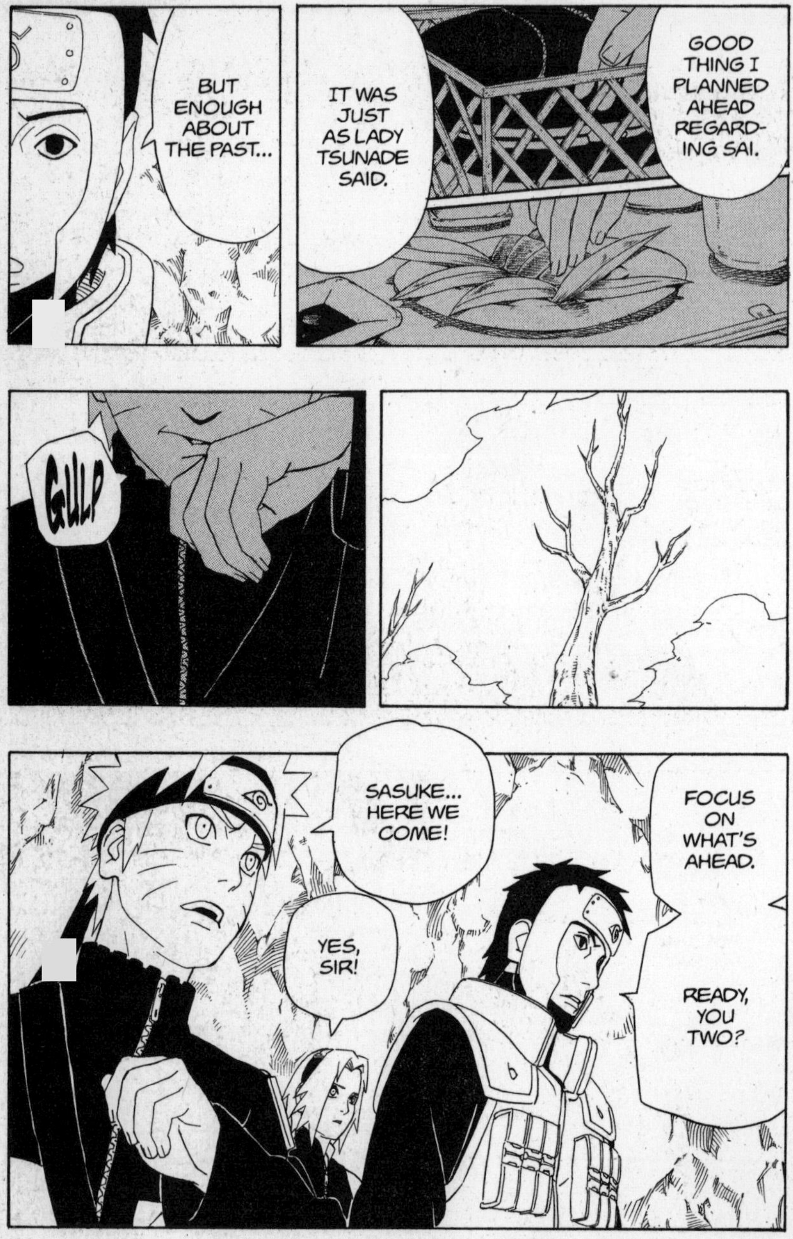

GOOD THING I PLANNED AHEAD REGARD-ING SAI.
IT WAS JUST AS LADY TSUNADE SAID.
BUT ENOUGH ABOUT THE PAST...
GULP
FOCUS ON WHAT'S AHEAD.
READY, YOU TWO?
SASUKE... HERE WE COME!
YES, SIR!

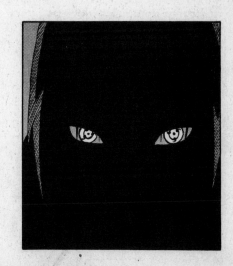

Number 302: Infiltration...!!

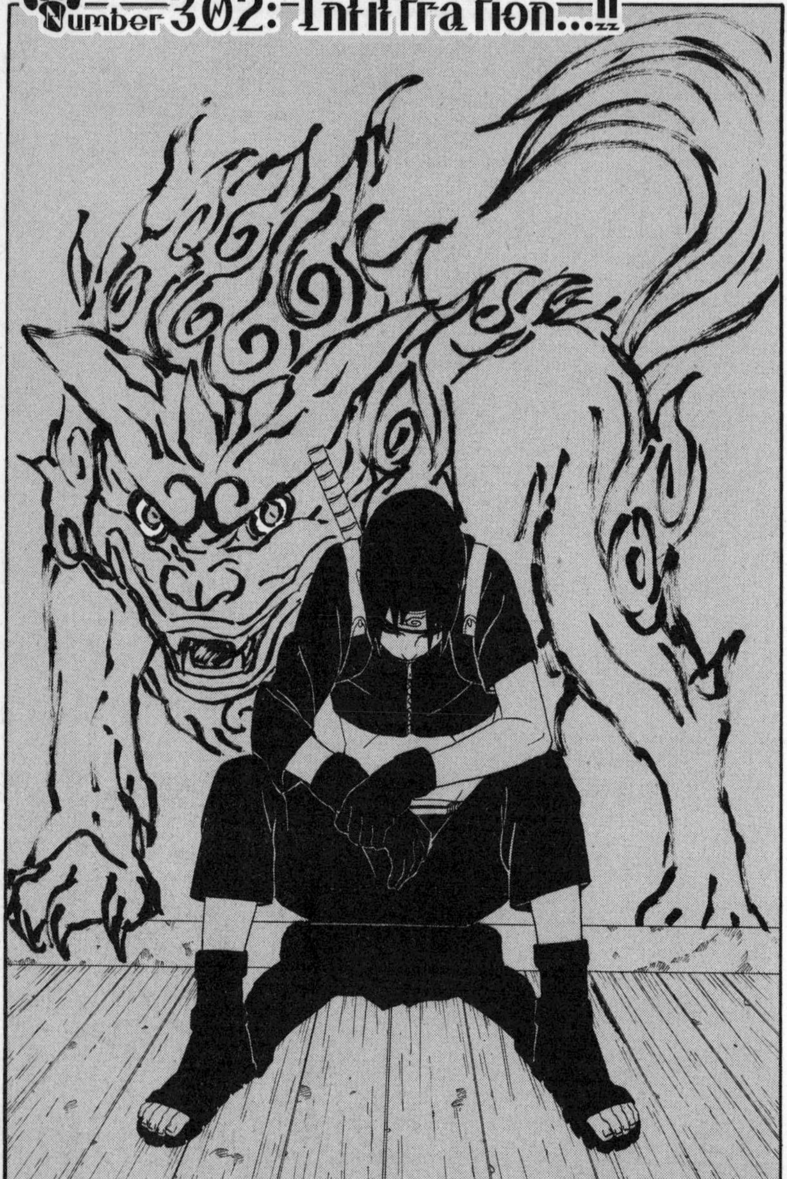

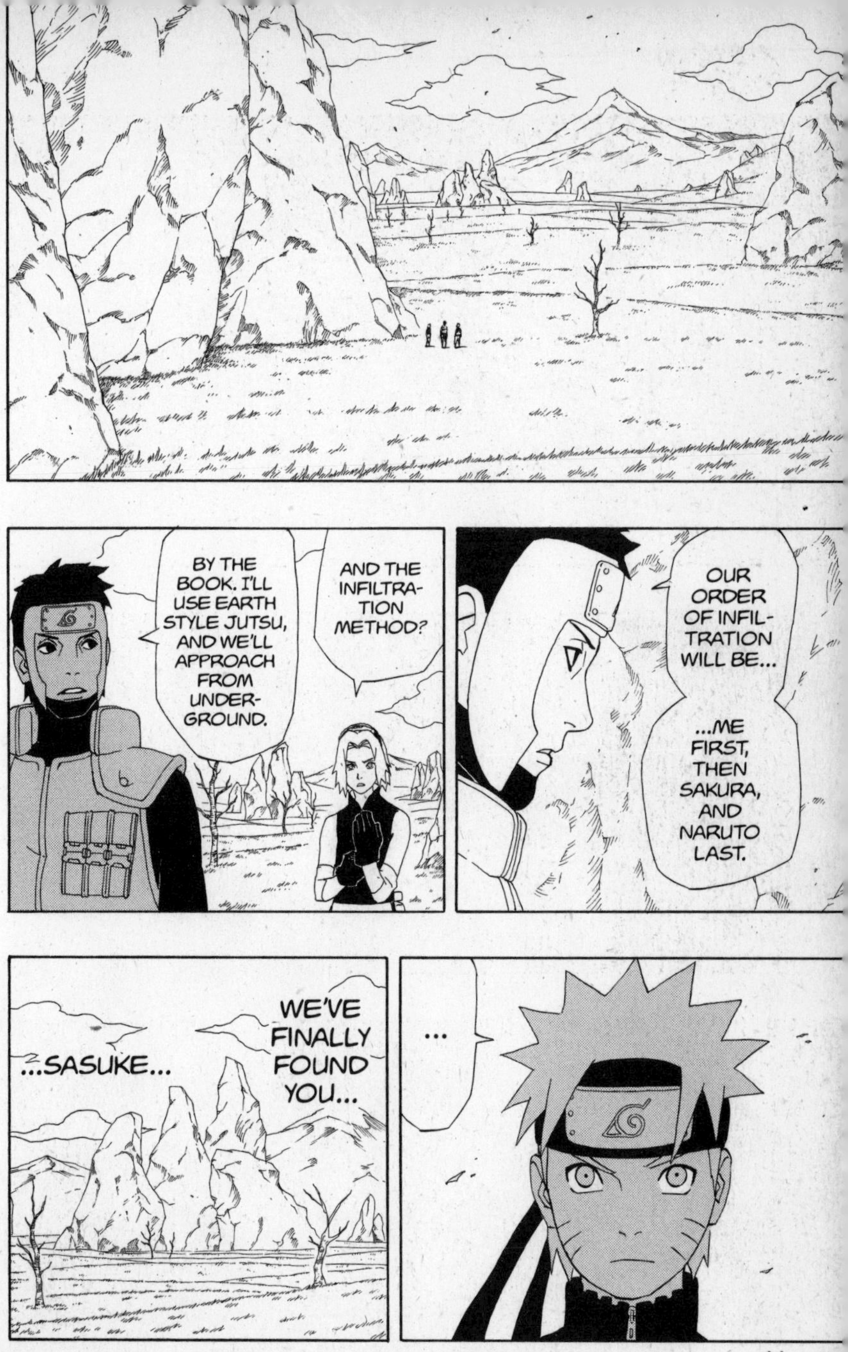
OUR ORDER OF INFILTRATION WILL BE...
...ME FIRST, THEN SAKURA, AND NARUTO LAST.
AND THE INFILTRATION METHOD?
BY THE BOOK. I'LL USE EARTH STYLE JUTSU, AND WE'LL APPROACH FROM UNDERGROUND.
...
WE'VE FINALLY FOUND YOU...
...SASUKE...

READ THIS WAY

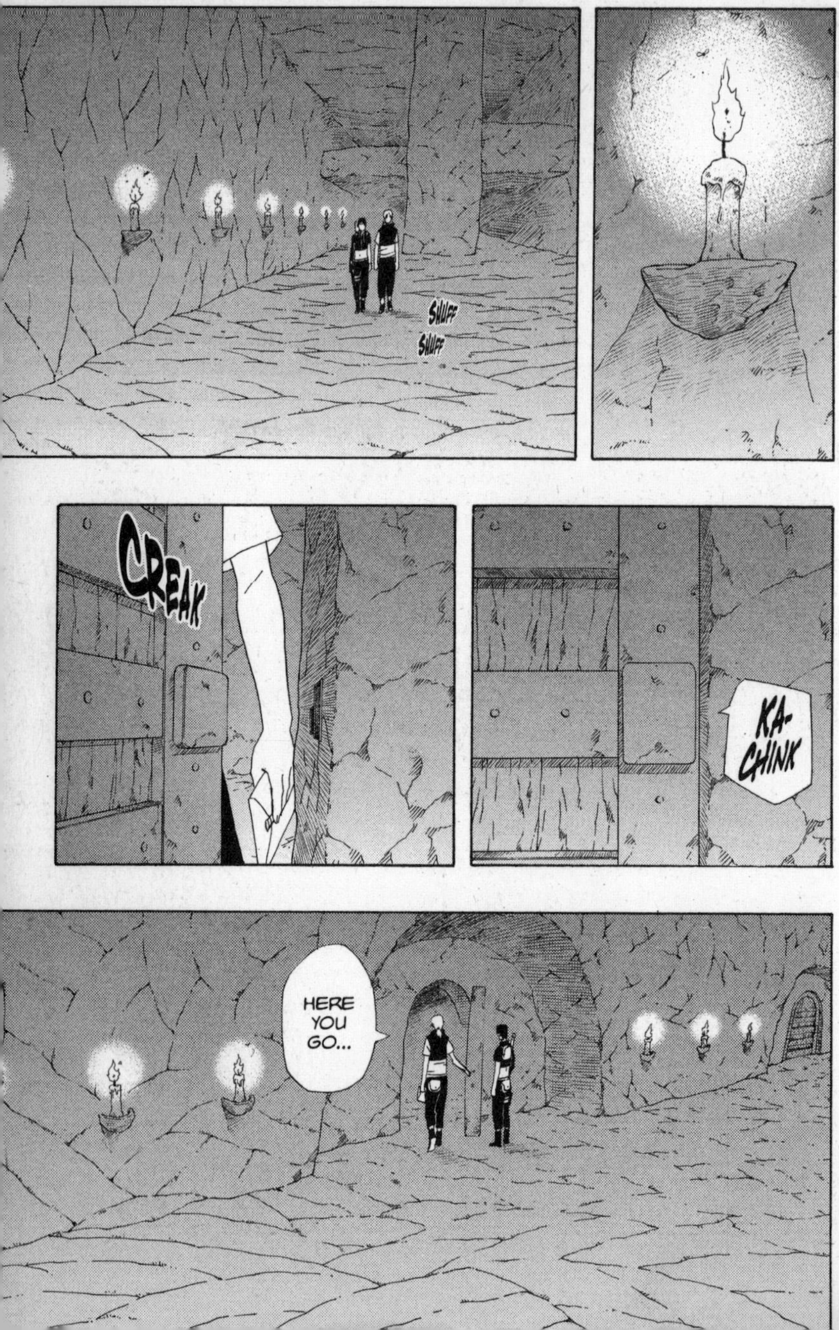
SHUFF
SHUFF
KA-CHINK
CREAK
HERE YOU GO...

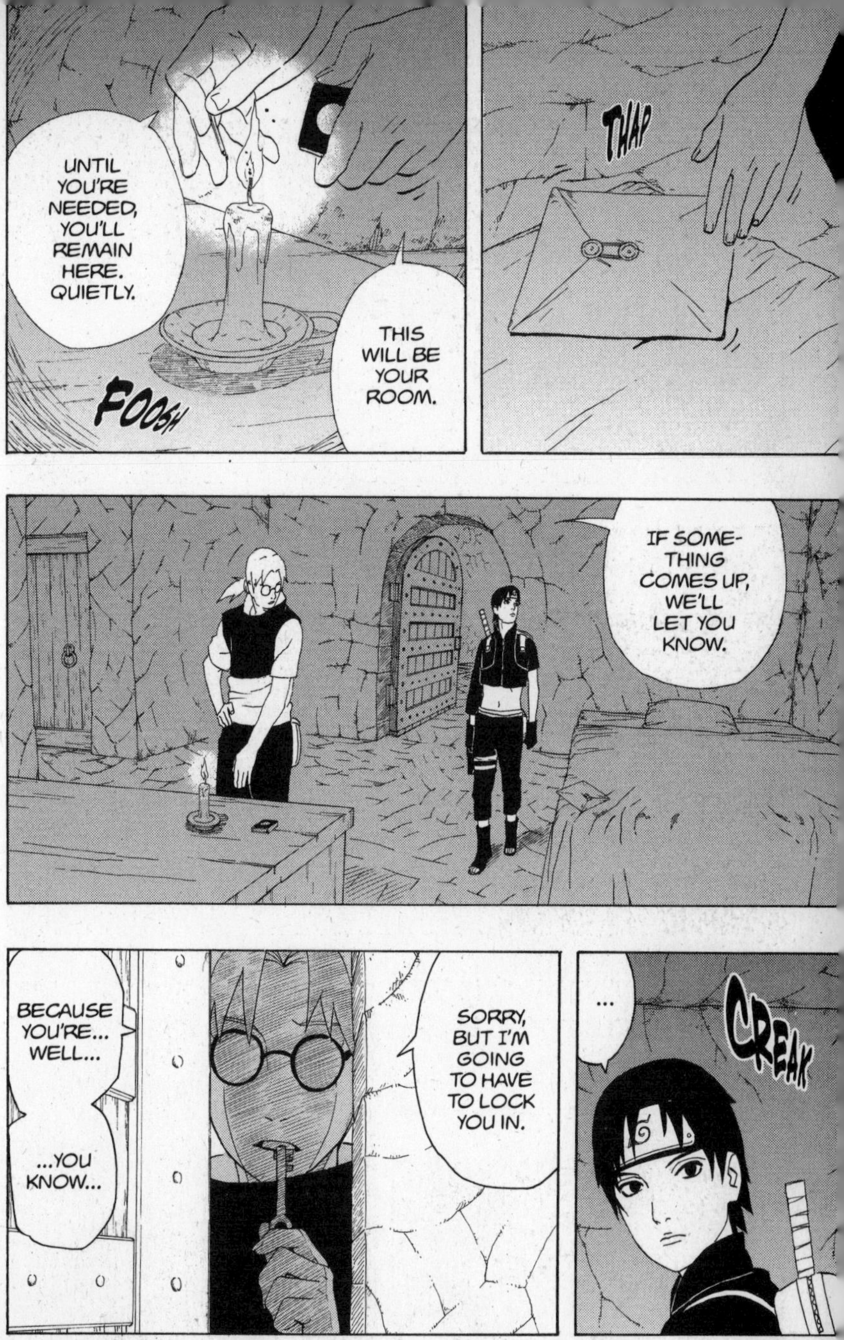
THAP
THIS WILL BE YOUR ROOM.
UNTIL YOU'RE NEEDED, YOU'LL REMAIN HERE. QUIETLY.
FOOSH
IF SOME-THING COMES UP, WE'LL LET YOU KNOW.
...
CREAK
SORRY, BUT I'M GOING TO HAVE TO LOCK YOU IN.
BECAUSE YOU'RE... WELL...
...YOU KNOW...

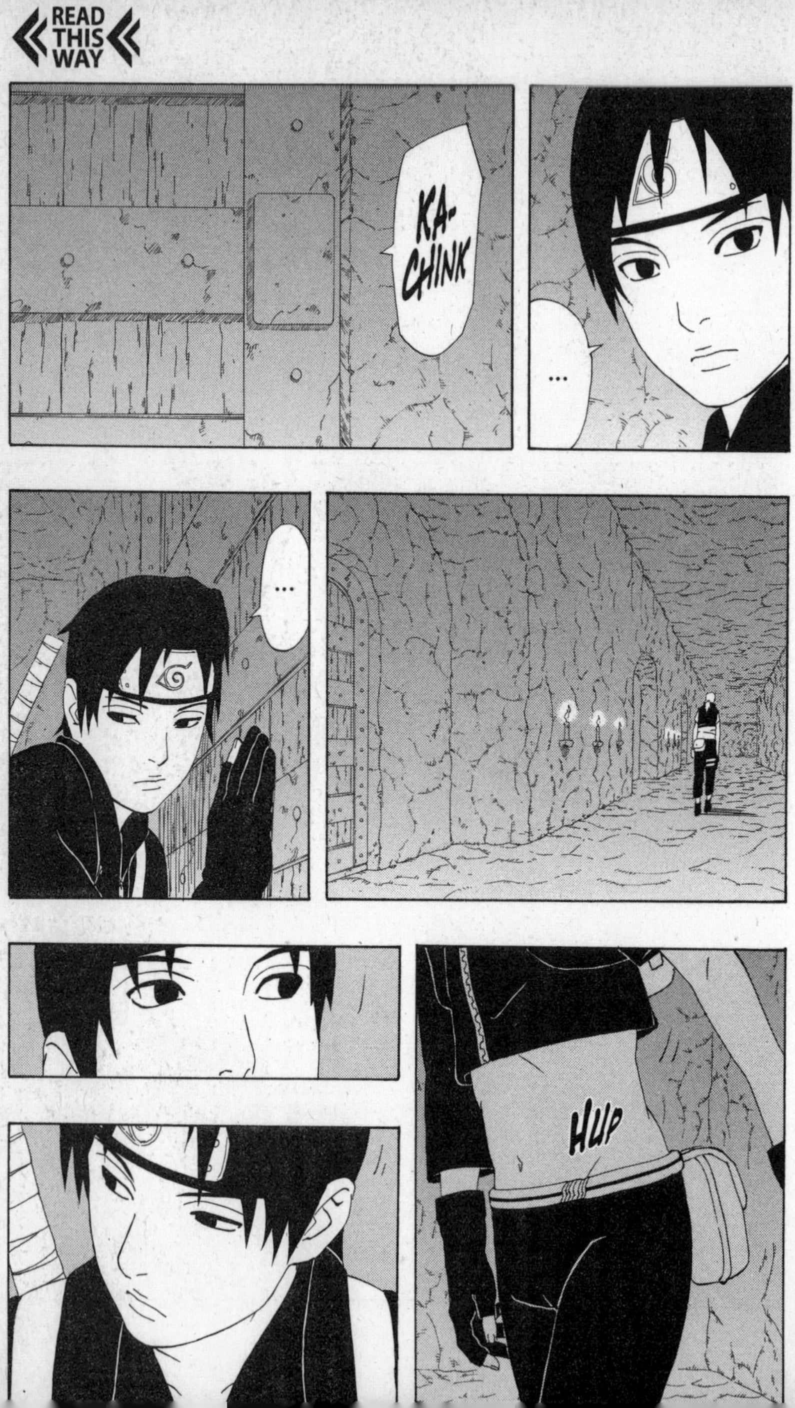
READ THIS WAY
...
KA-CHINK
...
HUP

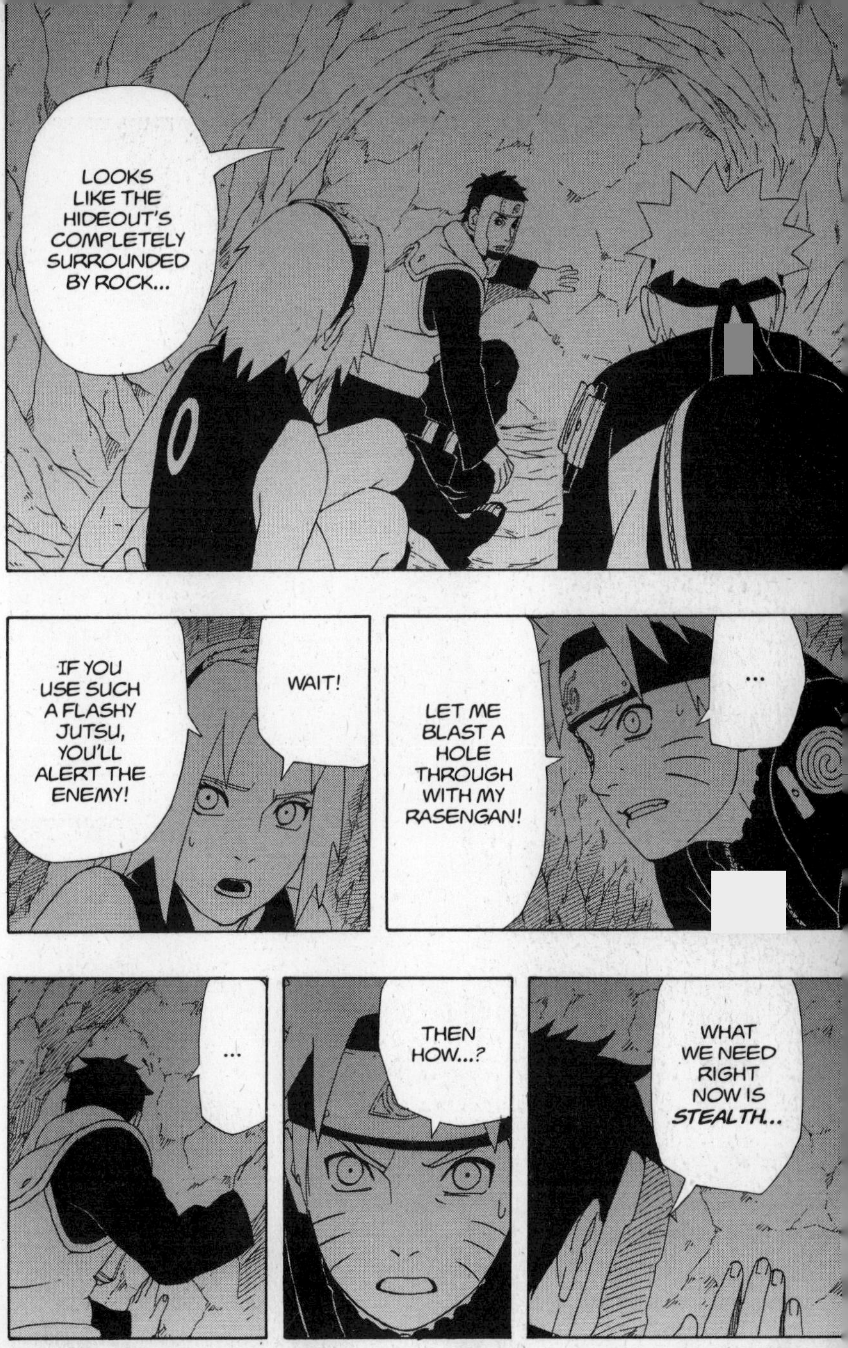
LOOKS LIKE THE HIDEOUT'S COMPLETELY SURROUNDED BY ROCK...
...
LET ME BLAST A HOLE THROUGH WITH MY RASENGAN!
WAIT!
IF YOU USE SUCH A FLASHY JUTSU, YOU'LL ALERT THE ENEMY!
WHAT WE NEED RIGHT NOW IS *STEALTH*...
THEN HOW...?
...

READ THIS WAY

?
FOUND IT...
THE MORE SOLID THE ROCK FACE...
...THE LESS FORCE NEED BE APPLIED TO A SMALL FISSURE, AND...
ZWOOP...
ZWOOP...
SPLISH
CRACK CRACK CRACK
ZWOOP...
CLACK
CLACK CLACK
VOILA! THERE YOU GO.

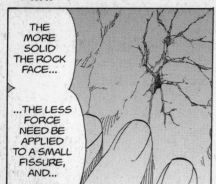

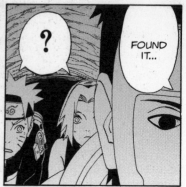

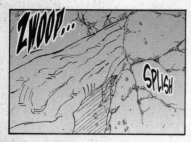

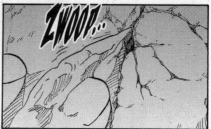

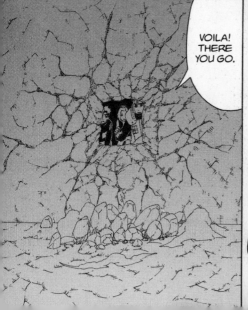

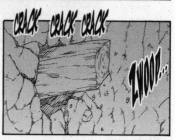

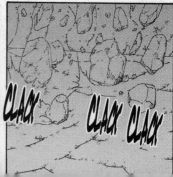

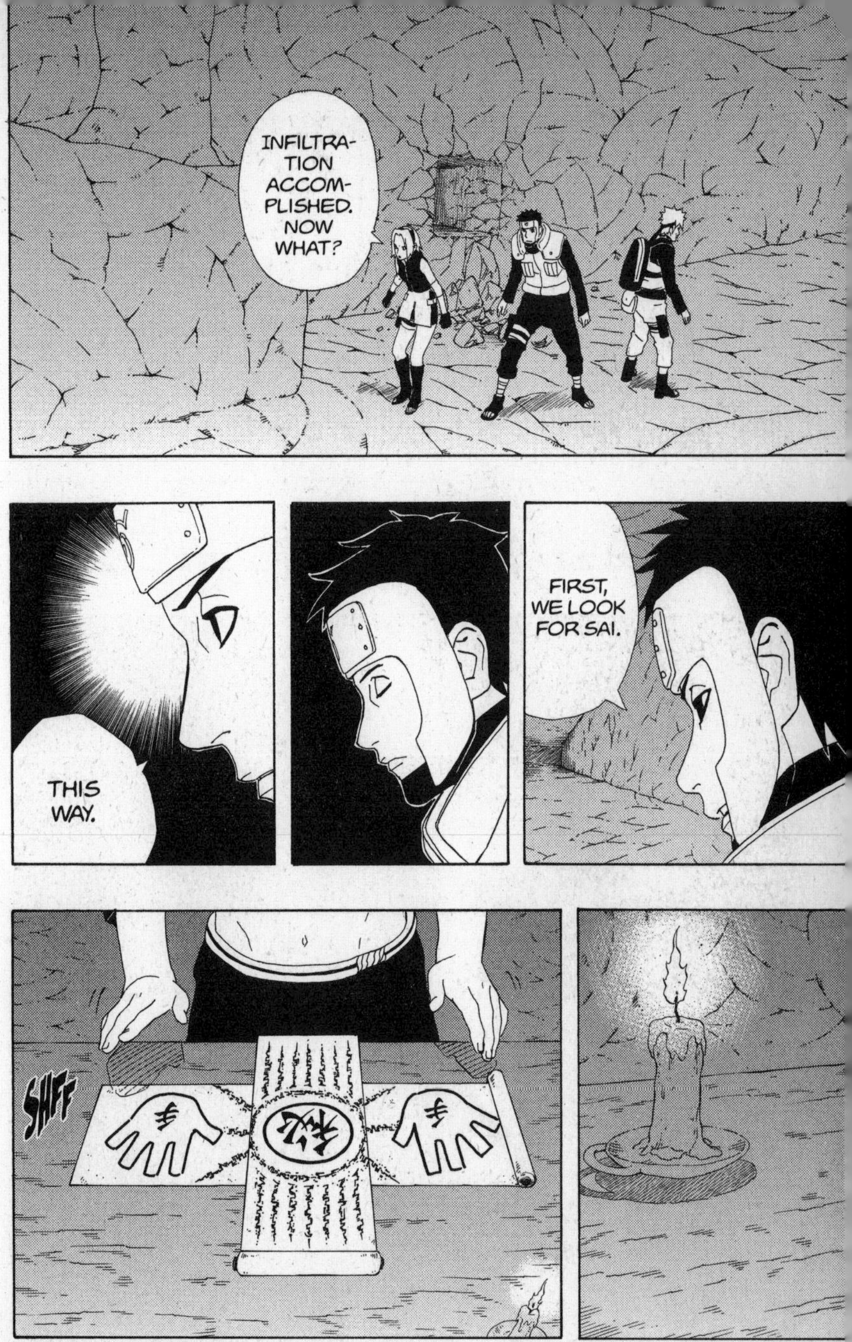
INFILTRATION ACCOMPLISHED. NOW WHAT?
FIRST, WE LOOK FOR SAI.
THIS WAY.
SHFF

(HAND) (SECRET) (HAND)

READ THIS WAY

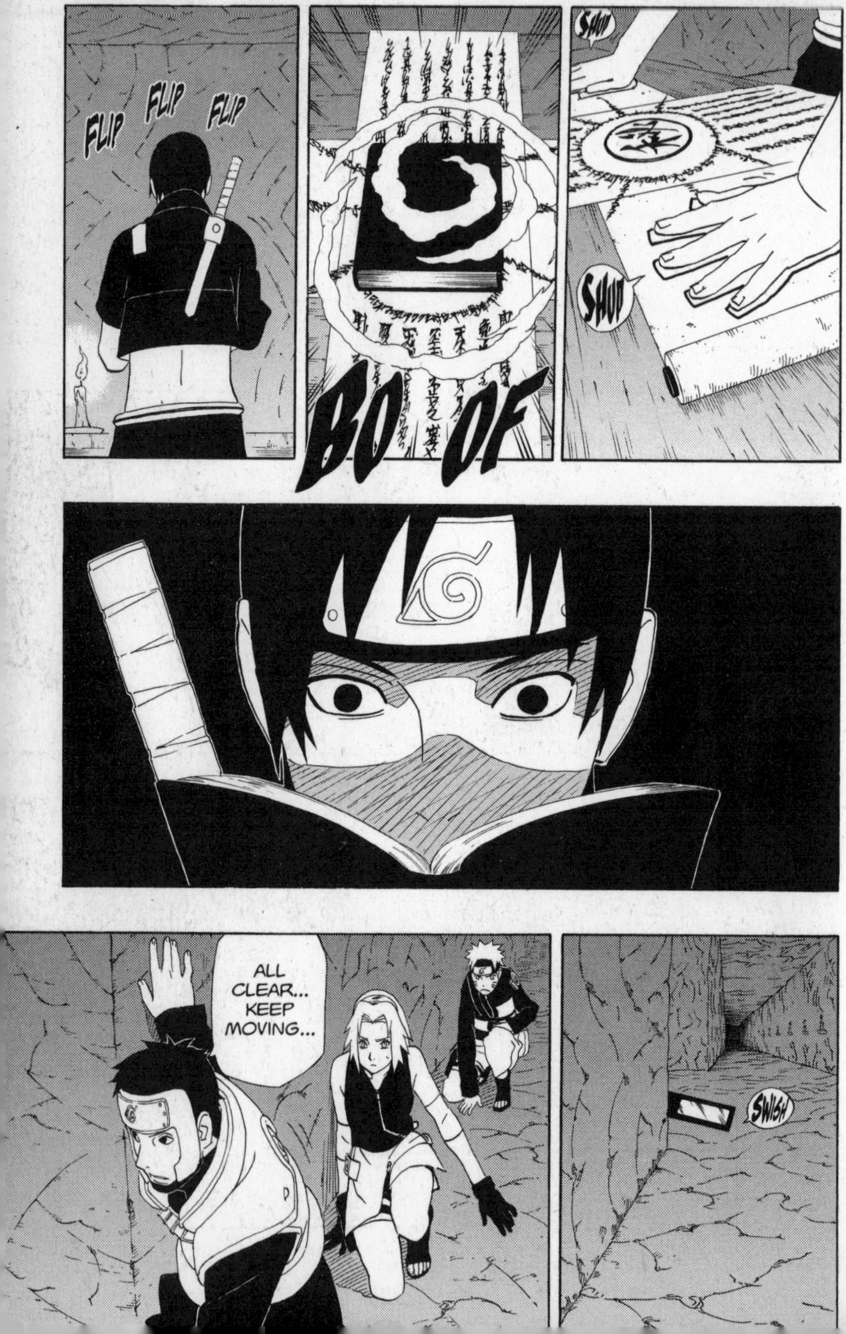
SHUP
SHUP
BOOF
FLIP FLIP FLIP
SWISH
ALL CLEAR... KEEP MOVING...

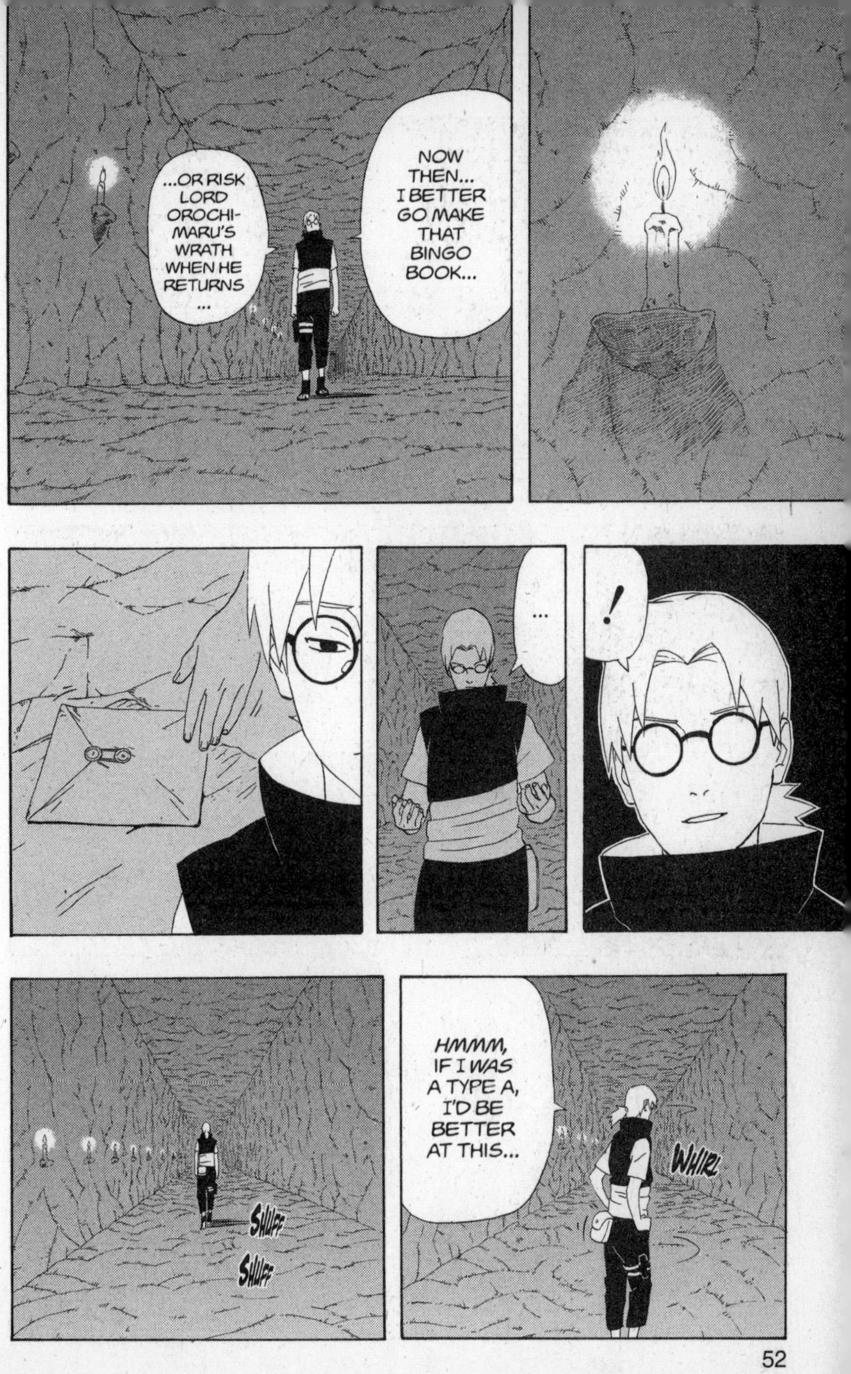

NOW THEN... I BETTER GO MAKE THAT BINGO BOOK...
...OR RISK LORD OROCHIMARU'S WRATH WHEN HE RETURNS...
!
...
HMMM, IF I WAS A TYPE A, I'D BE BETTER AT THIS...
WHIRL
SHUFF
SHUFF

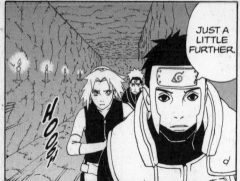

JUST A LITTLE FURTHER.

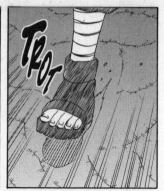

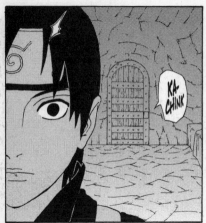

KA-CHINK

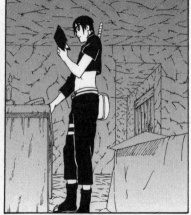

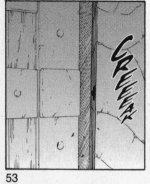

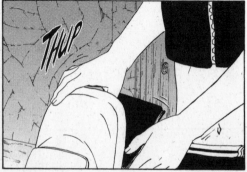

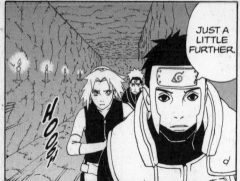

JUST A LITTLE FURTHER.

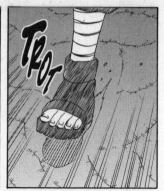

TROT

HOO...

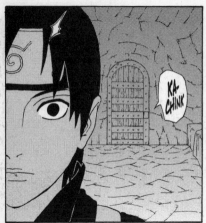

KA-CHINK

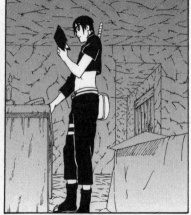

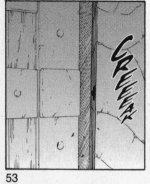

CREEEAK

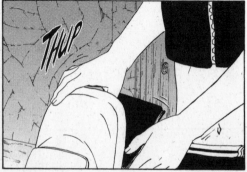

THUP

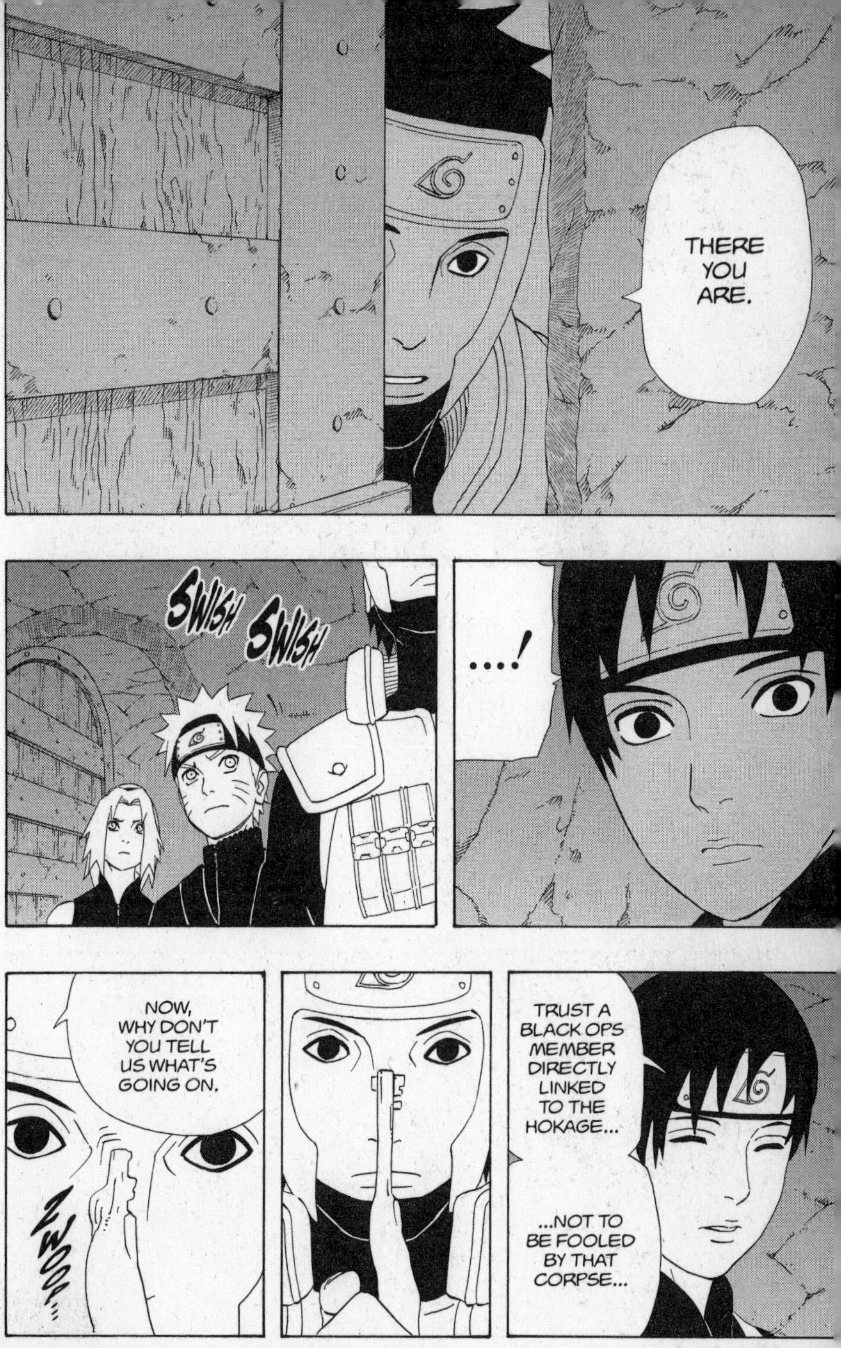
THERE YOU ARE.
...!
SWISH SWISH
TRUST A BLACK OPS MEMBER DIRECTLY LINKED TO THE HOKAGE...
...NOT TO BE FOOLED BY THAT CORPSE...
NOW, WHY DON'T YOU TELL US WHAT'S GOING ON.
ZWOOP...

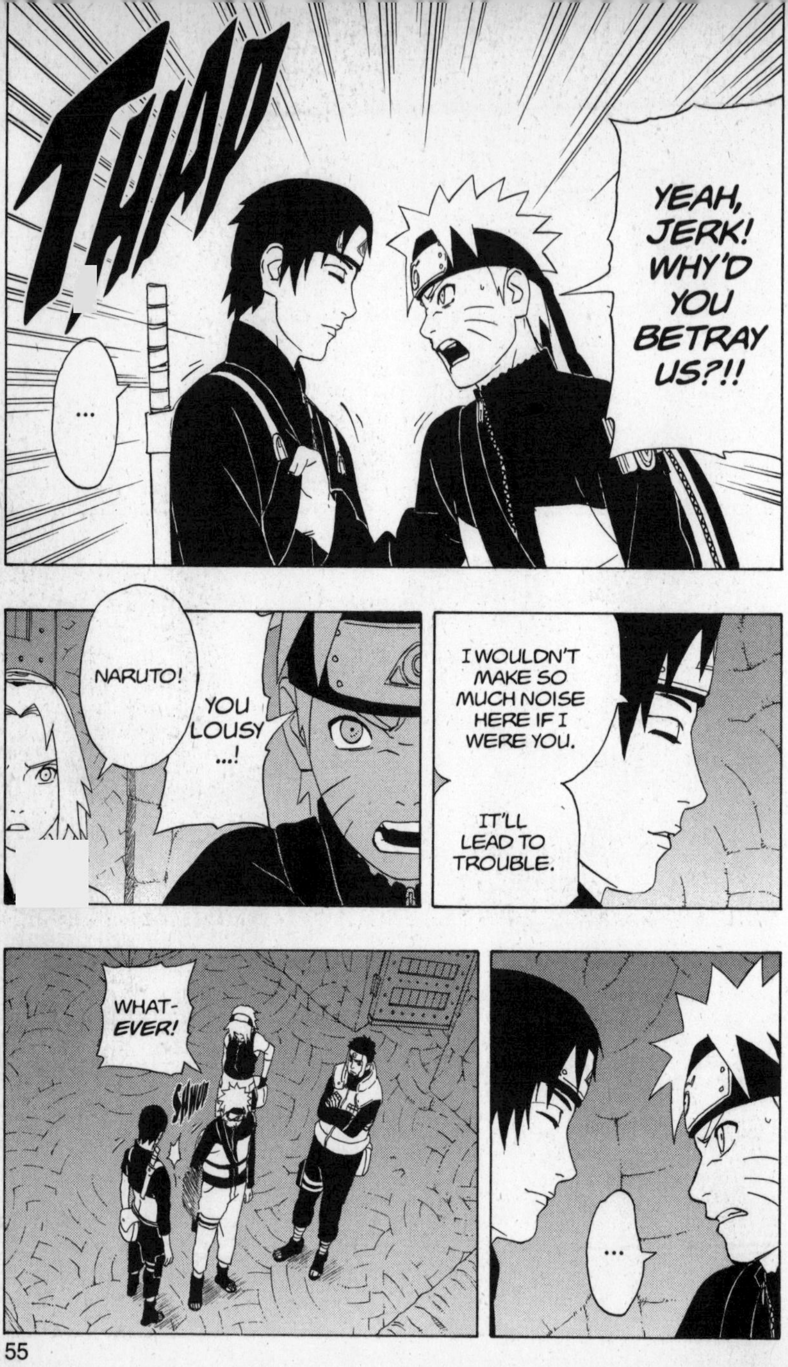
YEAH, JERK! WHY'D YOU BETRAY US?!!
TAPP
...
I WOULDN'T MAKE SO MUCH NOISE HERE IF I WERE YOU.
IT'LL LEAD TO TROUBLE.
YOU LOUSY ...!
NARUTO!
...
WHAT-EVER!

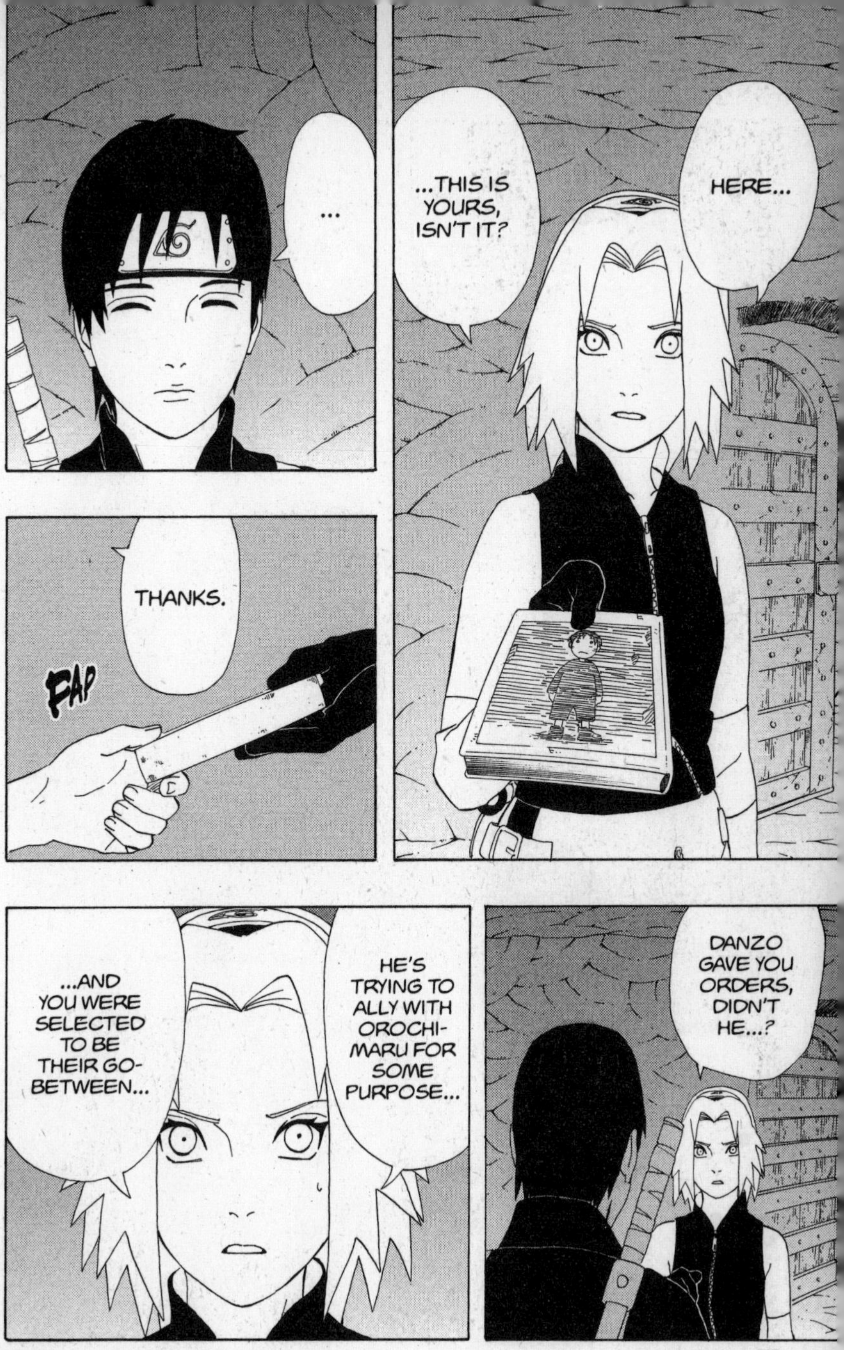
HERE...
...THIS IS YOURS, ISN'T IT?
...
THANKS.
FAP
DANZO GAVE YOU ORDERS, DIDN'T HE...?
HE'S TRYING TO ALLY WITH OROCHI-MARU FOR SOME PURPOSE...
...AND YOU WERE SELECTED TO BE THEIR GO-BETWEEN...

READ THIS WAY

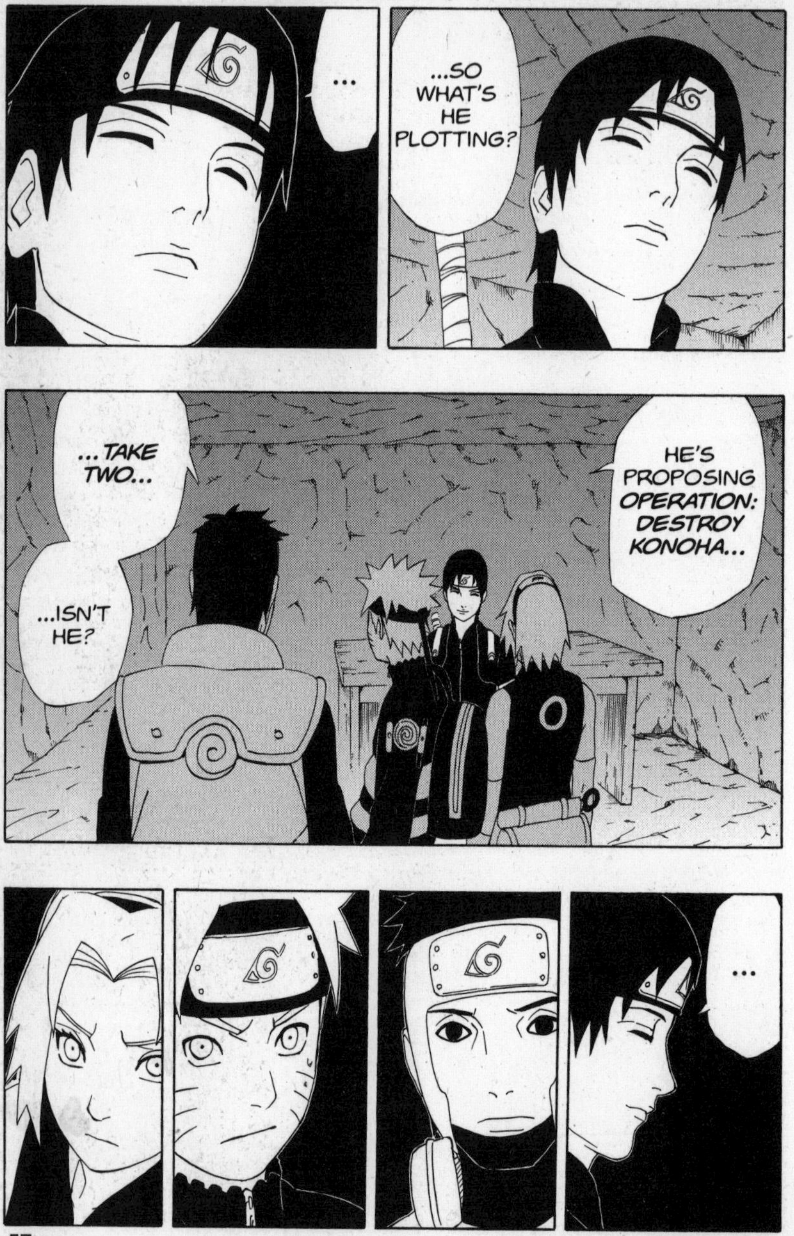
...SO WHAT'S HE PLOTTING?
...
HE'S PROPOSING OPERATION: DESTROY KONOHA...
...TAKE TWO...
...ISN'T HE?
...

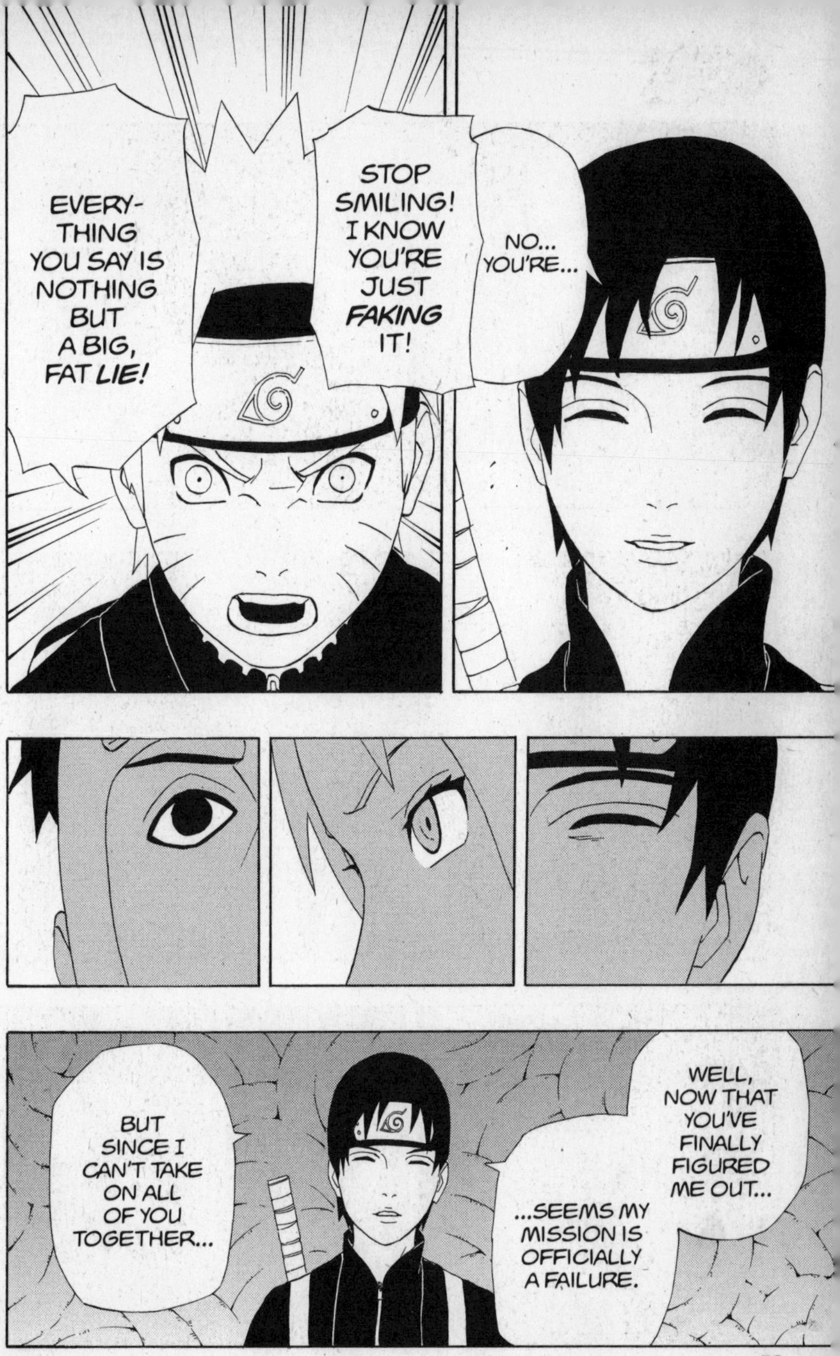

NO... YOU'RE...
STOP SMILING! I KNOW YOU'RE JUST FAKING IT!
EVERY-THING YOU SAY IS NOTHING BUT A BIG, FAT LIE!
WELL, NOW THAT YOU'VE FINALLY FIGURED ME OUT...
...SEEMS MY MISSION IS OFFICIALLY A FAILURE.
BUT SINCE I CAN'T TAKE ON ALL OF YOU TOGETHER...

READ THIS WAY

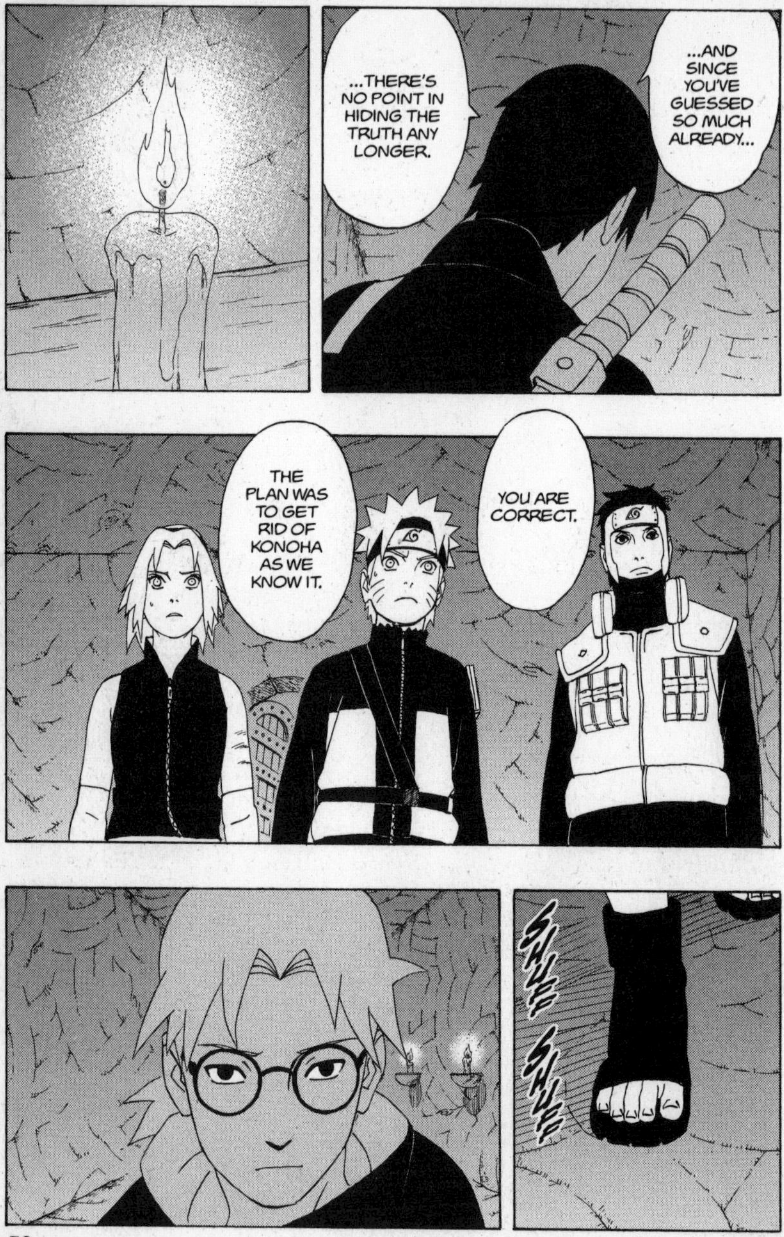
...AND SINCE YOU'VE GUESSED SO MUCH ALREADY...
...THERE'S NO POINT IN HIDING THE TRUTH ANY LONGER.
YOU ARE CORRECT.
THE PLAN WAS TO GET RID OF KONOHA AS WE KNOW IT.
SHUFF SHUFF

NARUTO

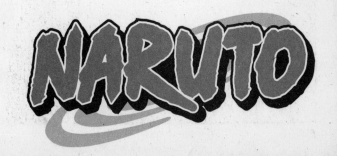

Number 303: Sai's Betrayal!!

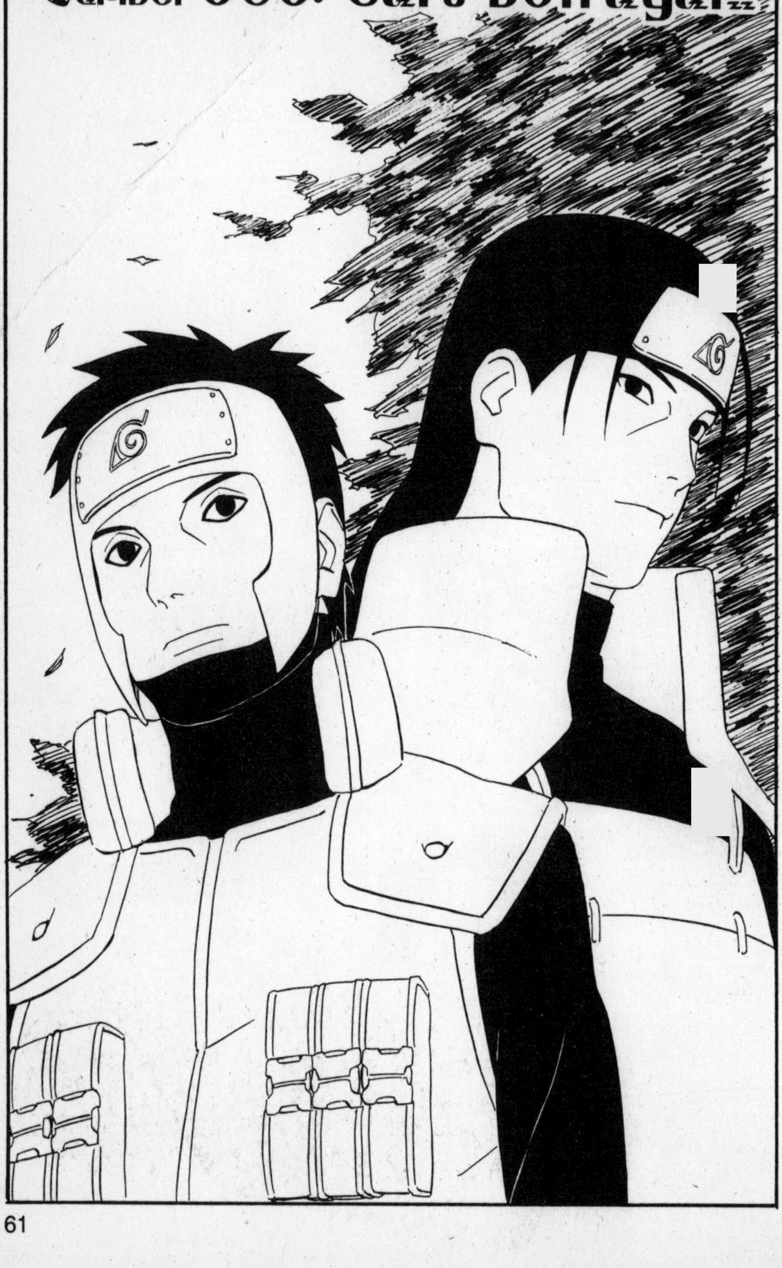

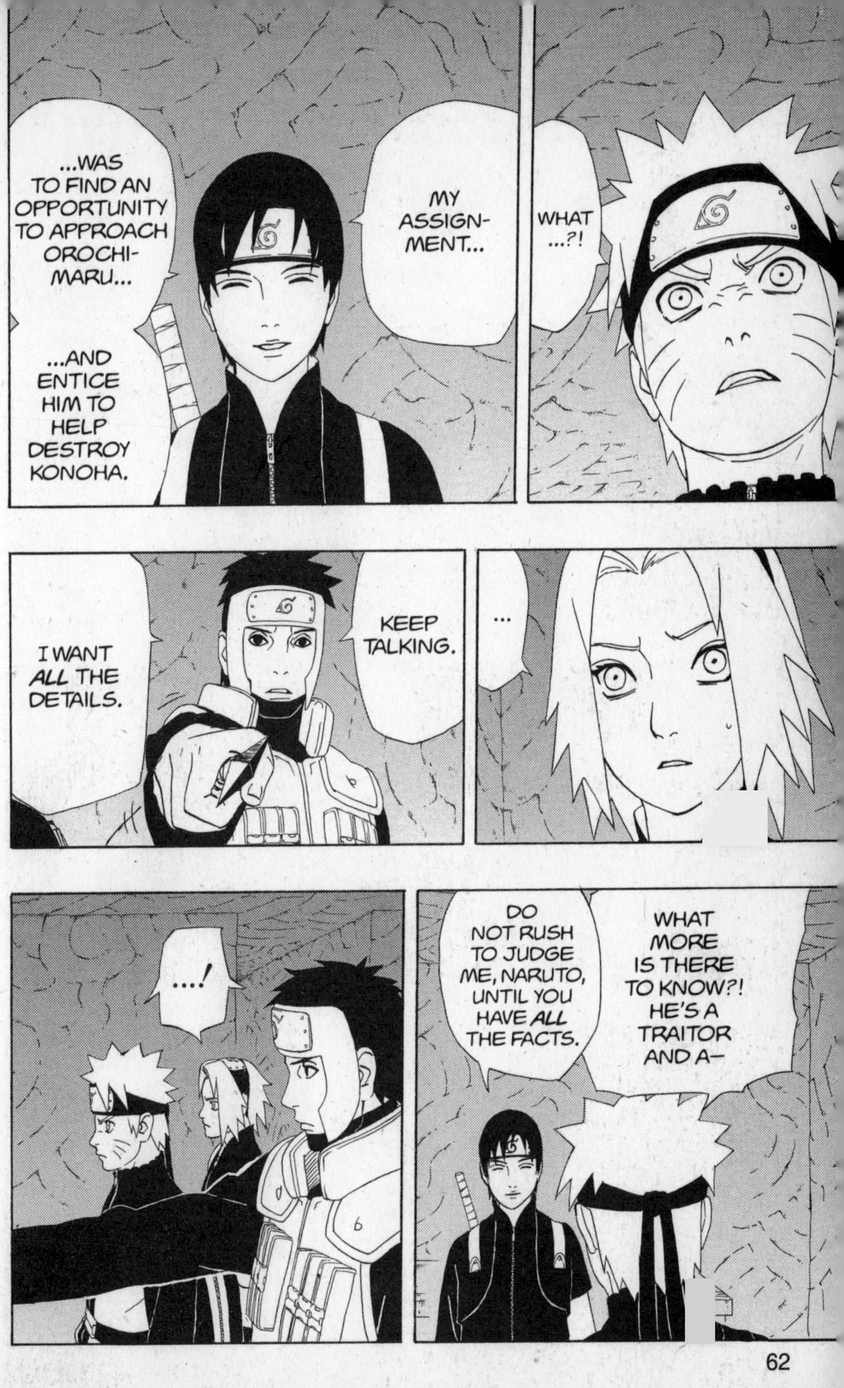
WHAT ...?!
MY ASSIGN-MENT...
...WAS TO FIND AN OPPORTUNITY TO APPROACH OROCHI-MARU...
...AND ENTICE HIM TO HELP DESTROY KONOHA.
...
KEEP TALKING.
I WANT ALL THE DETAILS.
WHAT MORE IS THERE TO KNOW?! HE'S A TRAITOR AND A—
DO NOT RUSH TO JUDGE ME, NARUTO, UNTIL YOU HAVE ALL THE FACTS.
...!

READ THIS WAY

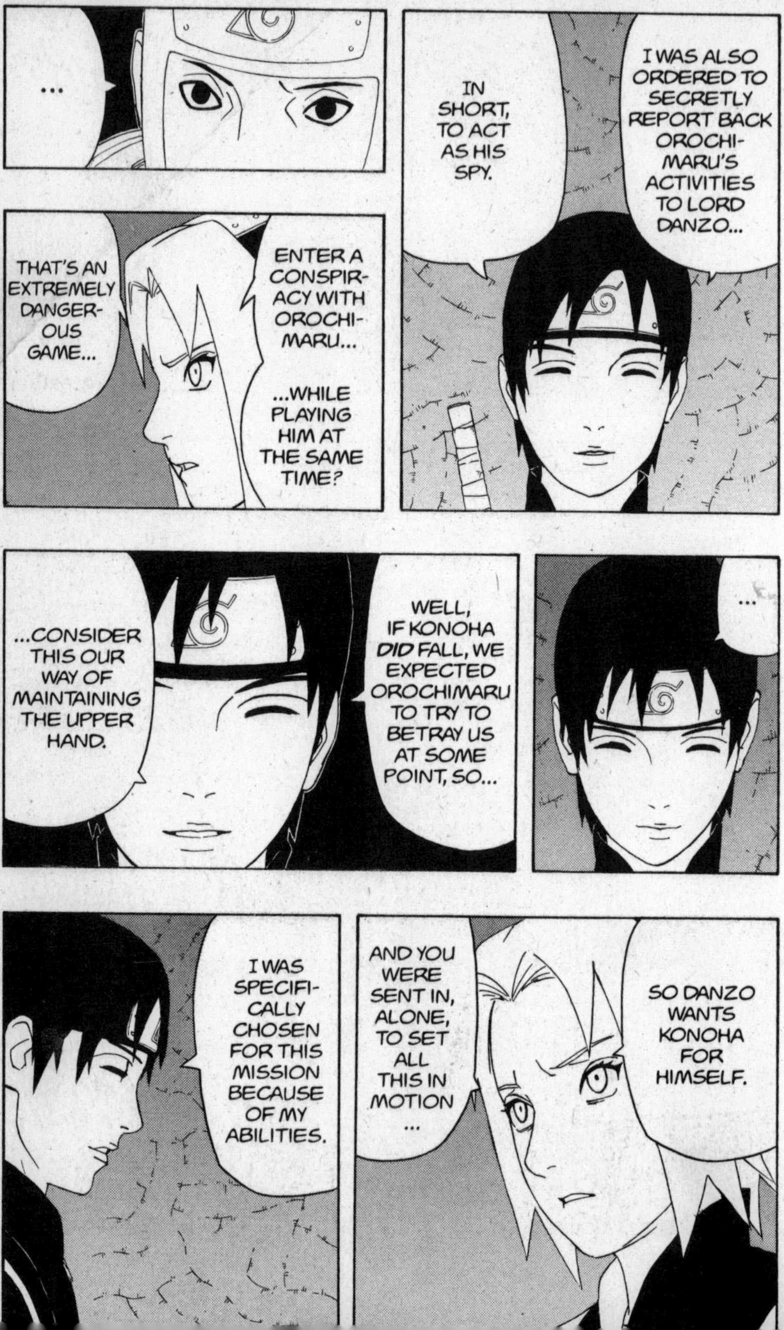
I WAS ALSO ORDERED TO SECRETLY REPORT BACK OROCHIMARU'S ACTIVITIES TO LORD DANZO...
IN SHORT, TO ACT AS HIS SPY.
...
ENTER A CONSPIRACY WITH OROCHIMARU...
...WHILE PLAYING HIM AT THE SAME TIME?
THAT'S AN EXTREMELY DANGEROUS GAME...
...
WELL, IF KONOHA *DID* FALL, WE EXPECTED OROCHIMARU TO TRY TO BETRAY US AT SOME POINT, SO...
...CONSIDER THIS OUR WAY OF MAINTAINING THE UPPER HAND.
SO DANZO WANTS KONOHA FOR HIMSELF.
AND YOU WERE SENT IN, ALONE, TO SET ALL THIS IN MOTION...
I WAS SPECIFICALLY CHOSEN FOR THIS MISSION BECAUSE OF MY ABILITIES.

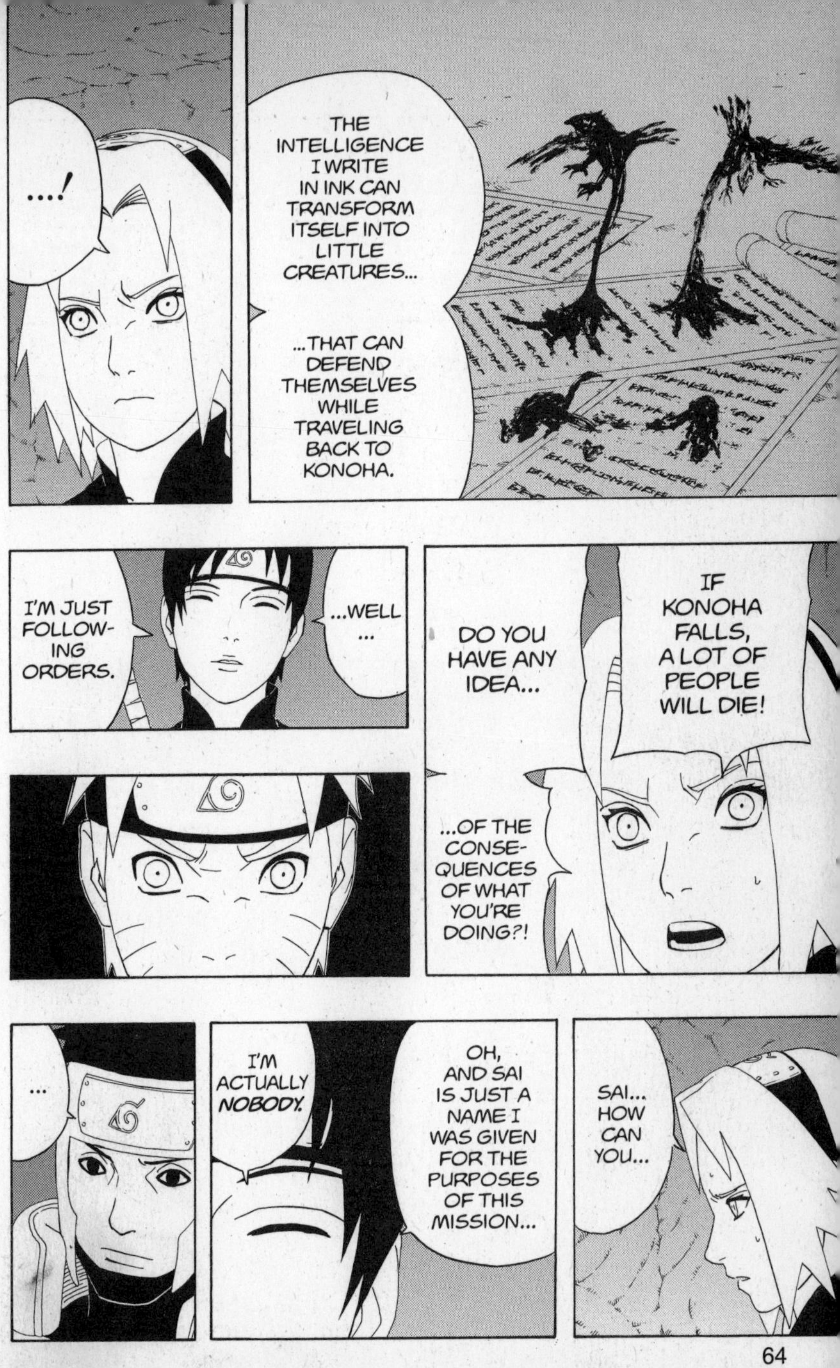
THE INTELLIGENCE I WRITE IN INK CAN TRANSFORM ITSELF INTO LITTLE CREATURES...
...THAT CAN DEFEND THEMSELVES WHILE TRAVELING BACK TO KONOHA.
....!
IF KONOHA FALLS, A LOT OF PEOPLE WILL DIE!
DO YOU HAVE ANY IDEA...
...OF THE CONSE-QUENCES OF WHAT YOU'RE DOING?!
...WELL ...
I'M JUST FOLLOW-ING ORDERS.
SAI... HOW CAN YOU...
OH, AND SAI IS JUST A NAME I WAS GIVEN FOR THE PURPOSES OF THIS MISSION...
I'M ACTUALLY *NOBODY.*
...

READ THIS WAY

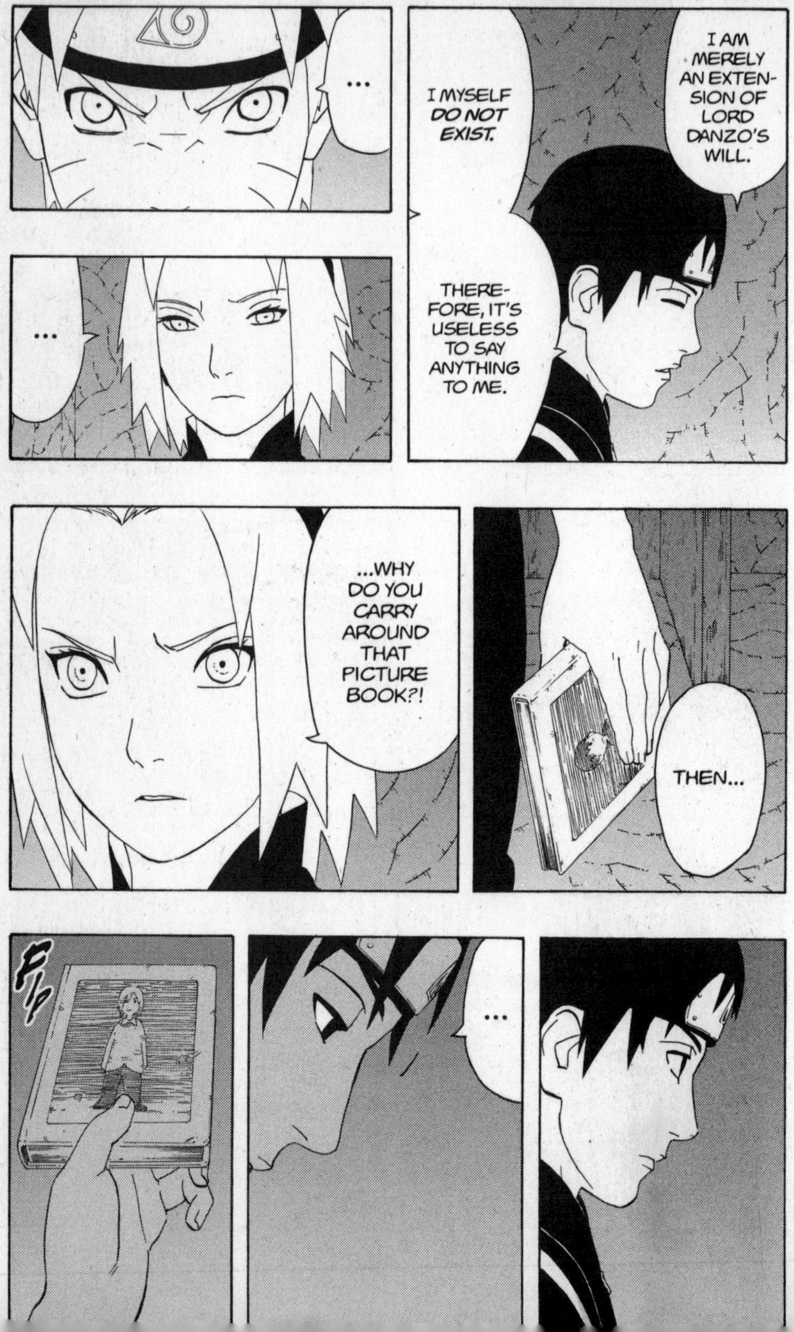

I AM MERELY AN EXTENSION OF LORD DANZO'S WILL.
I MYSELF DO NOT EXIST.
THEREFORE, IT'S USELESS TO SAY ANYTHING TO ME.
...
...
THEN...
...WHY DO YOU CARRY AROUND THAT PICTURE BOOK?!
...

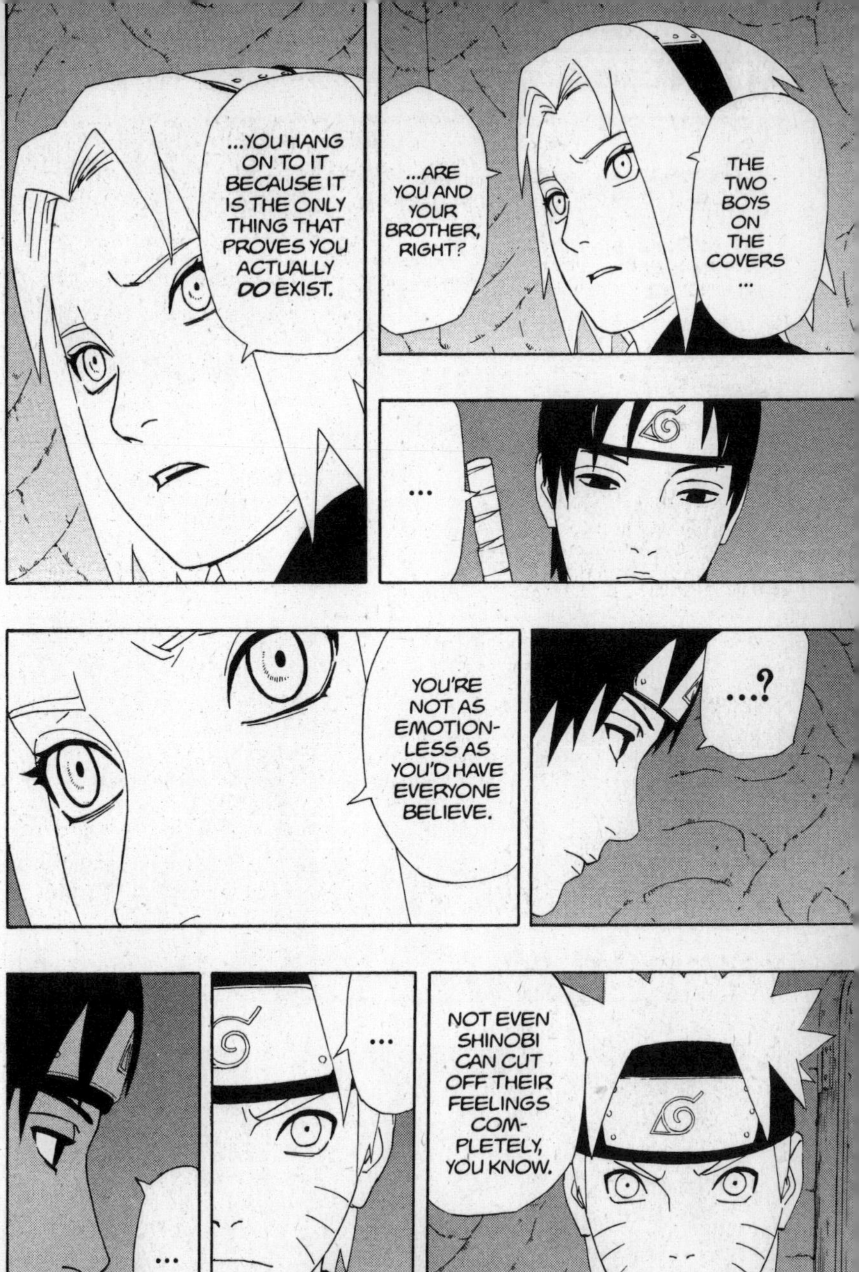
THE TWO BOYS ON THE COVERS...
...ARE YOU AND YOUR BROTHER, RIGHT?
...
...YOU HANG ON TO IT BECAUSE IT IS THE ONLY THING THAT PROVES YOU ACTUALLY *DO* EXIST.
...?
YOU'RE NOT AS EMOTION-LESS AS YOU'D HAVE EVERYONE BELIEVE.
NOT EVEN SHINOBI CAN CUT OFF THEIR FEELINGS COM-PLETELY, YOU KNOW.
...
...

READ THIS WAY

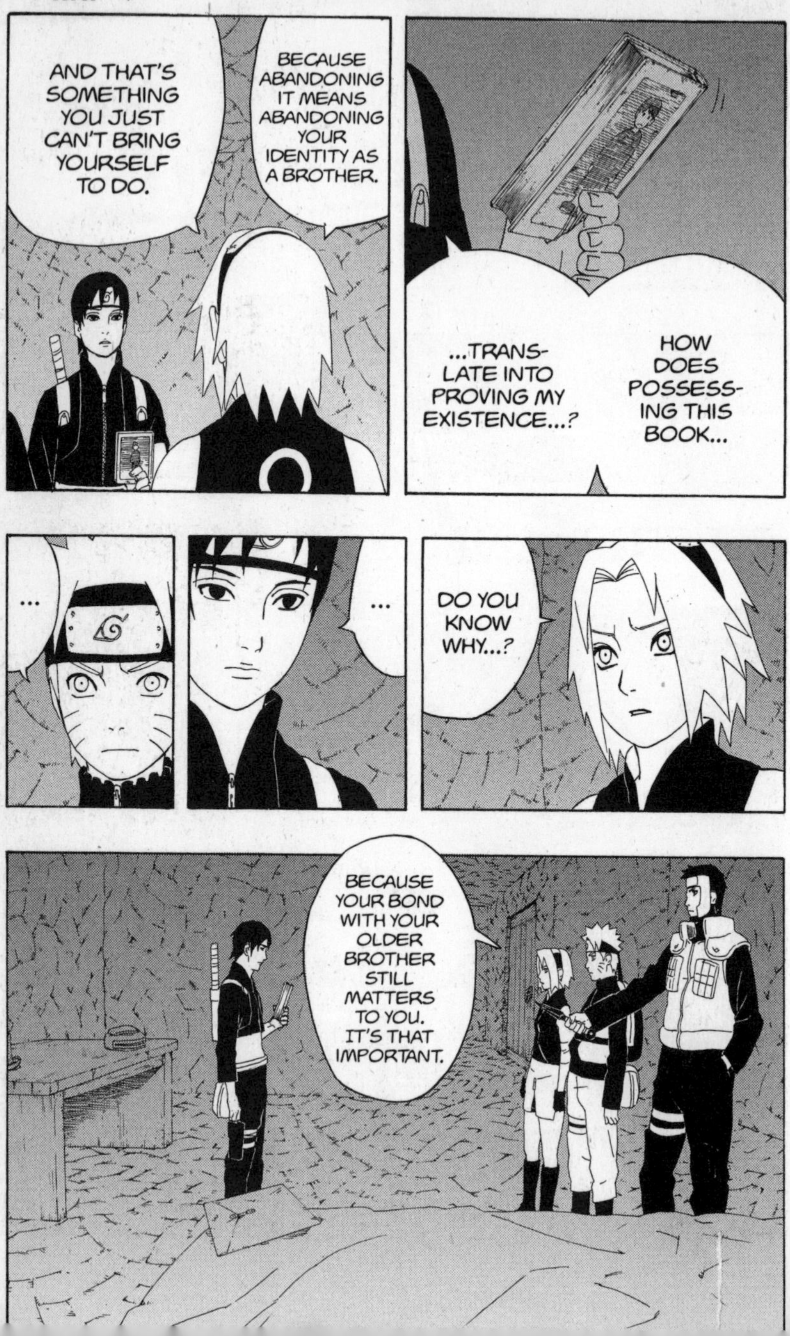
HOW DOES POSSESS-ING THIS BOOK...
...TRANS-LATE INTO PROVING MY EXISTENCE...?
BECAUSE ABANDONING IT MEANS ABANDONING YOUR IDENTITY AS A BROTHER.
AND THAT'S SOMETHING YOU JUST CAN'T BRING YOURSELF TO DO.
DO YOU KNOW WHY...?
...
...
BECAUSE YOUR BOND WITH YOUR OLDER BROTHER STILL MATTERS TO YOU. IT'S THAT IMPORTANT.

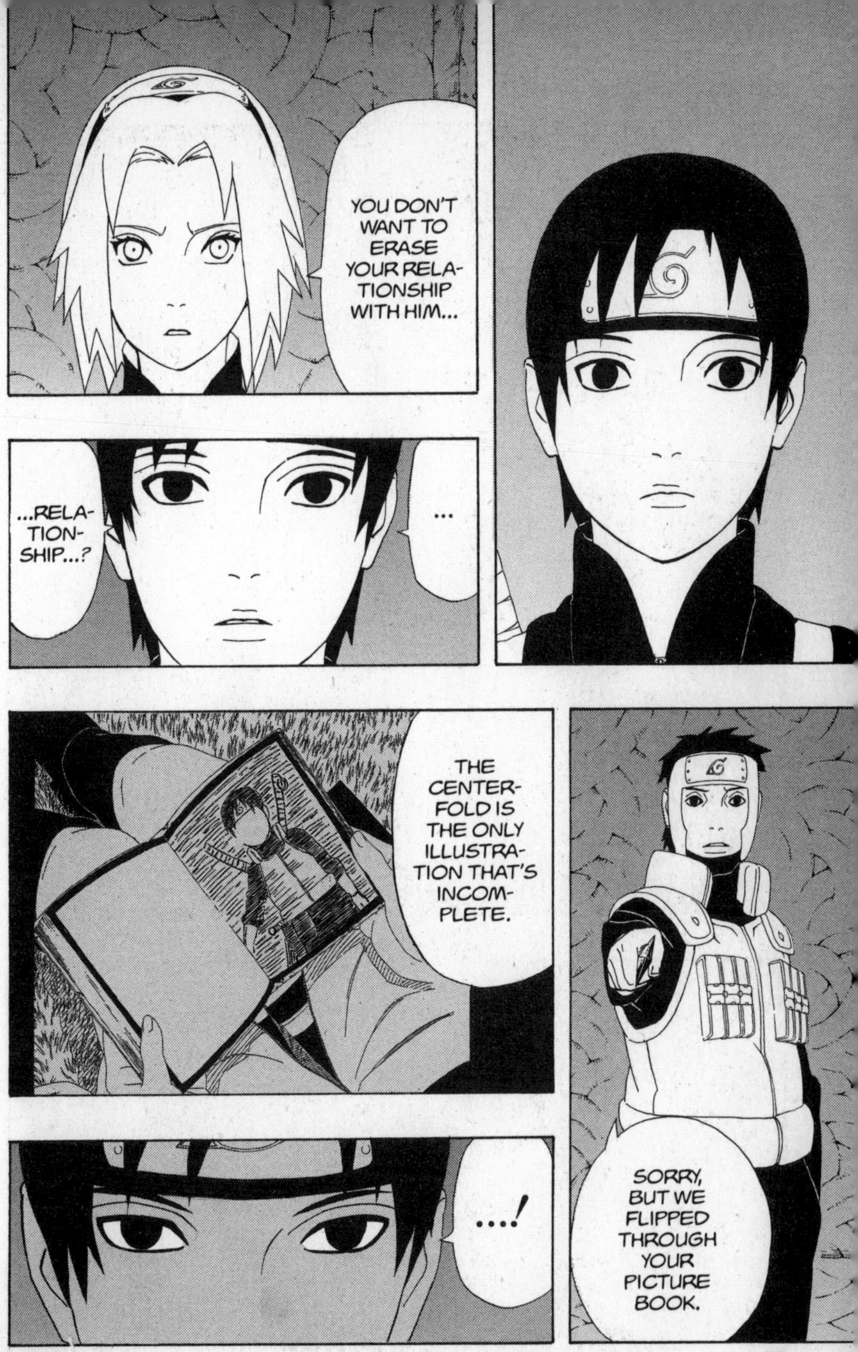
YOU DON'T WANT TO ERASE YOUR RELATIONSHIP WITH HIM...
...
...RELATIONSHIP...?
SORRY, BUT WE FLIPPED THROUGH YOUR PICTURE BOOK.
THE CENTERFOLD IS THE ONLY ILLUSTRATION THAT'S INCOMPLETE.
...!

READ THIS WAY

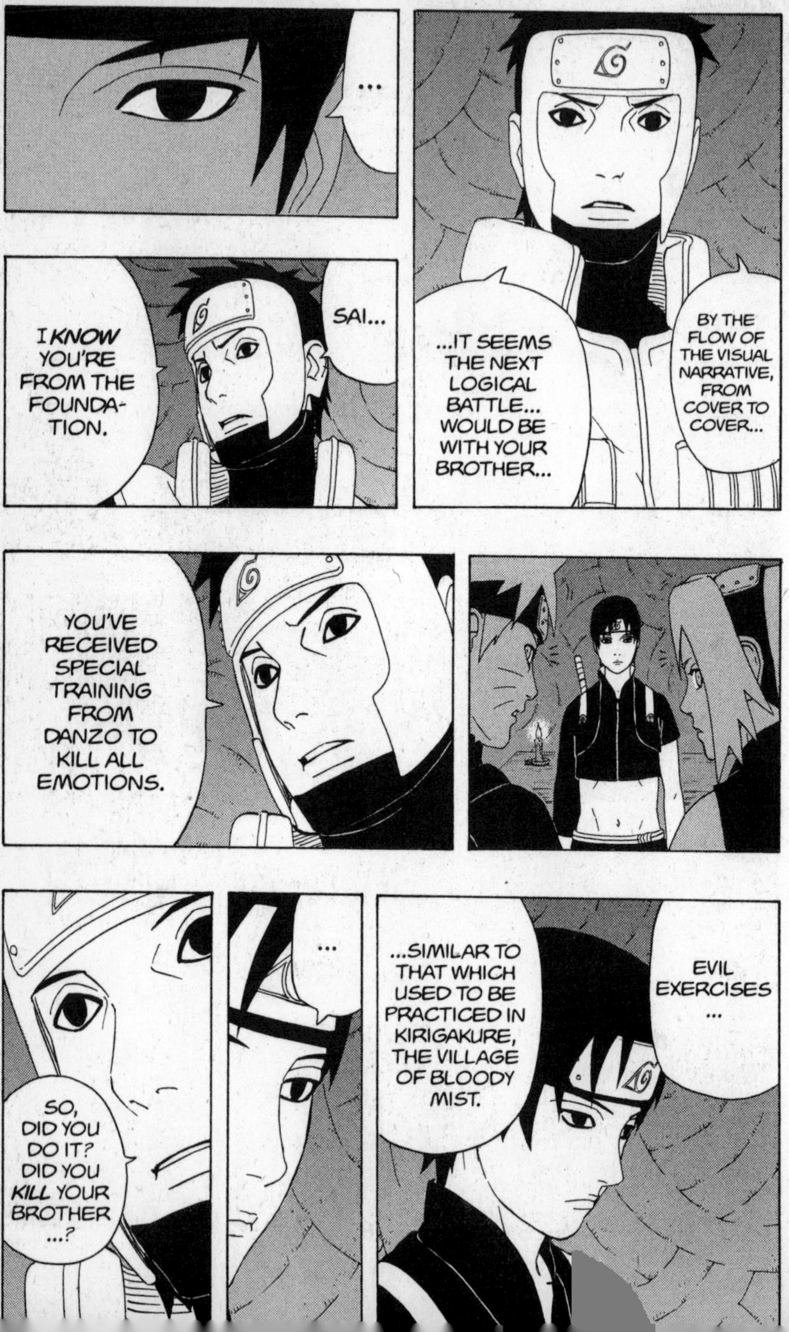

BY THE FLOW OF THE VISUAL NARRATIVE, FROM COVER TO COVER...
...IT SEEMS THE NEXT LOGICAL BATTLE... WOULD BE WITH YOUR BROTHER...
...
SAI...
I *KNOW* YOU'RE FROM THE FOUNDA-TION.
YOU'VE RECEIVED SPECIAL TRAINING FROM DANZO TO KILL ALL EMOTIONS.
EVIL EXERCISES ...
...SIMILAR TO THAT WHICH USED TO BE PRACTICED IN KIRIGAKURE, THE VILLAGE OF BLOODY MIST.
...
SO, DID YOU DO IT? DID YOU *KILL* YOUR BROTHER ...?

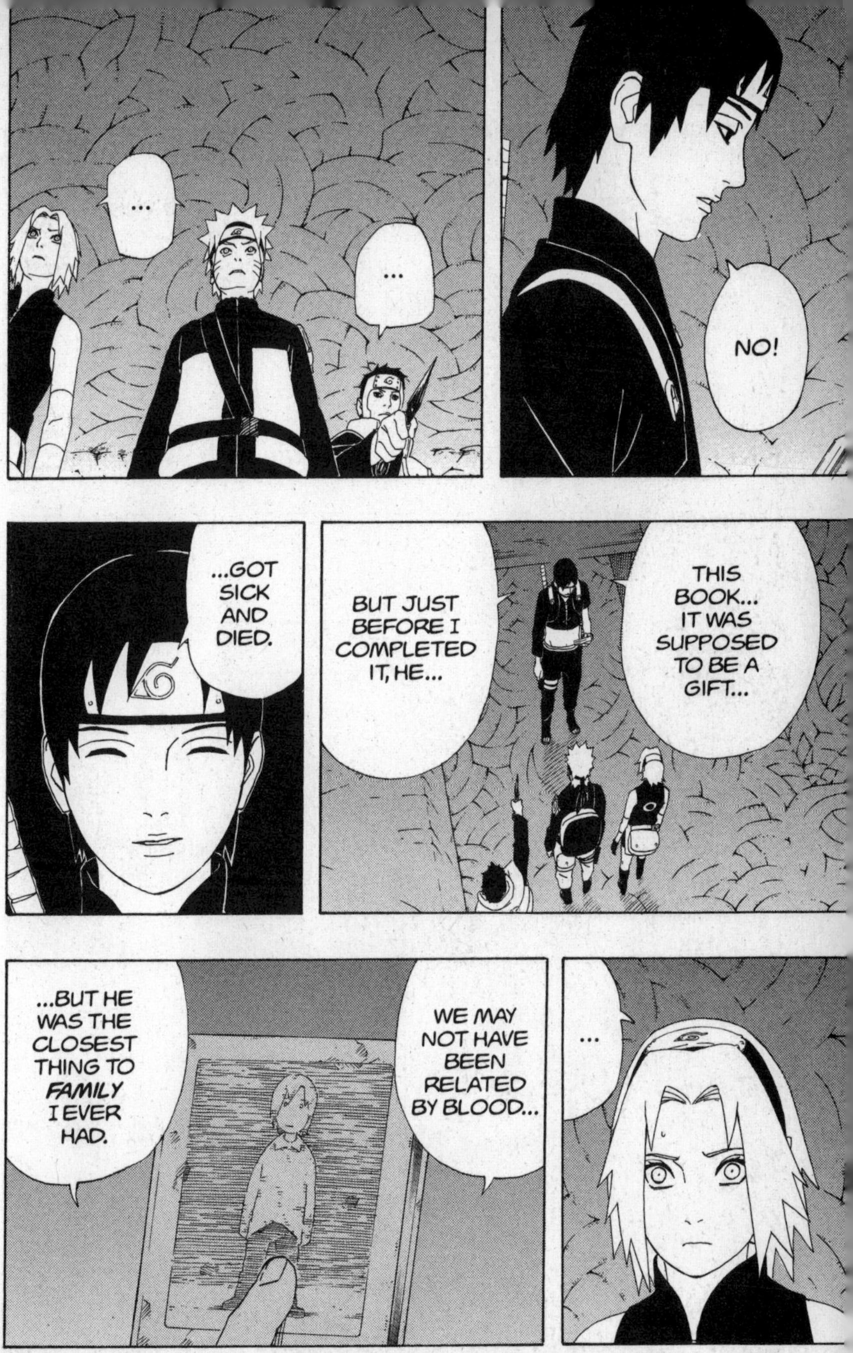
NO!
...
...
THIS BOOK... IT WAS SUPPOSED TO BE A GIFT...
BUT JUST BEFORE I COMPLETED IT, HE...
...GOT SICK AND DIED.
...
WE MAY NOT HAVE BEEN RELATED BY BLOOD...
...BUT HE WAS THE CLOSEST THING TO *FAMILY* I EVER HAD.

READ THIS WAY

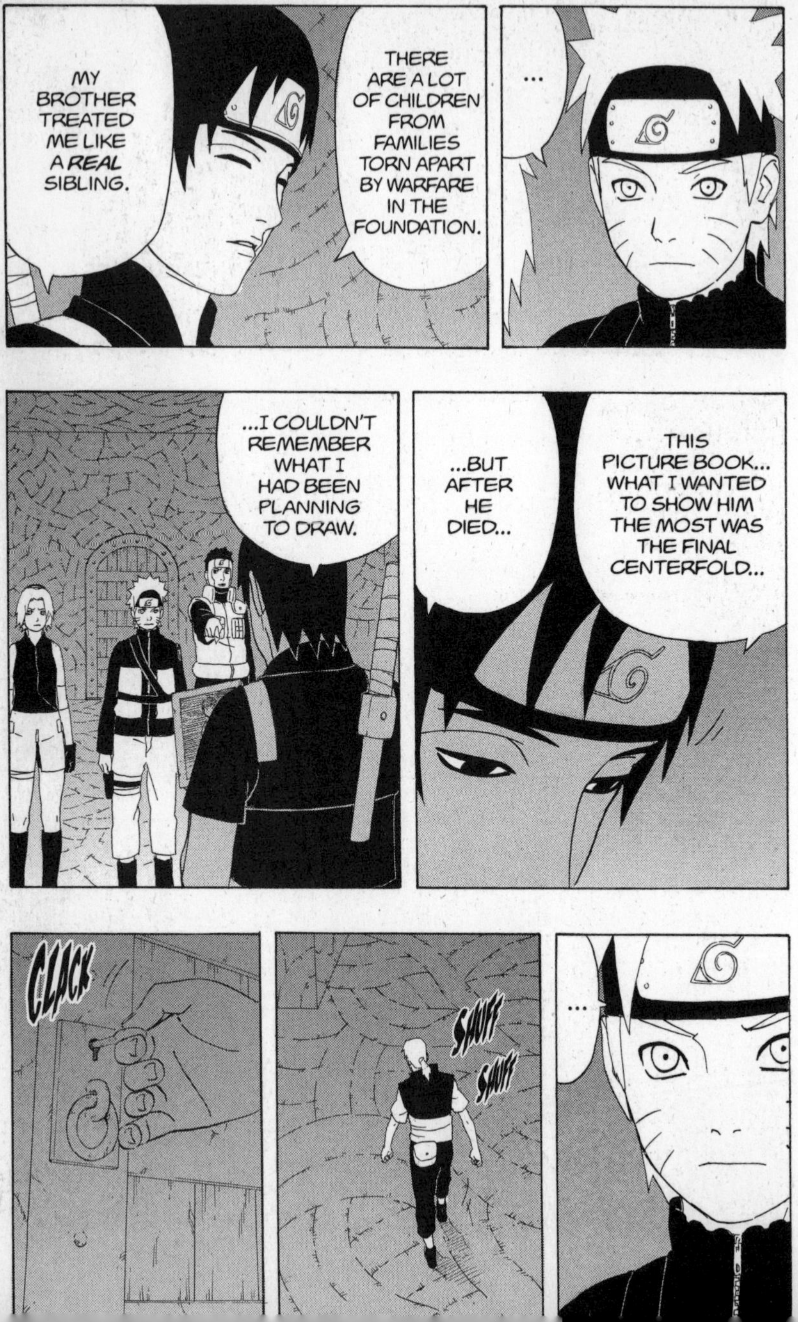
...
THERE ARE A LOT OF CHILDREN FROM FAMILIES TORN APART BY WARFARE IN THE FOUNDATION.
MY BROTHER TREATED ME LIKE A *REAL* SIBLING.
THIS PICTURE BOOK... WHAT I WANTED TO SHOW HIM THE MOST WAS THE FINAL CENTERFOLD...
...BUT AFTER HE DIED...
...I COULDN'T REMEMBER WHAT I HAD BEEN PLANNING TO DRAW.
...
SHUFF
SHUFF
CLACK

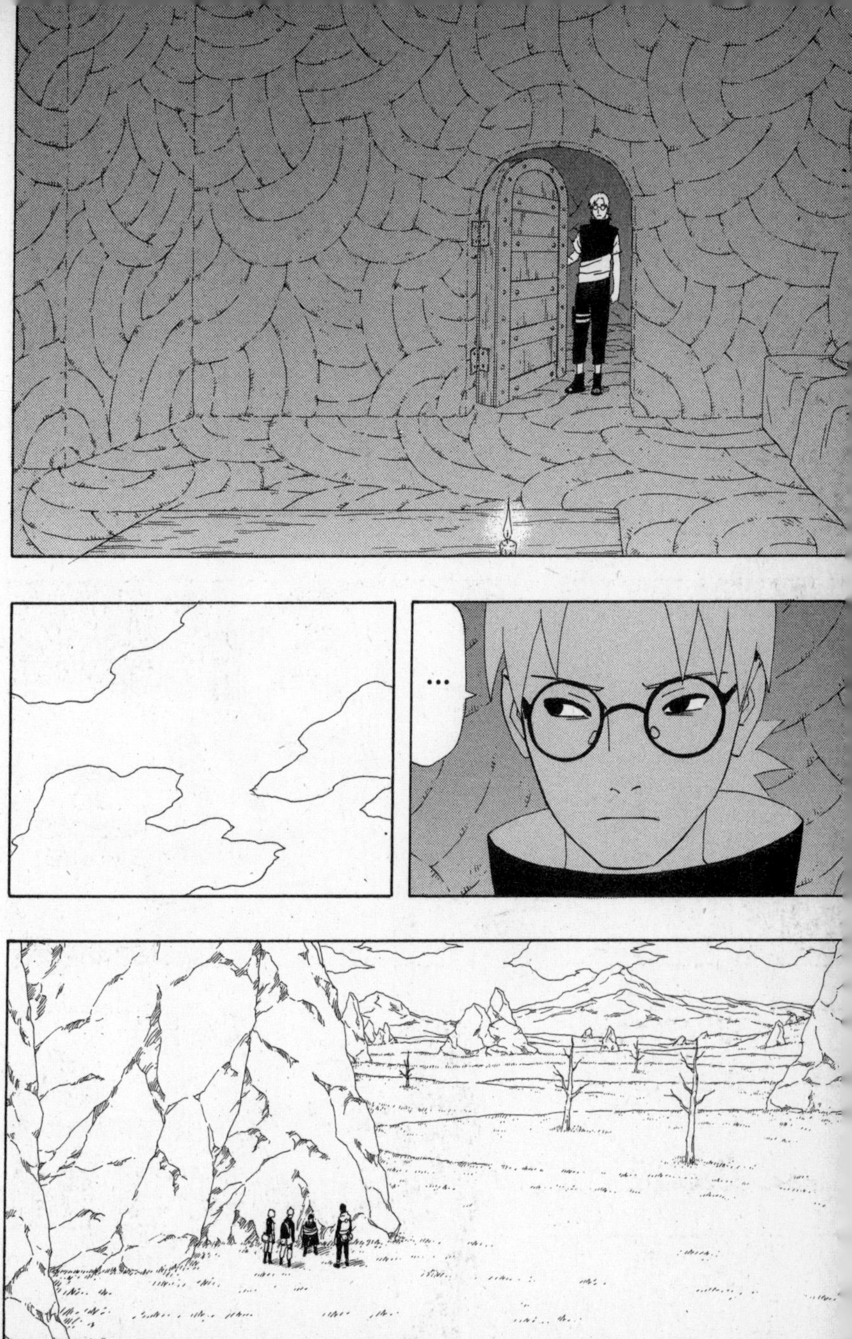
...

READ THIS WAY

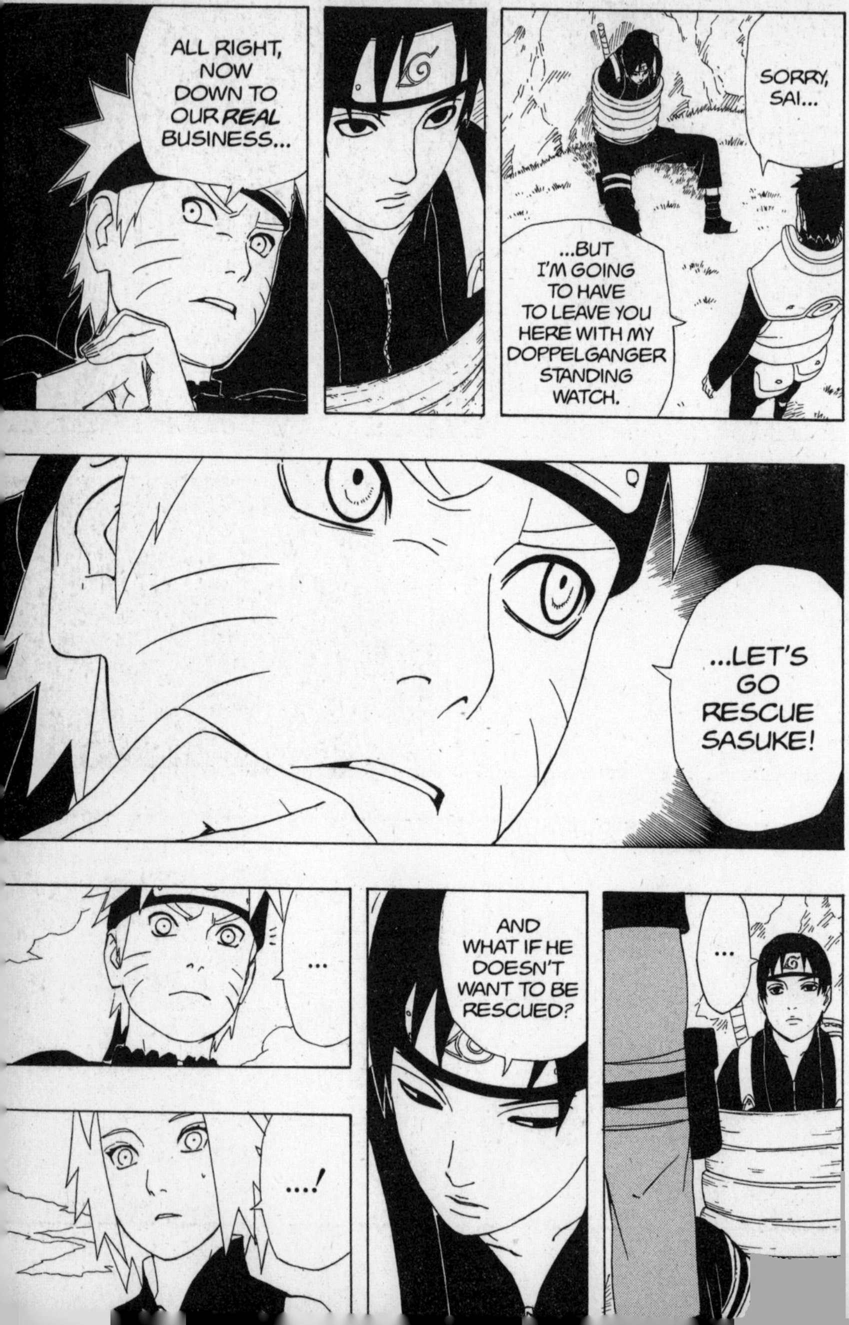
SORRY, SAI...
...BUT I'M GOING TO HAVE TO LEAVE YOU HERE WITH MY DOPPELGANGER STANDING WATCH.
ALL RIGHT, NOW DOWN TO OUR *REAL* BUSINESS...
...LET'S GO RESCUE SASUKE!
...
AND WHAT IF HE DOESN'T WANT TO BE RESCUED?
...
...!

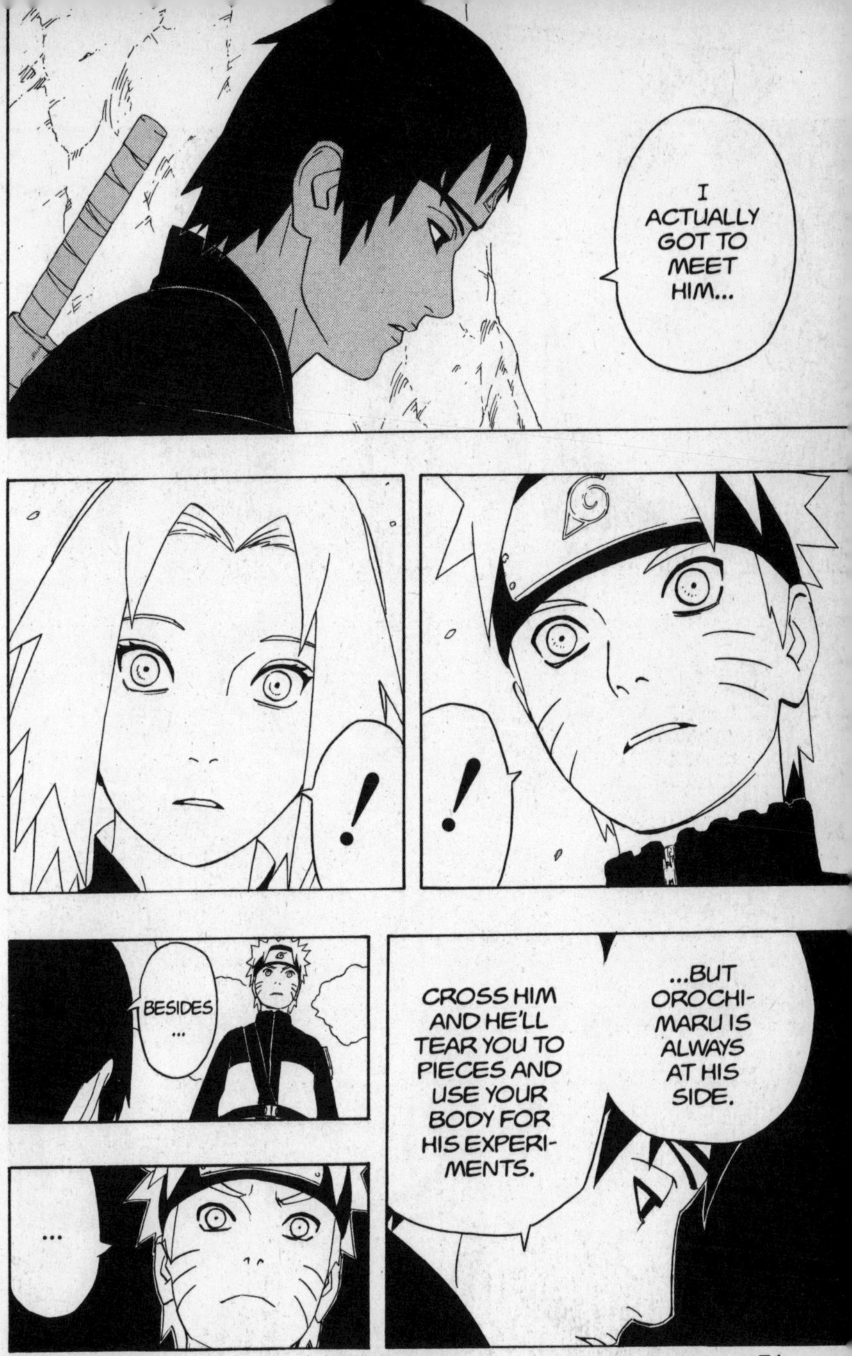
I ACTUALLY GOT TO MEET HIM...
!
!
...BUT OROCHIMARU IS ALWAYS AT HIS SIDE.
CROSS HIM AND HE'LL TEAR YOU TO PIECES AND USE YOUR BODY FOR HIS EXPERIMENTS.
BESIDES...
...

READ THIS WAY

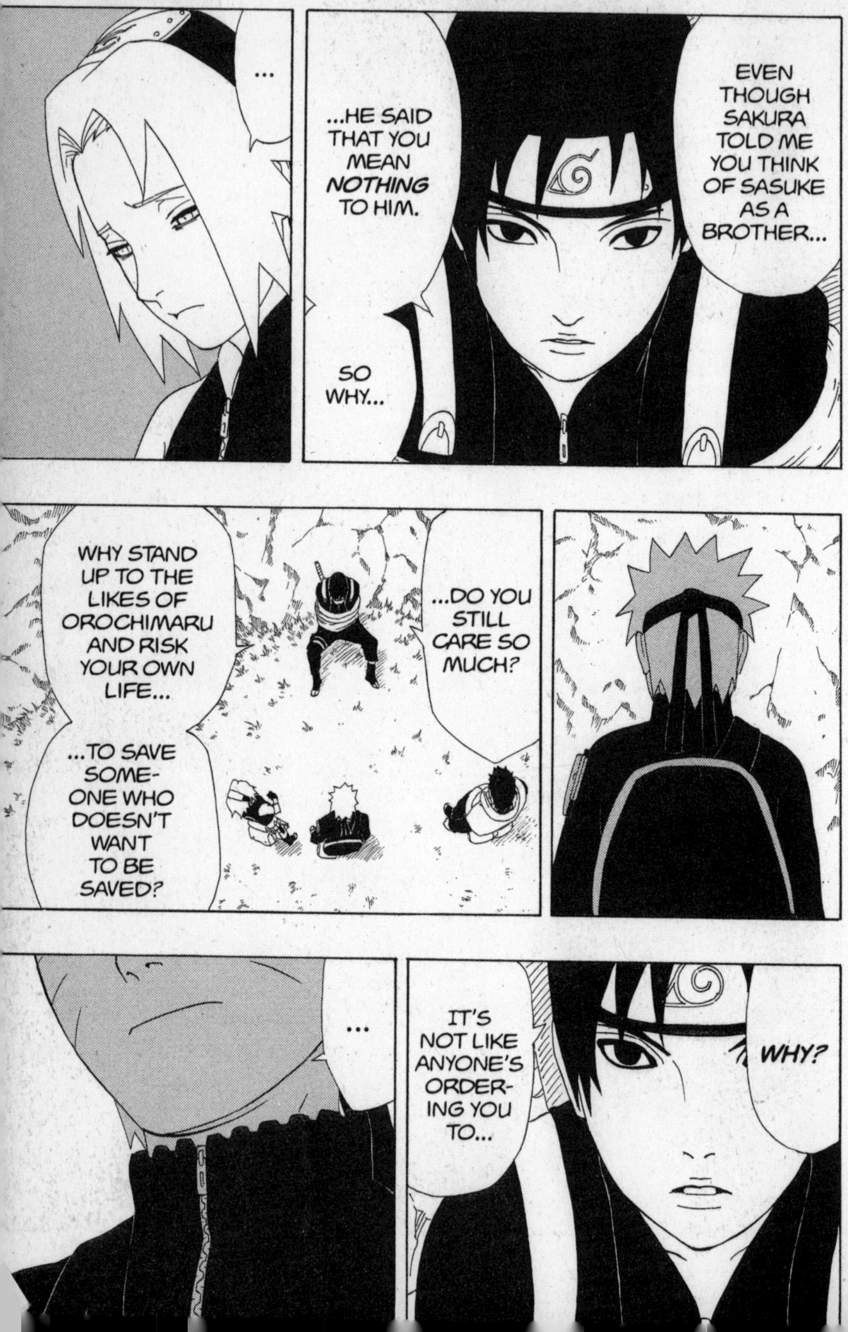
EVEN THOUGH SAKURA TOLD ME YOU THINK OF SASUKE AS A BROTHER...
...HE SAID THAT YOU MEAN *NOTHING* TO HIM.
SO WHY...
...
...DO YOU STILL CARE SO MUCH?
WHY STAND UP TO THE LIKES OF OROCHIMARU AND RISK YOUR OWN LIFE...
...TO SAVE SOME-ONE WHO DOESN'T WANT TO BE SAVED?
WHY?
IT'S NOT LIKE ANYONE'S ORDER-ING YOU TO...
...

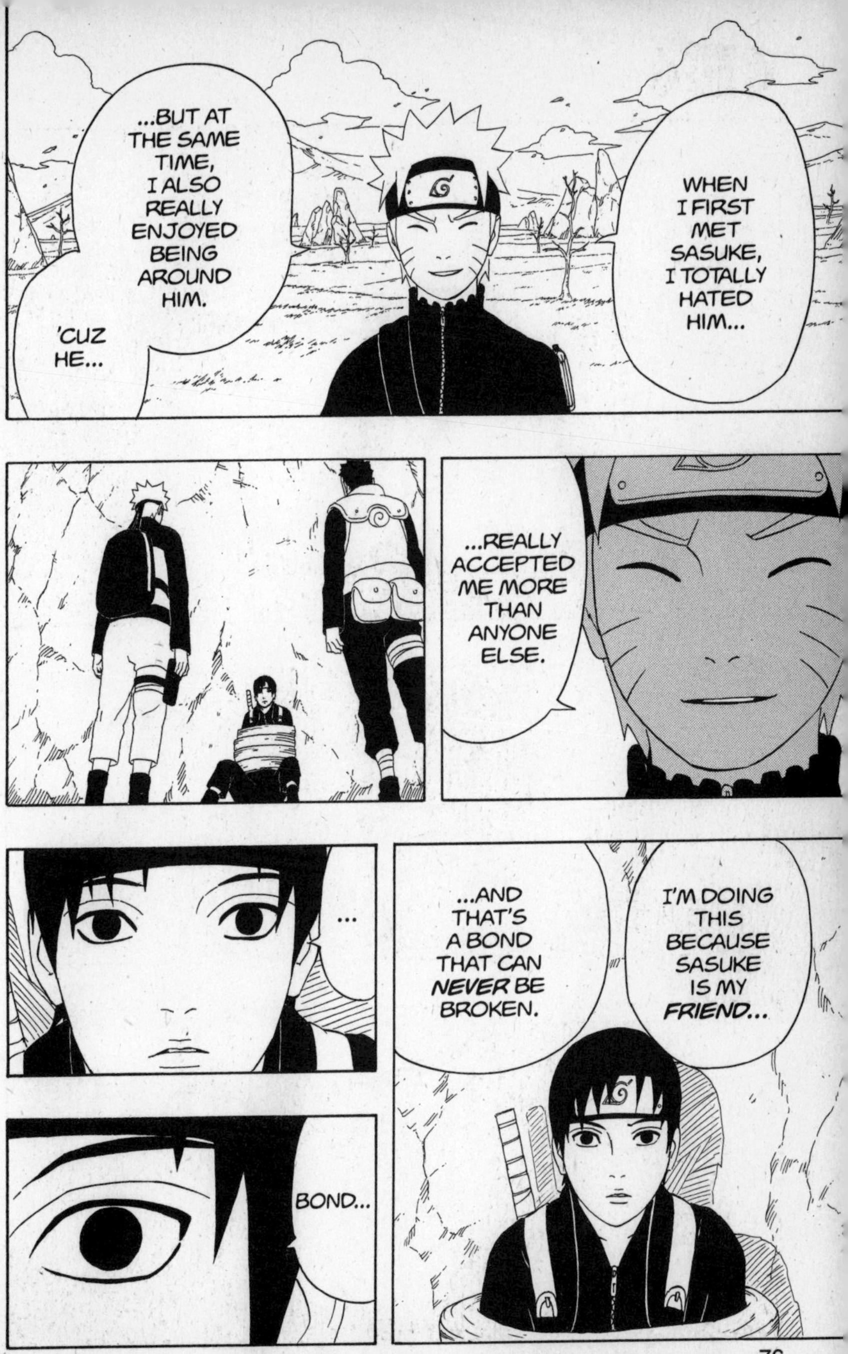
WHEN I FIRST MET SASUKE, I TOTALLY HATED HIM...
...BUT AT THE SAME TIME, I ALSO REALLY ENJOYED BEING AROUND HIM.
'CUZ HE...
...REALLY ACCEPTED ME MORE THAN ANYONE ELSE.
I'M DOING THIS BECAUSE SASUKE IS MY *FRIEND*...
...AND THAT'S A BOND THAT CAN *NEVER* BE BROKEN.
...
BOND...

READ THIS WAY

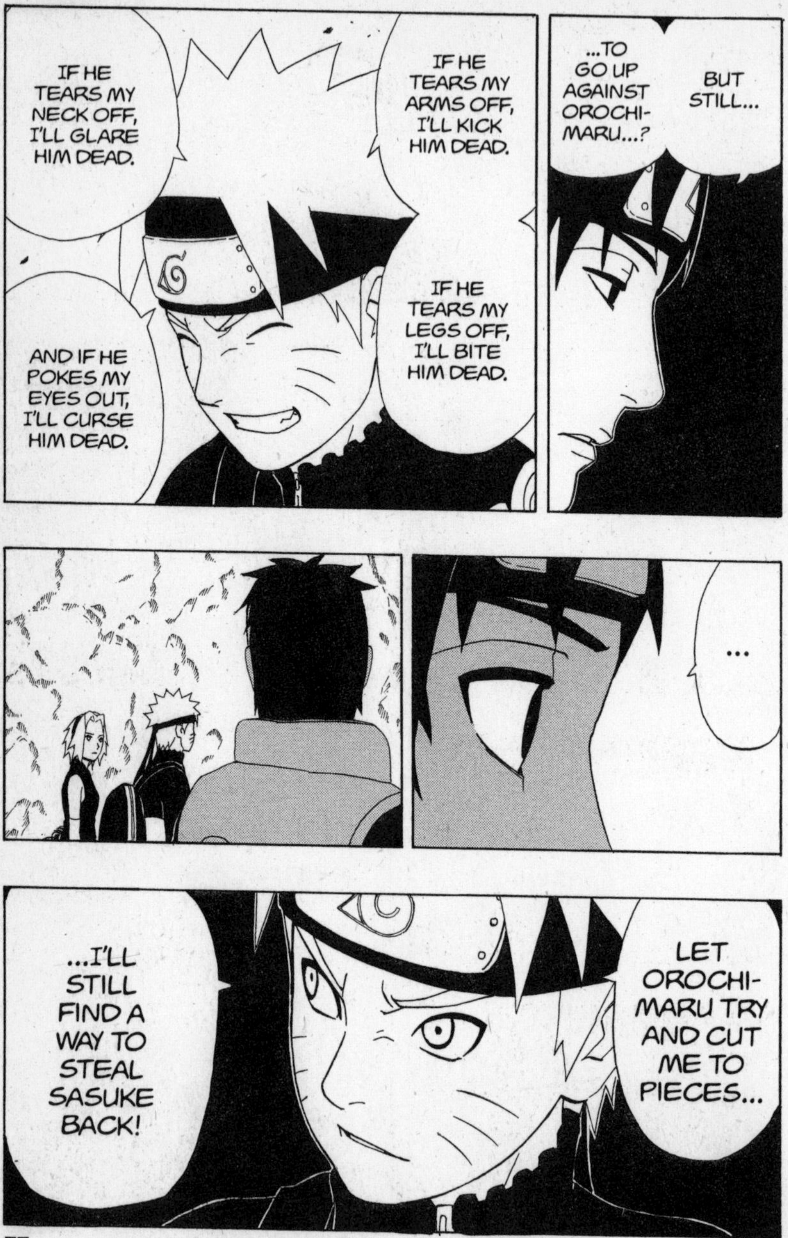
BUT STILL...
...TO GO UP AGAINST OROCHI-MARU...?
IF HE TEARS MY ARMS OFF, I'LL KICK HIM DEAD.
IF HE TEARS MY NECK OFF, I'LL GLARE HIM DEAD.
IF HE TEARS MY LEGS OFF, I'LL BITE HIM DEAD.
AND IF HE POKES MY EYES OUT, I'LL CURSE HIM DEAD.
...
LET OROCHI-MARU TRY AND CUT ME TO PIECES...
...I'LL STILL FIND A WAY TO STEAL SASUKE BACK!

NARUTO

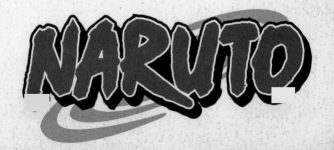

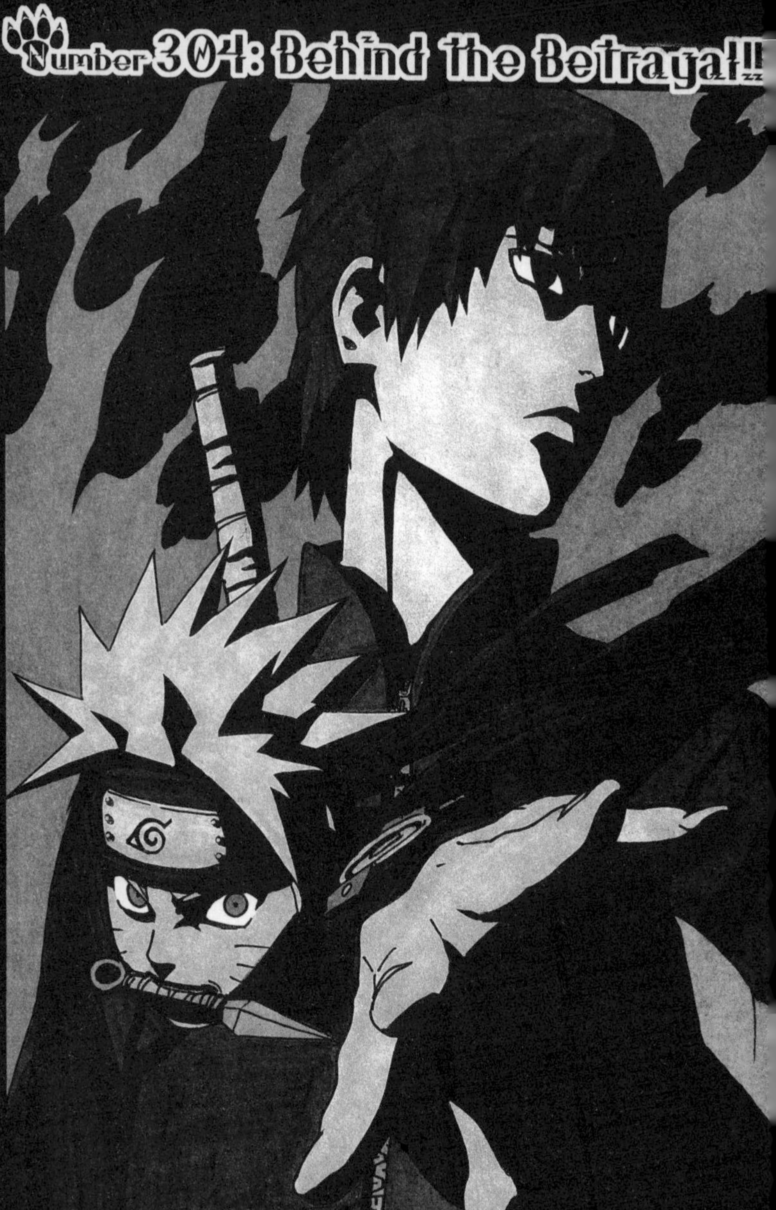
Number 304: Behind the Betrayal!!

NARUTO

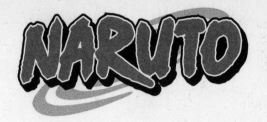

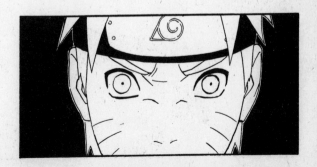

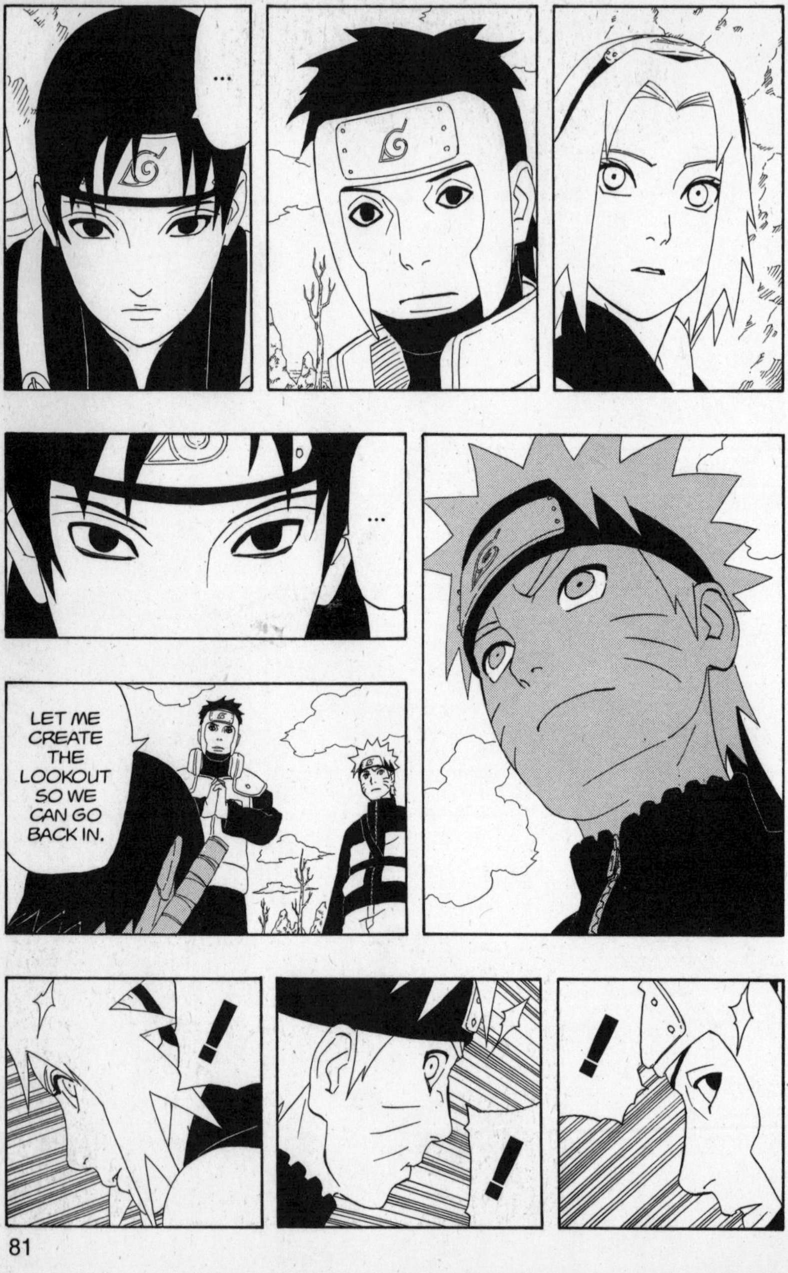
...
...
LET ME CREATE THE LOOKOUT SO WE CAN GO BACK IN.
!
!
!
!

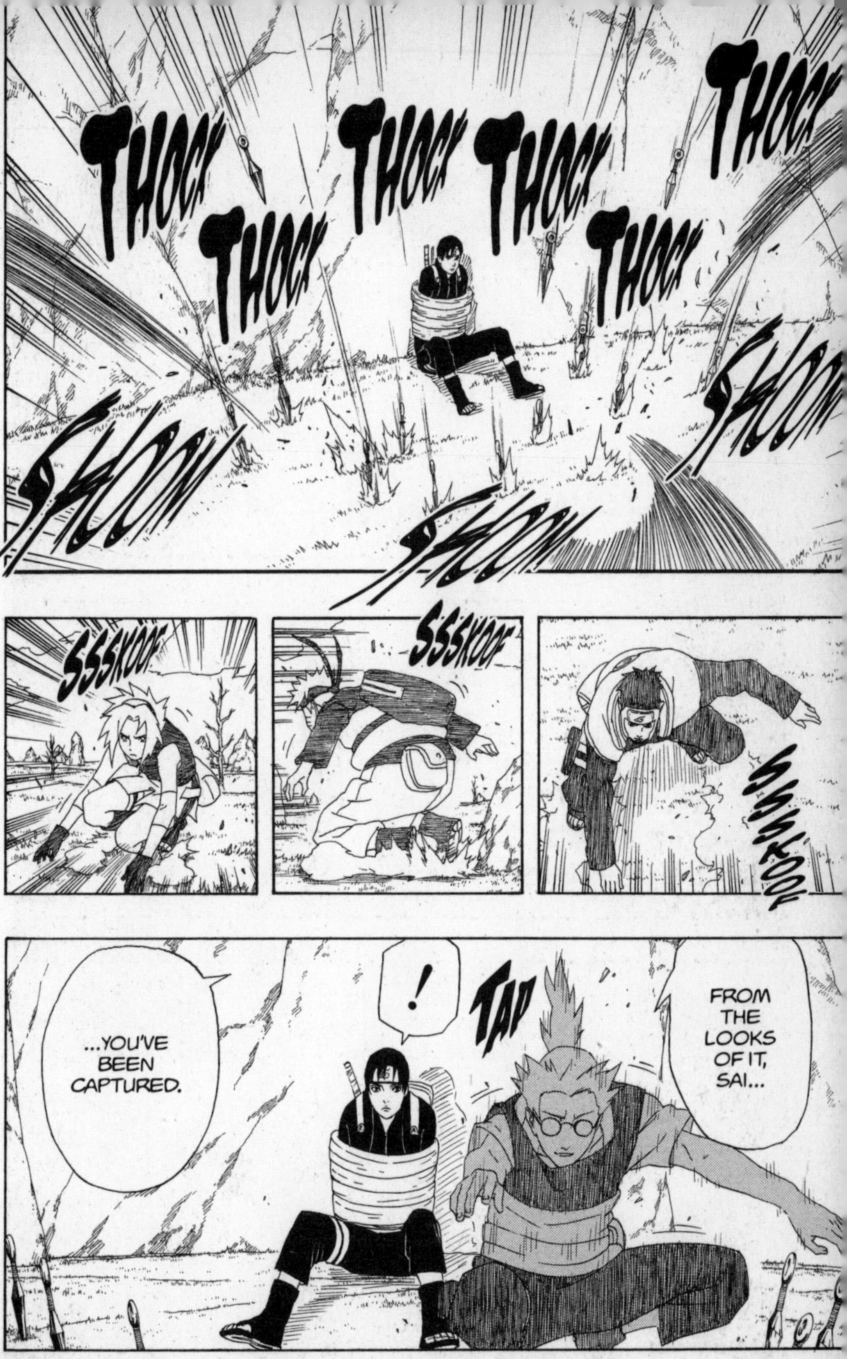
THOCK
THOCK
THOCK
THOCK
THOCK
THOCK
THOCK
SHOOM
SHOOM
SHOOM
SSSKOOF
SSSKOOF
SSSKOOF
FROM THE LOOKS OF IT, SAI...
TAP
!
...YOU'VE BEEN CAPTURED.

READ THIS WAY

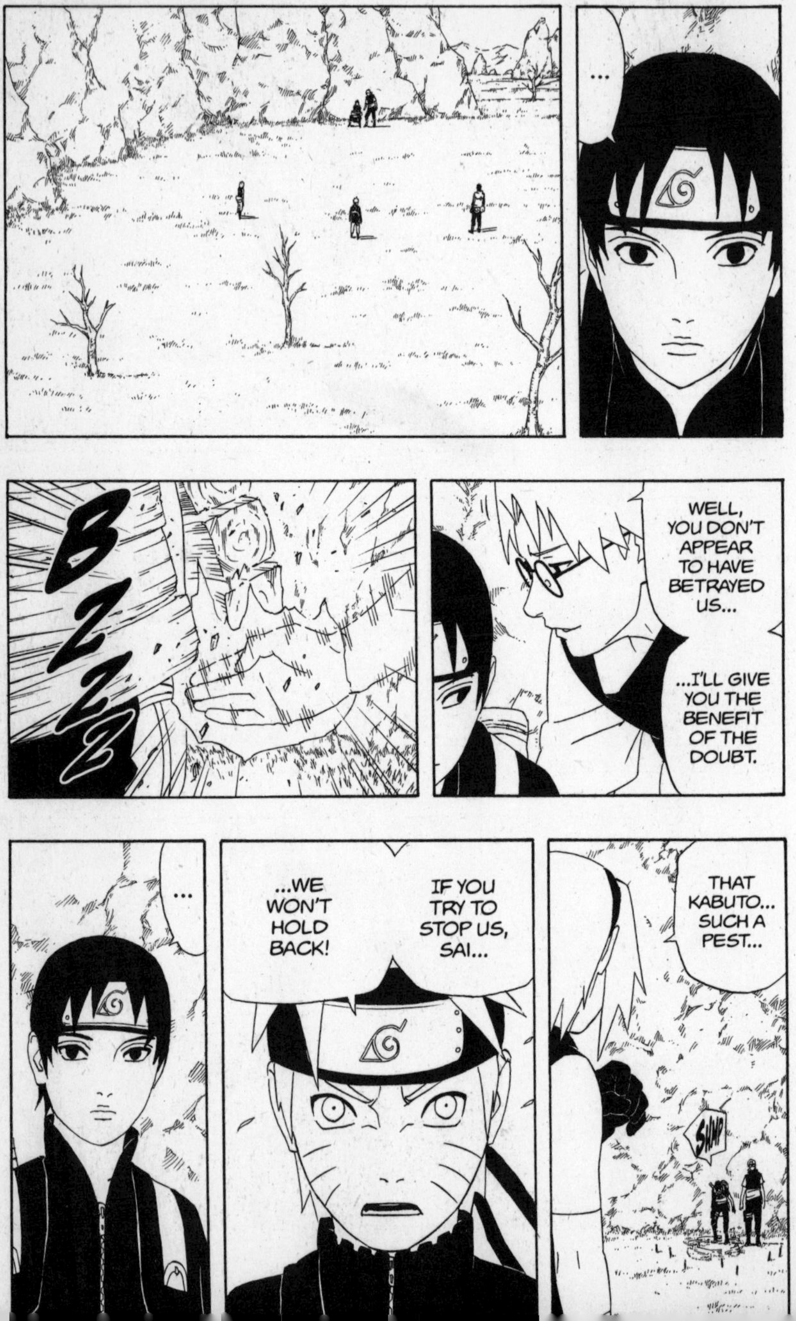
...
WELL, YOU DON'T APPEAR TO HAVE BETRAYED US...
...I'LL GIVE YOU THE BENEFIT OF THE DOUBT.
BZZZZ
THAT KABUTO... SUCH A PEST...
SHMP
IF YOU TRY TO STOP US, SAI...
...WE WON'T HOLD BACK!
...

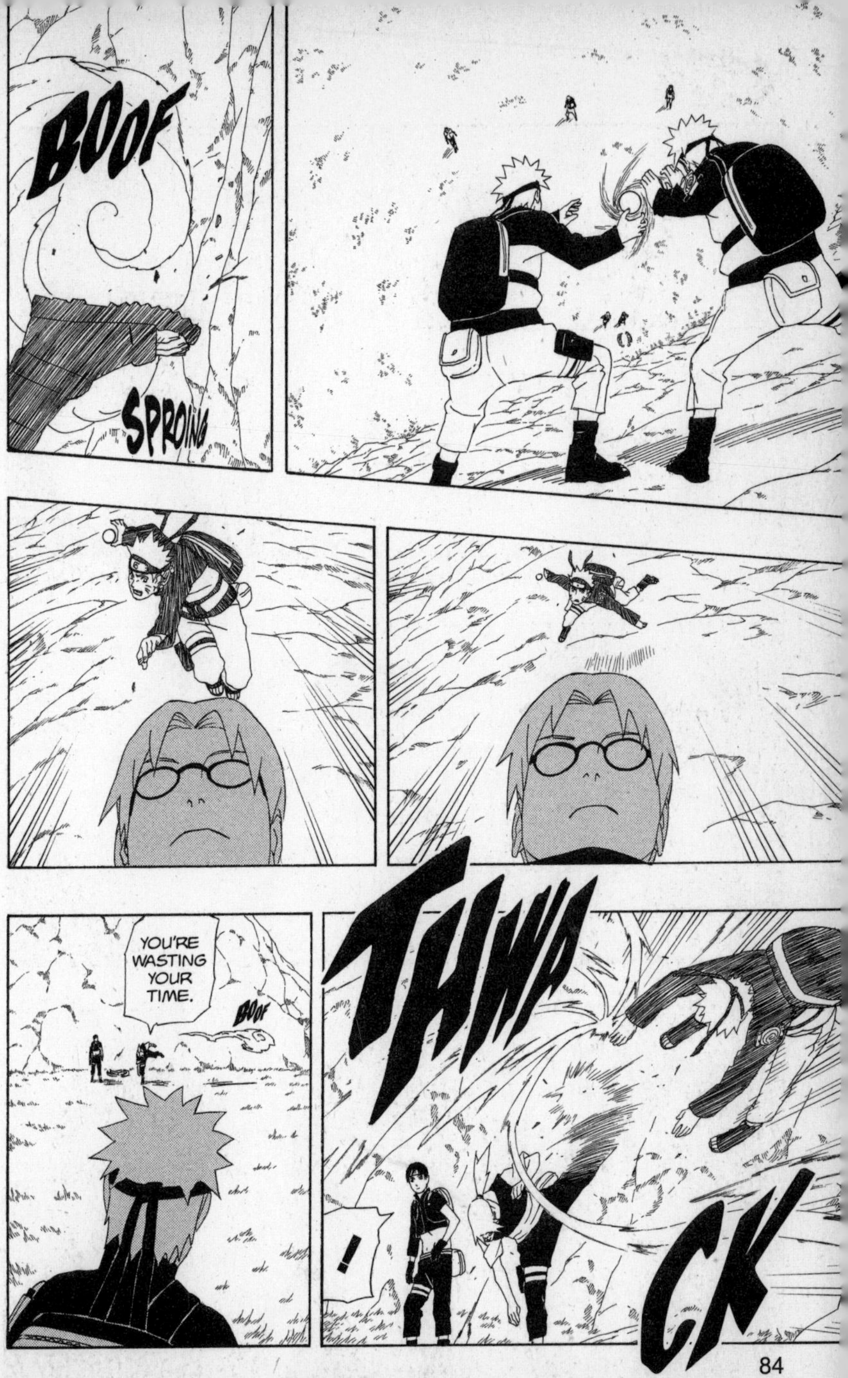
BOOF
SPROING
THWA
CK
!
YOU'RE WASTING YOUR TIME.
BOOF

READ THIS WAY

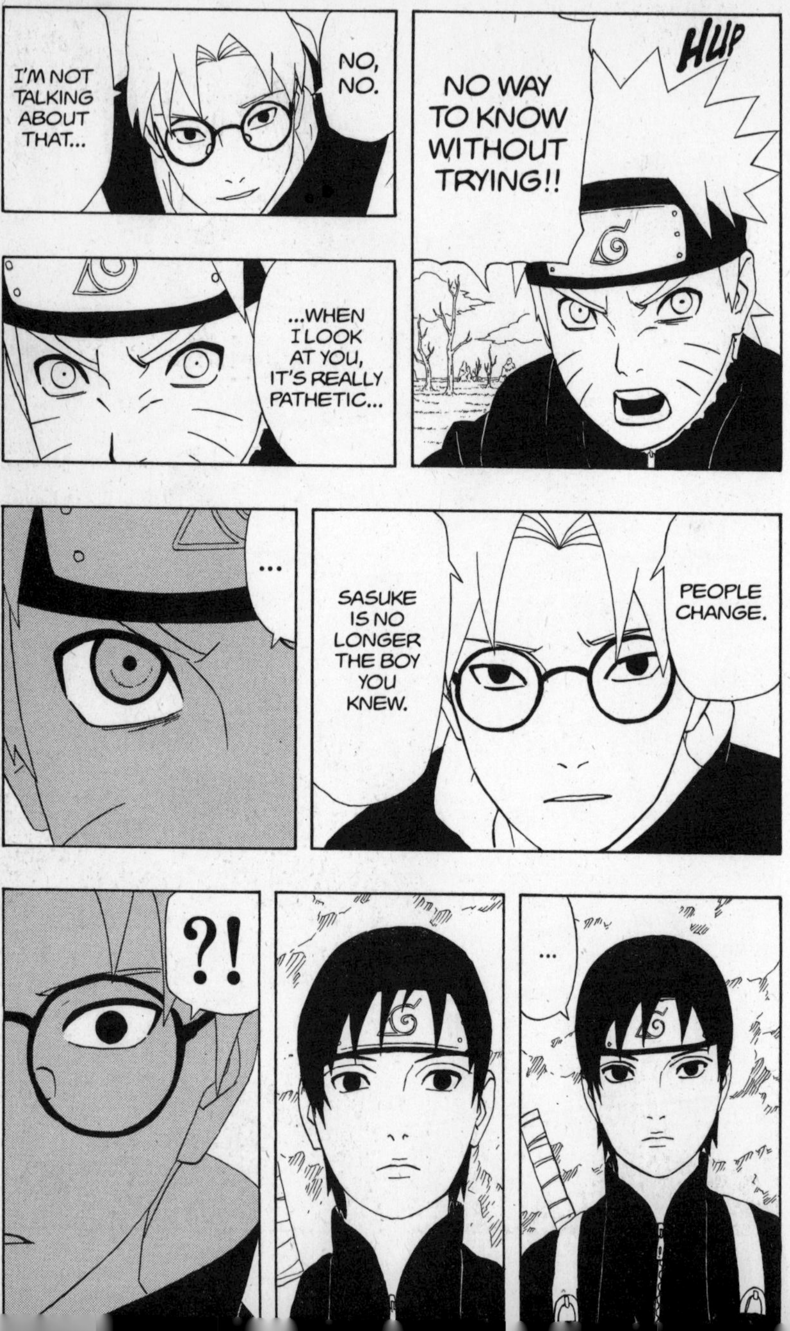
HUP
NO WAY TO KNOW WITHOUT TRYING!!
NO, NO.
I'M NOT TALKING ABOUT THAT...
...WHEN I LOOK AT YOU, IT'S REALLY PATHETIC...
PEOPLE CHANGE.
SASUKE IS NO LONGER THE BOY YOU KNEW.
...
...
?!

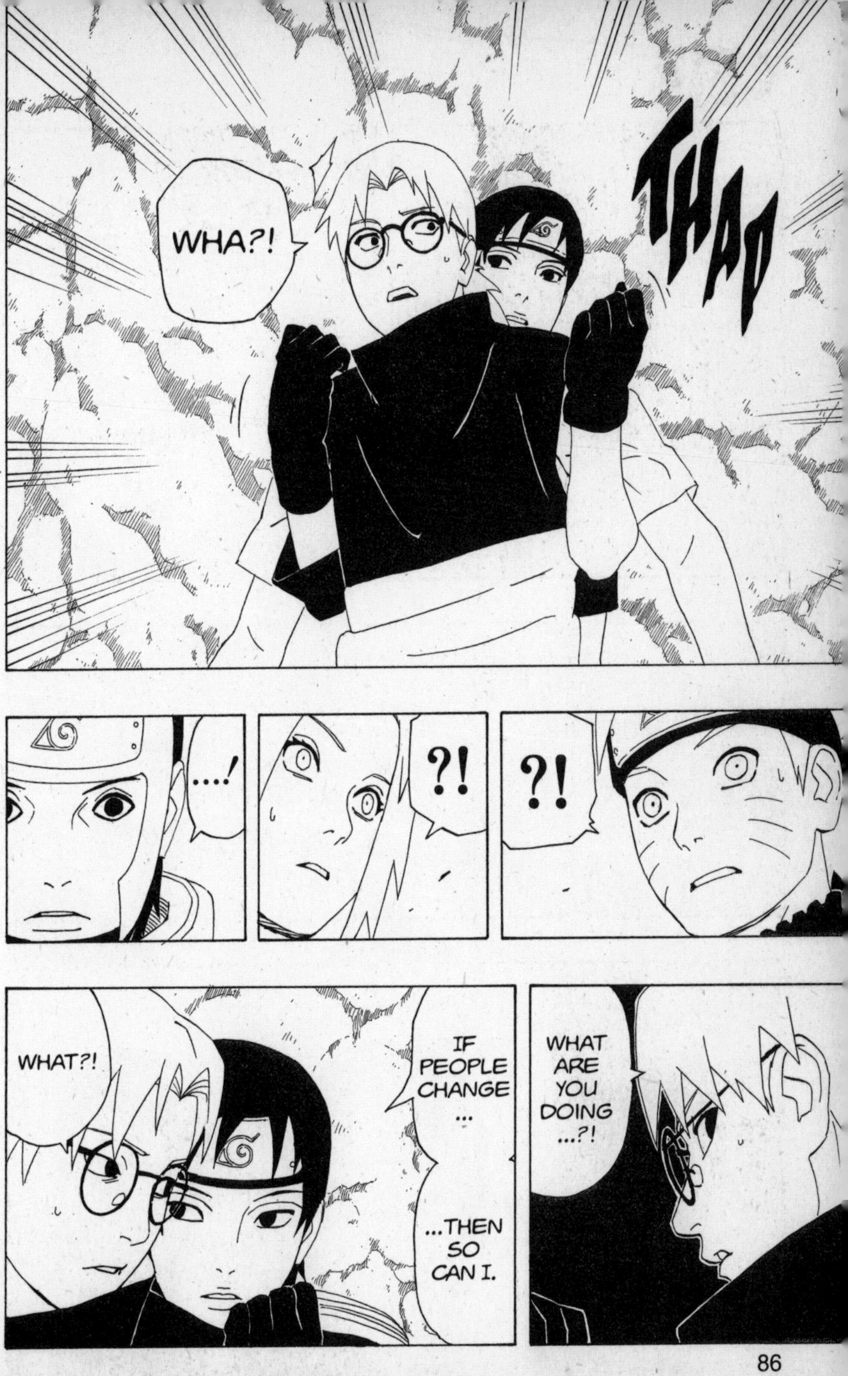
THAP
WHA?!
?!
?!
...!
WHAT ARE YOU DOING ...?!
IF PEOPLE CHANGE ...
WHAT?!
...THEN SO CAN I.

READ THIS WAY

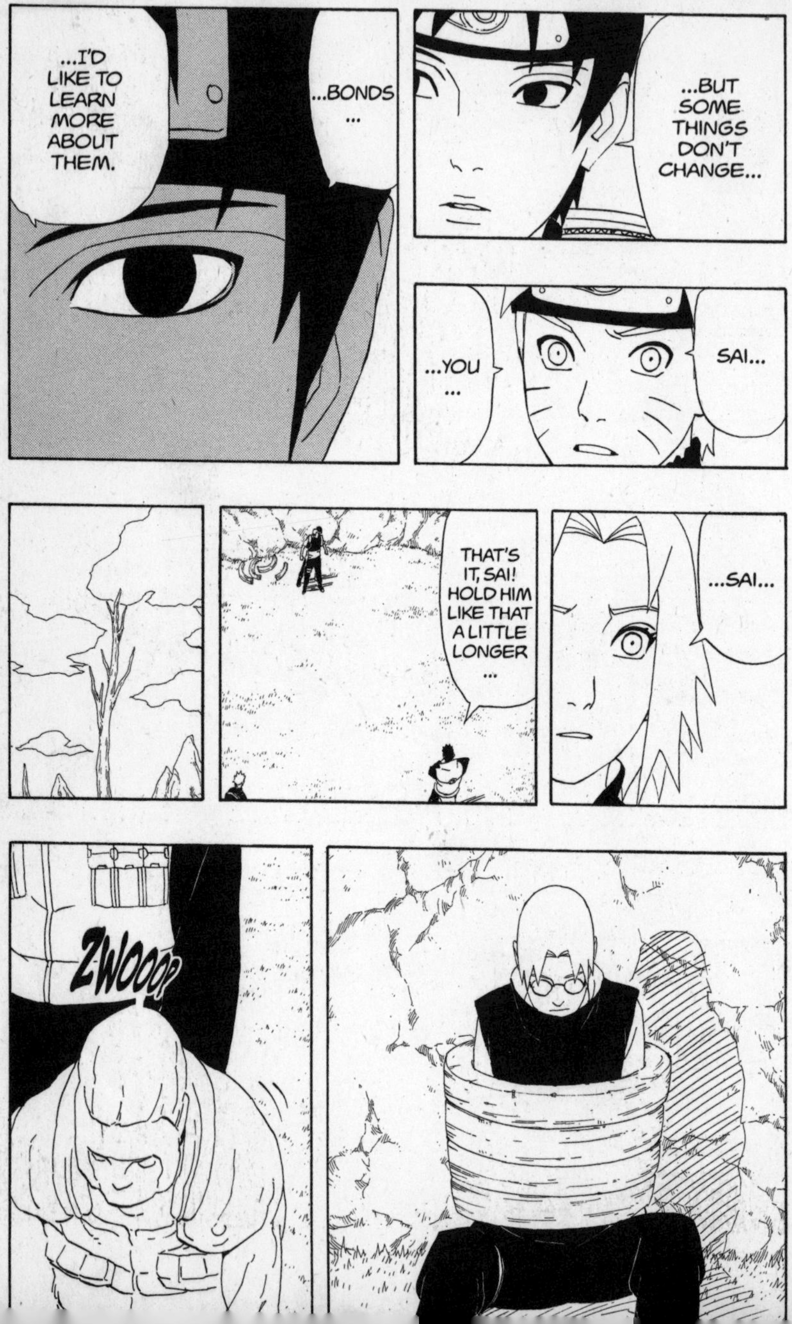

...BUT SOME THINGS DON'T CHANGE...
SAI...
...YOU ...
...BONDS ...
...I'D LIKE TO LEARN MORE ABOUT THEM.
...SAI...
THAT'S IT, SAI! HOLD HIM LIKE THAT A LITTLE LONGER ...
ZWOOOP

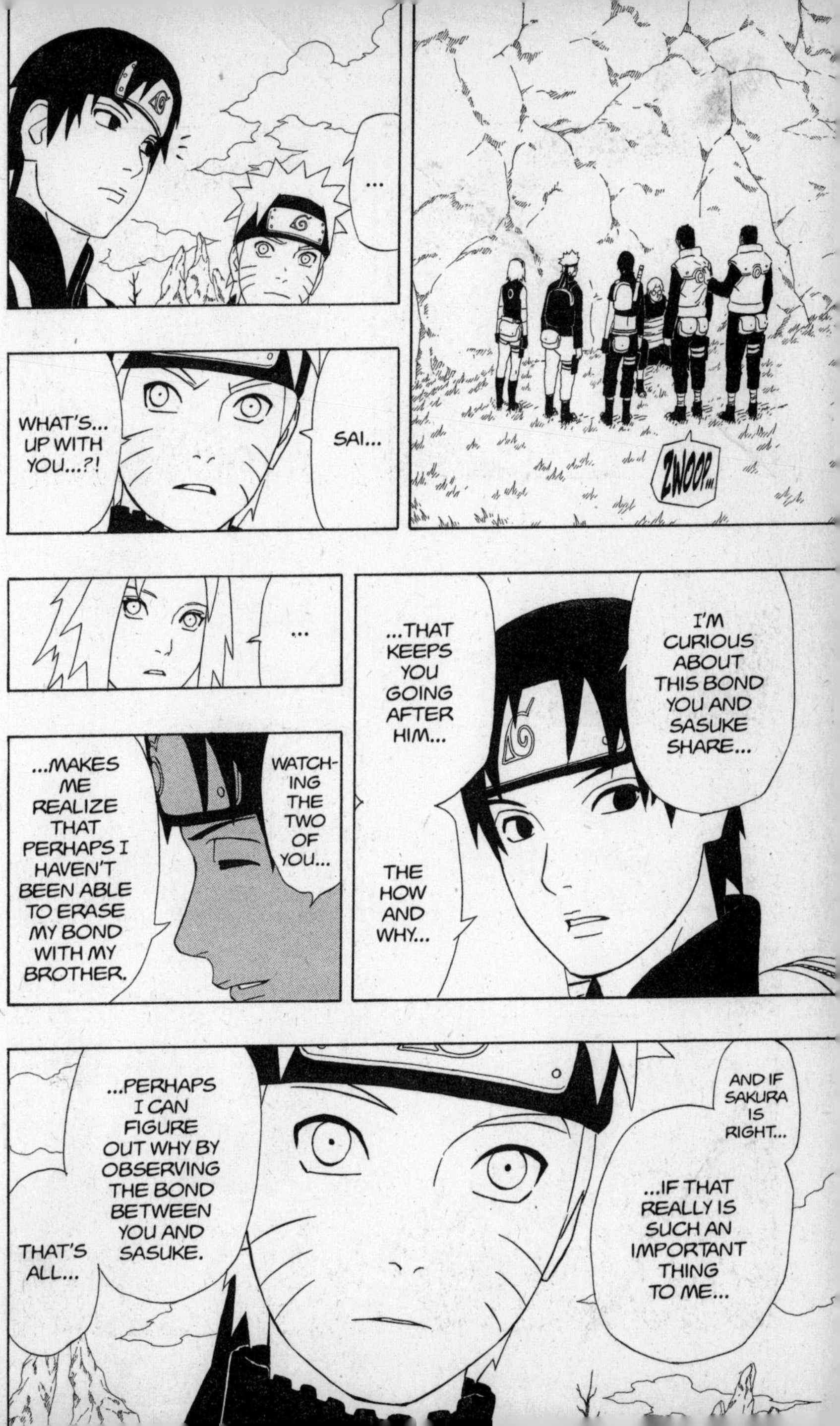
ZWOOP...
...
SAI...
WHAT'S... UP WITH YOU...?!
I'M CURIOUS ABOUT THIS BOND YOU AND SASUKE SHARE...
...THAT KEEPS YOU GOING AFTER HIM...
THE HOW AND WHY...
...
WATCHING THE TWO OF YOU...
...MAKES ME REALIZE THAT PERHAPS I HAVEN'T BEEN ABLE TO ERASE MY BOND WITH MY BROTHER.
AND IF SAKURA IS RIGHT...
...IF THAT REALLY IS SUCH AN IMPORTANT THING TO ME...
...PERHAPS I CAN FIGURE OUT WHY BY OBSERVING THE BOND BETWEEN YOU AND SASUKE.
THAT'S ALL...

READ THIS WAY

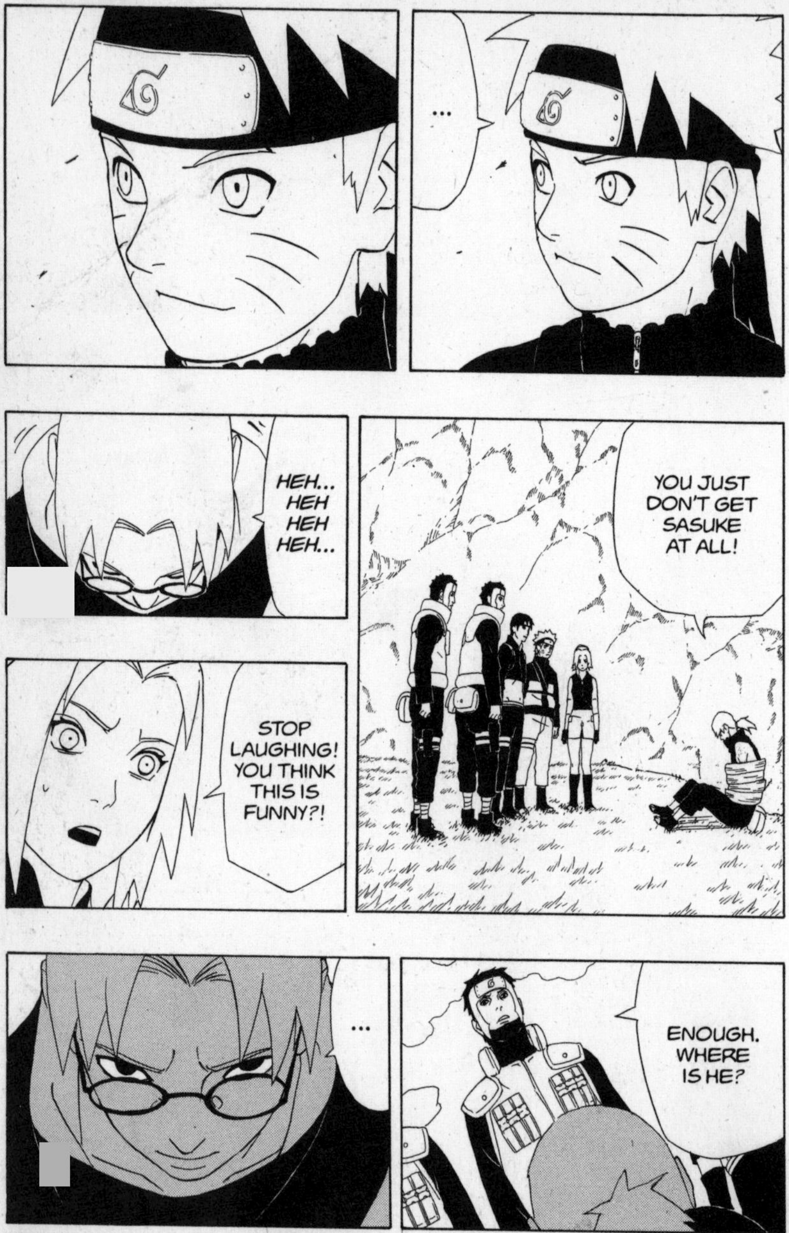
...
YOU JUST DON'T GET SASUKE AT ALL!
HEH... HEH HEH HEH...
STOP LAUGHING! YOU THINK THIS IS FUNNY?!
ENOUGH. WHERE IS HE?
...

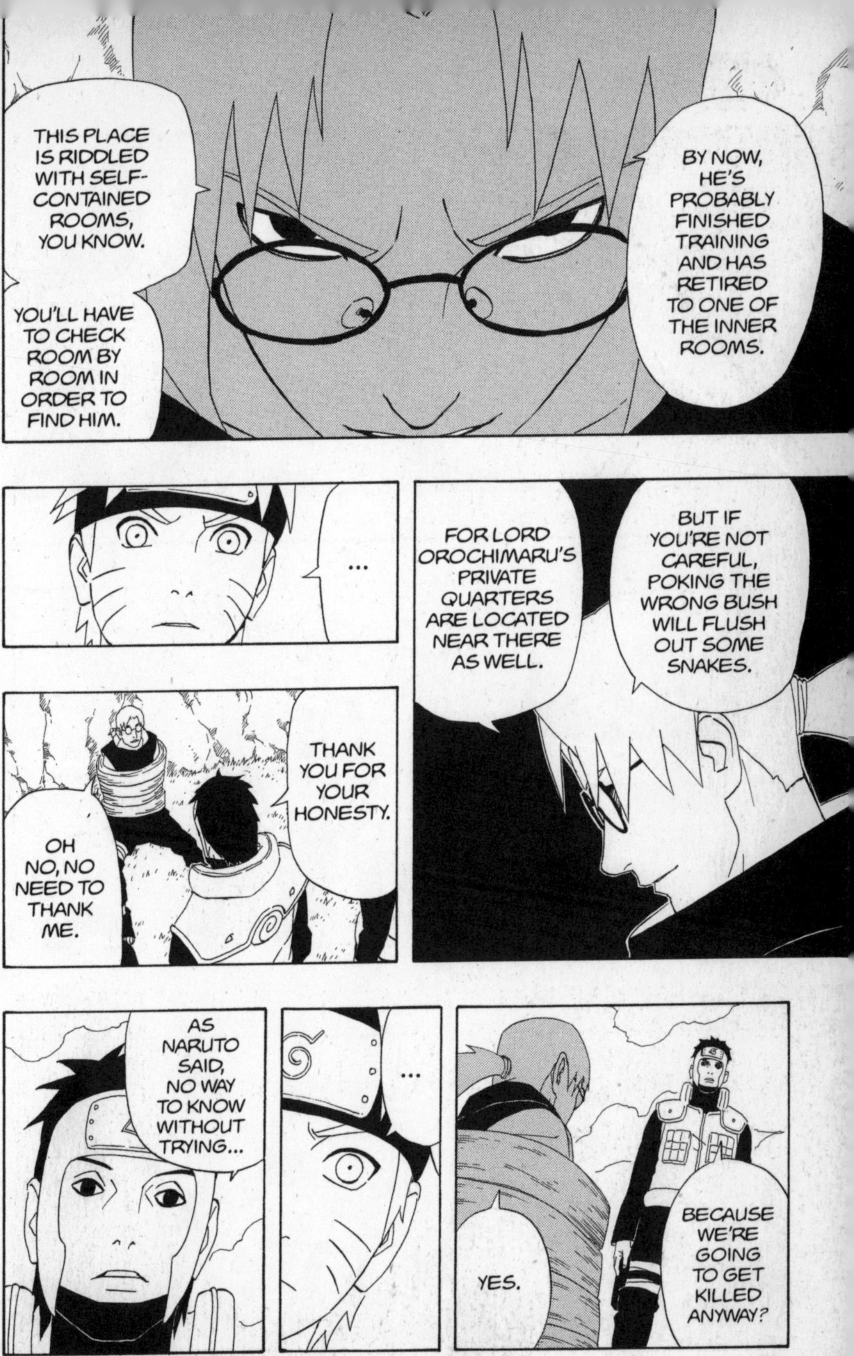
BY NOW, HE'S PROBABLY FINISHED TRAINING AND HAS RETIRED TO ONE OF THE INNER ROOMS.
THIS PLACE IS RIDDLED WITH SELF-CONTAINED ROOMS, YOU KNOW.
YOU'LL HAVE TO CHECK ROOM BY ROOM IN ORDER TO FIND HIM.
BUT IF YOU'RE NOT CAREFUL, POKING THE WRONG BUSH WILL FLUSH OUT SOME SNAKES.
FOR LORD OROCHIMARU'S PRIVATE QUARTERS ARE LOCATED NEAR THERE AS WELL.
...
THANK YOU FOR YOUR HONESTY.
OH NO, NO NEED TO THANK ME.
BECAUSE WE'RE GOING TO GET KILLED ANYWAY?
YES.
...
AS NARUTO SAID, NO WAY TO KNOW WITHOUT TRYING...

READ THIS WAY

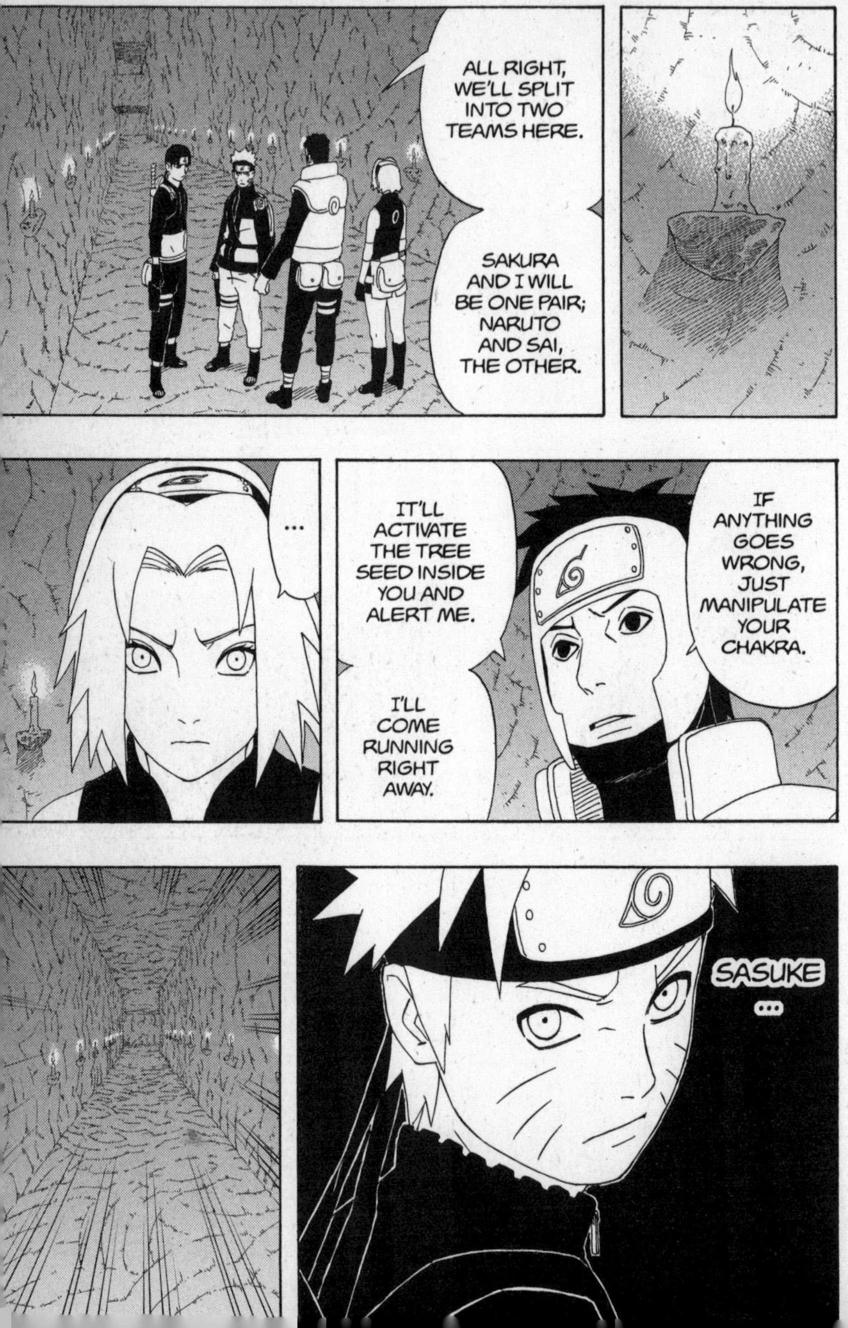

ALL RIGHT, WE'LL SPLIT INTO TWO TEAMS HERE.
SAKURA AND I WILL BE ONE PAIR; NARUTO AND SAI, THE OTHER.
IF ANYTHING GOES WRONG, JUST MANIPULATE YOUR CHAKRA.
IT'LL ACTIVATE THE TREE SEED INSIDE YOU AND ALERT ME.
I'LL COME RUNNING RIGHT AWAY.
...
SASUKE ...

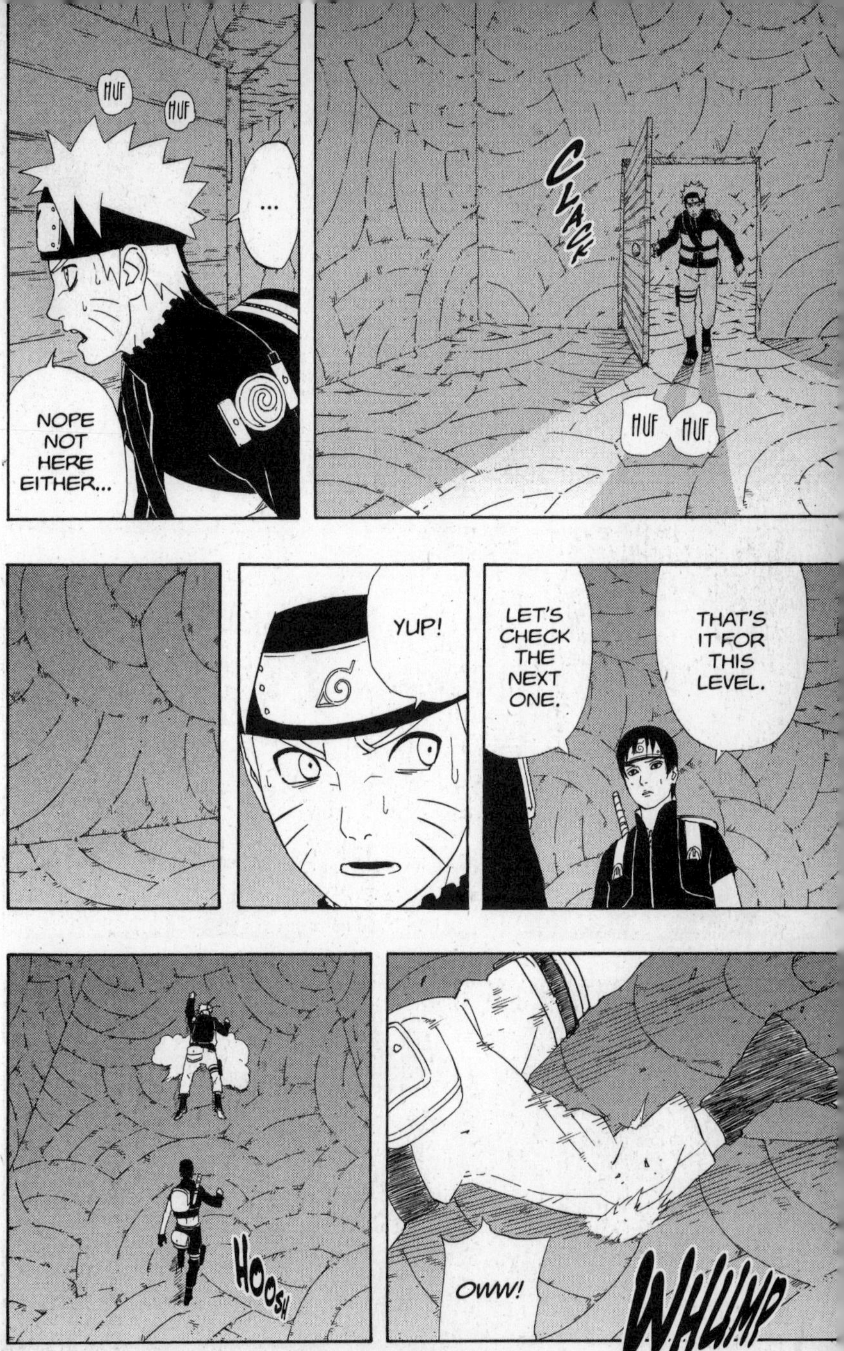
CLACK
HUF
HUF
HUF
HUF
...
NOPE NOT HERE EITHER...
THAT'S IT FOR THIS LEVEL.
LET'S CHECK THE NEXT ONE.
YUP!
OWW!
WHUMP
HOOSH

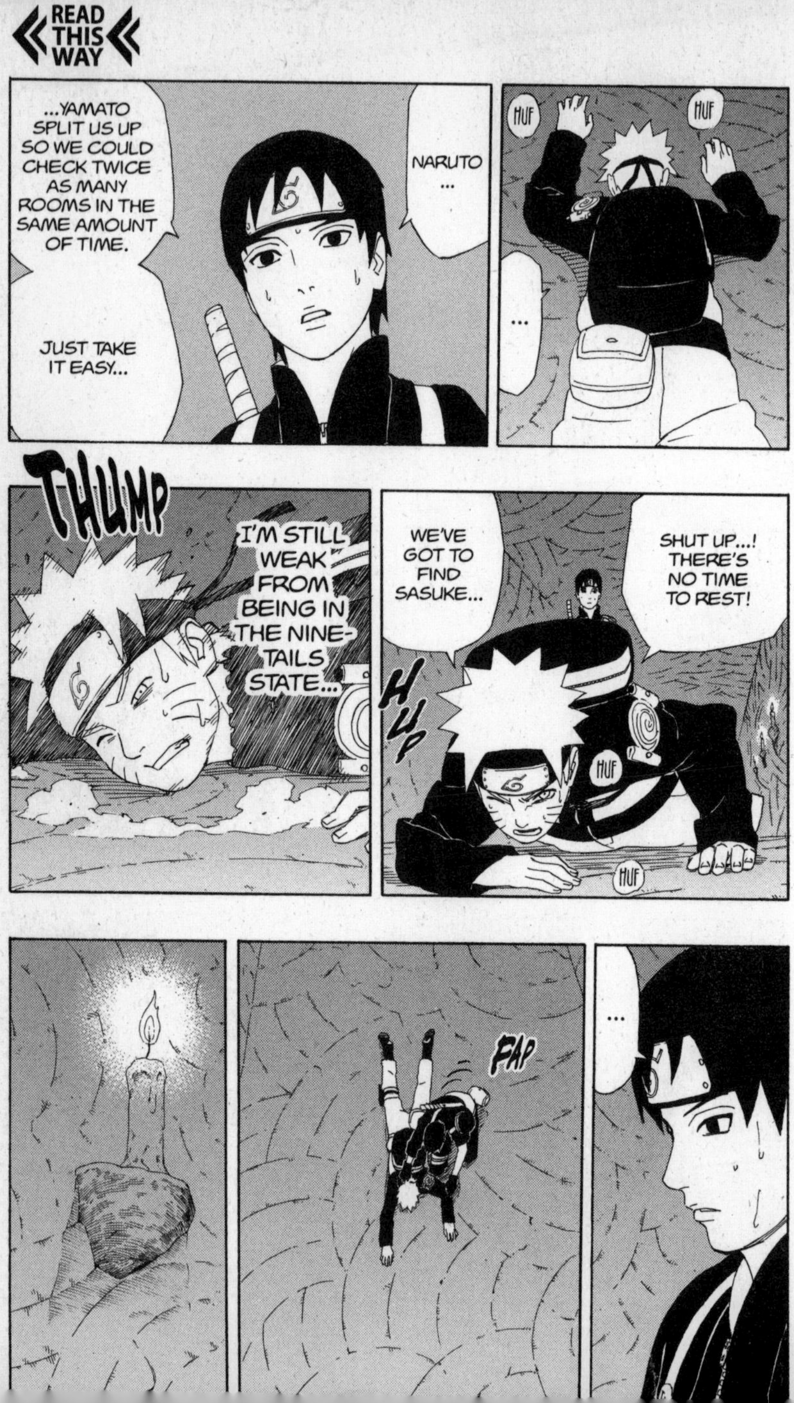
READ THIS WAY
HUF
HUF
...
NARUTO ...
...YAMATO SPLIT US UP SO WE COULD CHECK TWICE AS MANY ROOMS IN THE SAME AMOUNT OF TIME.
JUST TAKE IT EASY...
SHUT UP...! THERE'S NO TIME TO REST!
WE'VE GOT TO FIND SASUKE...
HUP
HUF
HUF
THUMP
I'M STILL WEAK FROM BEING IN THE NINE-TAILS STATE...
...
FAP

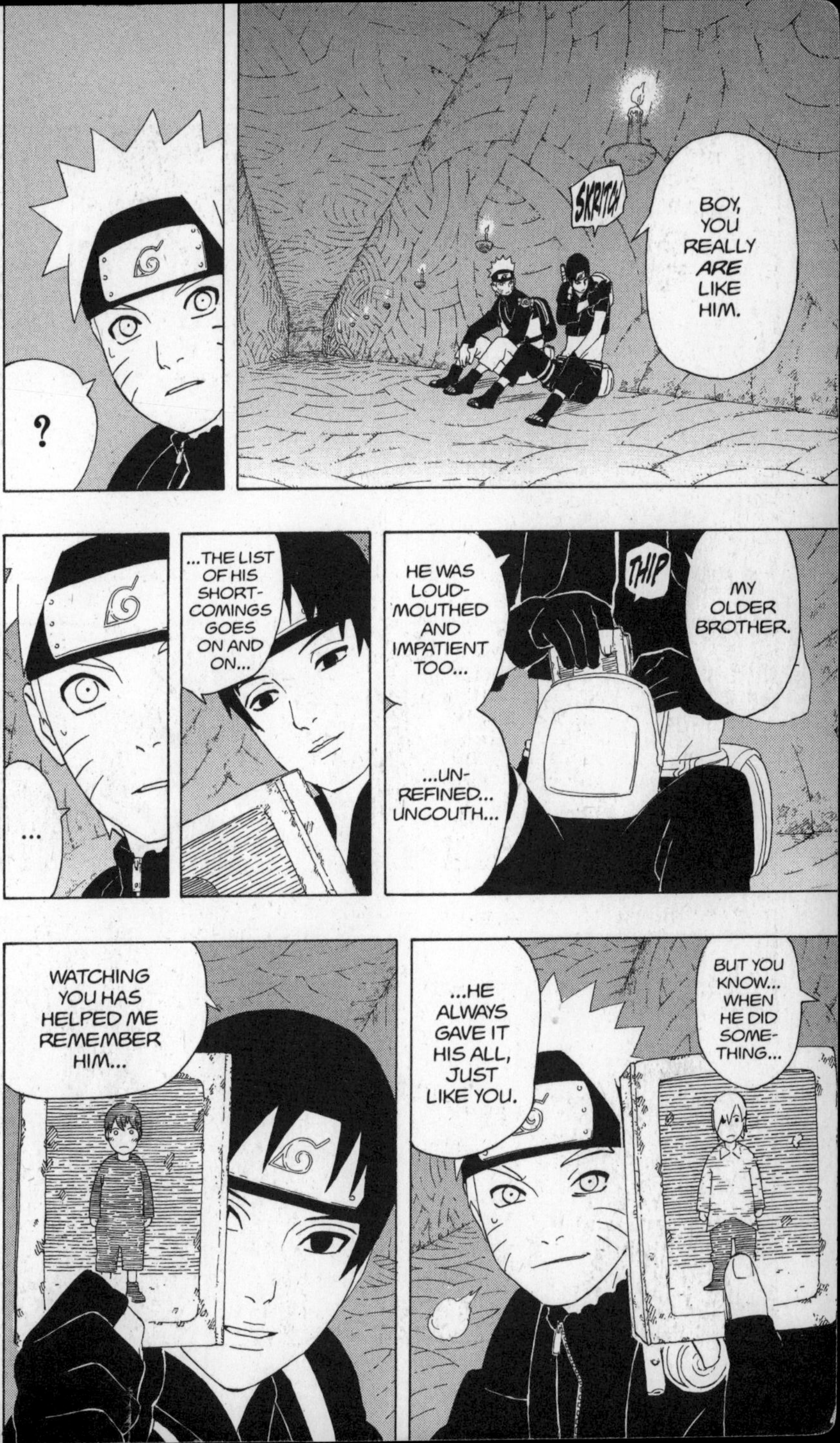
SKRITCH
BOY, YOU REALLY ARE LIKE HIM.
?
THIP
MY OLDER BROTHER.
HE WAS LOUD-MOUTHED AND IMPATIENT TOO...
...UN-REFINED... UNCOUTH...
...THE LIST OF HIS SHORT-COMINGS GOES ON AND ON...
...
BUT YOU KNOW... WHEN HE DID SOME-THING...
...HE ALWAYS GAVE IT HIS ALL, JUST LIKE YOU.
WATCHING YOU HAS HELPED ME REMEMBER HIM...

READ THIS WAY

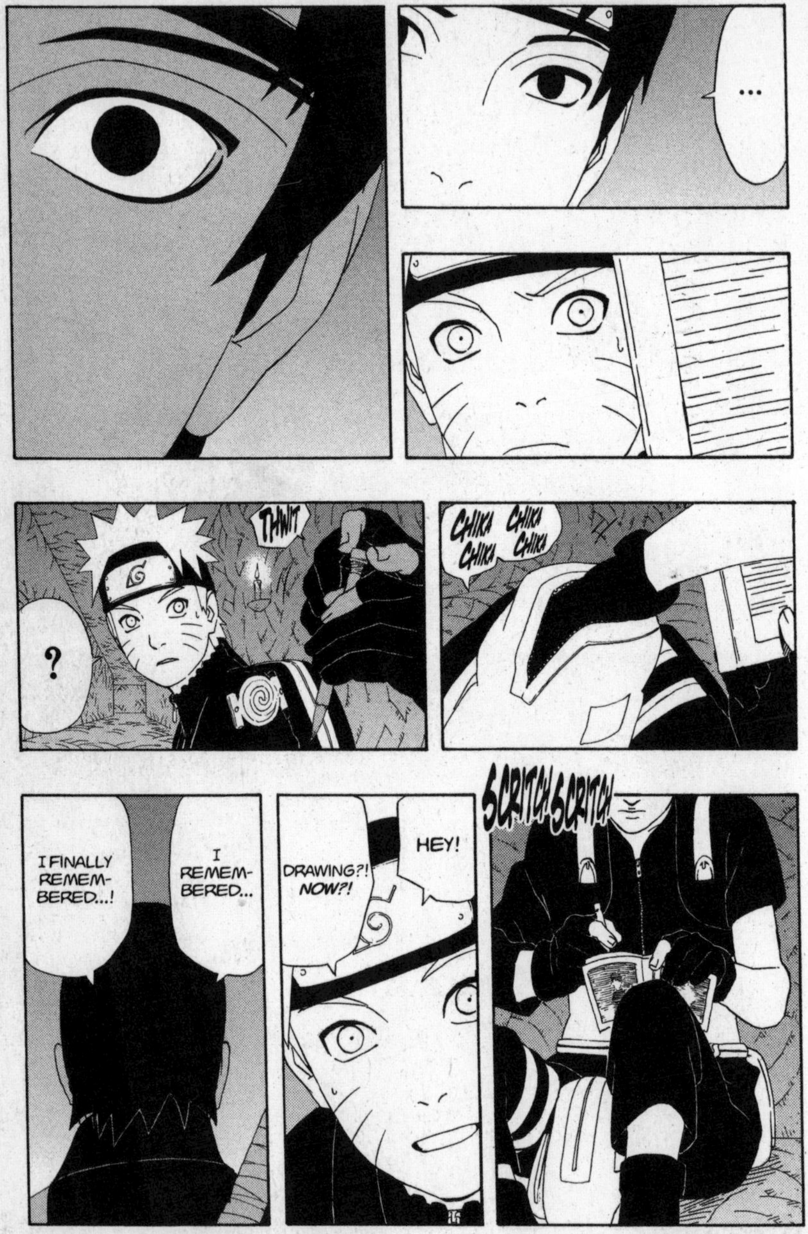

...
CHIKA CHIKA CHIKA CHIKA
THWIT
?
SCRITCH SCRITCH
HEY!
DRAWING?! NOW?!
I REMEMBERED...
I FINALLY REMEMBERED...!

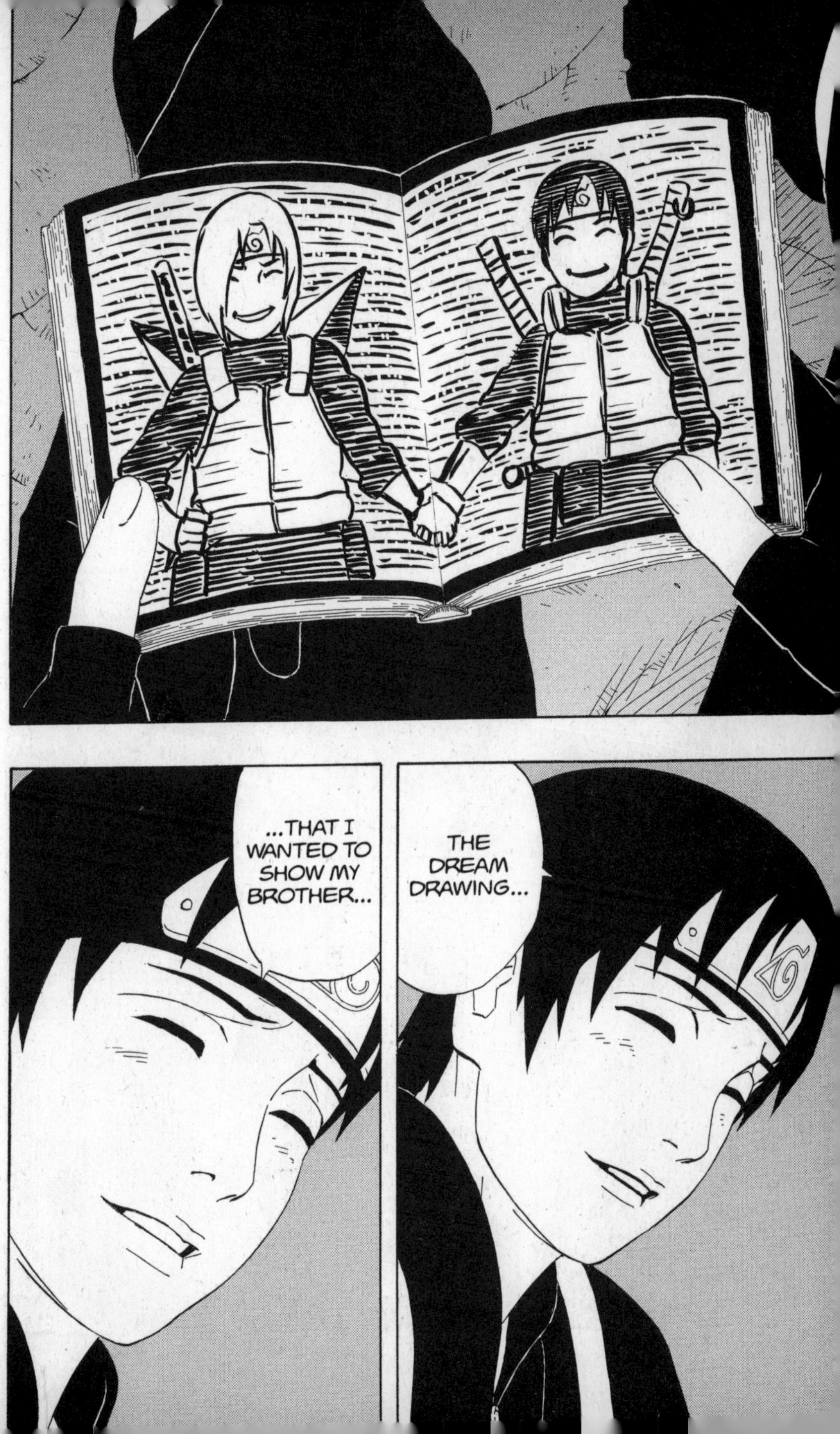
THE DREAM DRAWING...
...THAT I WANTED TO SHOW MY BROTHER...

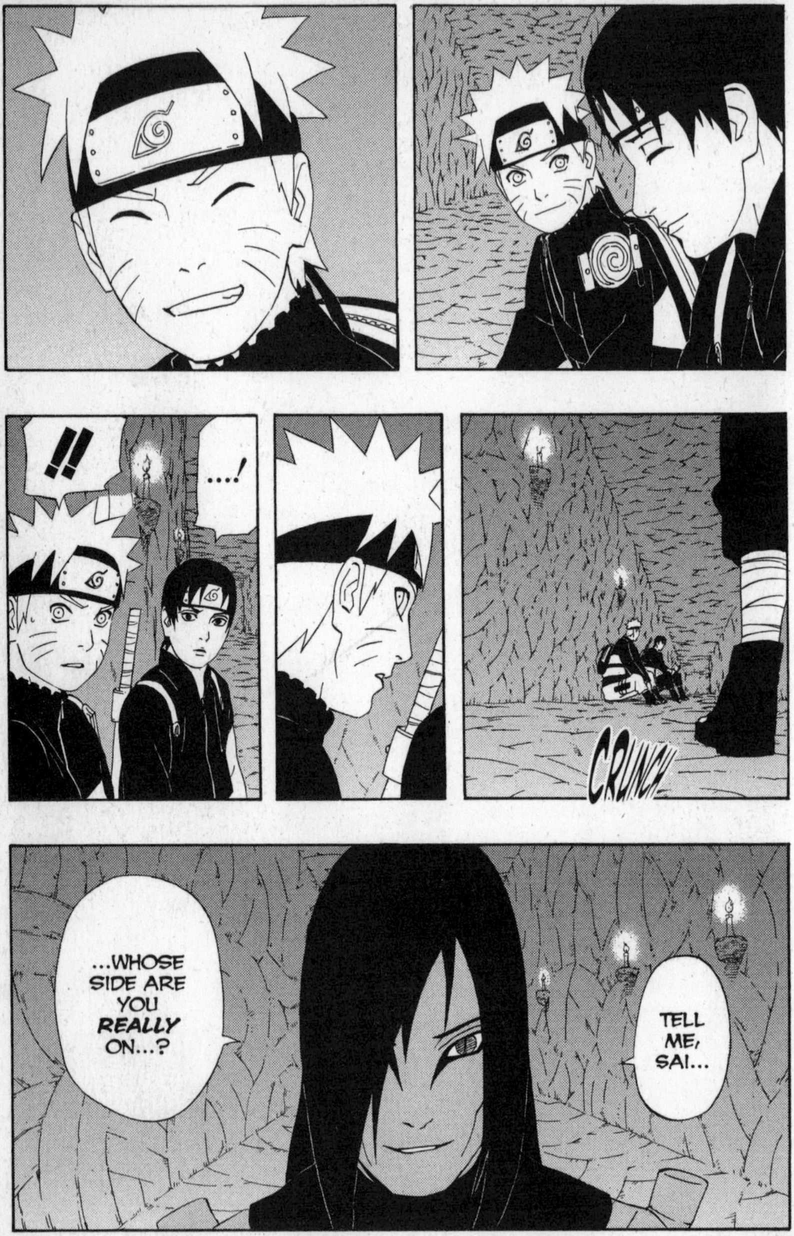
...!
!!
CRUNCH
TELL ME, SAI...
...WHOSE SIDE ARE YOU *REALLY* ON...?

NARUTO

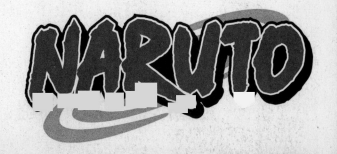

Number 305: Our Bond

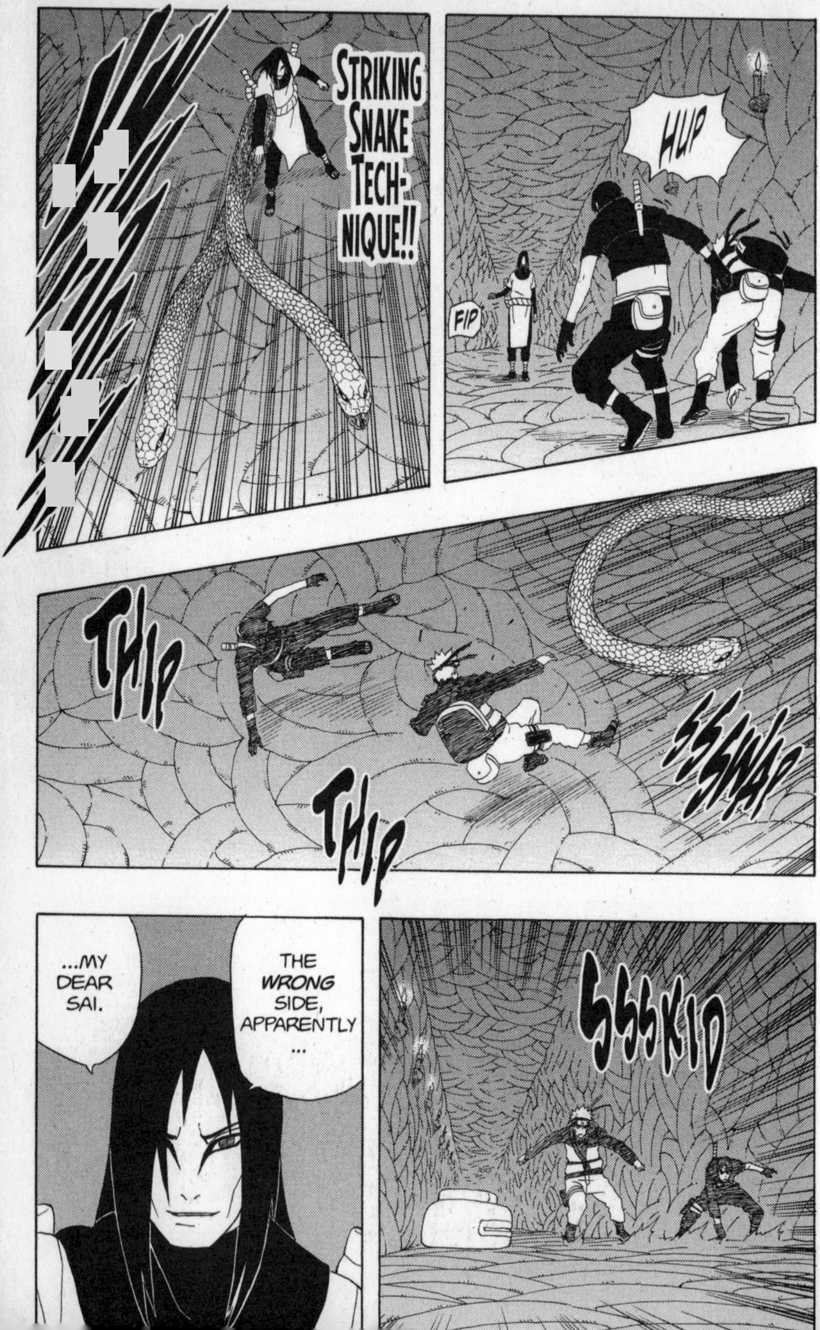
HUP
FIP
STRIKING SNAKE TECHNIQUE!!
SSSWAP
THIP
THIP
SSSKID
THE WRONG SIDE, APPARENTLY...
...MY DEAR SAI.

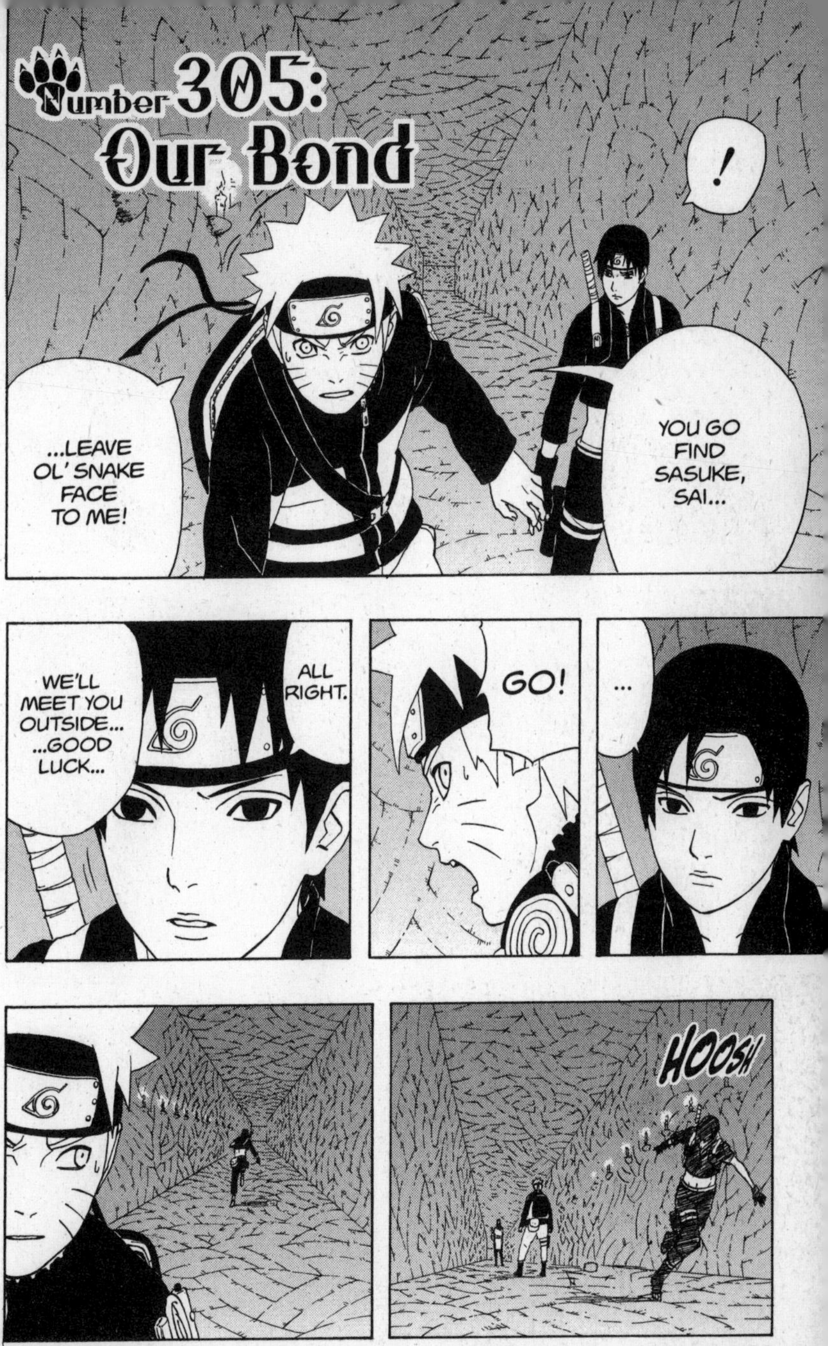
Number 305: Our Bond
!
YOU GO FIND SASUKE, SAI...
...LEAVE OL' SNAKE FACE TO ME!
...
GO!
ALL RIGHT.
WE'LL MEET YOU OUTSIDE... ...GOOD LUCK...
HOOSH

READ THIS WAY

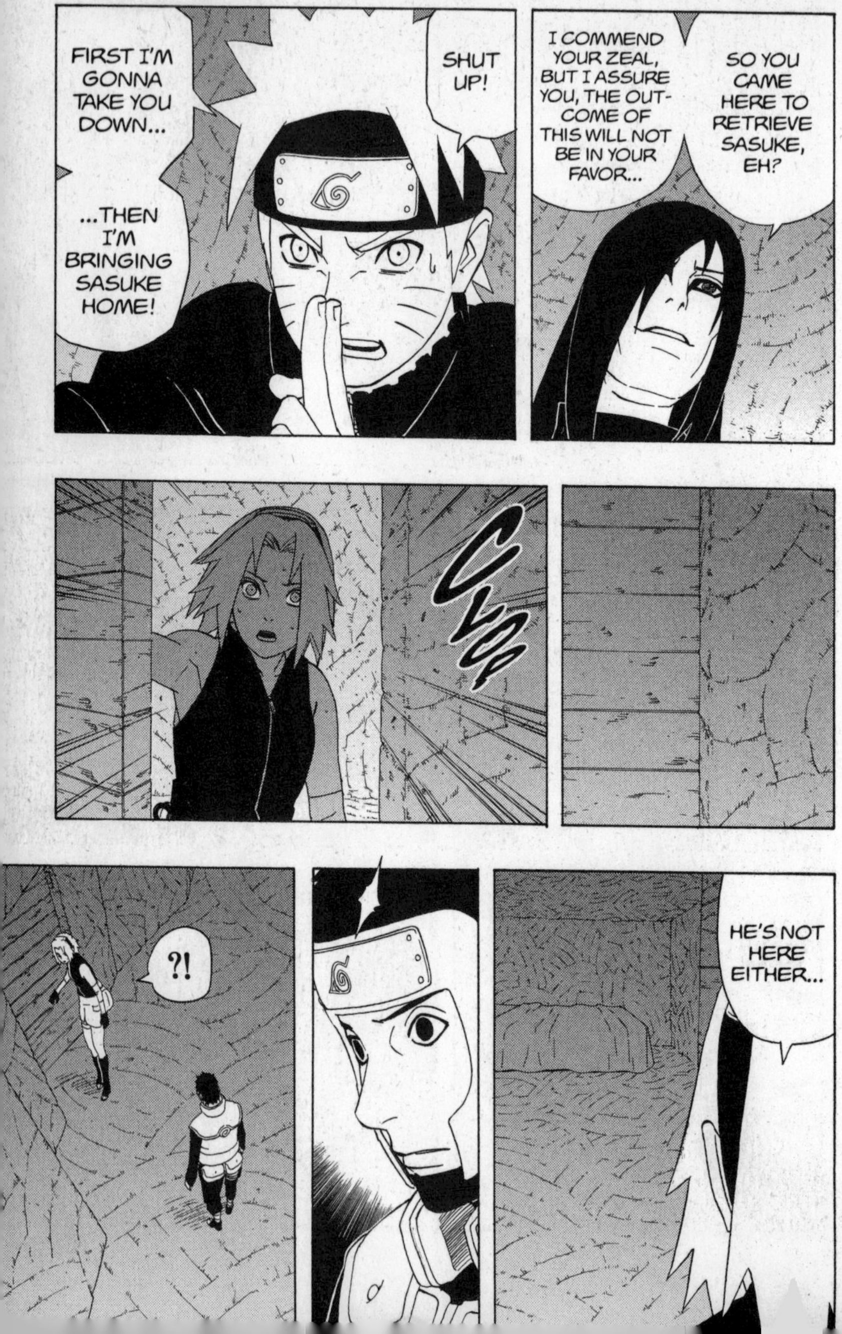
SO YOU CAME HERE TO RETRIEVE SASUKE, EH?
I COMMEND YOUR ZEAL, BUT I ASSURE YOU, THE OUT-COME OF THIS WILL NOT BE IN YOUR FAVOR...
SHUT UP!
FIRST I'M GONNA TAKE YOU DOWN...
...THEN I'M BRINGING SASUKE HOME!
HE'S NOT HERE EITHER...
?!

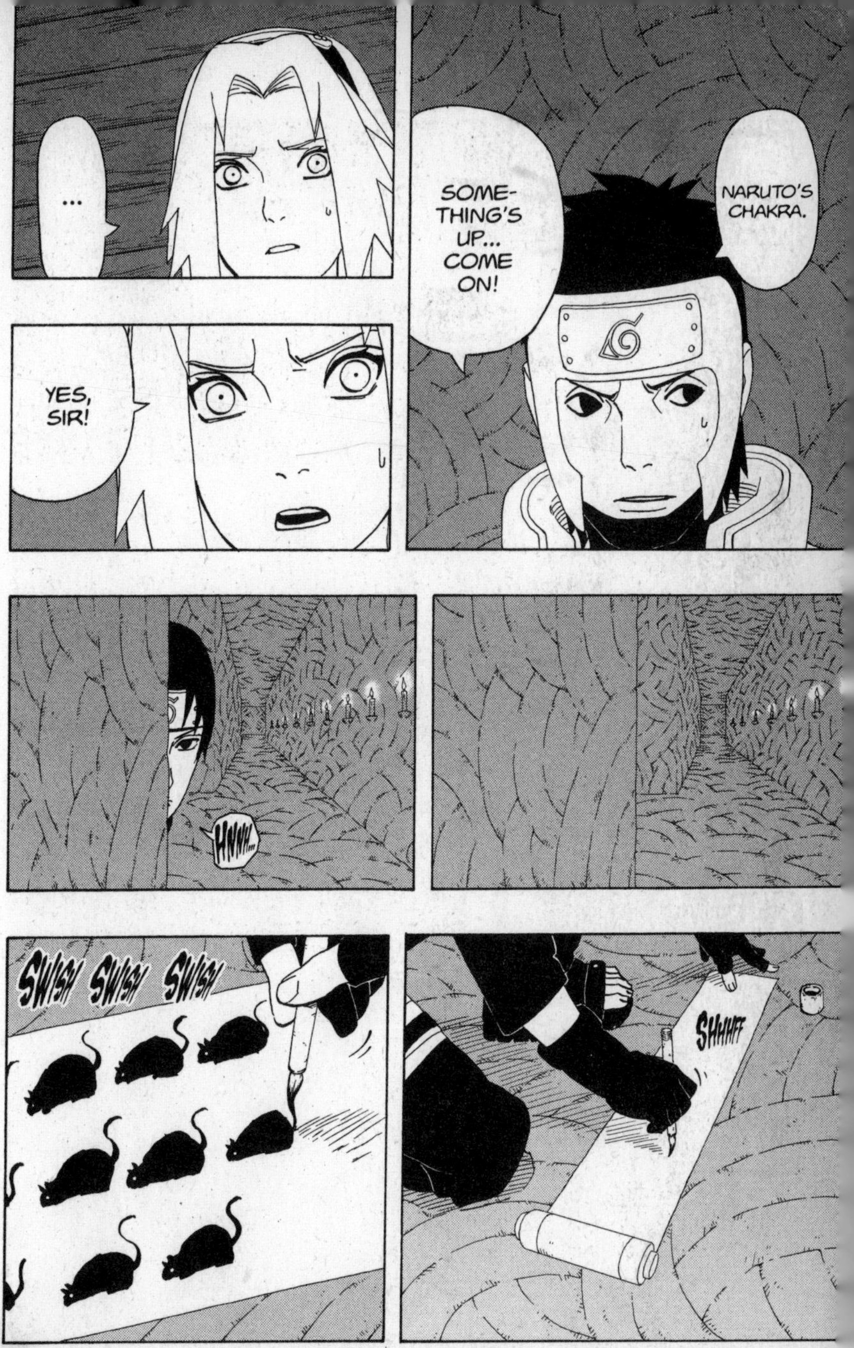
NARUTO'S CHAKRA.
SOME-THING'S UP... COME ON!
...
YES, SIR!
HNNH...
SHHHFF
SWISH SWISH SWISH

READ THIS WAY

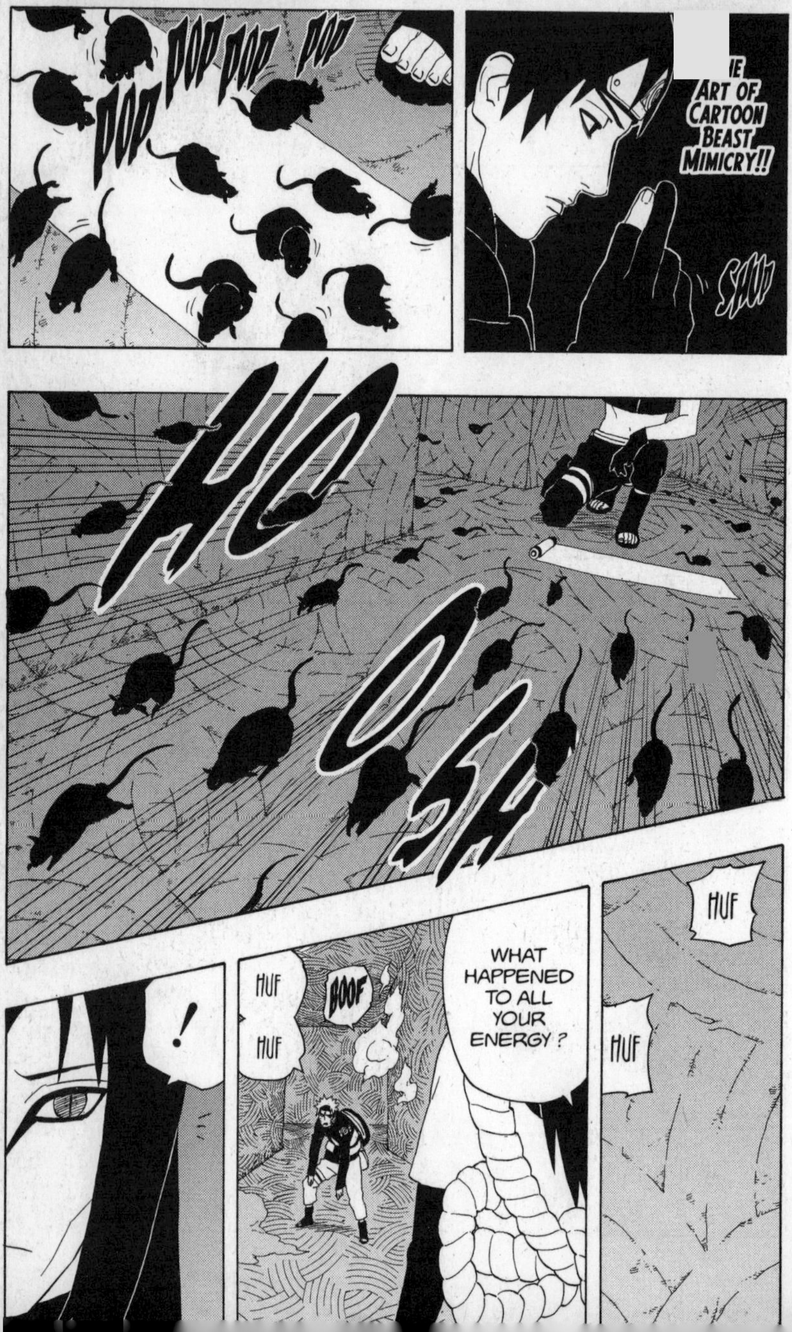
Art of Cartoon Beast Mimicry!!
SHUP
POP POP POP POP POP
HOOSH
HUF
HUF
WHAT HAPPENED TO ALL YOUR ENERGY ?
HUF
HUF
BOOF
!

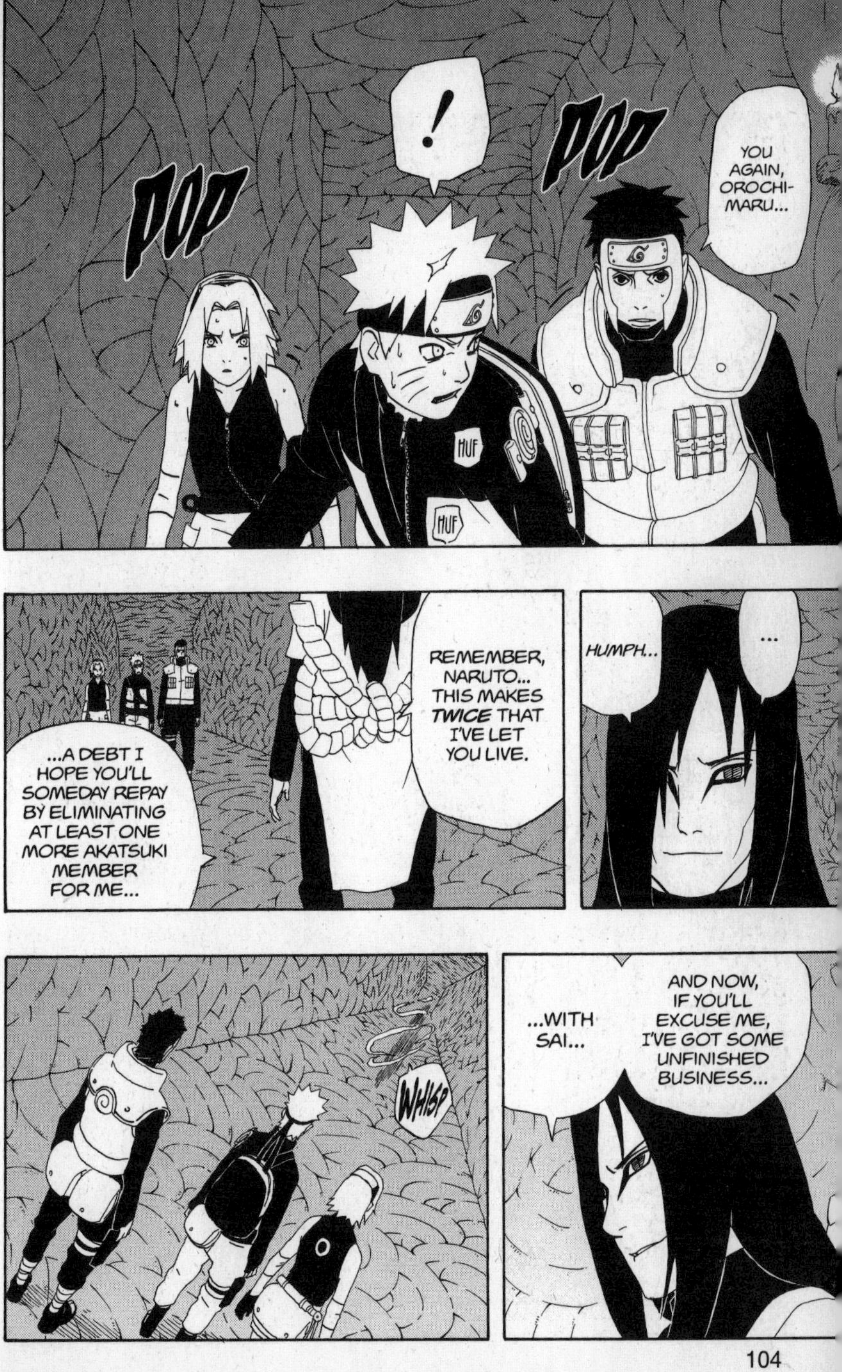
YOU AGAIN, OROCHI-MARU...
POP
!
POP
...
HUMPH...
REMEMBER, NARUTO... THIS MAKES *TWICE* THAT I'VE LET YOU LIVE.
...A DEBT I HOPE YOU'LL SOMEDAY REPAY BY ELIMINATING AT LEAST ONE MORE AKATSUKI MEMBER FOR ME...
AND NOW, IF YOU'LL EXCUSE ME, I'VE GOT SOME UNFINISHED BUSINESS...
...WITH SAI...
WHISP

READ THIS WAY

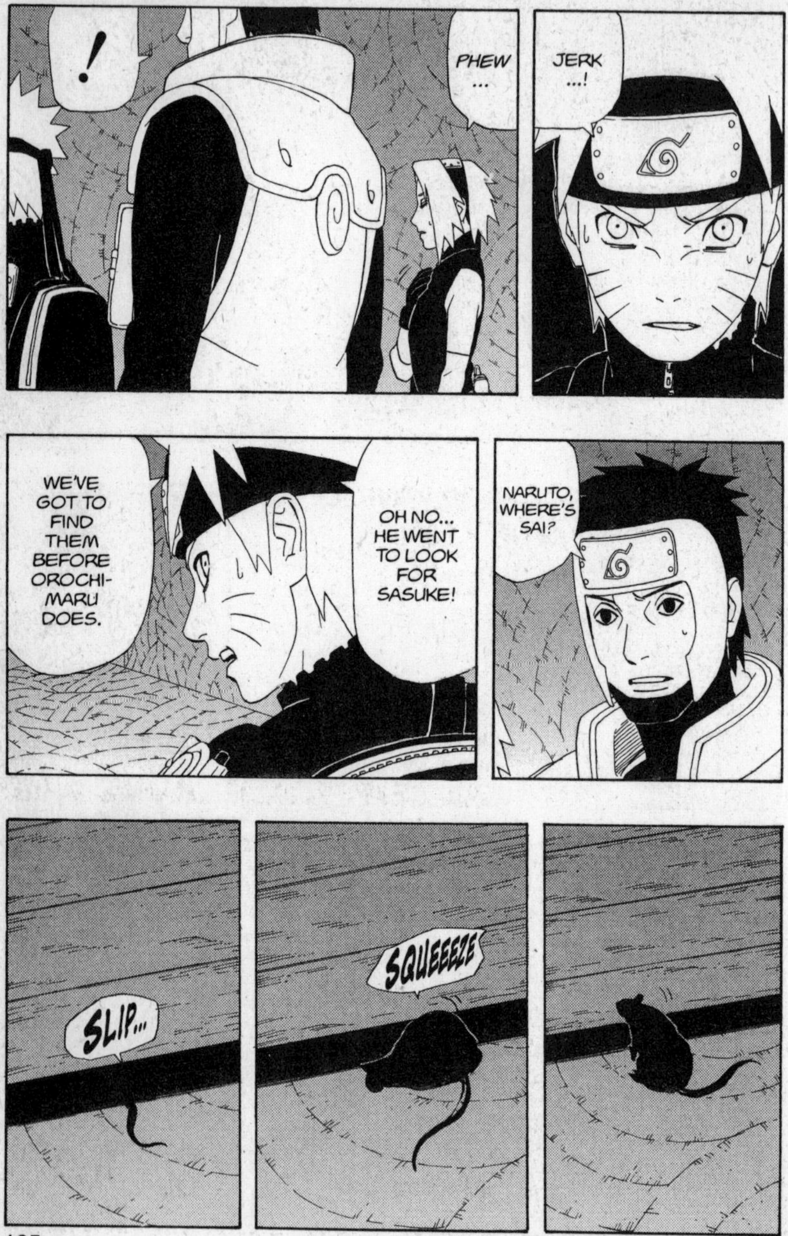
JERK ...!
PHEW ...
!
NARUTO, WHERE'S SAI?
OH NO... HE WENT TO LOOK FOR SASUKE!
WE'VE GOT TO FIND THEM BEFORE OROCHI-MARU DOES.
SQUEEEZE
SLIP...

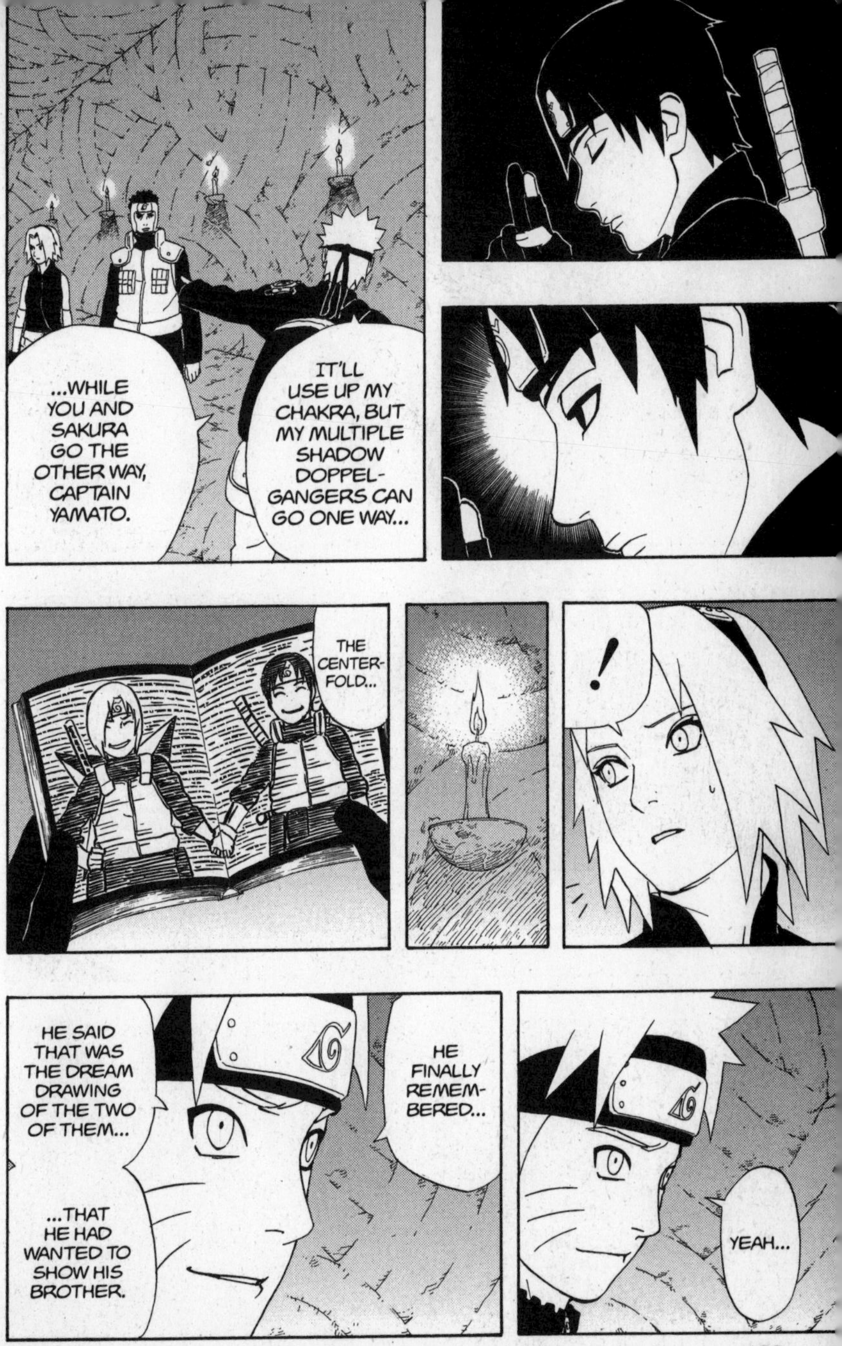
IT'LL USE UP MY CHAKRA, BUT MY MULTIPLE SHADOW DOPPEL-GANGERS CAN GO ONE WAY...
...WHILE YOU AND SAKURA GO THE OTHER WAY, CAPTAIN YAMATO.
!
THE CENTER-FOLD...
YEAH...
HE FINALLY REMEM-BERED...
HE SAID THAT WAS THE DREAM DRAWING OF THE TWO OF THEM...
...THAT HE HAD WANTED TO SHOW HIS BROTHER.

READ THIS WAY

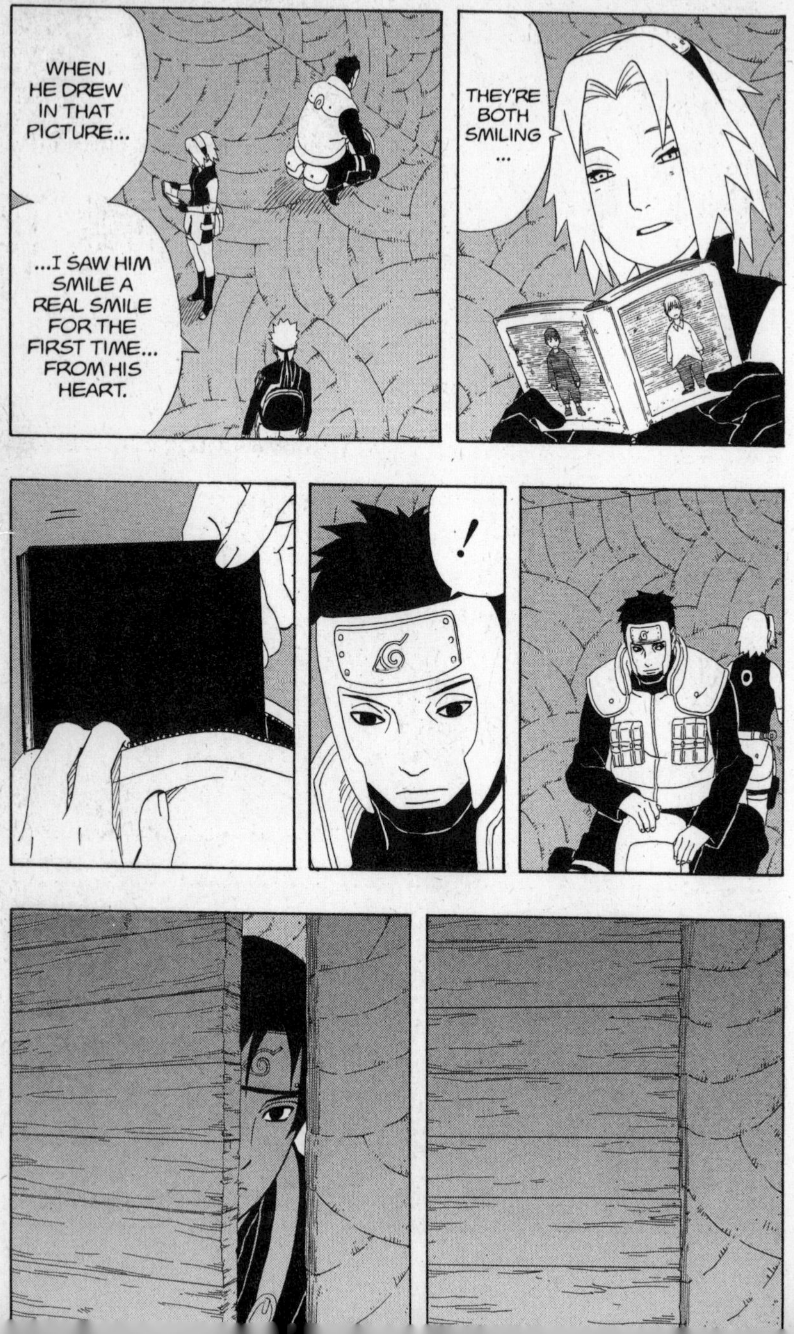
THEY'RE BOTH SMILING ...
WHEN HE DREW IN THAT PICTURE...
...I SAW HIM SMILE A REAL SMILE FOR THE FIRST TIME... FROM HIS HEART.
!

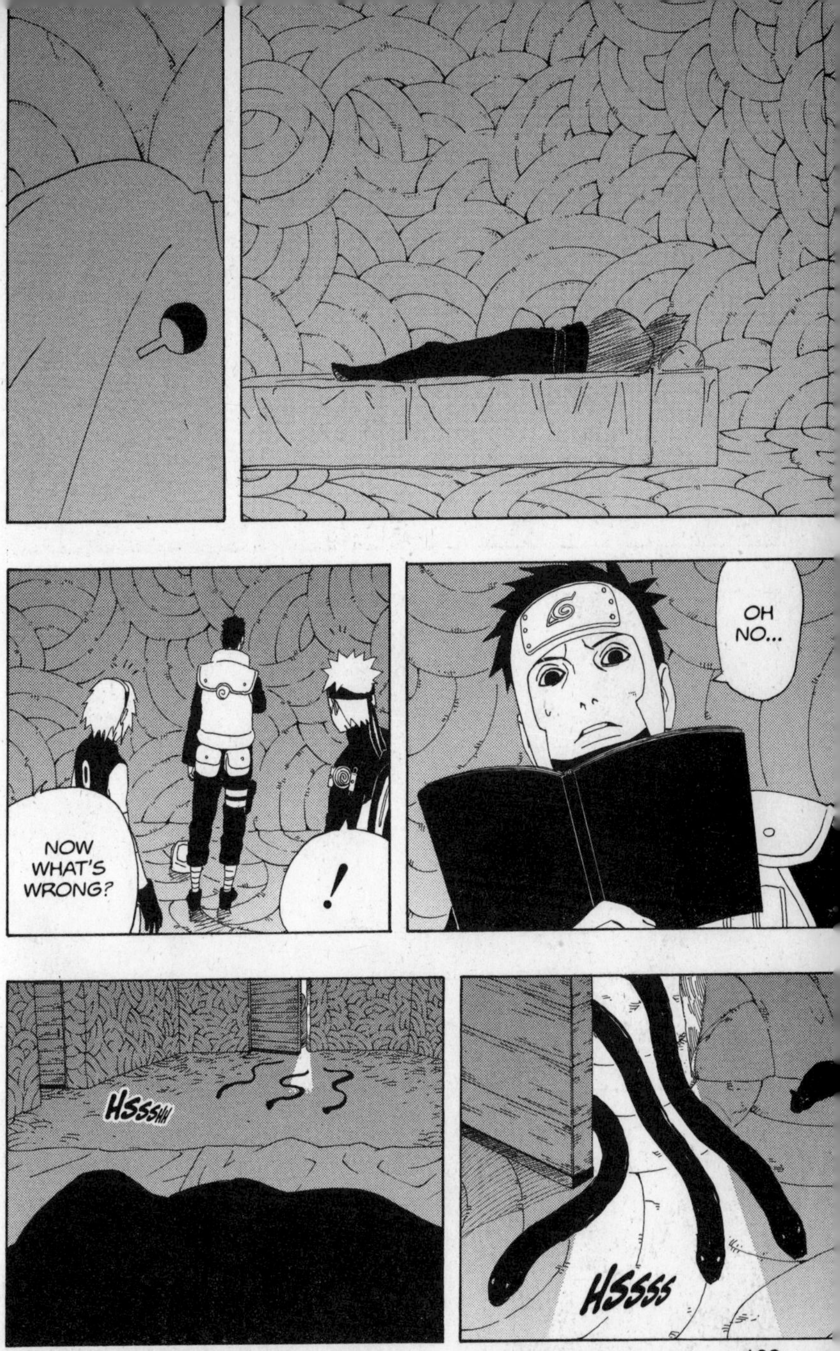
OH NO...
!
NOW WHAT'S WRONG?
HSSSS
HSSSHH

READ THIS WAY

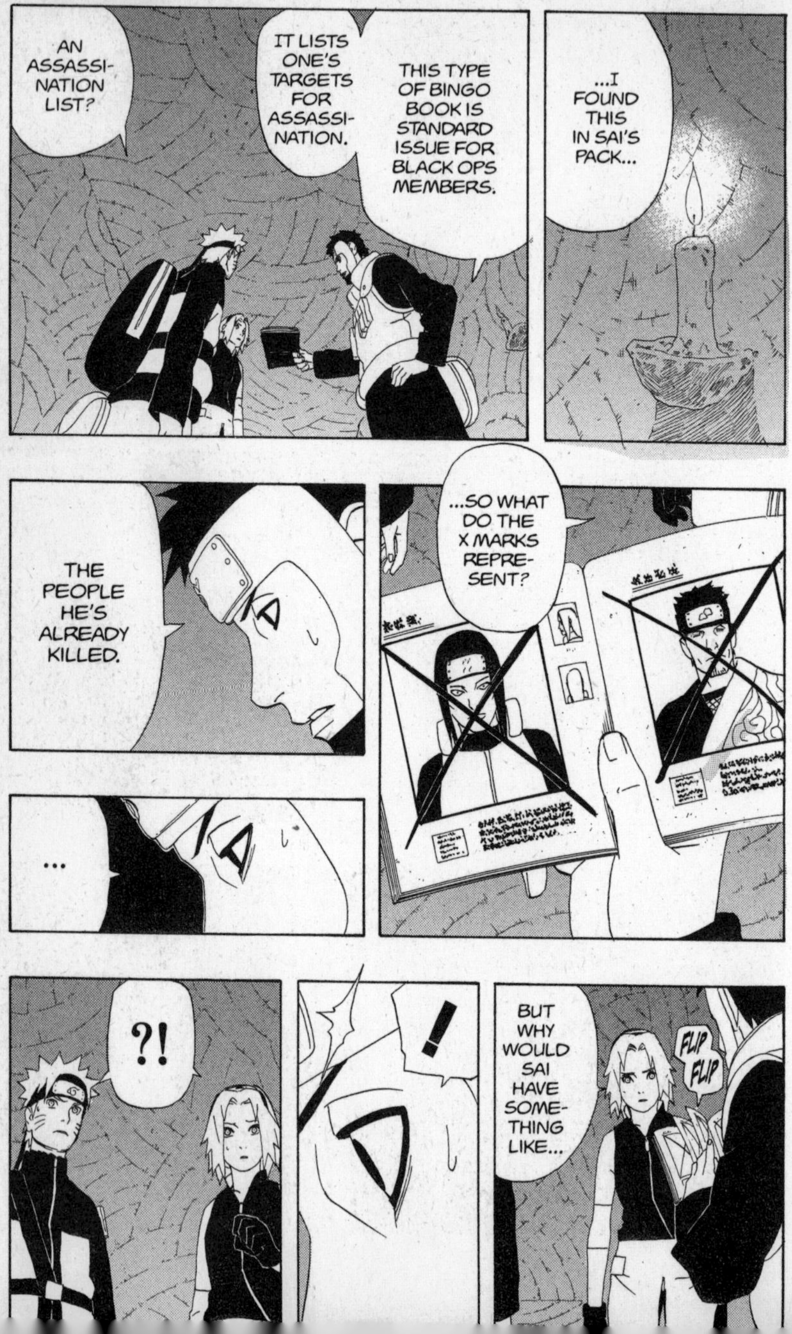
...I FOUND THIS IN SAI'S PACK...
THIS TYPE OF BINGO BOOK IS STANDARD ISSUE FOR BLACK OPS MEMBERS.
IT LISTS ONE'S TARGETS FOR ASSASSINATION.
AN ASSASSINATION LIST?
...SO WHAT DO THE X MARKS REPRESENT?
THE PEOPLE HE'S ALREADY KILLED.
...
FLIP FLIP
BUT WHY WOULD SAI HAVE SOMETHING LIKE...
!
?!

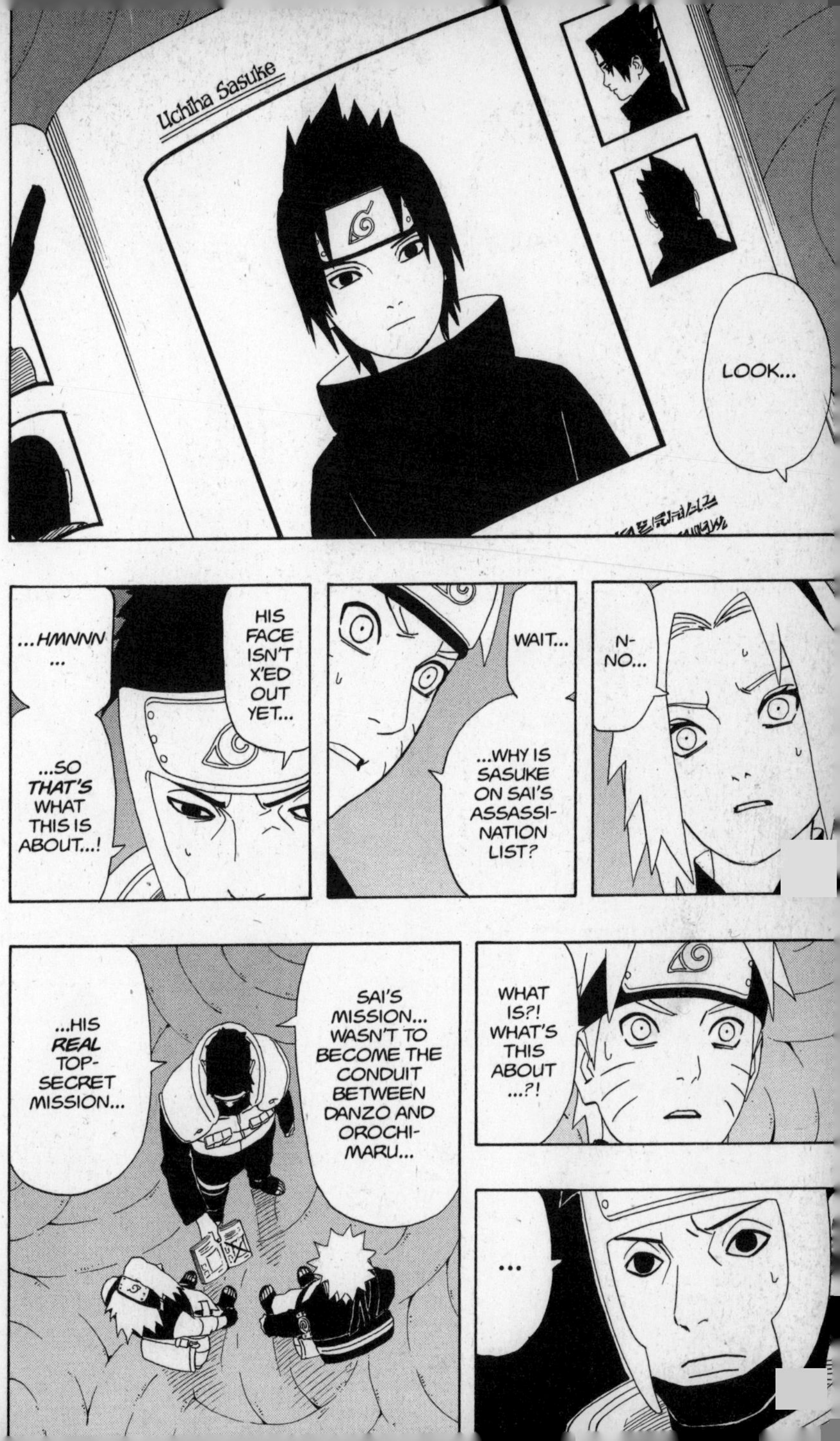
Uchiha Sasuke
LOOK...
N- NO...
WAIT...
...WHY IS SASUKE ON SAI'S ASSASSI- NATION LIST?
HIS FACE ISN'T X'ED OUT YET...
...HMNNN ...
...SO *THAT'S* WHAT THIS IS ABOUT...!
WHAT IS?! WHAT'S THIS ABOUT ...?!
...
SAI'S MISSION... WASN'T TO BECOME THE CONDUIT BETWEEN DANZO AND OROCHI- MARU...
...HIS *REAL* TOP- SECRET MISSION...

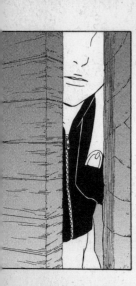

...IS TO ASSASSINATE SASUKE.
HSSS
BUT...
...BUT THAT'S NOT POSSIBLE!
I MEAN, JUST NOW HE SAID HE WAS GOING TO RESCUE SASUKE...!
AND I SAW HIM SMILE FROM HIS HEART...
...I REALLY THINK HE'S CHANGED...
UNLESS IT WAS ALL JUST AN ACT TO DRAW YOU OUT...

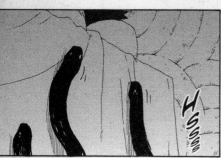

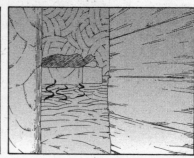

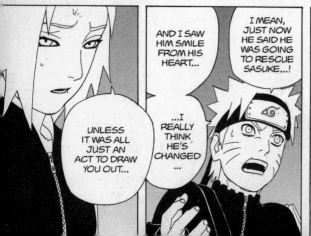

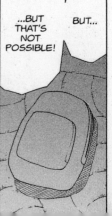

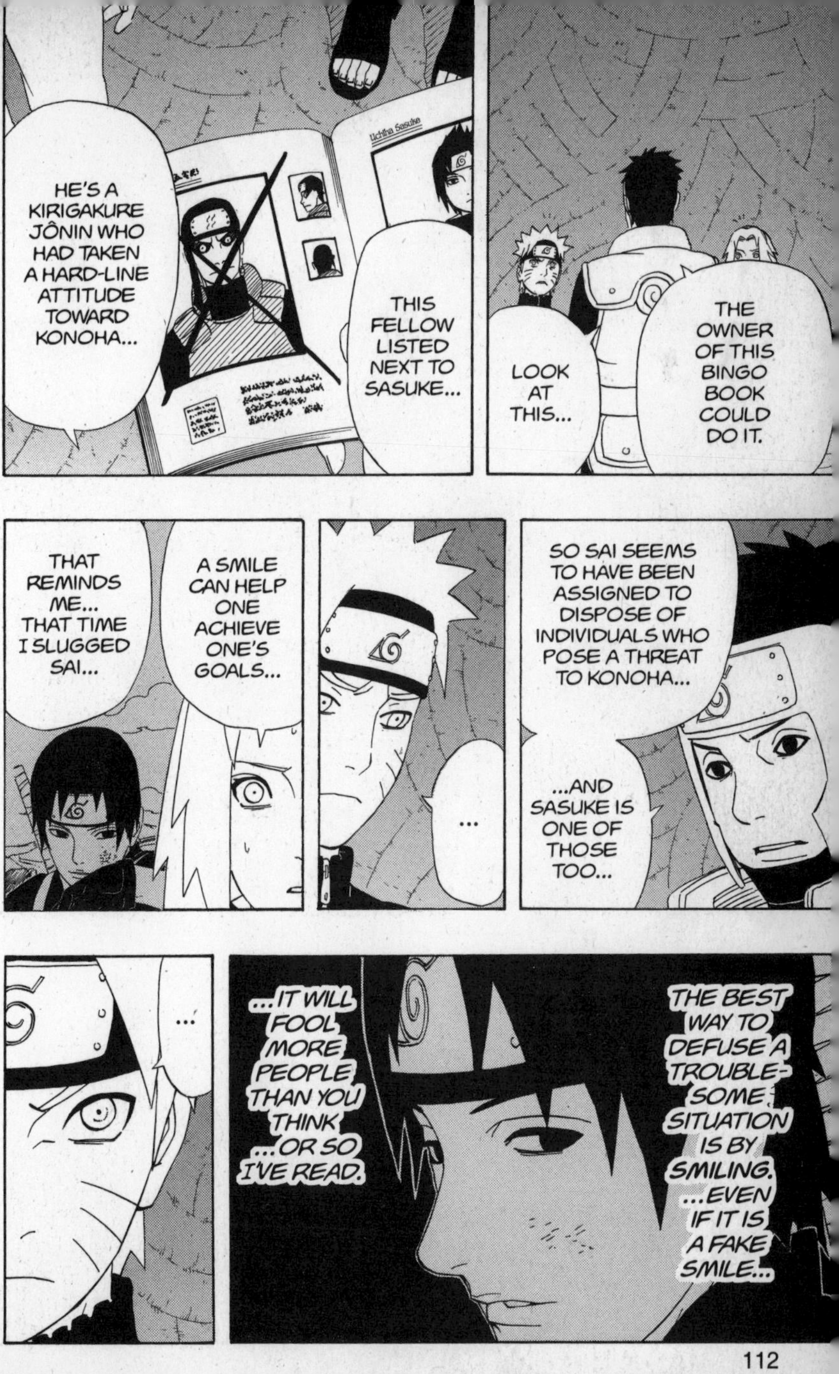
THE OWNER OF THIS BINGO BOOK COULD DO IT.
LOOK AT THIS...
THIS FELLOW LISTED NEXT TO SASUKE...
HE'S A KIRIGAKURE JÔNIN WHO HAD TAKEN A HARD-LINE ATTITUDE TOWARD KONOHA...
SO SAI SEEMS TO HAVE BEEN ASSIGNED TO DISPOSE OF INDIVIDUALS WHO POSE A THREAT TO KONOHA...
...AND SASUKE IS ONE OF THOSE TOO...
...
A SMILE CAN HELP ONE ACHIEVE ONE'S GOALS...
THAT REMINDS ME... THAT TIME I SLUGGED SAI...
THE BEST WAY TO DEFUSE A TROUBLE-SOME SITUATION IS BY SMILING. ...EVEN IF IT IS A FAKE SMILE...
...IT WILL FOOL MORE PEOPLE THAN YOU THINK ...OR SO I'VE READ.
...

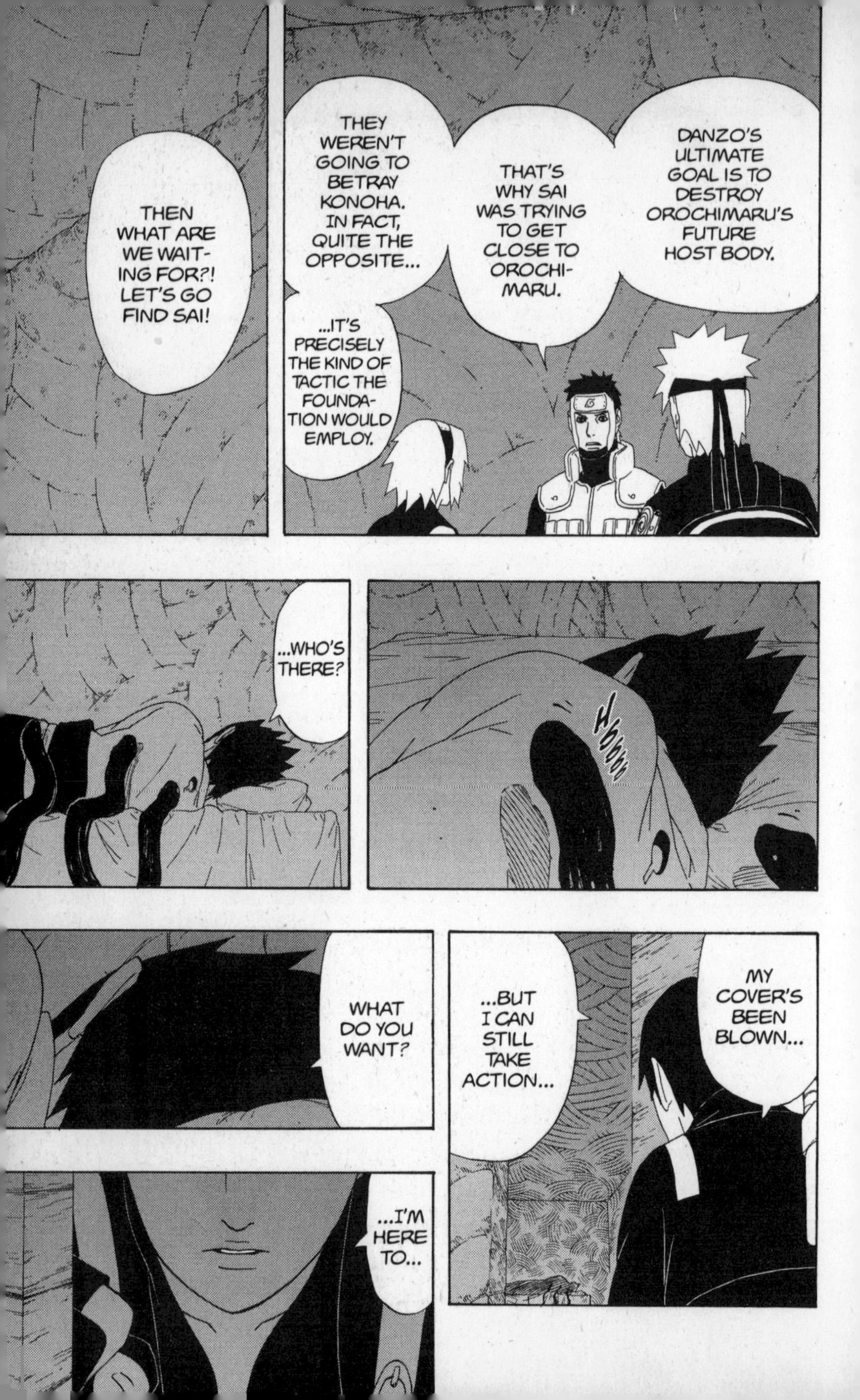
DANZO'S ULTIMATE GOAL IS TO DESTROY OROCHIMARU'S FUTURE HOST BODY.
THAT'S WHY SAI WAS TRYING TO GET CLOSE TO OROCHIMARU.
THEY WEREN'T GOING TO BETRAY KONOHA. IN FACT, QUITE THE OPPOSITE...
...IT'S PRECISELY THE KIND OF TACTIC THE FOUNDATION WOULD EMPLOY.
THEN WHAT ARE WE WAITING FOR?! LET'S GO FIND SAI!
...WHO'S THERE?
MY COVER'S BEEN BLOWN...
...BUT I CAN STILL TAKE ACTION...
WHAT DO YOU WANT?
...I'M HERE TO...

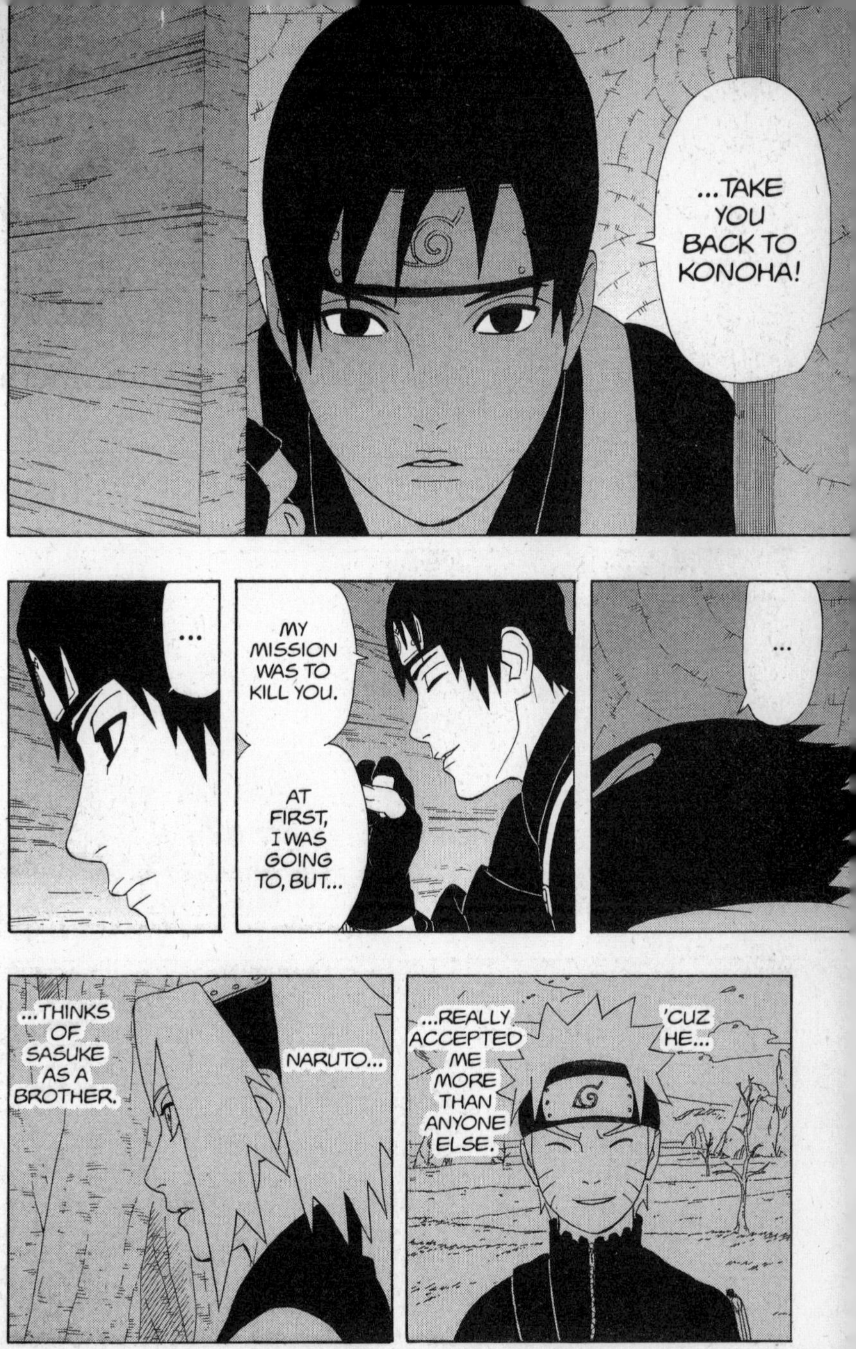
...TAKE YOU BACK TO KONOHA!
...
MY MISSION WAS TO KILL YOU.
AT FIRST, I WAS GOING TO, BUT...
...
'CUZ HE...
...REALLY ACCEPTED ME MORE THAN ANYONE ELSE.
NARUTO...
...THINKS OF SASUKE AS A BROTHER.

READ THIS WAY

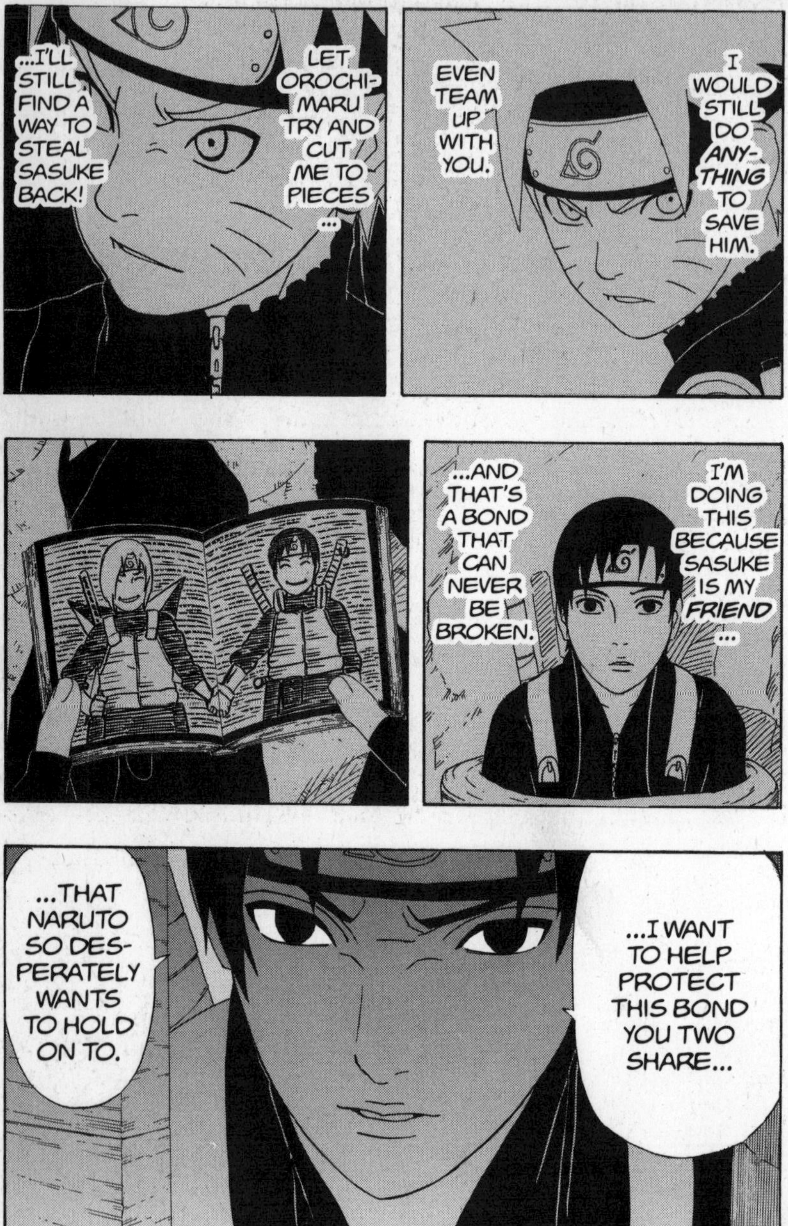
I WOULD STILL DO ANYTHING TO SAVE HIM.
EVEN TEAM UP WITH YOU.
LET OROCHIMARU TRY AND CUT ME TO PIECES...
...I'LL STILL FIND A WAY TO STEAL SASUKE BACK!
I'M DOING THIS BECAUSE SASUKE IS MY FRIEND...
...AND THAT'S A BOND THAT CAN NEVER BE BROKEN.
...I WANT TO HELP PROTECT THIS BOND YOU TWO SHARE...
...THAT NARUTO SO DESPERATELY WANTS TO HOLD ON TO.

NARUTO

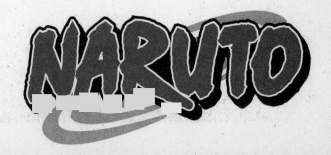

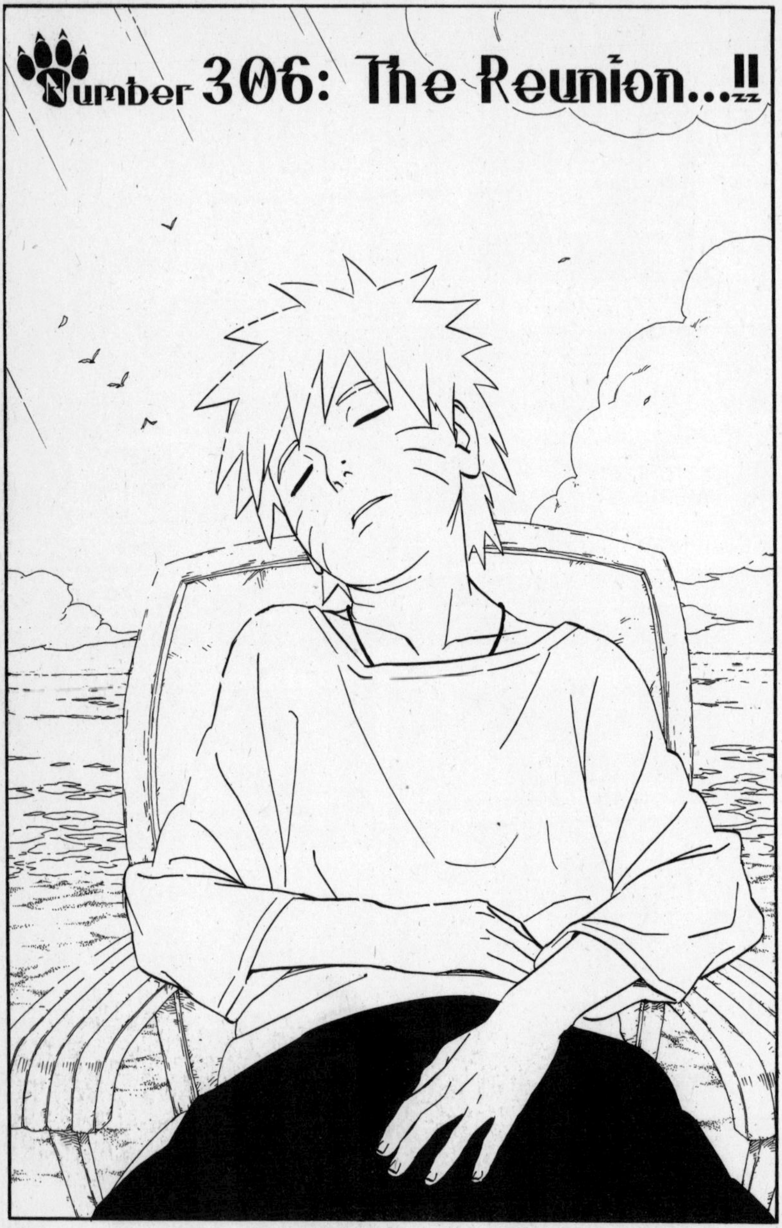
Number 306: The Reunion...!!
zzz

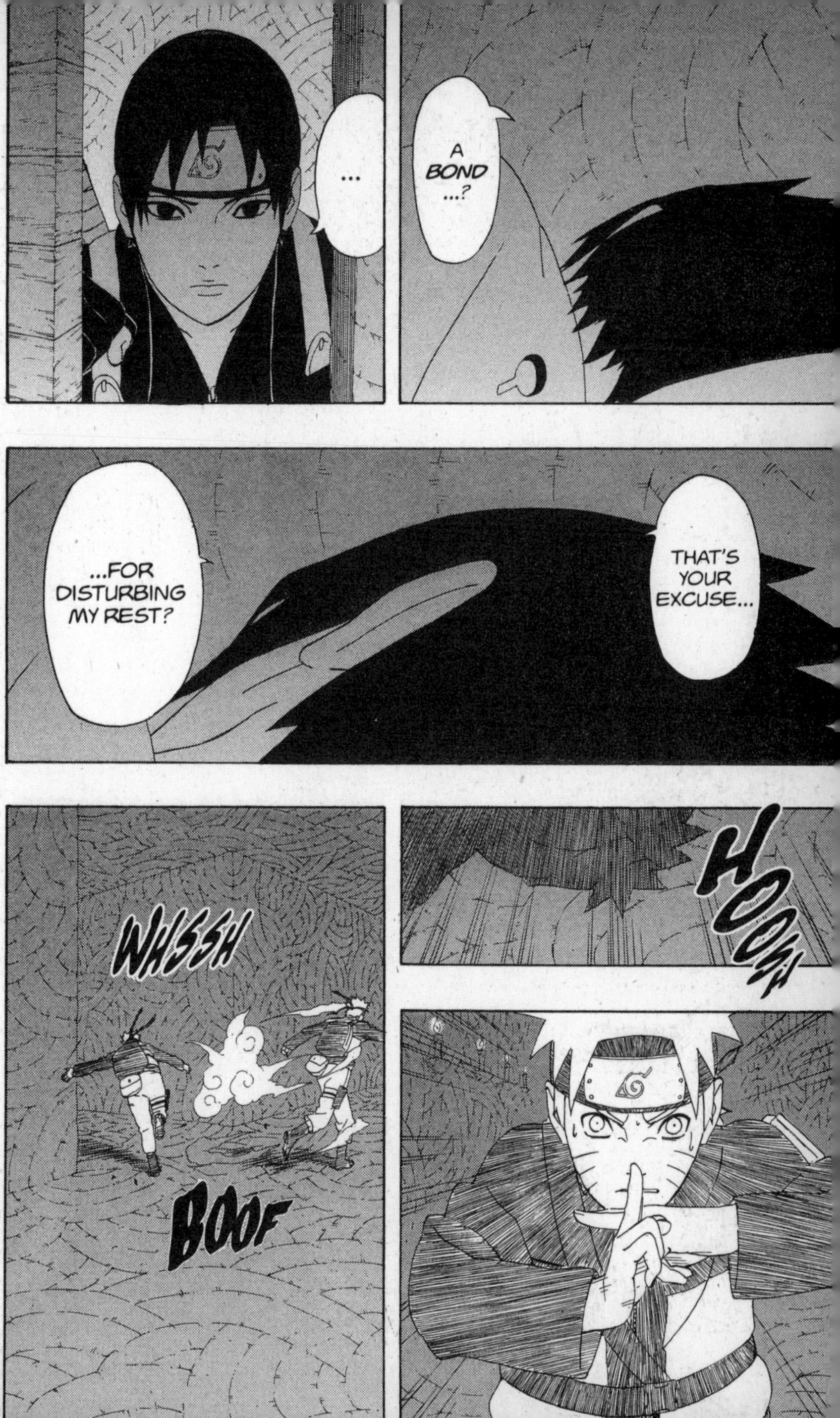
A BOND ...?
...
THAT'S YOUR EXCUSE...
...FOR DISTURBING MY REST?
HOOOSH
WHSSH
BOOF

READ THIS WAY

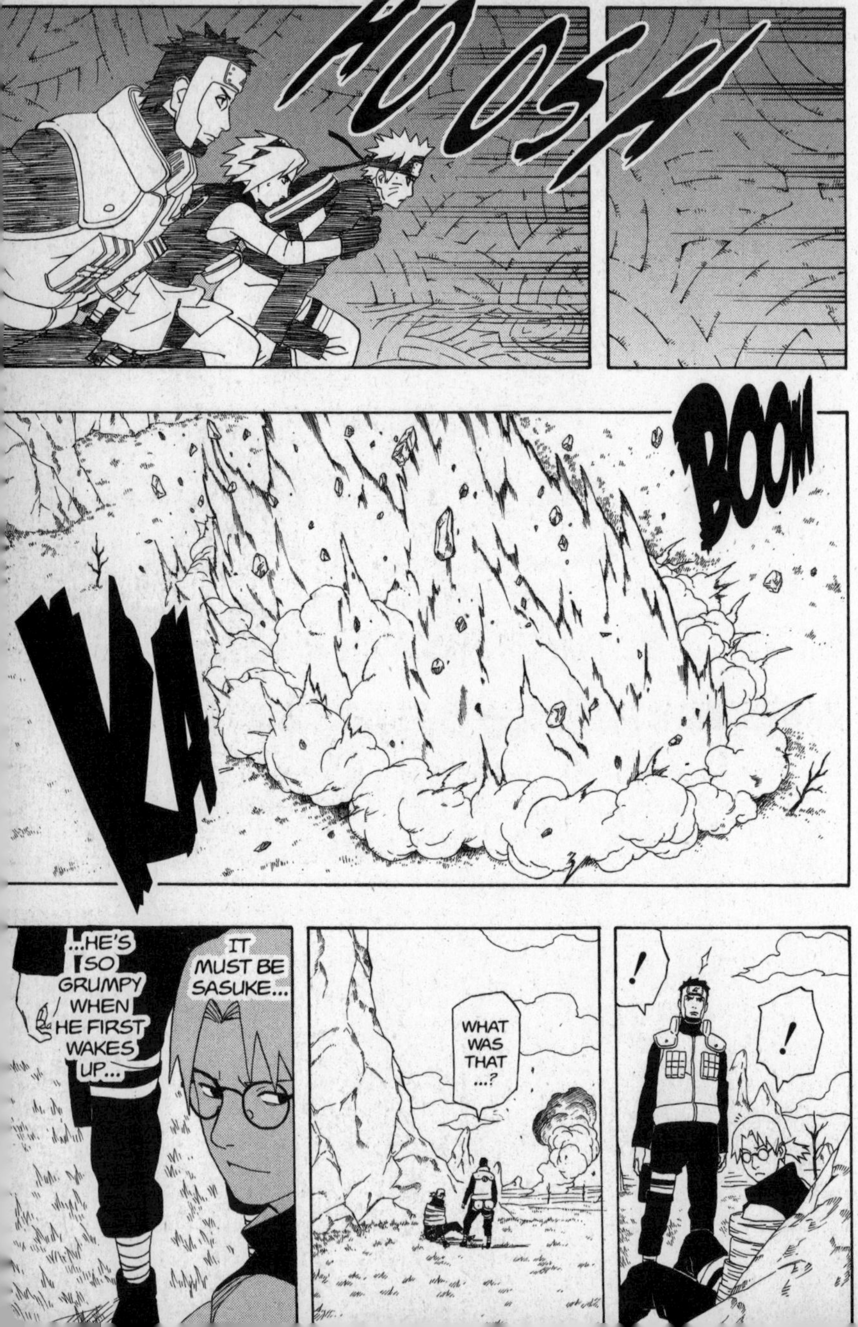
WHOOSH
BOOM
VA
!
!
WHAT WAS THAT ...?
IT MUST BE SASUKE...
...HE'S SO GRUMPY WHEN HE FIRST WAKES UP...

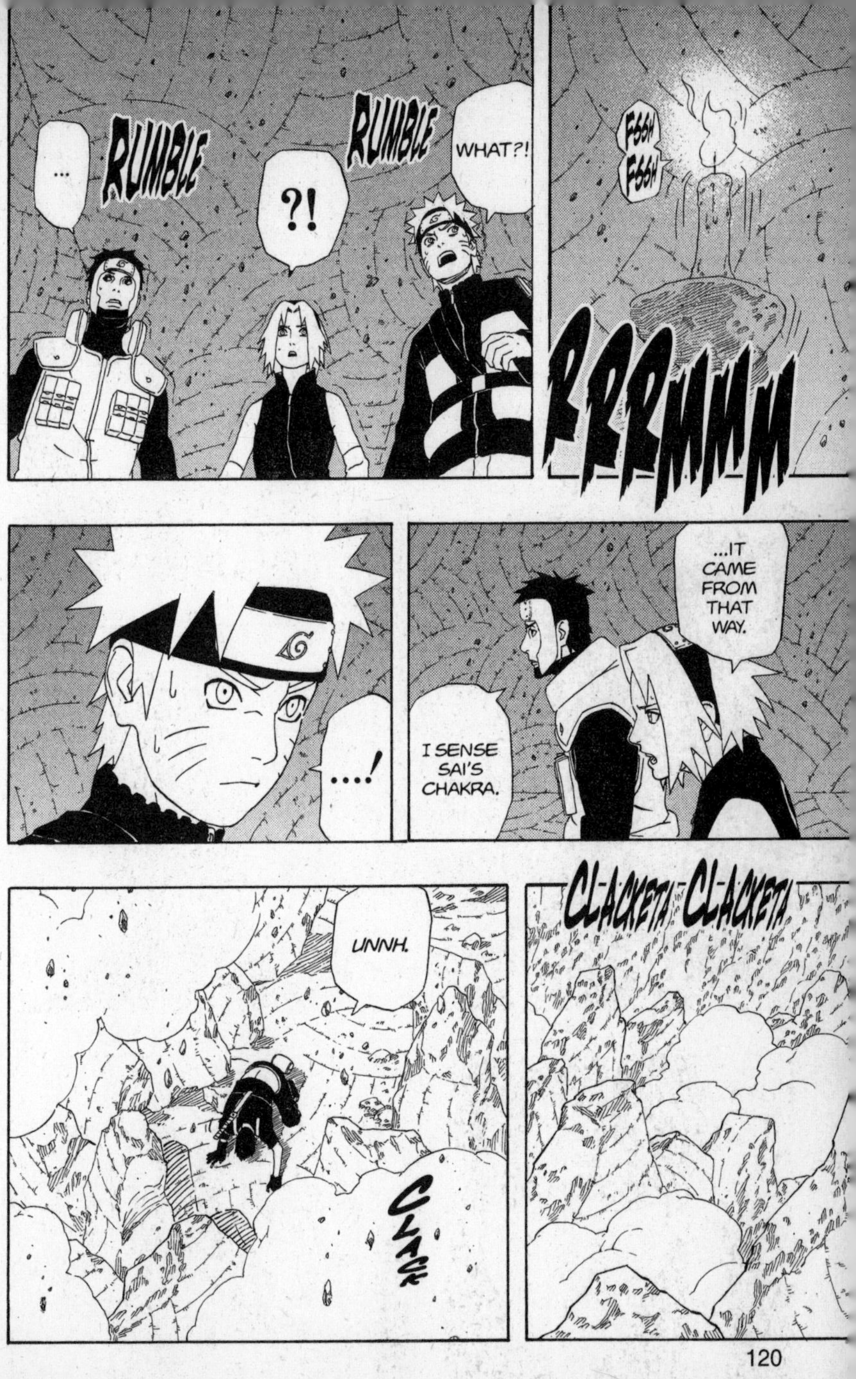
FSSH FSSH
RRRMMMM
WHAT?!
RUMBLE
?!
RUMBLE
...
...IT CAME FROM THAT WAY.
I SENSE SAI'S CHAKRA.
...!
CLACKETA CLACKETA
UNNH.
CLACK

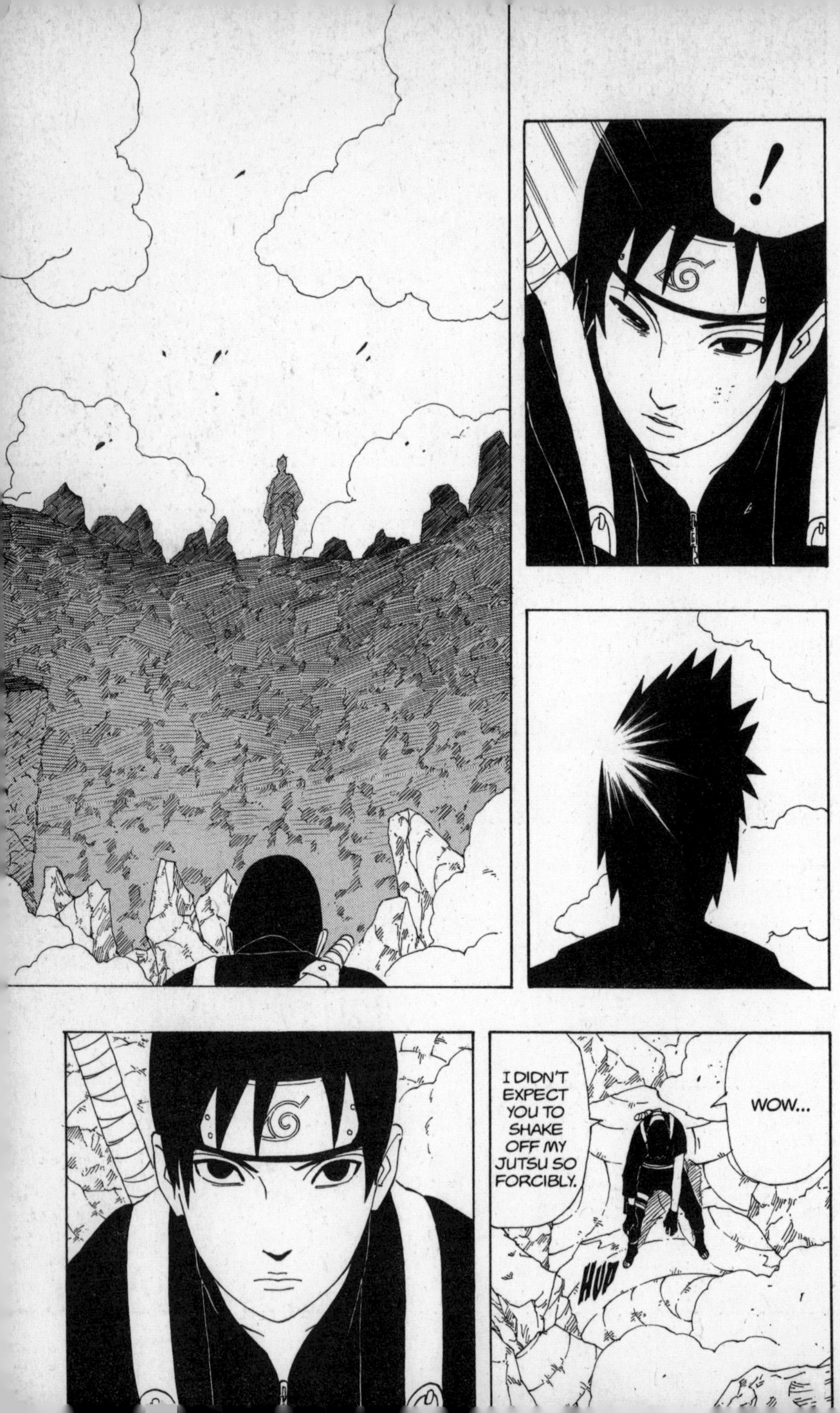
!
WOW...
I DIDN'T EXPECT YOU TO SHAKE OFF MY JUTSU SO FORCIBLY.
HUP

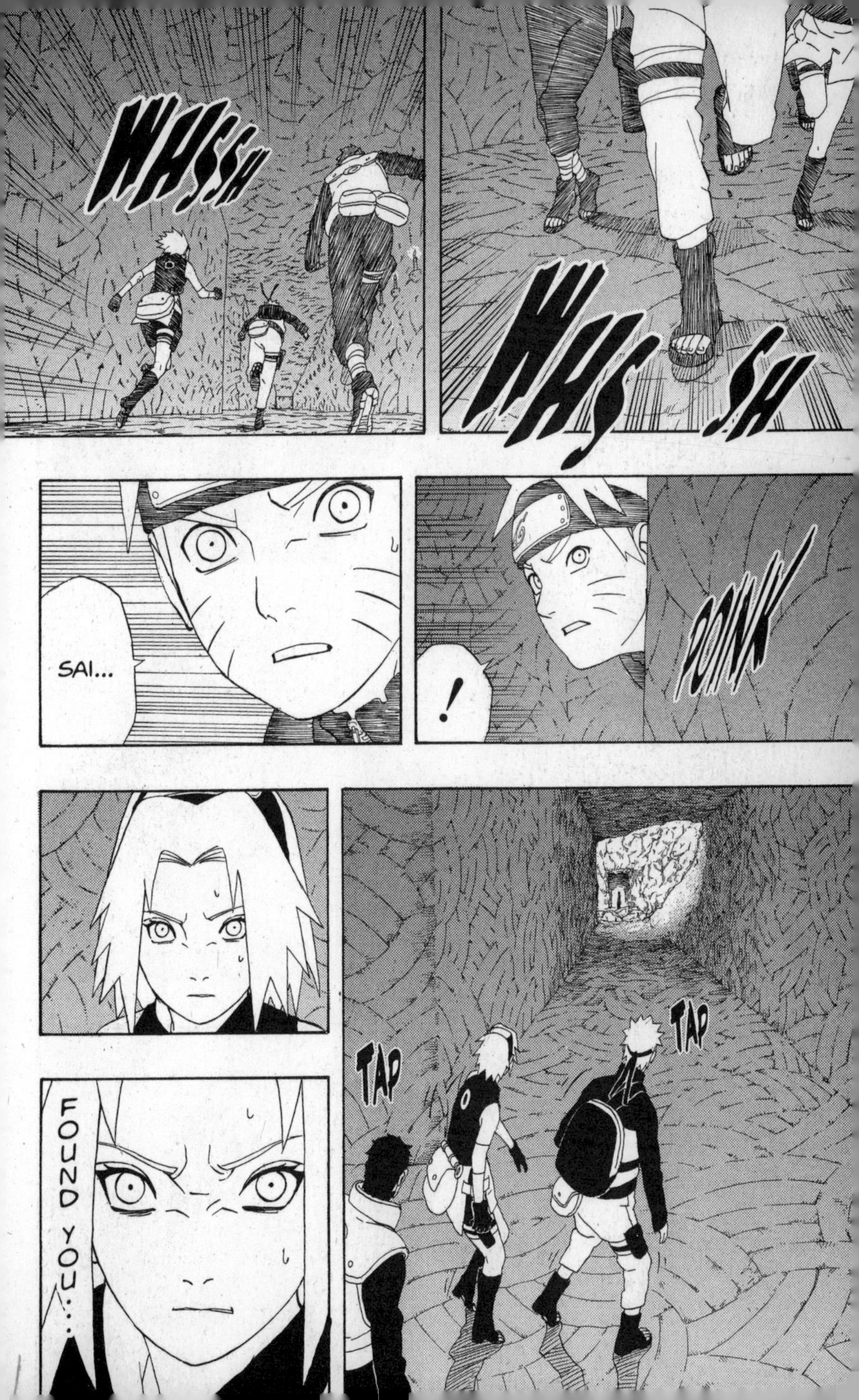
WHSSH
WHS SH
!
POINK
SAI...
TAP
TAP
FOUND YOU...

READ THIS WAY

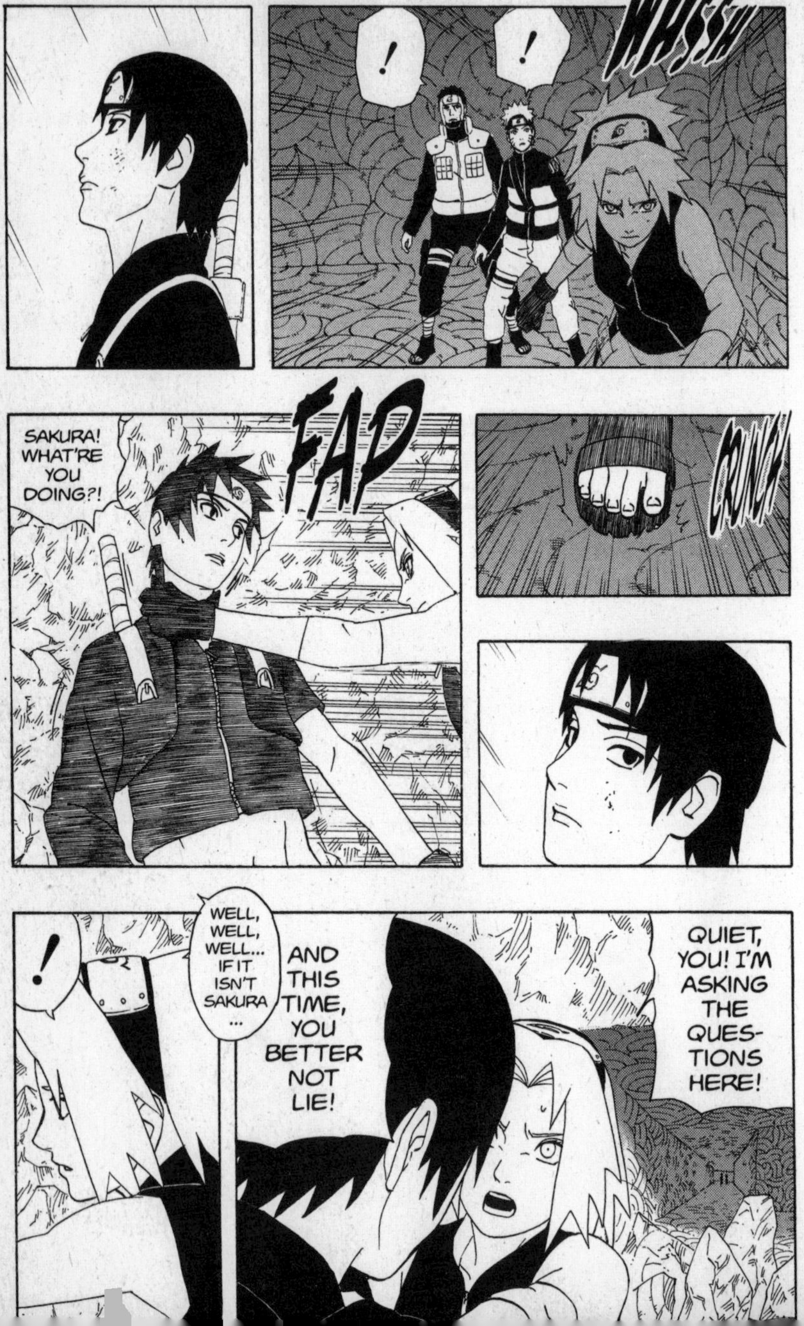
WHSSH
!
!
CRUNCH
FAP
SAKURA! WHAT'RE YOU DOING?!
QUIET, YOU! I'M ASKING THE QUES-TIONS HERE!
AND THIS TIME, YOU BETTER NOT LIE!
WELL, WELL, WELL... IF IT ISN'T SAKURA...
!

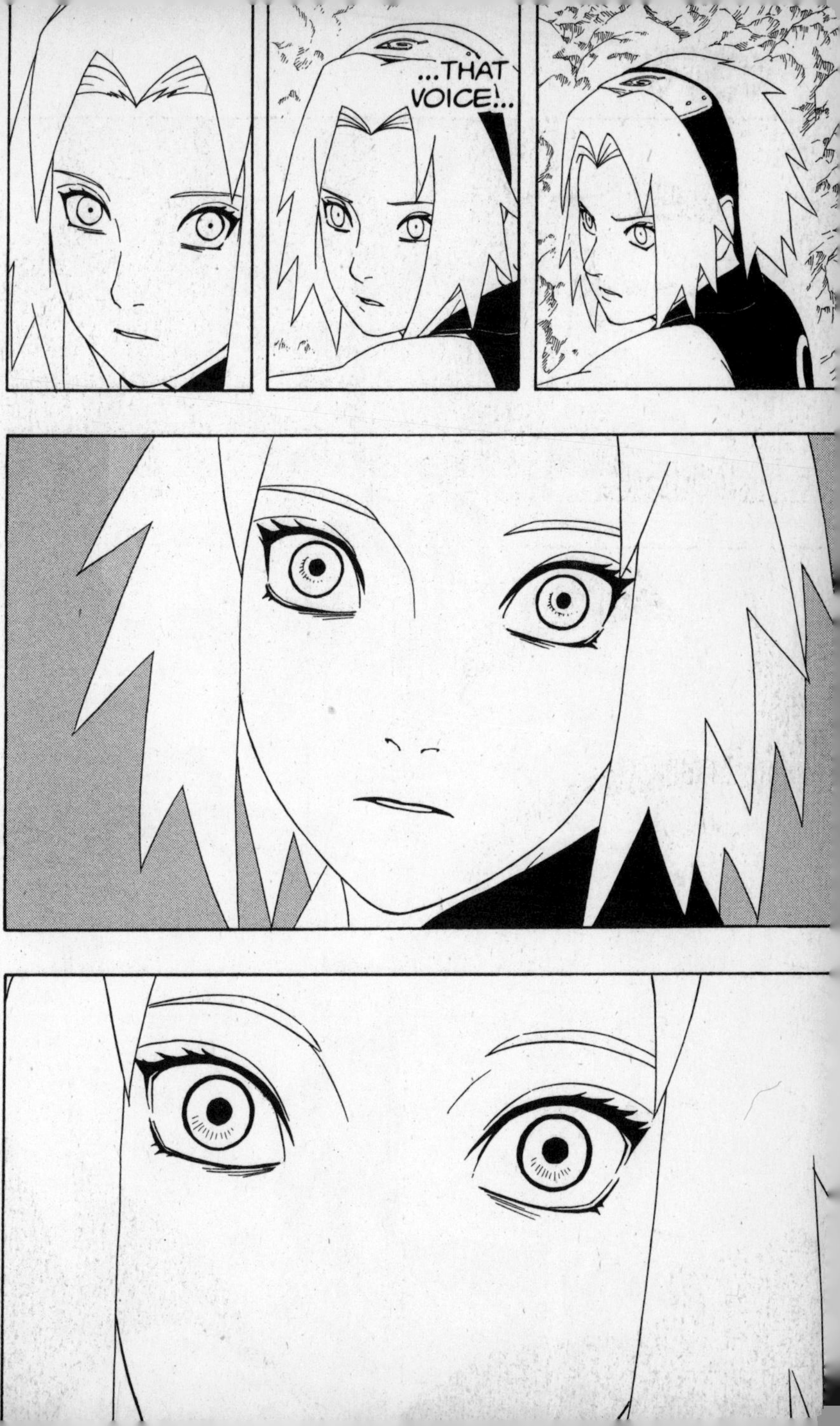
...THAT VOICE!...

READ THIS WAY

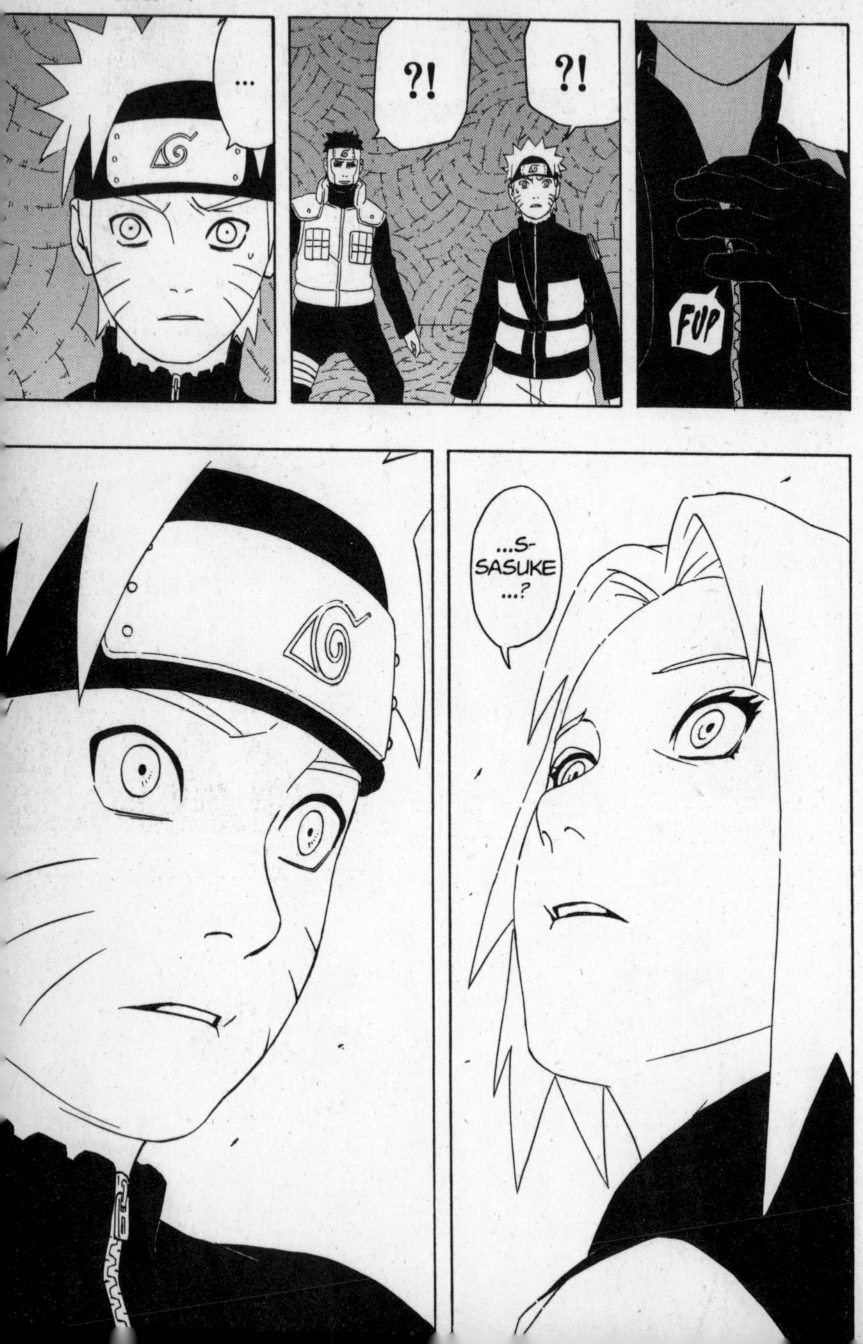
FUP
?!
?!
...
...S-
SASUKE
...?

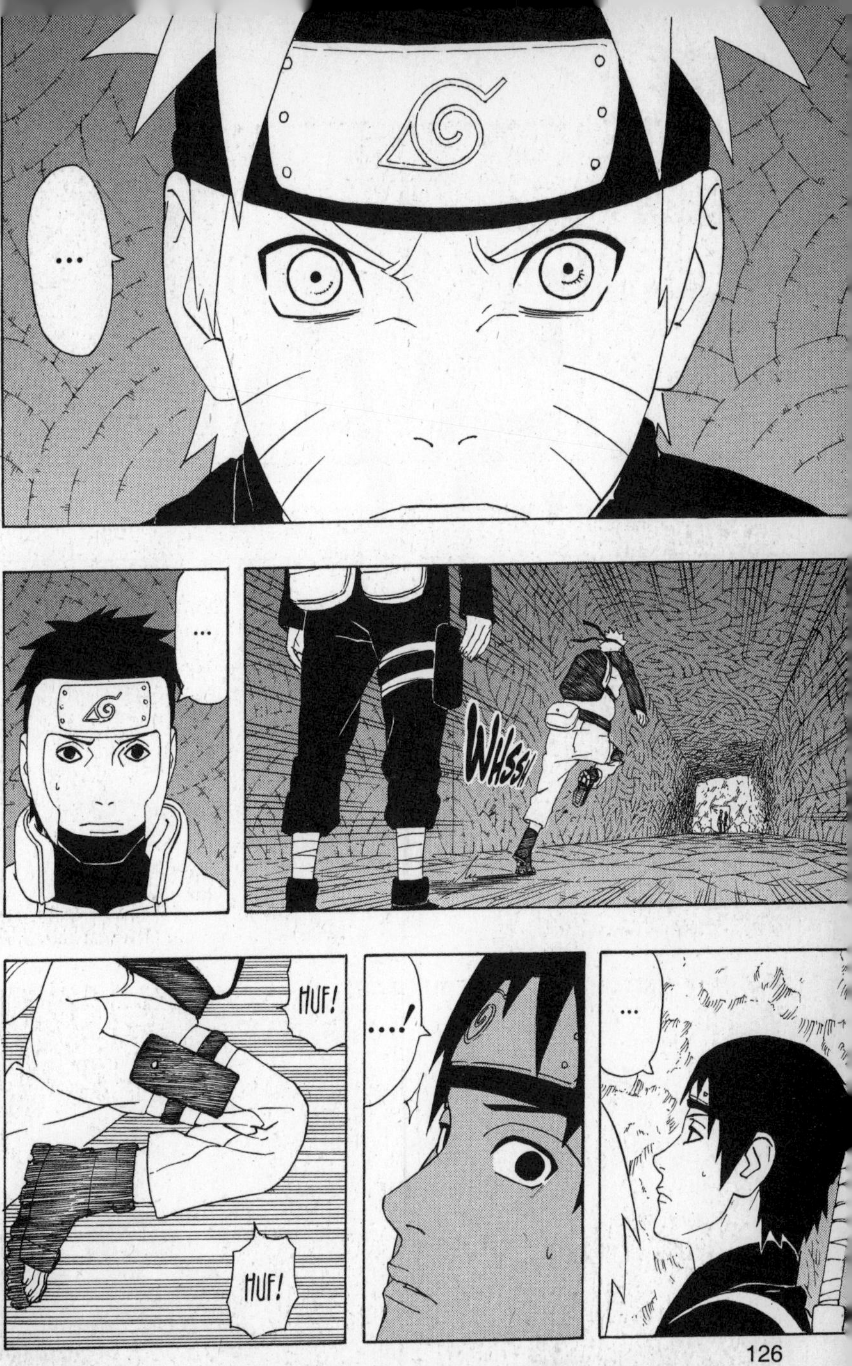
...
WHSSH
...
...
....!
HUF!
HUF!

READ THIS WAY

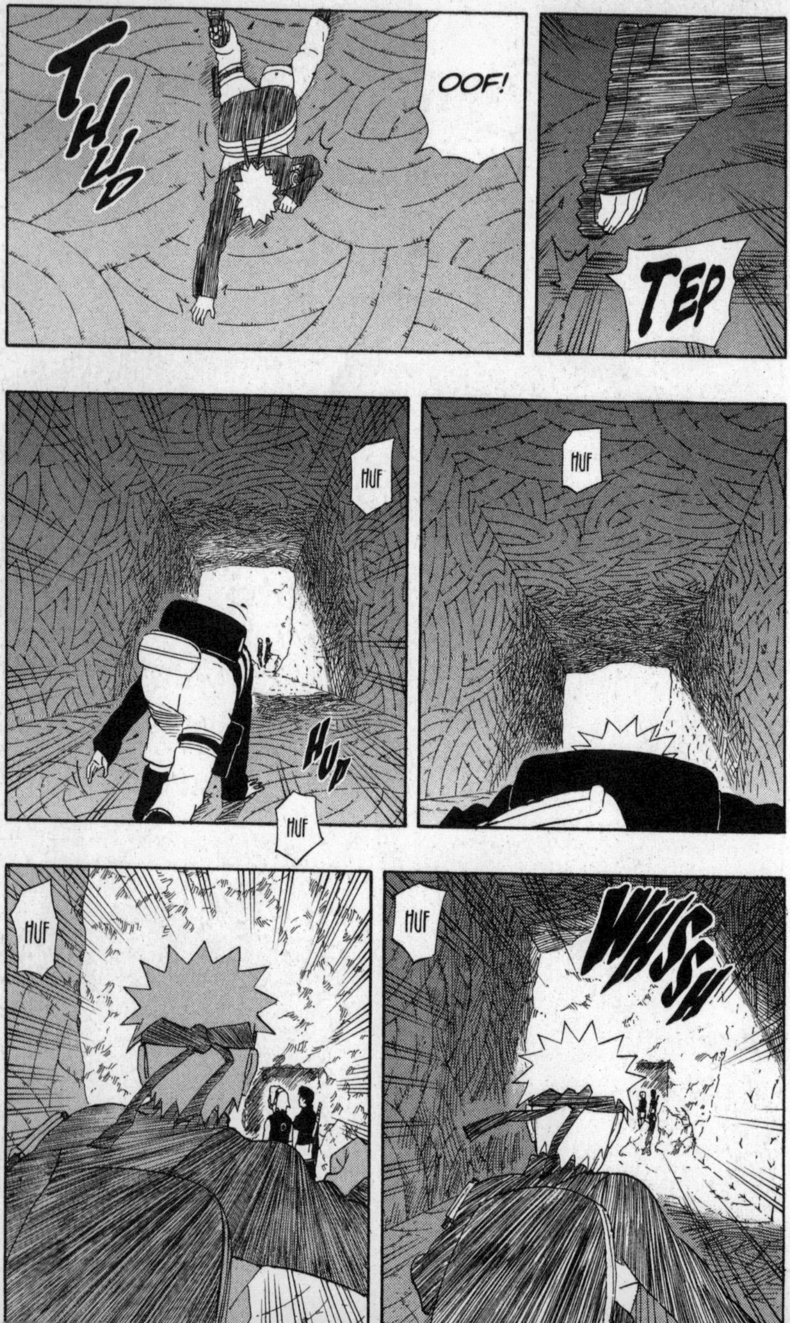
TEP
OOF!
THUD
HUF
HUF
HUD
HUF
WHSH
HUF
HUF

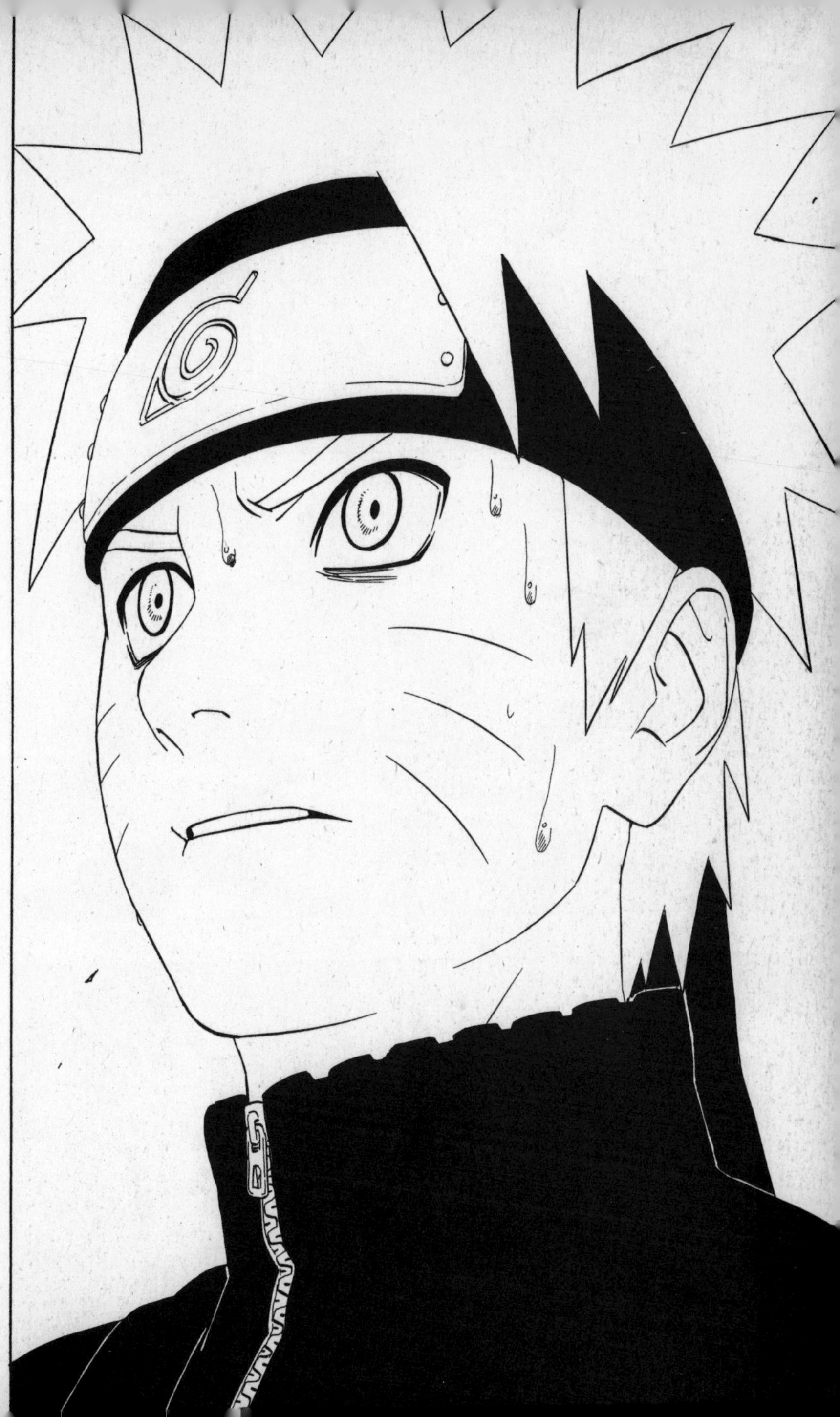

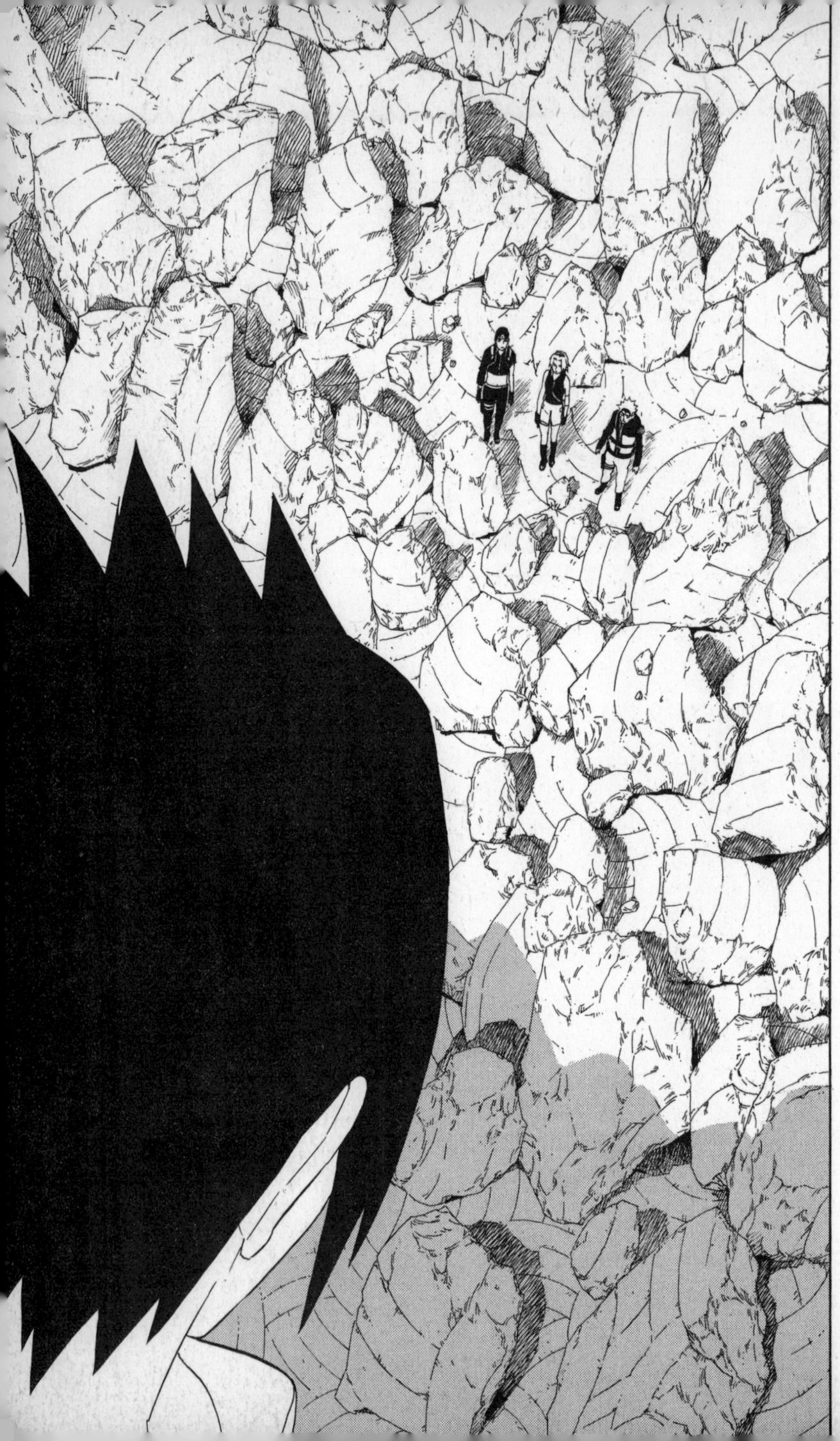

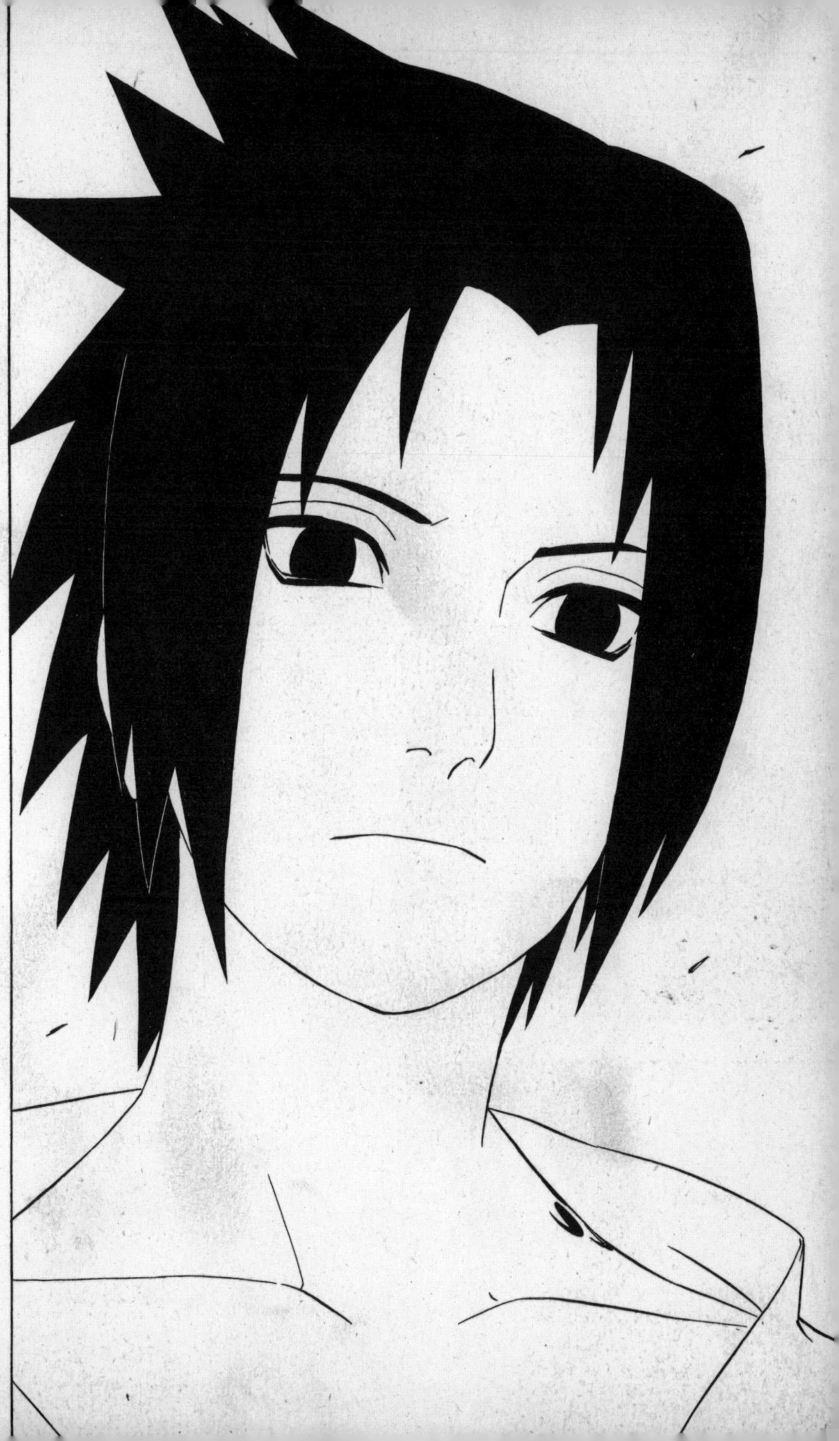

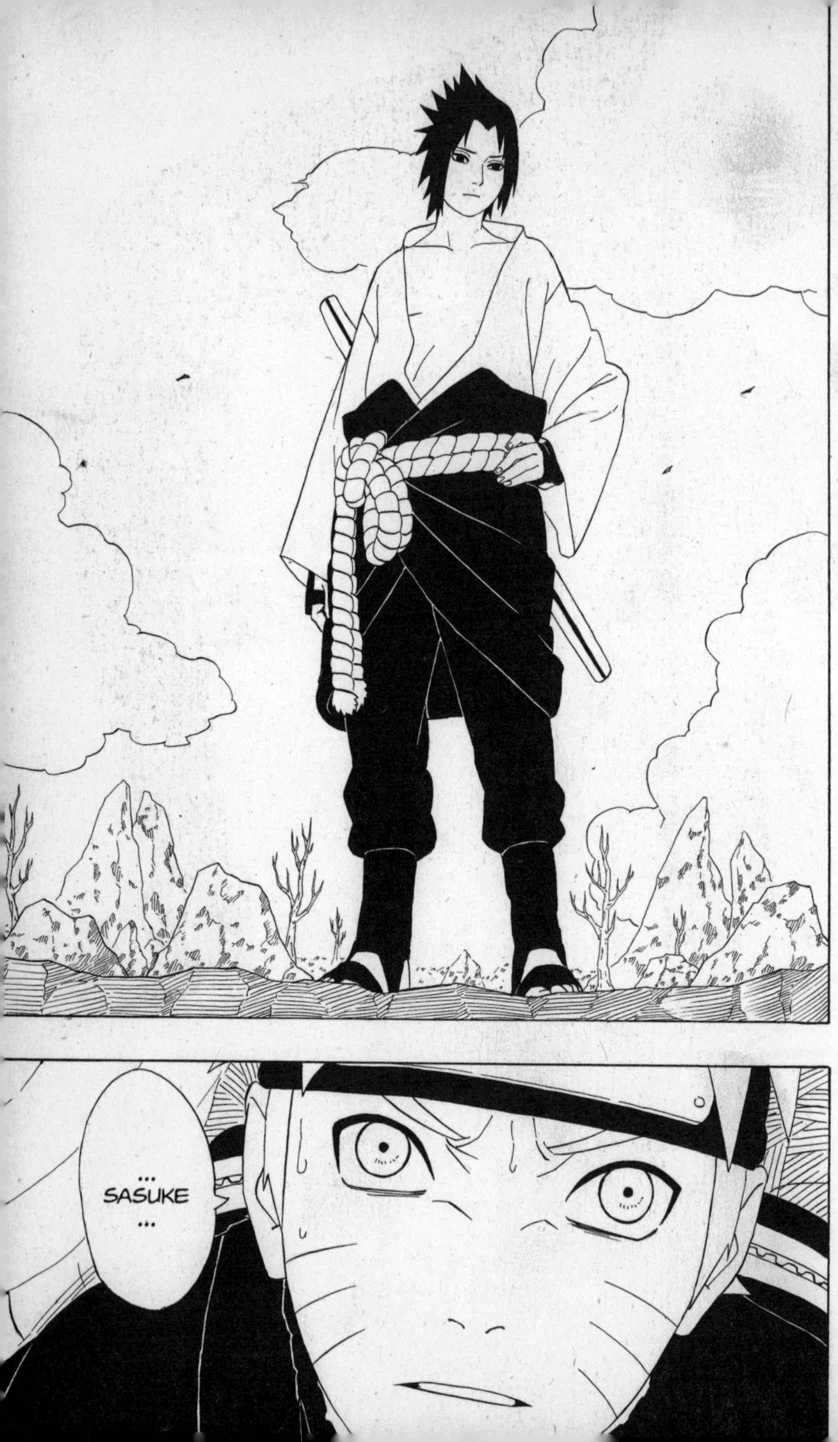
...
SASUKE
...

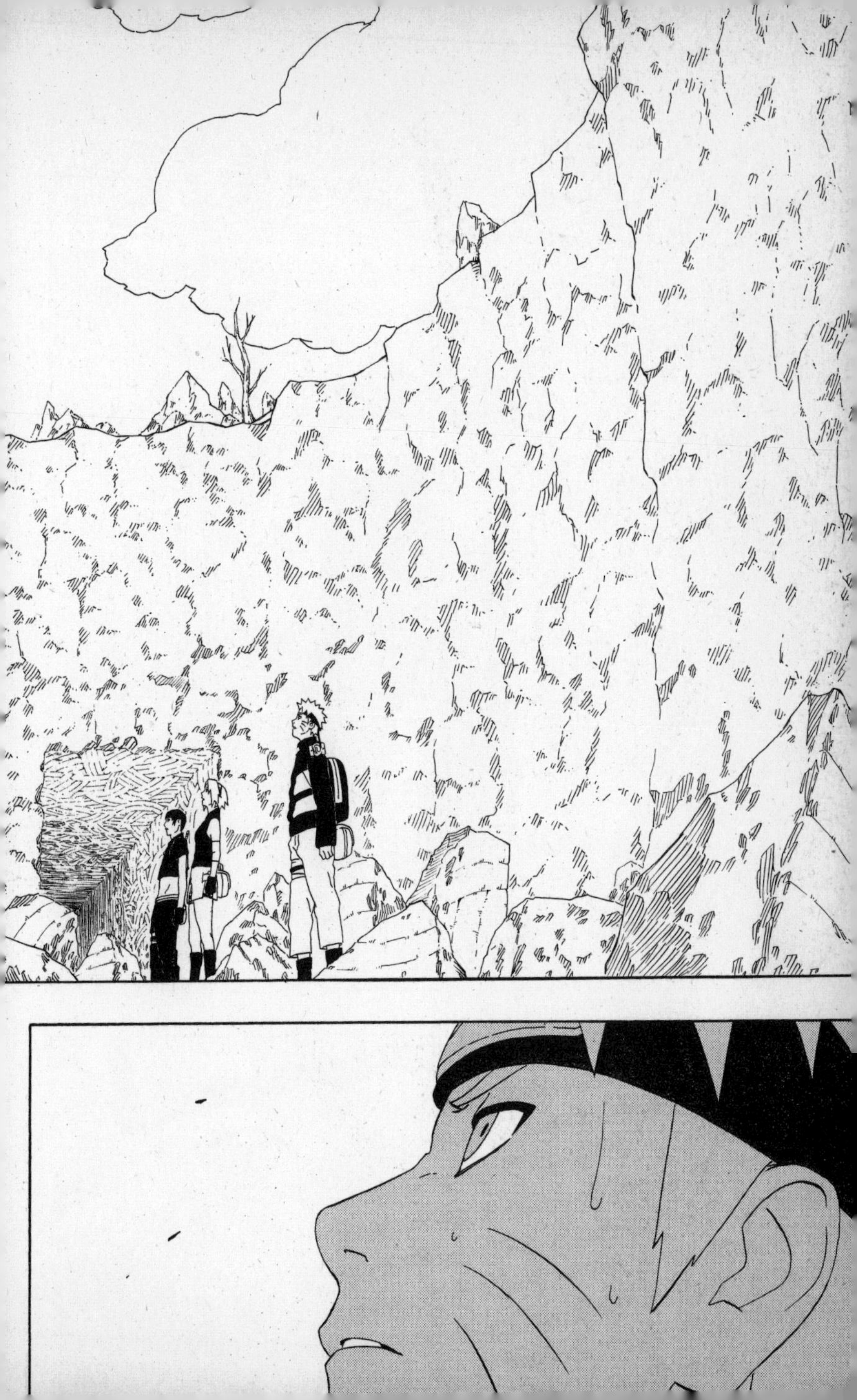

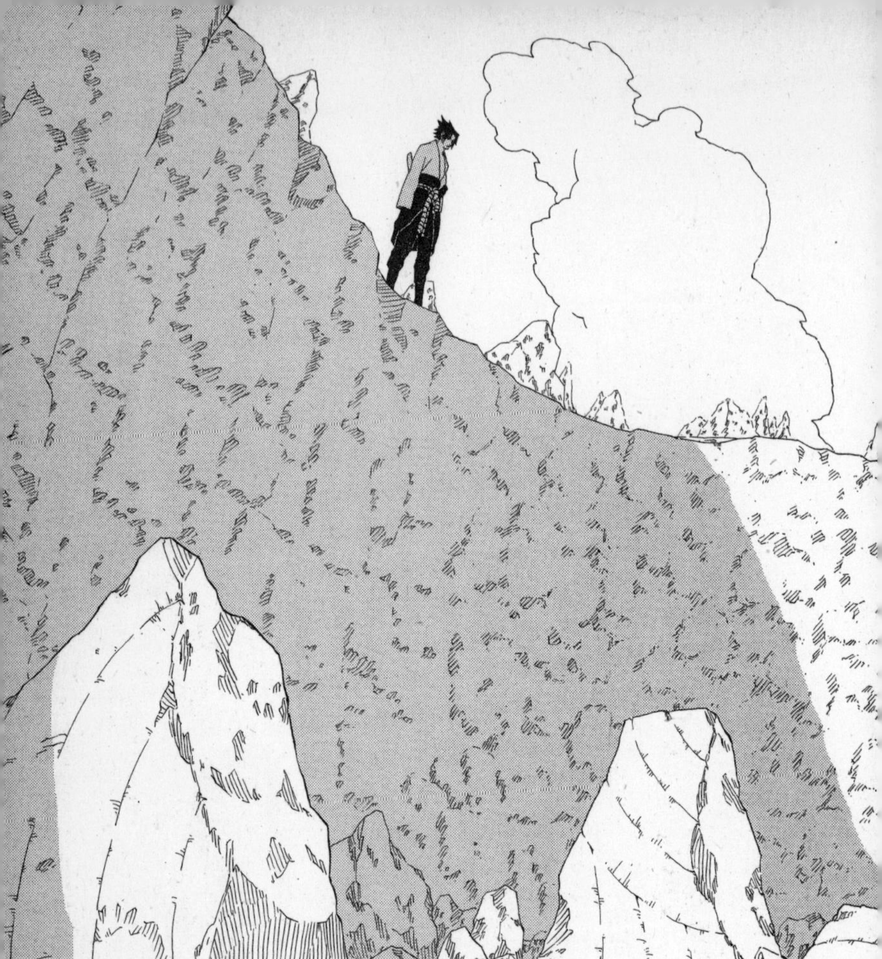
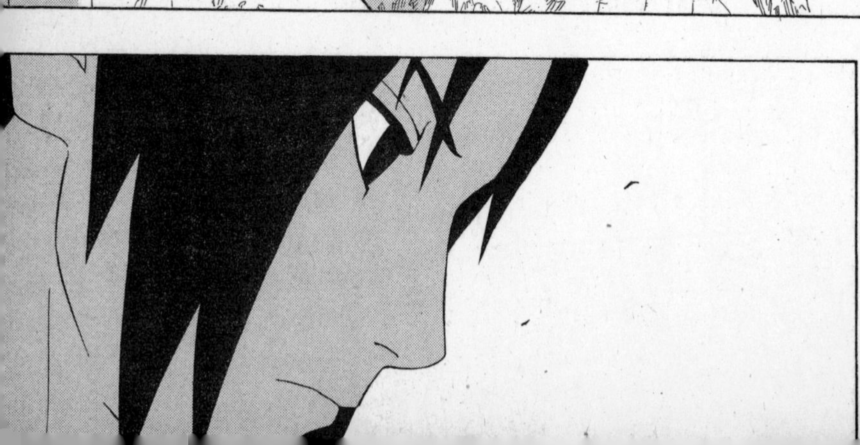

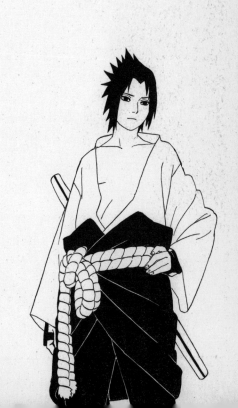

Number 307: On a Whim...!!

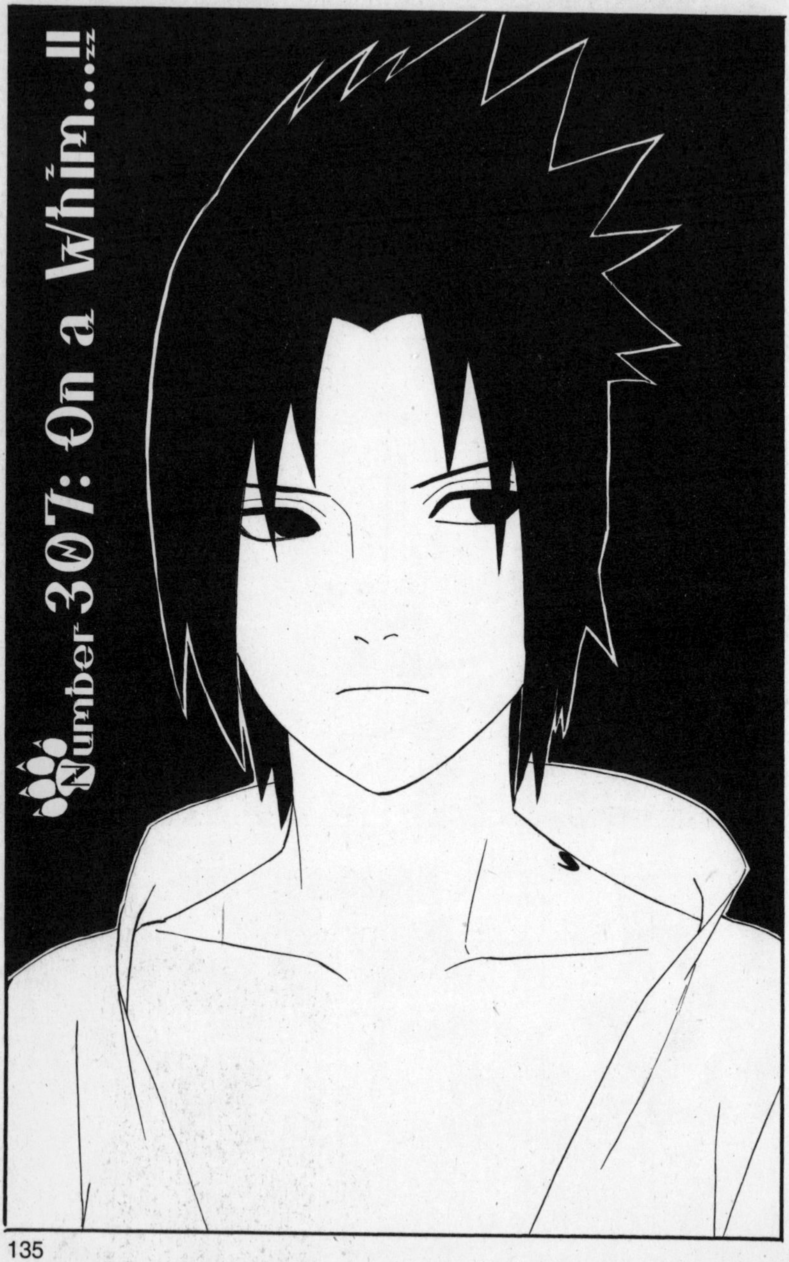

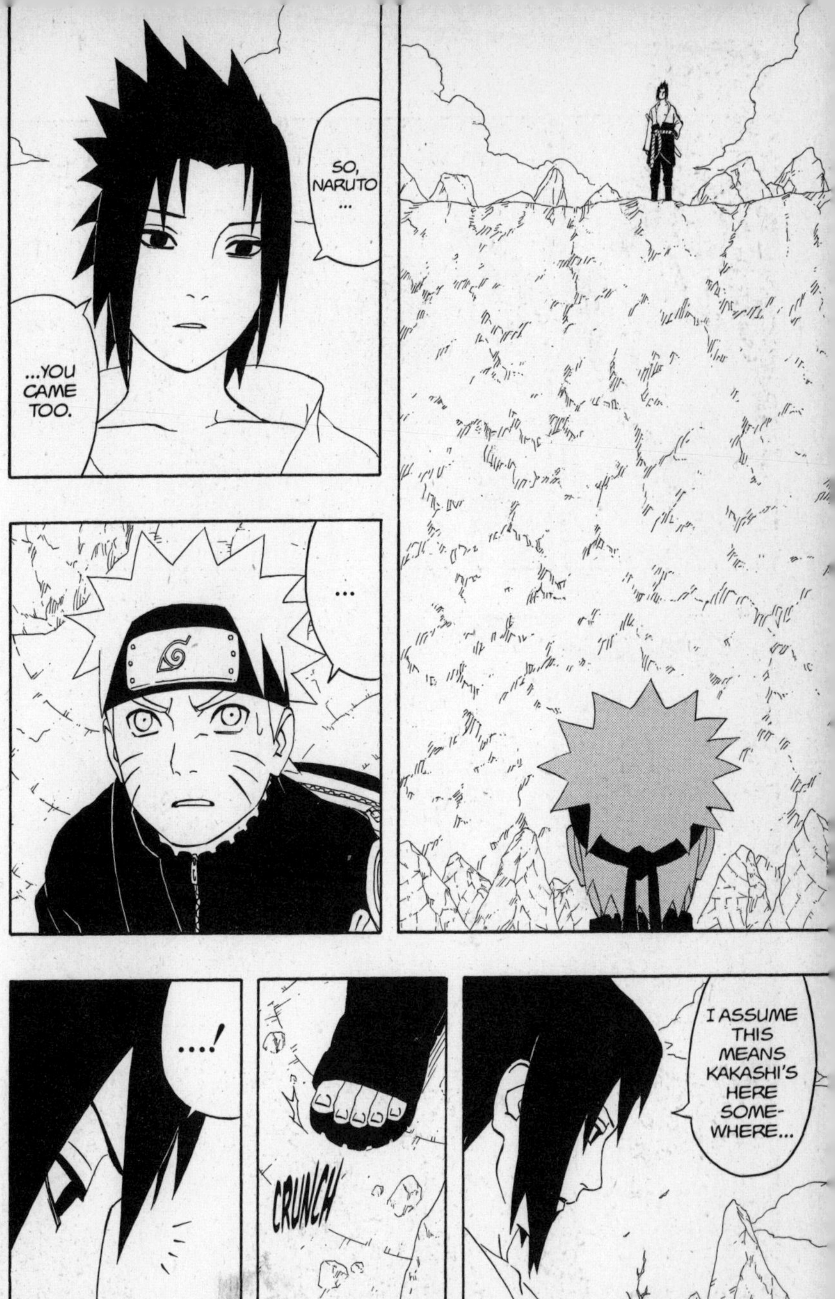
SO, NARUTO ...
...YOU CAME TOO.
...
I ASSUME THIS MEANS KAKASHI'S HERE SOME-WHERE...
CRUNCH
....!

READ THIS WAY

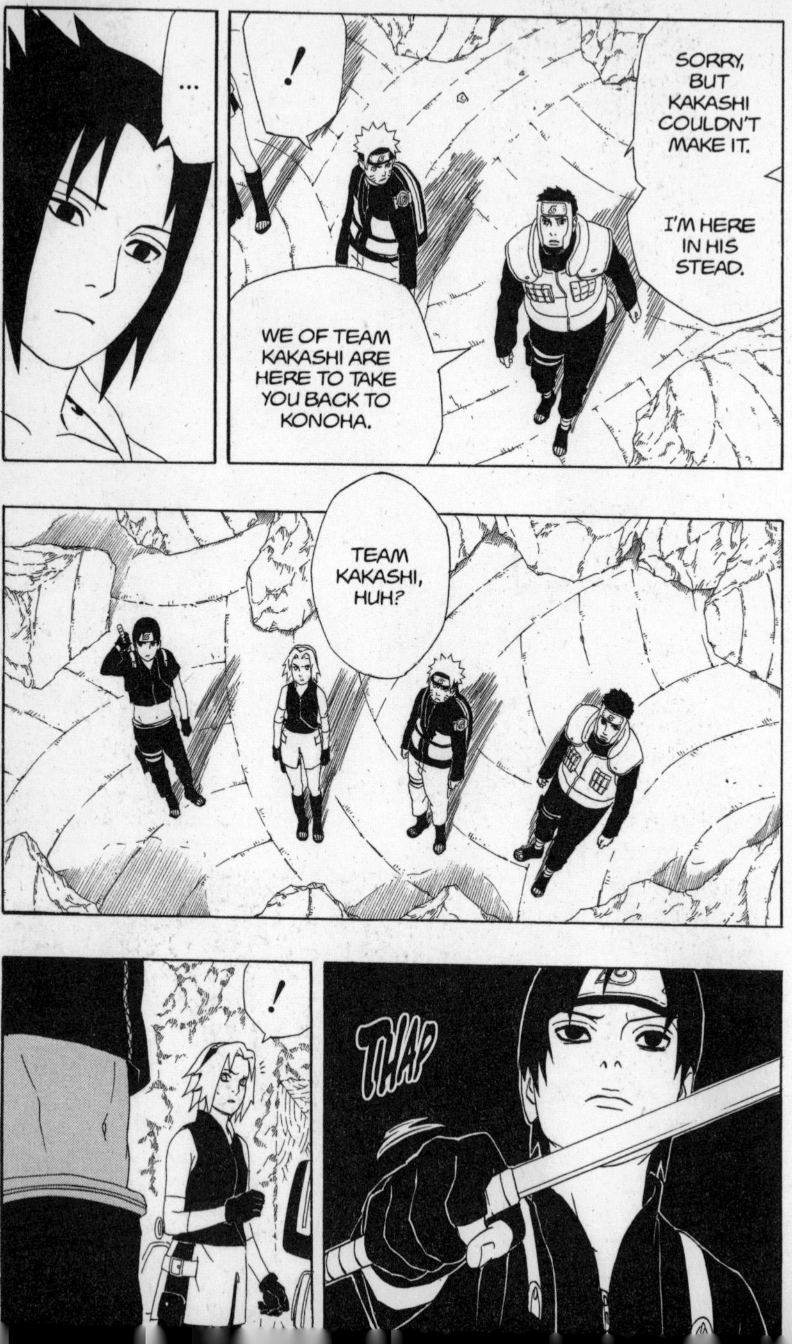
SORRY, BUT KAKASHI COULDN'T MAKE IT.
I'M HERE IN HIS STEAD.
!
WE OF TEAM KAKASHI ARE HERE TO TAKE YOU BACK TO KONOHA.
...
TEAM KAKASHI, HUH?
THAP
!

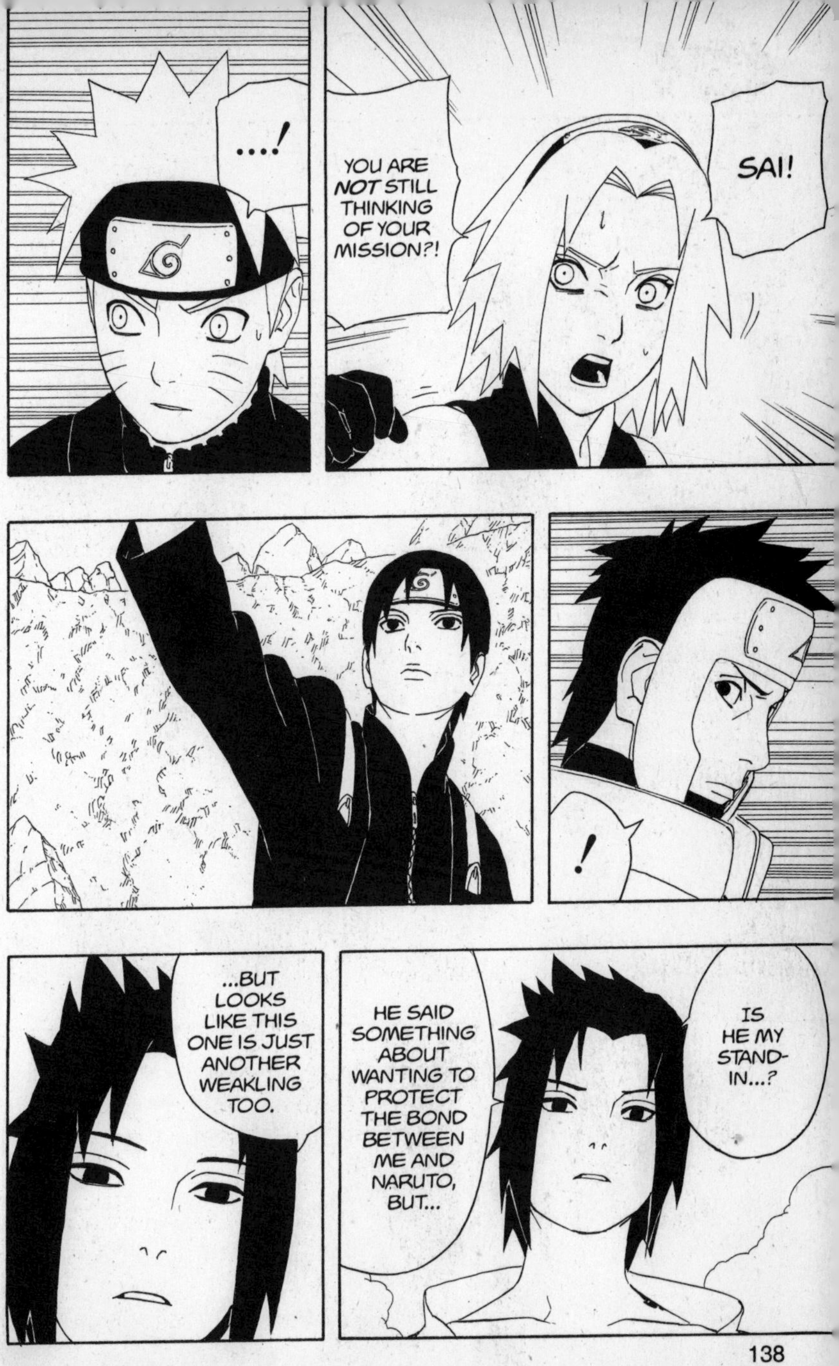
SAI!
YOU ARE *NOT* STILL THINKING OF YOUR MISSION?!
....!
!
IS HE MY STAND-IN...?
HE SAID SOMETHING ABOUT WANTING TO PROTECT THE BOND BETWEEN ME AND NARUTO, BUT...
...BUT LOOKS LIKE THIS ONE IS JUST ANOTHER WEAKLING TOO.

READ THIS WAY

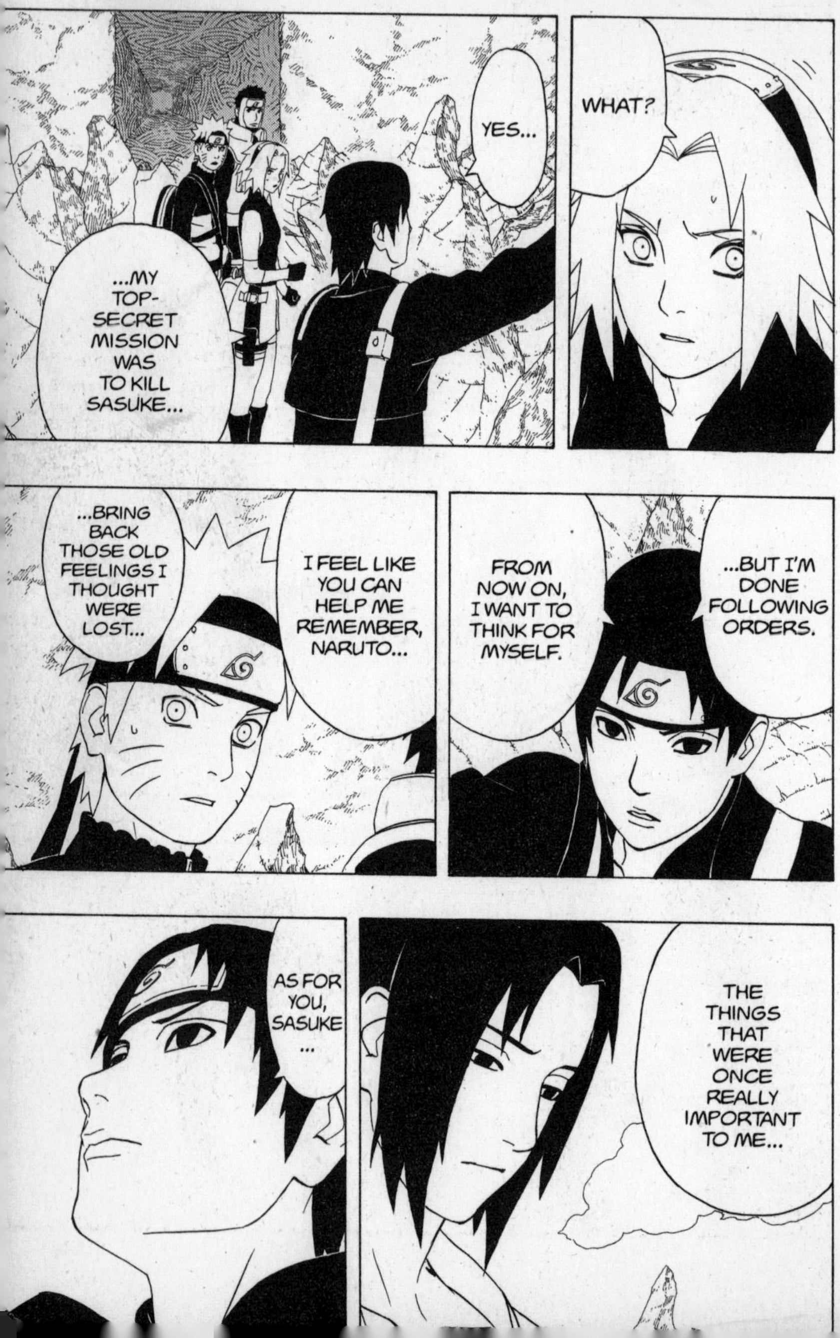
WHAT?
YES...
...MY TOP-SECRET MISSION WAS TO KILL SASUKE...
...BUT I'M DONE FOLLOWING ORDERS.
FROM NOW ON, I WANT TO THINK FOR MYSELF.
I FEEL LIKE YOU CAN HELP ME REMEMBER, NARUTO...
...BRING BACK THOSE OLD FEELINGS I THOUGHT WERE LOST...
THE THINGS THAT WERE ONCE REALLY IMPORTANT TO ME...
AS FOR YOU, SASUKE...

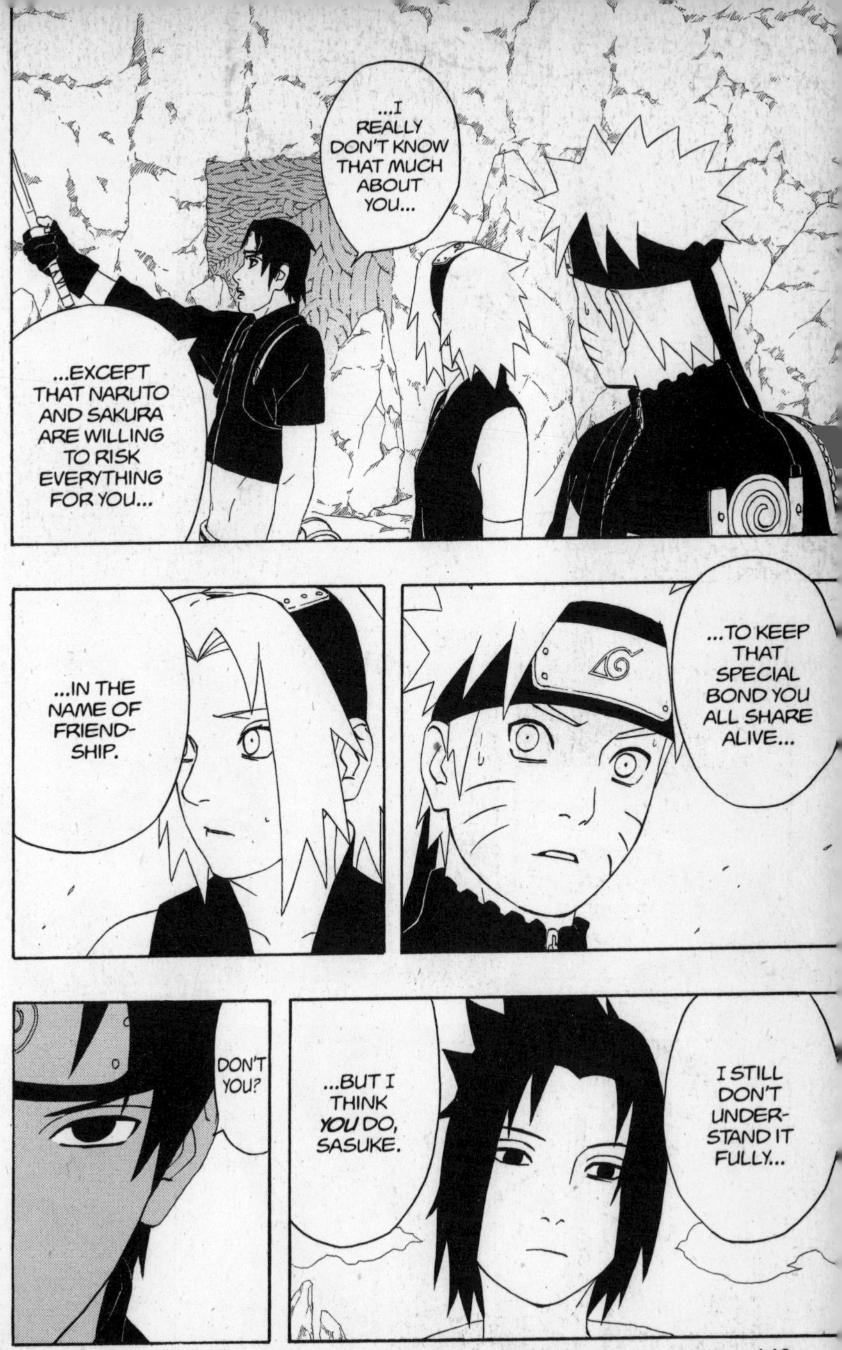
...I REALLY DON'T KNOW THAT MUCH ABOUT YOU...
...EXCEPT THAT NARUTO AND SAKURA ARE WILLING TO RISK EVERYTHING FOR YOU...
...TO KEEP THAT SPECIAL BOND YOU ALL SHARE ALIVE...
...IN THE NAME OF FRIEND-SHIP.
I STILL DON'T UNDER-STAND IT FULLY...
...BUT I THINK YOU DO, SASUKE.
DON'T YOU?

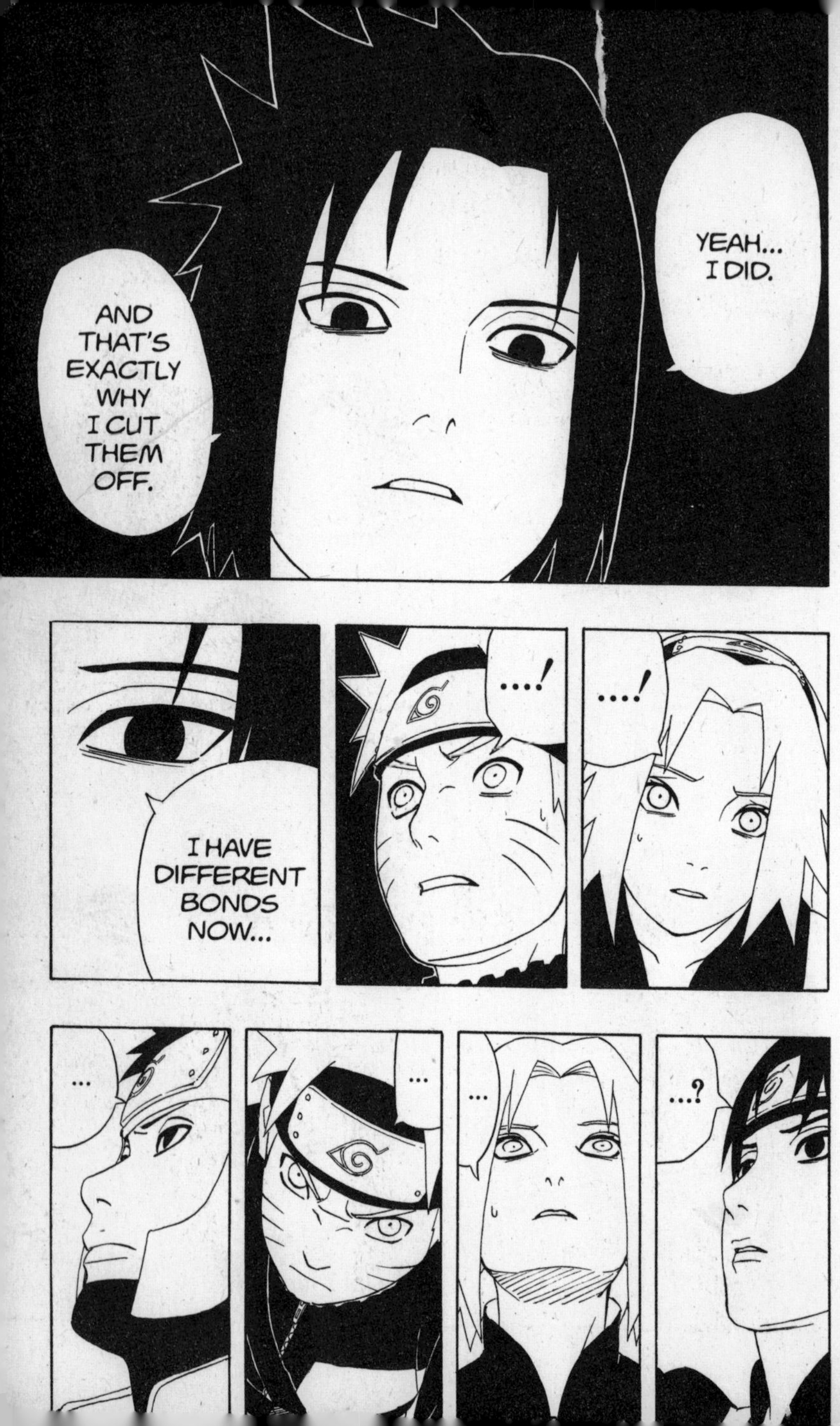
YEAH... I DID.
AND THAT'S EXACTLY WHY I CUT THEM OFF.
...!
...!
I HAVE DIFFERENT BONDS NOW...
...?
...
...
...

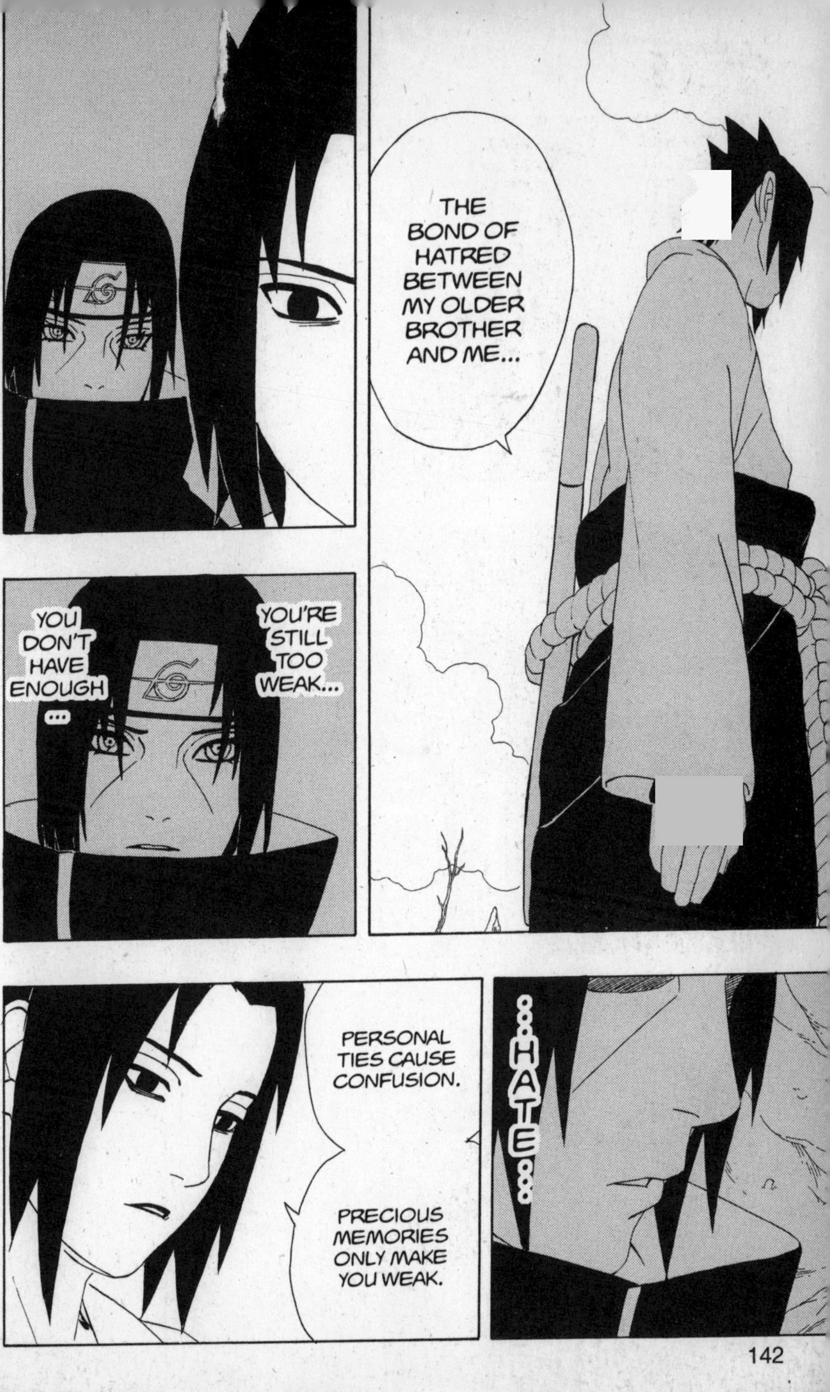
THE BOND OF HATRED BETWEEN MY OLDER BROTHER AND ME...
YOU'RE STILL TOO WEAK...
YOU DON'T HAVE ENOUGH ...
...HATE...
PERSONAL TIES CAUSE CONFUSION.
PRECIOUS MEMORIES ONLY MAKE YOU WEAK.

READ THIS WAY

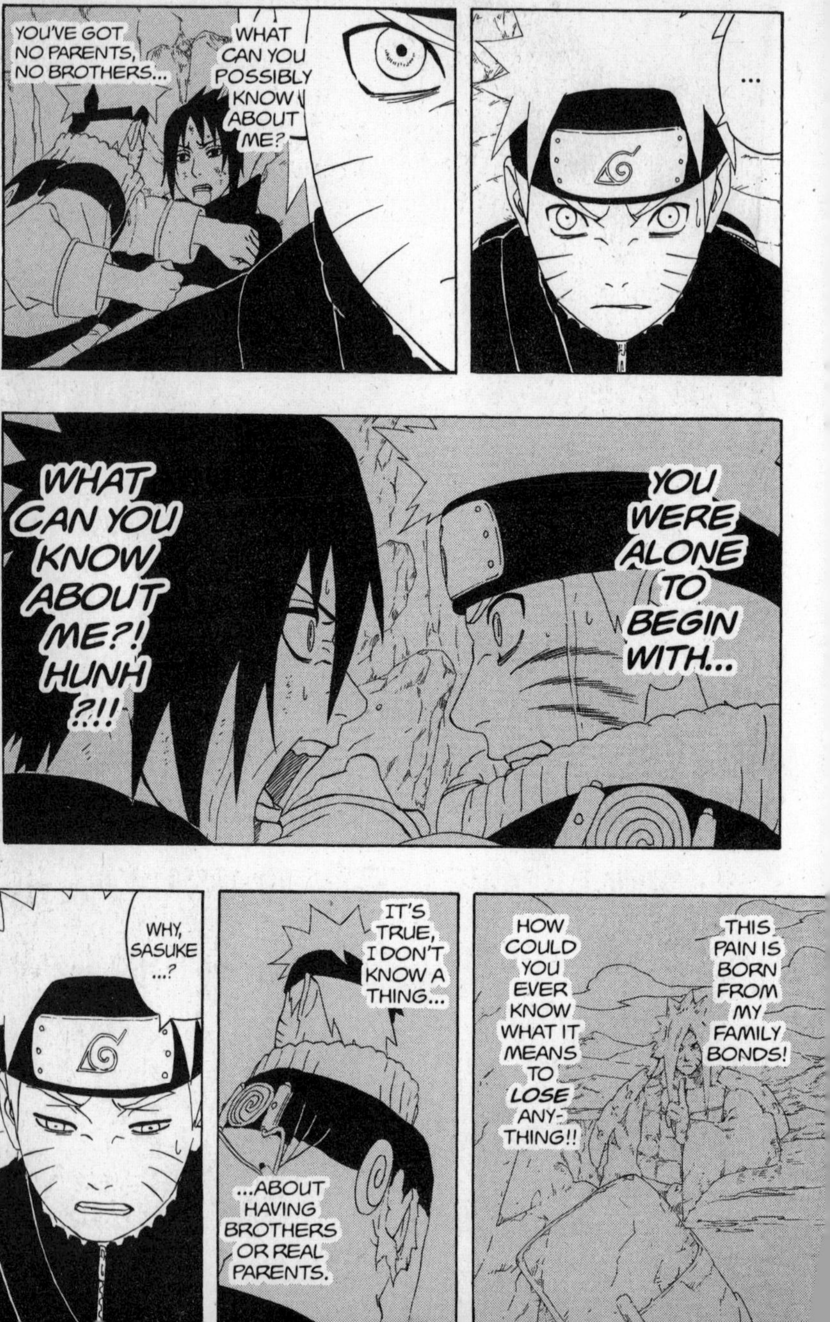
...
WHAT CAN YOU POSSIBLY KNOW ABOUT ME?
YOU'VE GOT NO PARENTS, NO BROTHERS...
YOU WERE ALONE TO BEGIN WITH...
WHAT CAN YOU KNOW ABOUT ME?! HUNH ?!!
THIS PAIN IS BORN FROM MY FAMILY BONDS!
HOW COULD YOU EVER KNOW WHAT IT MEANS TO LOSE ANYTHING!!
IT'S TRUE, I DON'T KNOW A THING...
...ABOUT HAVING BROTHERS OR REAL PARENTS.
WHY, SASUKE ...?

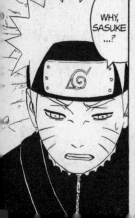

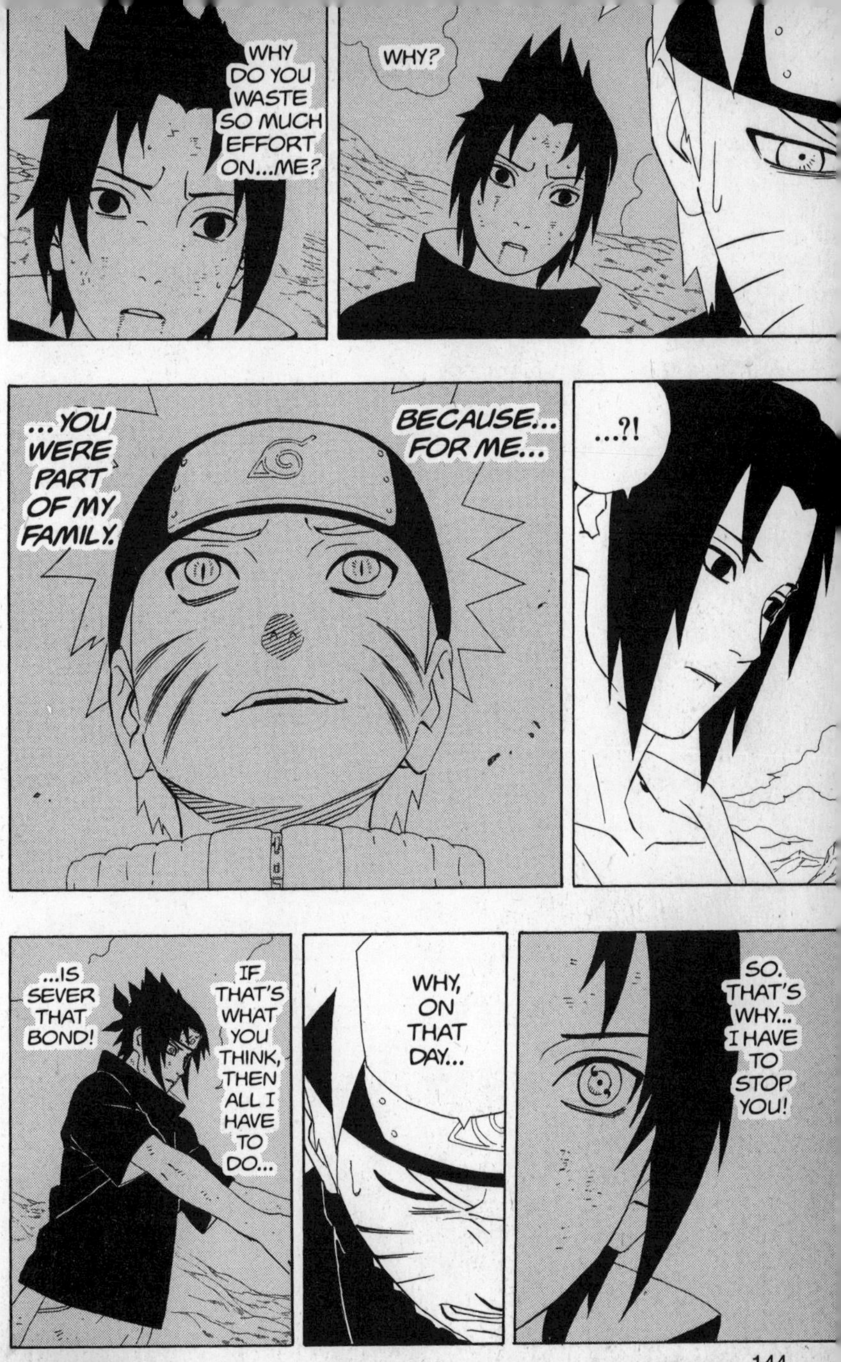
WHY?
WHY DO YOU WASTE SO MUCH EFFORT ON...ME?
...?!
BECAUSE... FOR ME...
...YOU WERE PART OF MY FAMILY.
SO. THAT'S WHY... I HAVE TO STOP YOU!
WHY, ON THAT DAY...
IF THAT'S WHAT YOU THINK, THEN ALL I HAVE TO DO...
...IS SEVER THAT BOND!

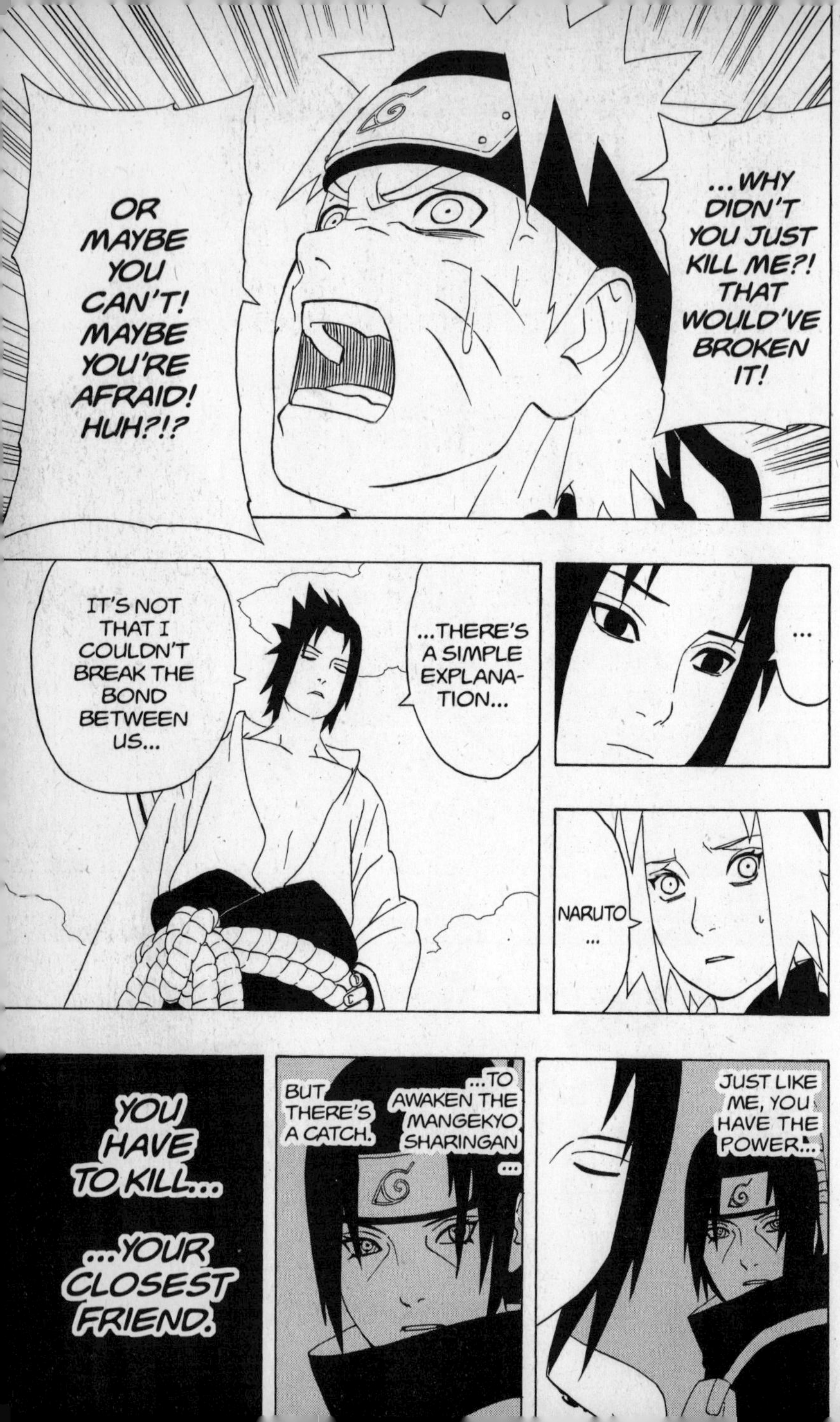
...WHY DIDN'T YOU JUST KILL ME?! THAT WOULD'VE BROKEN IT!
OR MAYBE YOU CAN'T! MAYBE YOU'RE AFRAID! HUH?!?
...
NARUTO ...
IT'S NOT THAT I COULDN'T BREAK THE BOND BETWEEN US...
...THERE'S A SIMPLE EXPLANATION...
JUST LIKE ME, YOU HAVE THE POWER...
...TO AWAKEN THE MANGEKYO SHARINGAN ...
BUT THERE'S A CATCH.
YOU HAVE TO KILL...
...YOUR CLOSEST FRIEND.

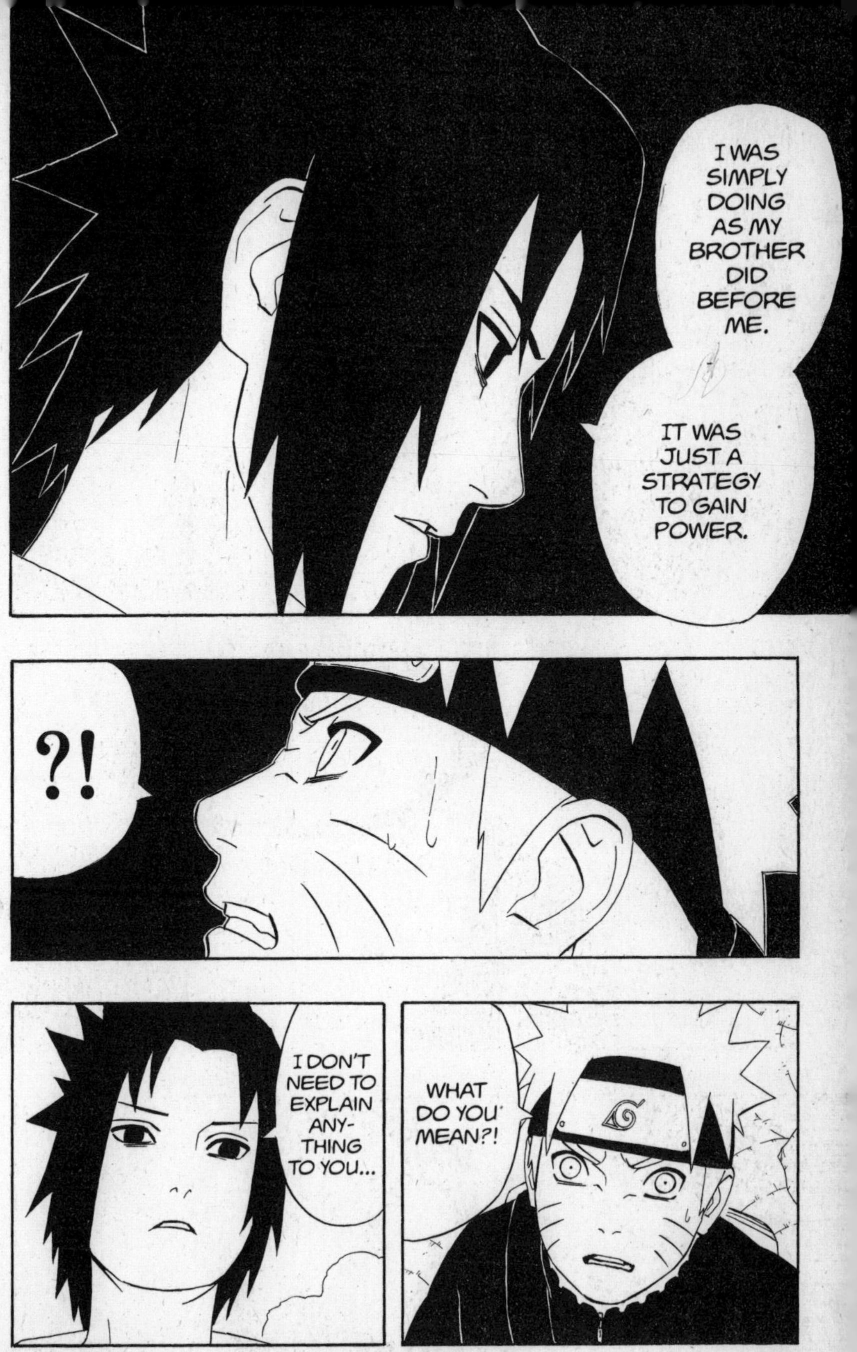
I WAS SIMPLY DOING AS MY BROTHER DID BEFORE ME.
IT WAS JUST A STRATEGY TO GAIN POWER.
?!
WHAT DO YOU MEAN?!
I DON'T NEED TO EXPLAIN ANY-THING TO YOU...

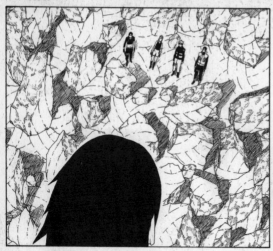

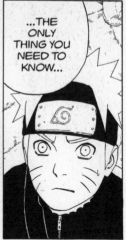

...THE ONLY THING YOU NEED TO KNOW...

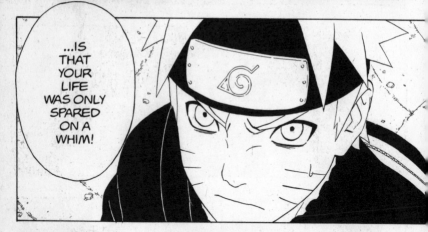

...IS THAT YOUR LIFE WAS ONLY SPARED ON A WHIM!

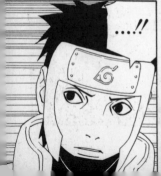

...!!

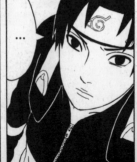

...

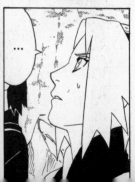

...

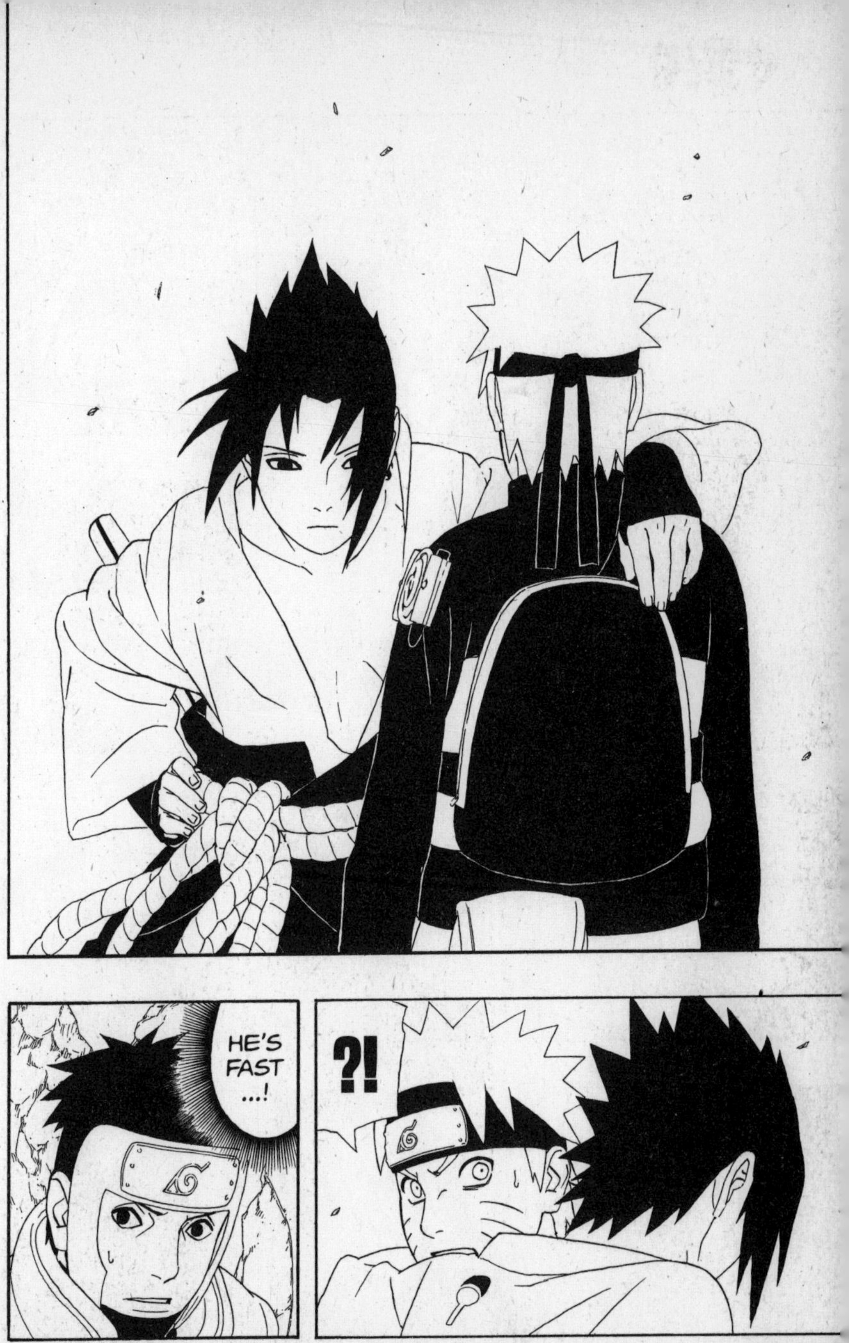
?!
HE'S FAST ...!

READ THIS WAY

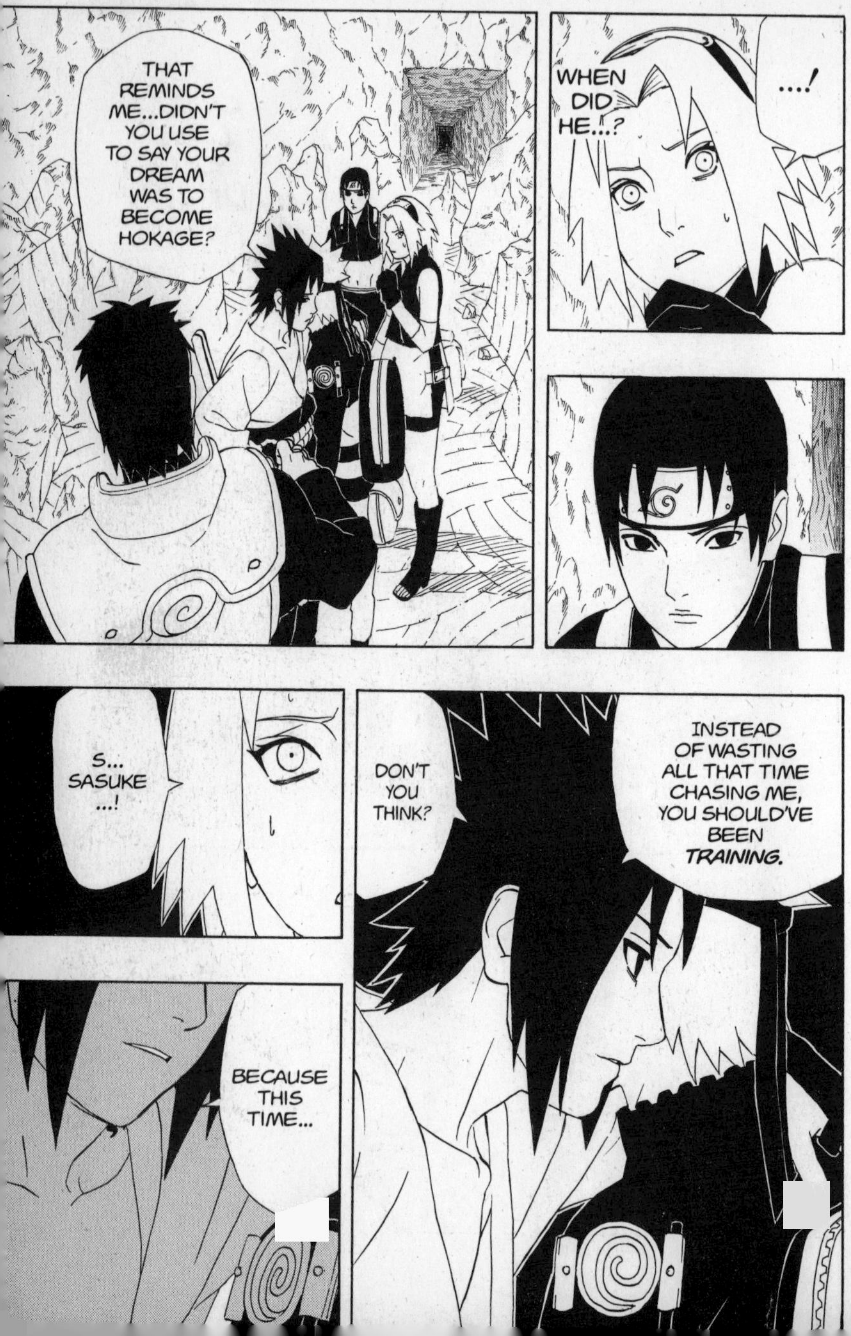
...!
WHEN DID HE...?
THAT REMINDS ME...DIDN'T YOU USE TO SAY YOUR DREAM WAS TO BECOME HOKAGE?
INSTEAD OF WASTING ALL THAT TIME CHASING ME, YOU SHOULD'VE BEEN *TRAINING.*
DON'T YOU THINK?
S... SASUKE ...!
BECAUSE THIS TIME...

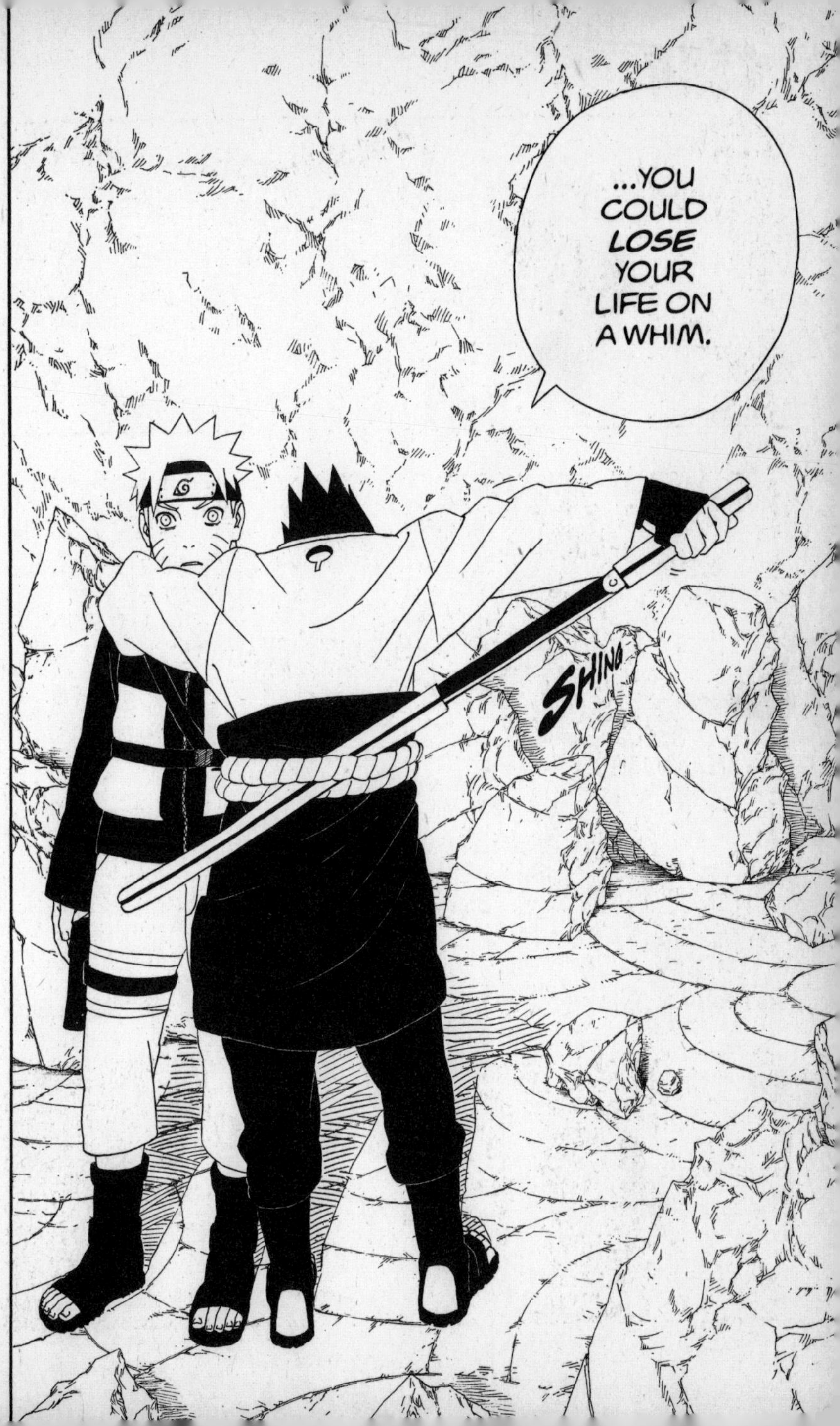
...YOU COULD LOSE YOUR LIFE ON A WHIM.
SHING

READ THIS WAY

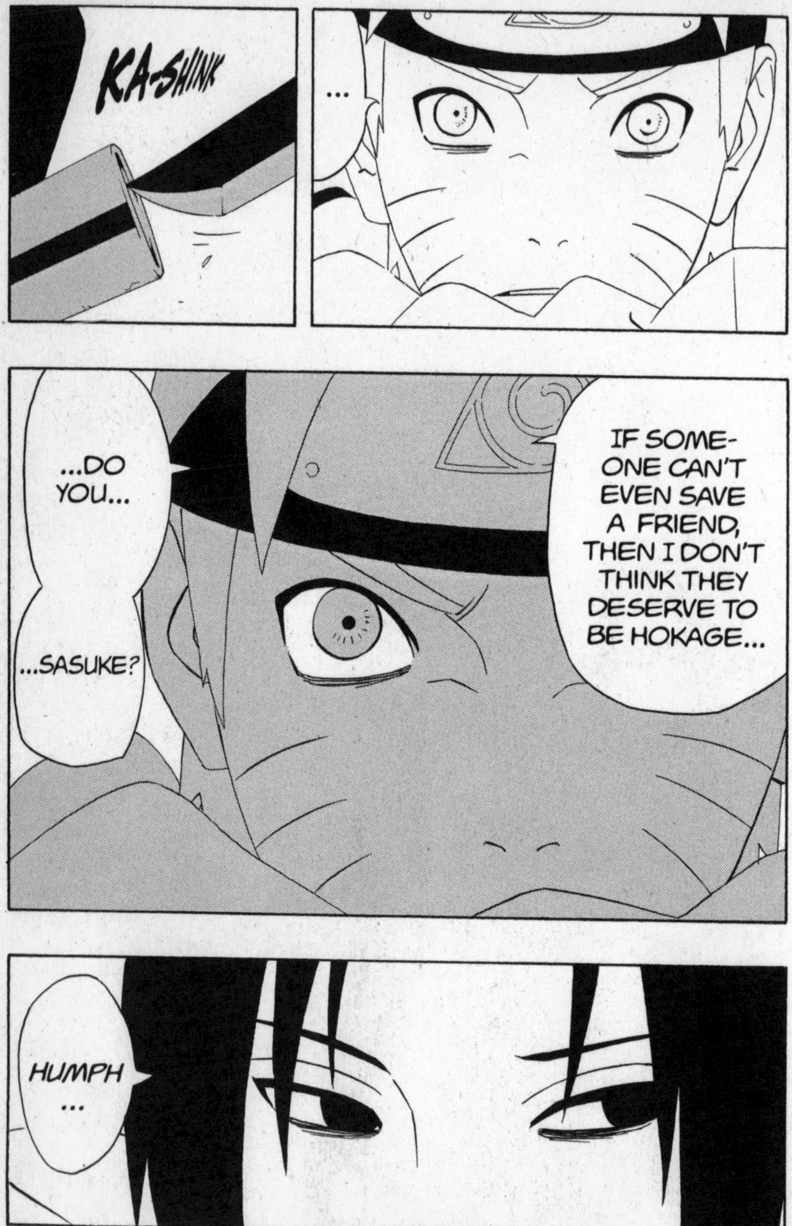
...
KA-SHINK
IF SOME-ONE CAN'T EVEN SAVE A FRIEND, THEN I DON'T THINK THEY DESERVE TO BE HOKAGE...
...DO YOU...
...SASUKE?
HUMPH ...

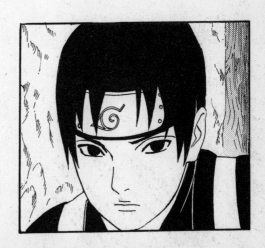

Number 308: Sasuke's Strength!!

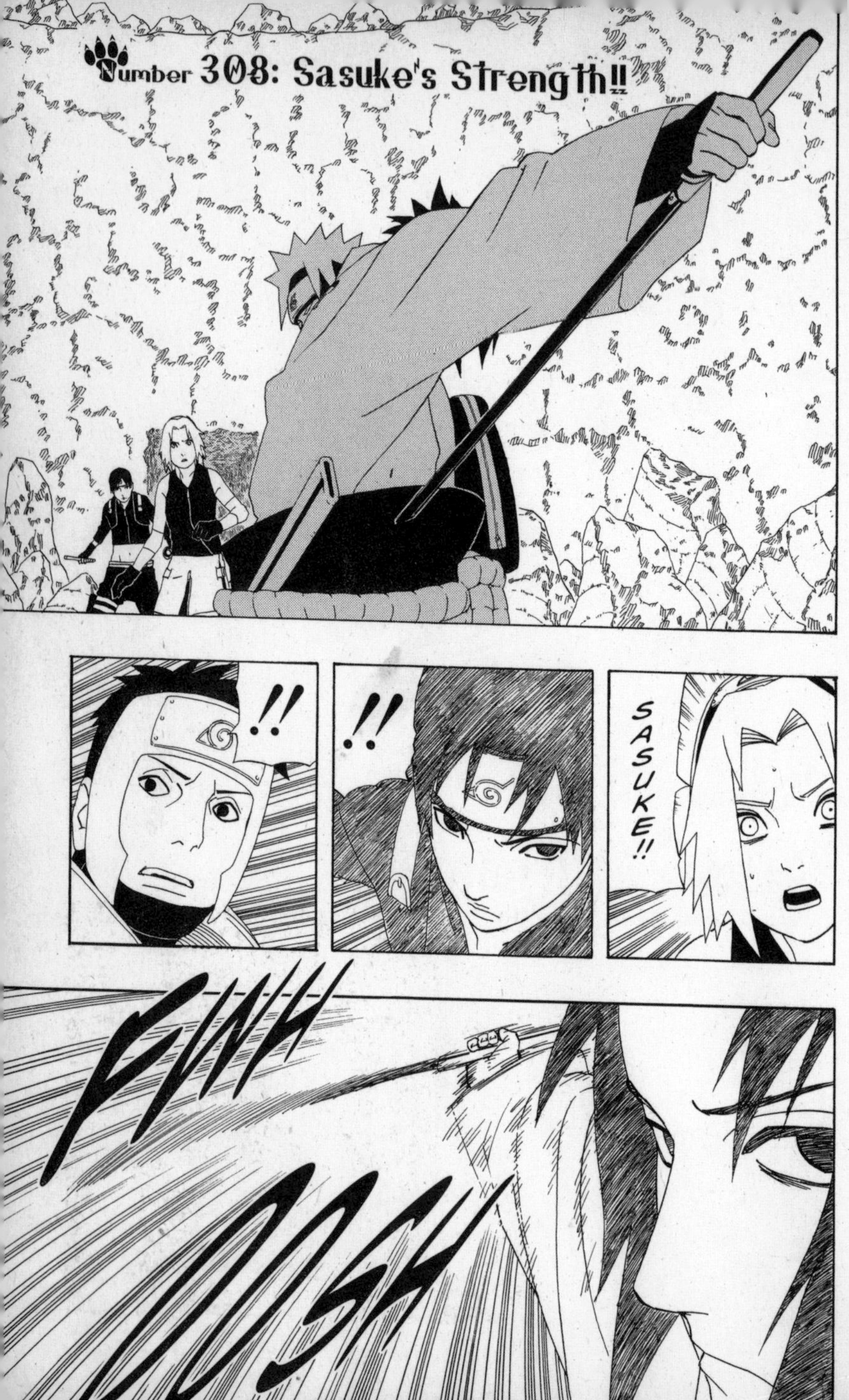
SASUKE!!
!!
!!
WOOSH

Number 308 Sasuke's Strength!!

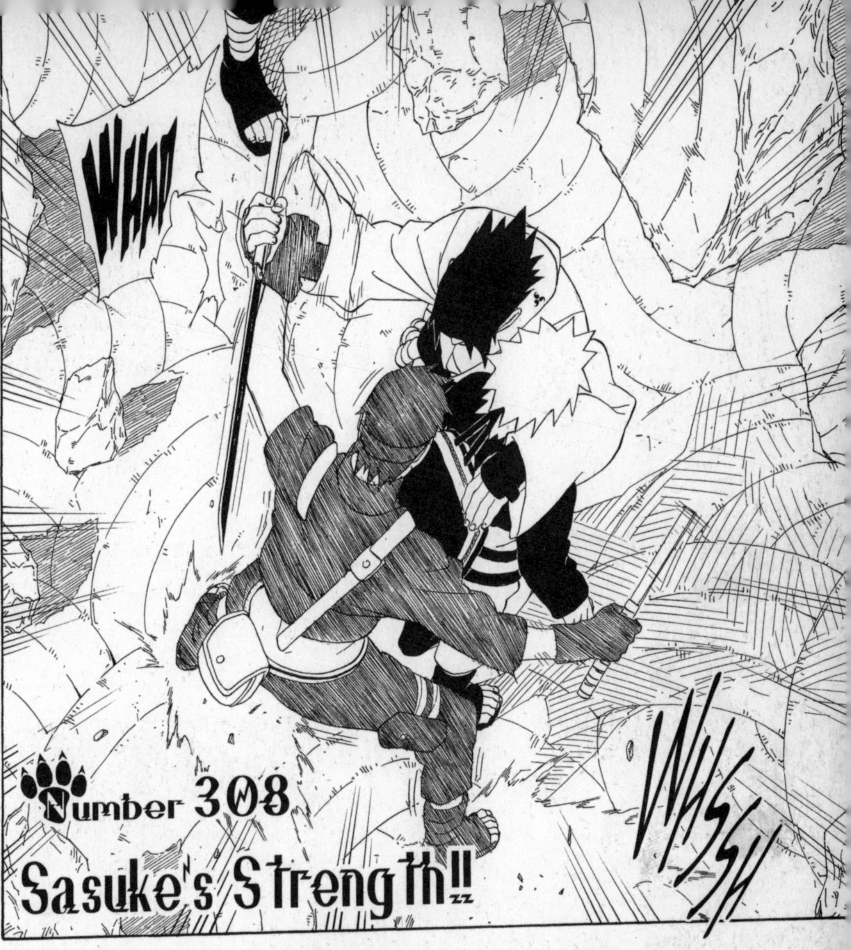
WHAP
WHSSH

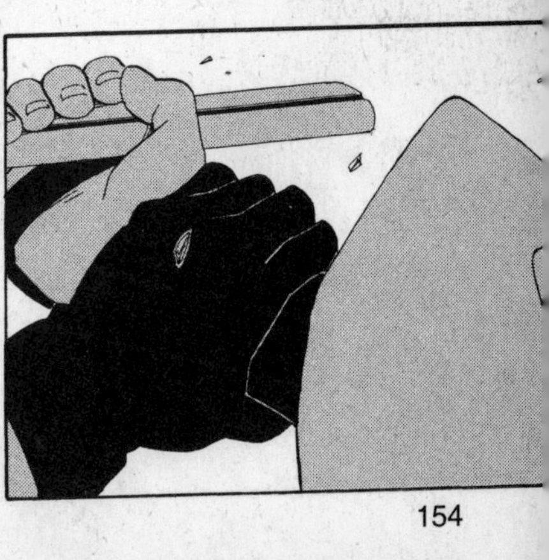

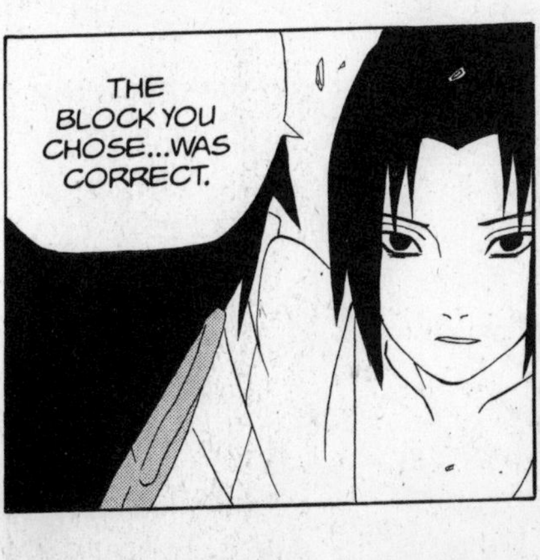
THE BLOCK YOU CHOSE...WAS CORRECT.

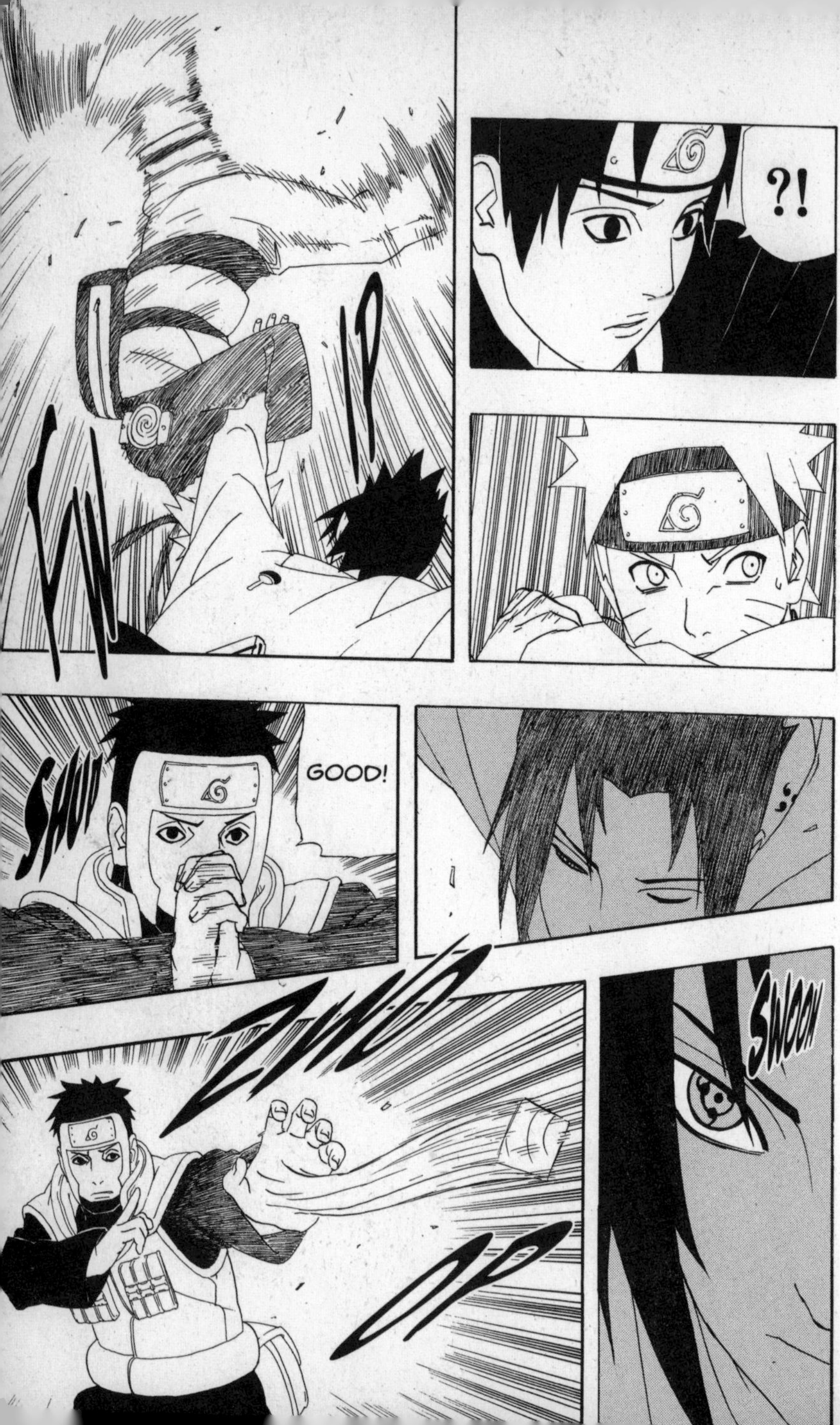
?!
GOOD!
SWOOH

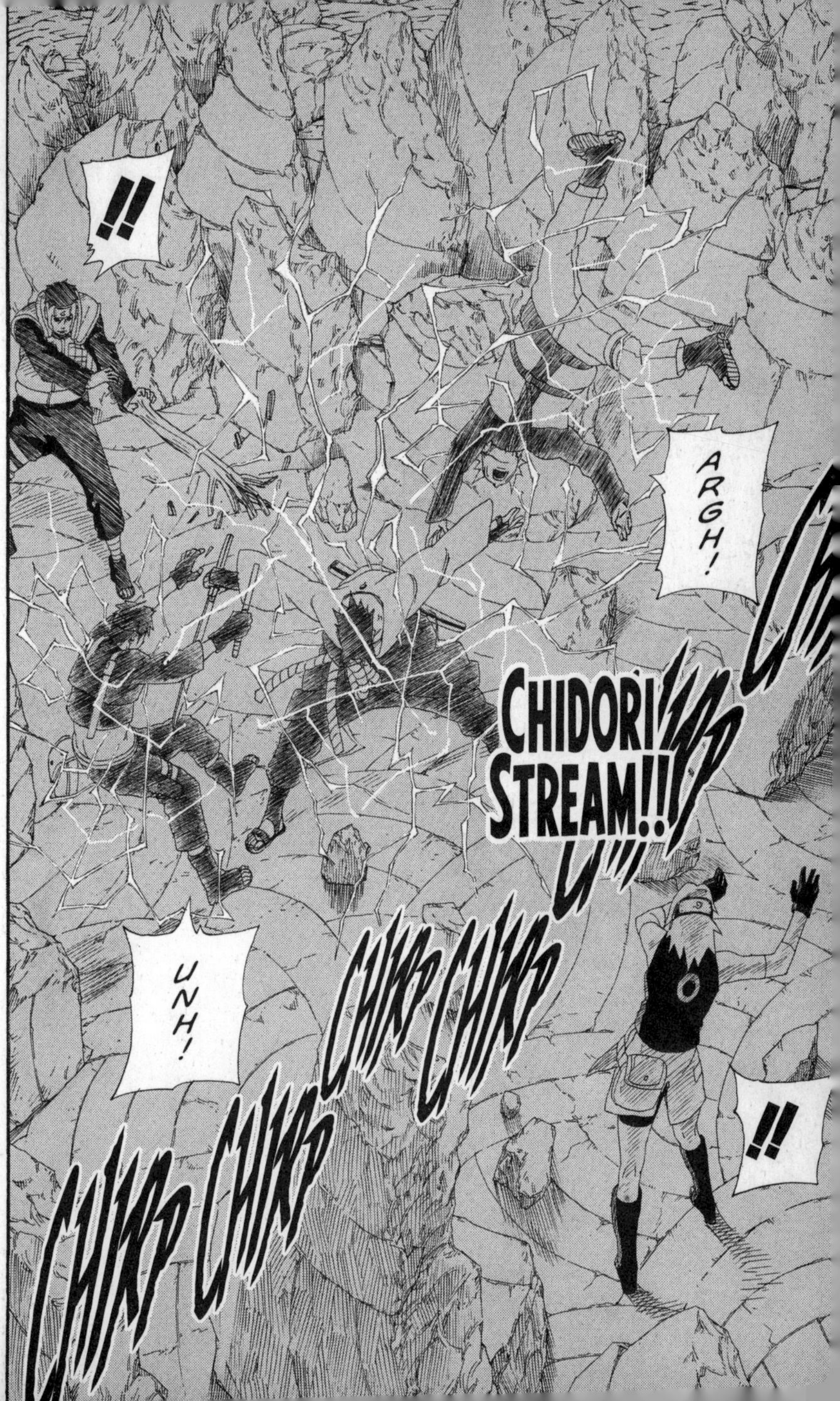
ARGH!
!!
CHIDORI STREAM!!
!!
UNH!
CHIRP CHIRP
CHIRP CHIRP

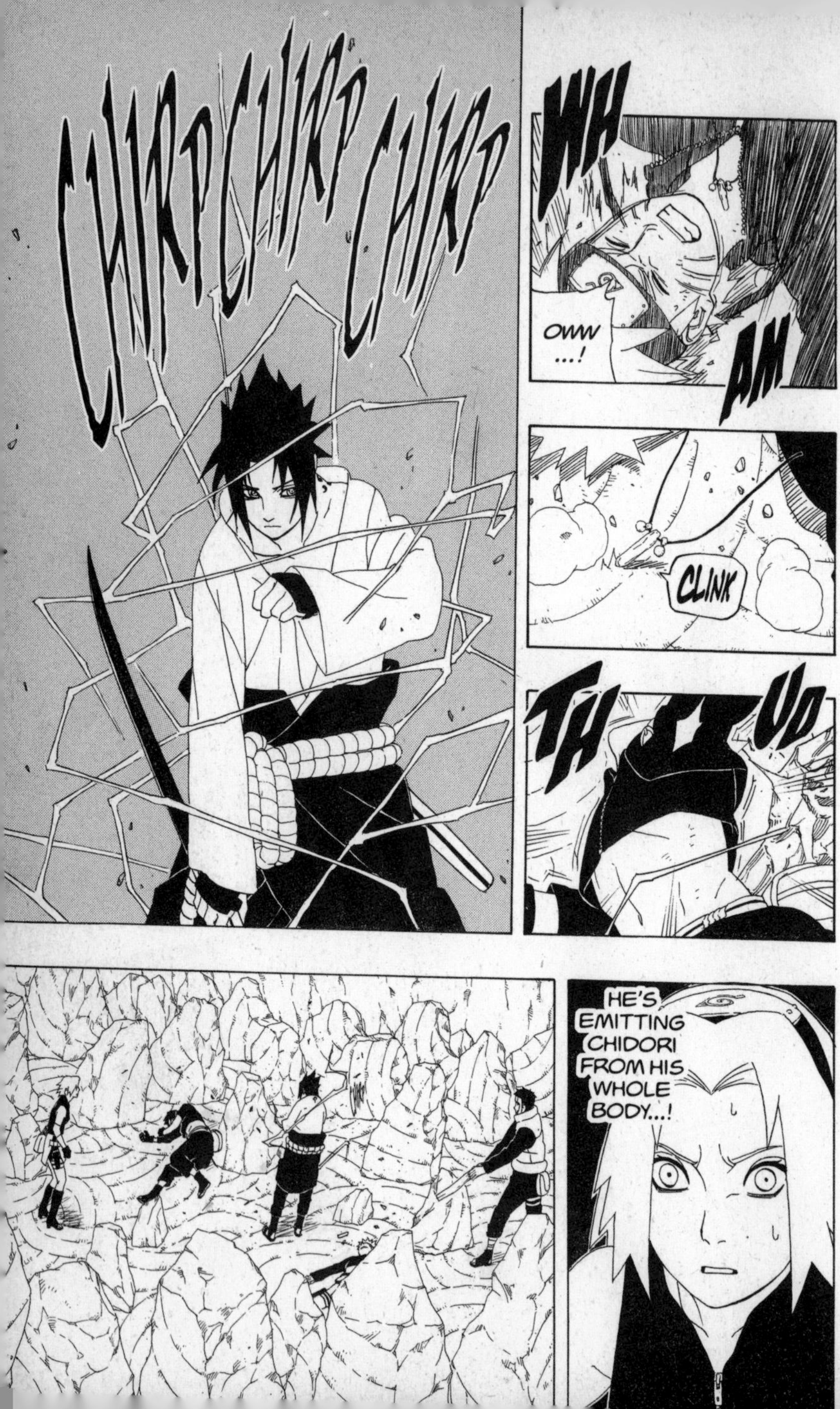
WHAM
OWW ...!
CLINK
THUD
CHIRP CHIRP CHIRP
HE'S EMITTING CHIDORI FROM HIS WHOLE BODY...!

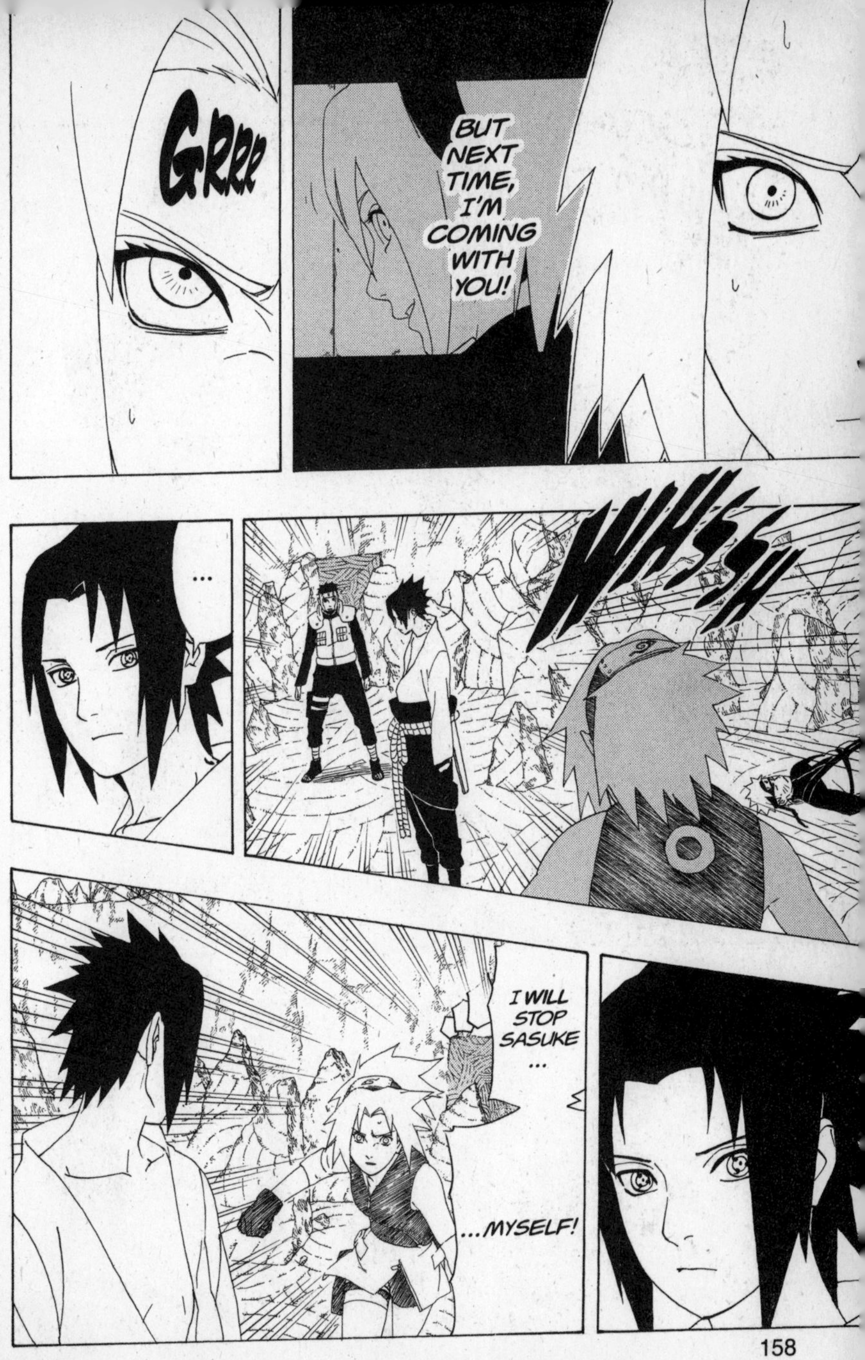
BUT NEXT TIME, I'M COMING WITH YOU!
GRRR
WHSSH
...
I WILL STOP SASUKE ...
...MYSELF!

WATCH OUT, SAKURA ...!

HIS EYES...

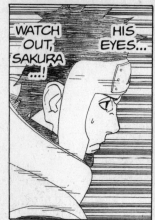

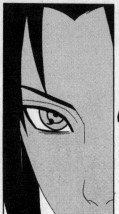

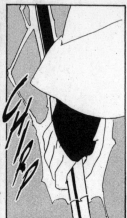

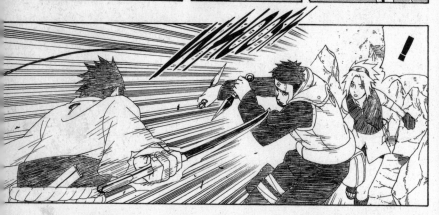

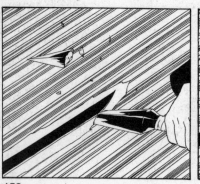

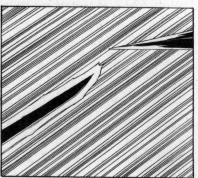

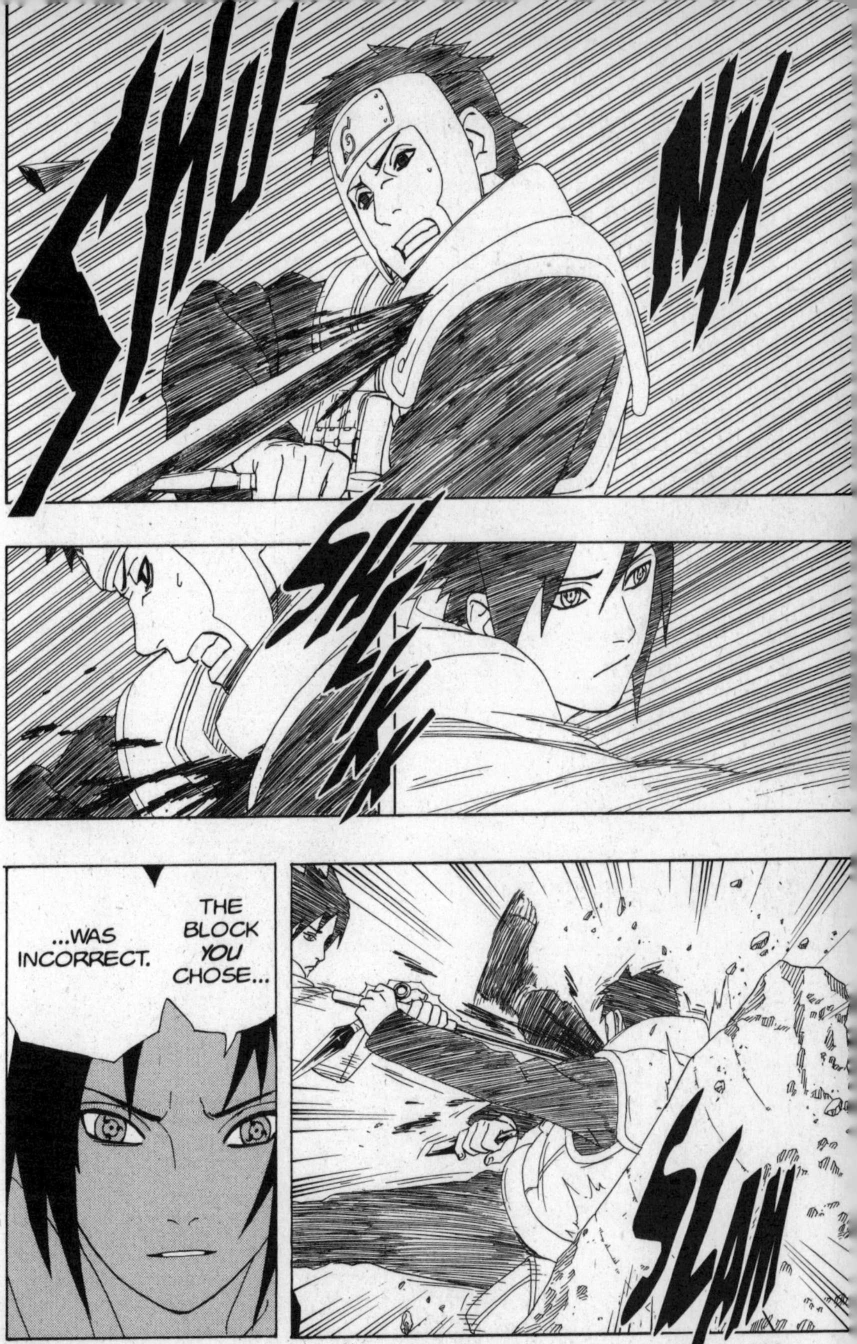
SLAM
THE BLOCK YOU CHOSE...
...WAS INCORRECT.

READ THIS WAY

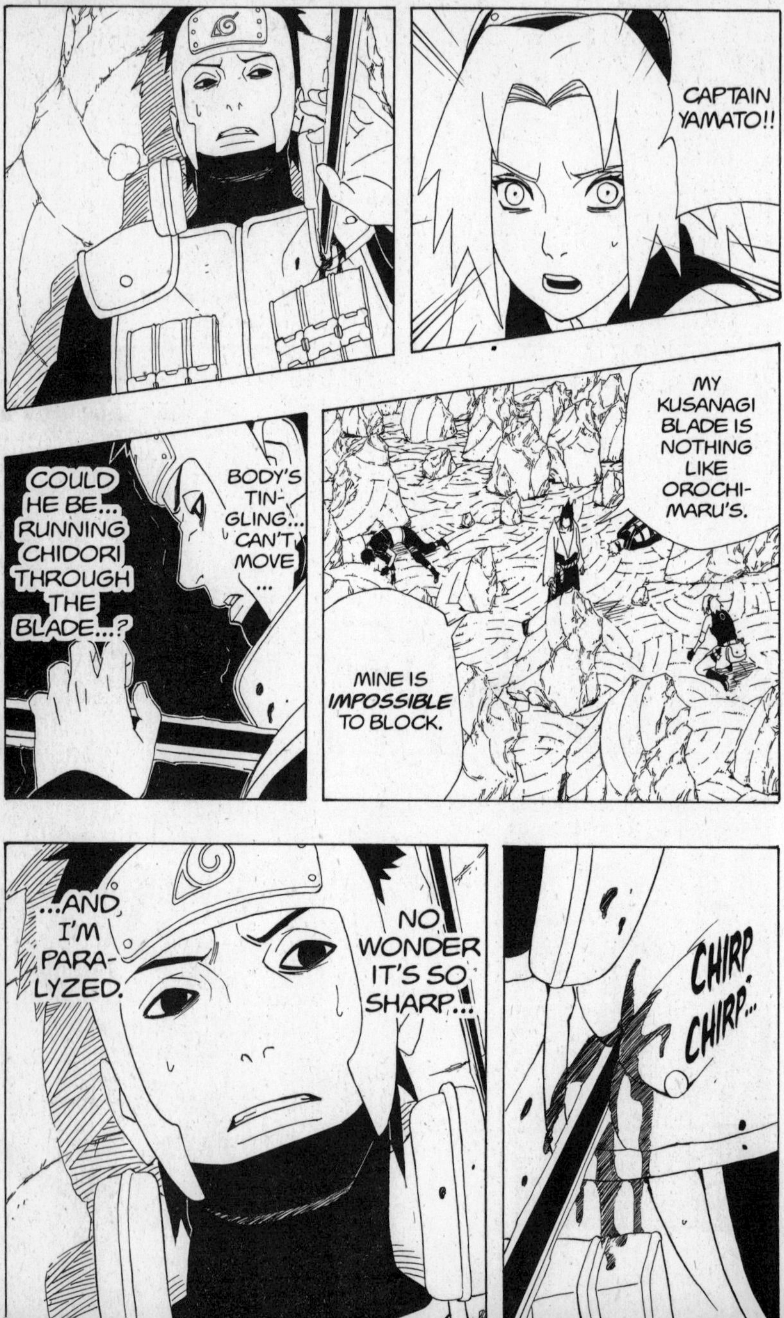
CAPTAIN YAMATO!!
MY KUSANAGI BLADE IS NOTHING LIKE OROCHI-MARU'S.
MINE IS *IMPOSSIBLE* TO BLOCK.
BODY'S TIN-GLING... CAN'T MOVE...
COULD HE BE... RUNNING CHIDORI THROUGH THE BLADE...?
CHIRP CHIRP...
NO WONDER IT'S SO SHARP...
...AND, I'M PARA-LYZED.

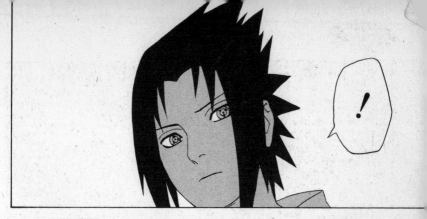

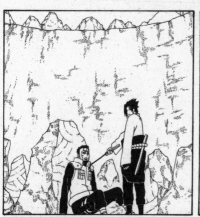

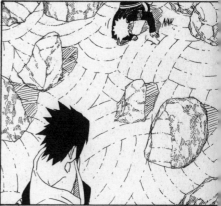

THIS IS YOUR CHANCE... NARUTO...

HEH HEH...

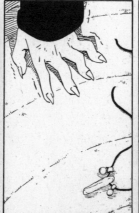

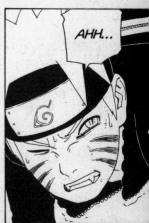

AHH...

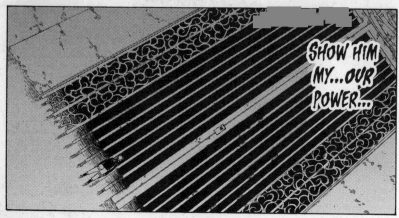

SHOW HIM MY...OUR POWER...

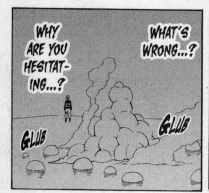

WHY ARE YOU HESITAT-ING...?

WHAT'S WRONG...?

GLUB

GLUB

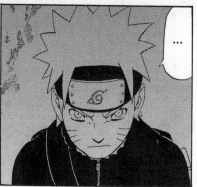

...

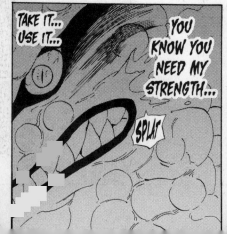

TAKE IT... USE IT...

YOU KNOW YOU NEED MY STRENGTH...

SPLAT

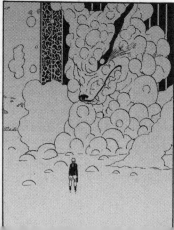

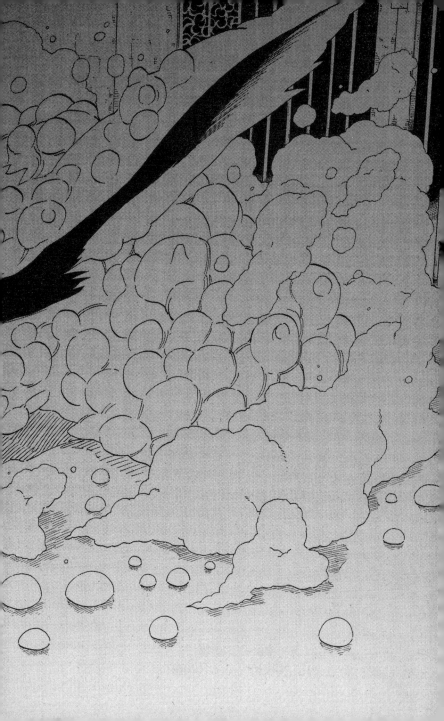

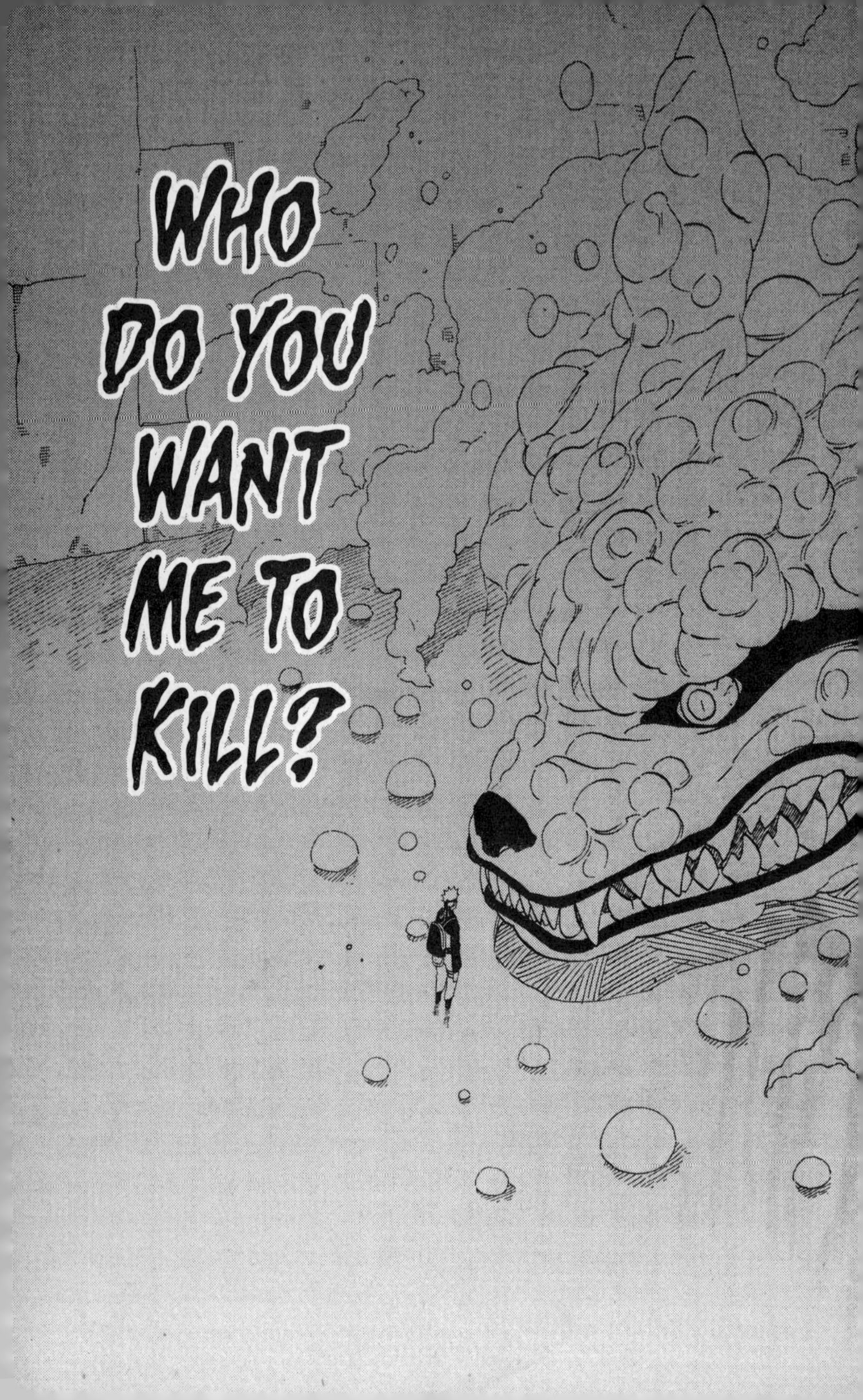
WHO DO YOU WANT ME TO KILL?

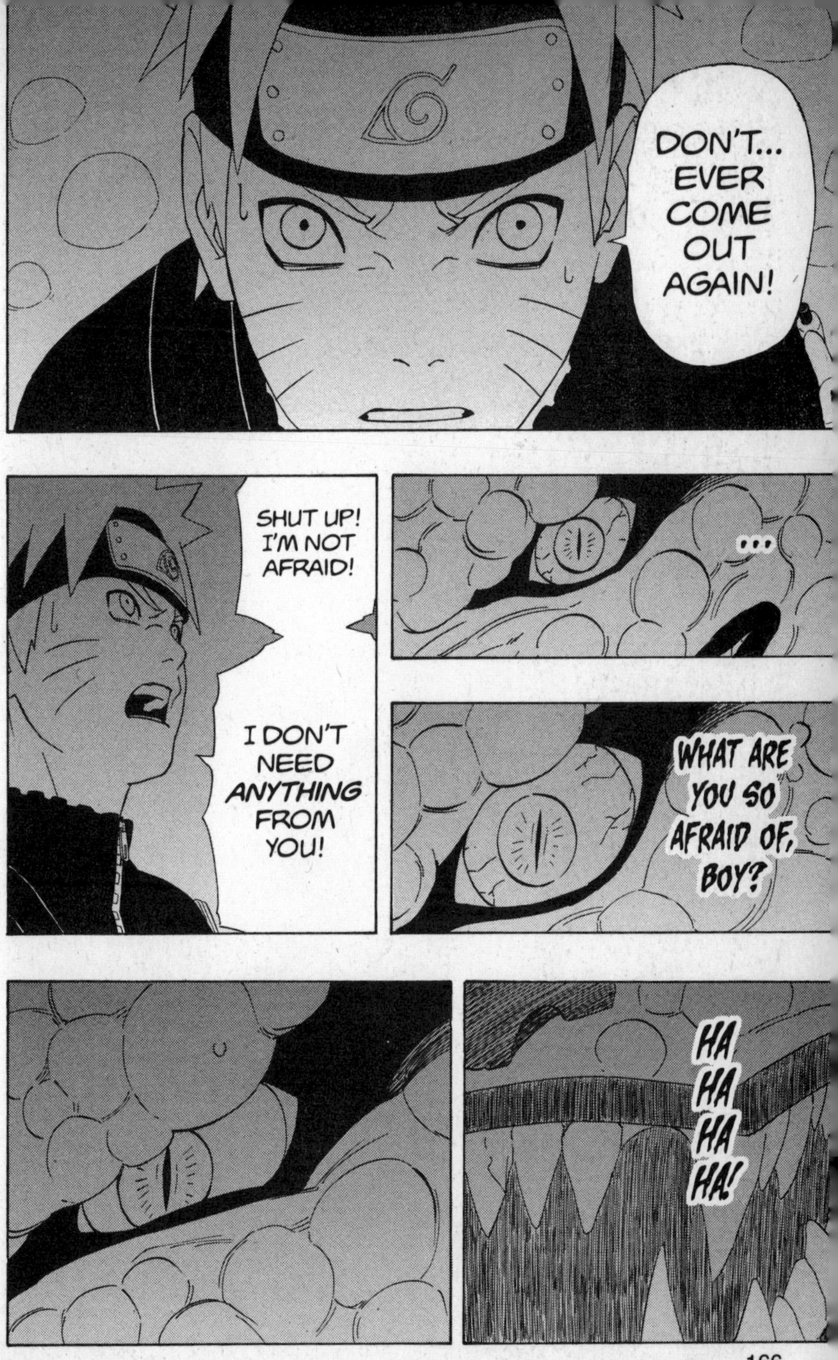
DON'T... EVER COME OUT AGAIN!
...
WHAT ARE YOU SO AFRAID OF, BOY?
SHUT UP! I'M NOT AFRAID!
I DON'T NEED ANYTHING FROM YOU!
HA HA HA HA!

READ THIS WAY

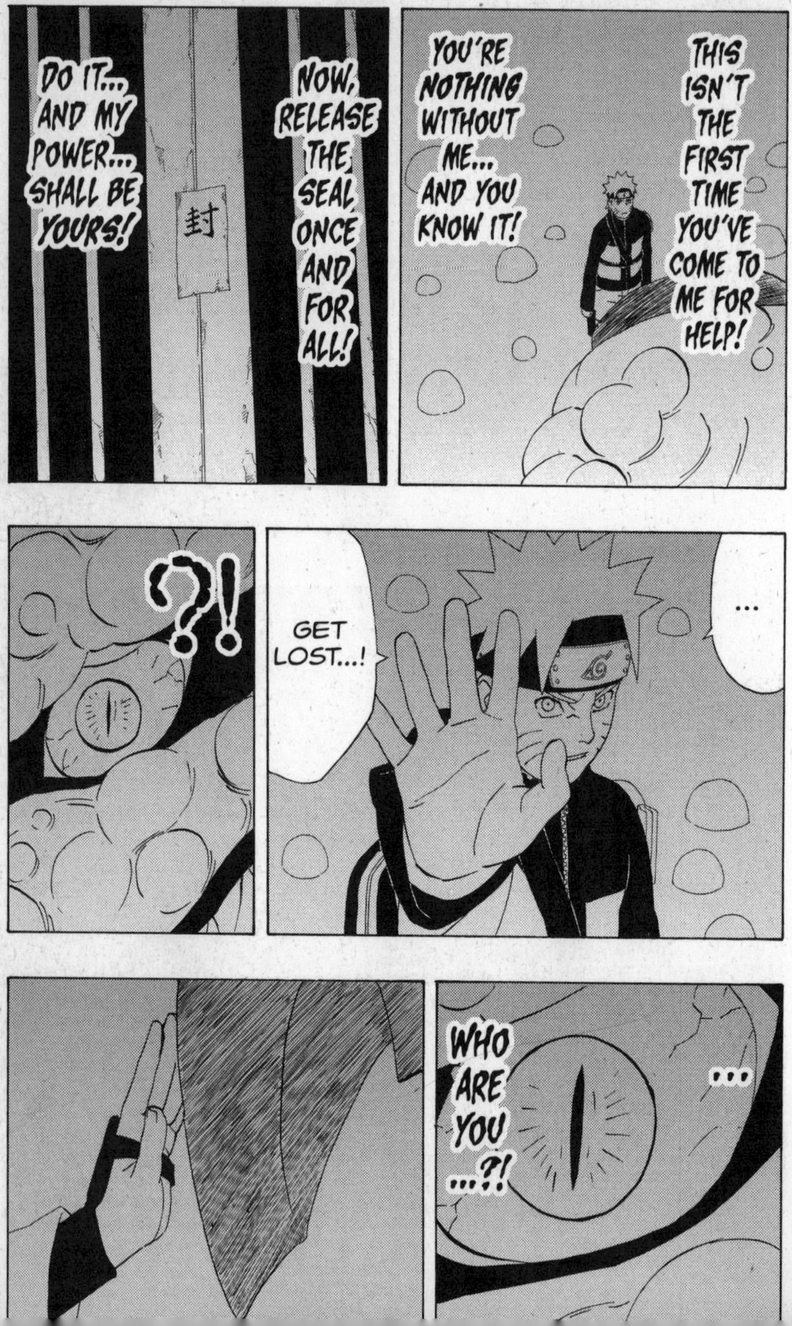
THIS ISN'T THE FIRST TIME YOU'VE COME TO ME FOR HELP!
YOU'RE NOTHING WITHOUT ME... AND YOU KNOW IT!
NOW, RELEASE THE SEAL ONCE AND FOR ALL!
封
DO IT... AND MY POWER... SHALL BE YOURS!
...
GET LOST...!
?!
...
WHO ARE YOU ...?!

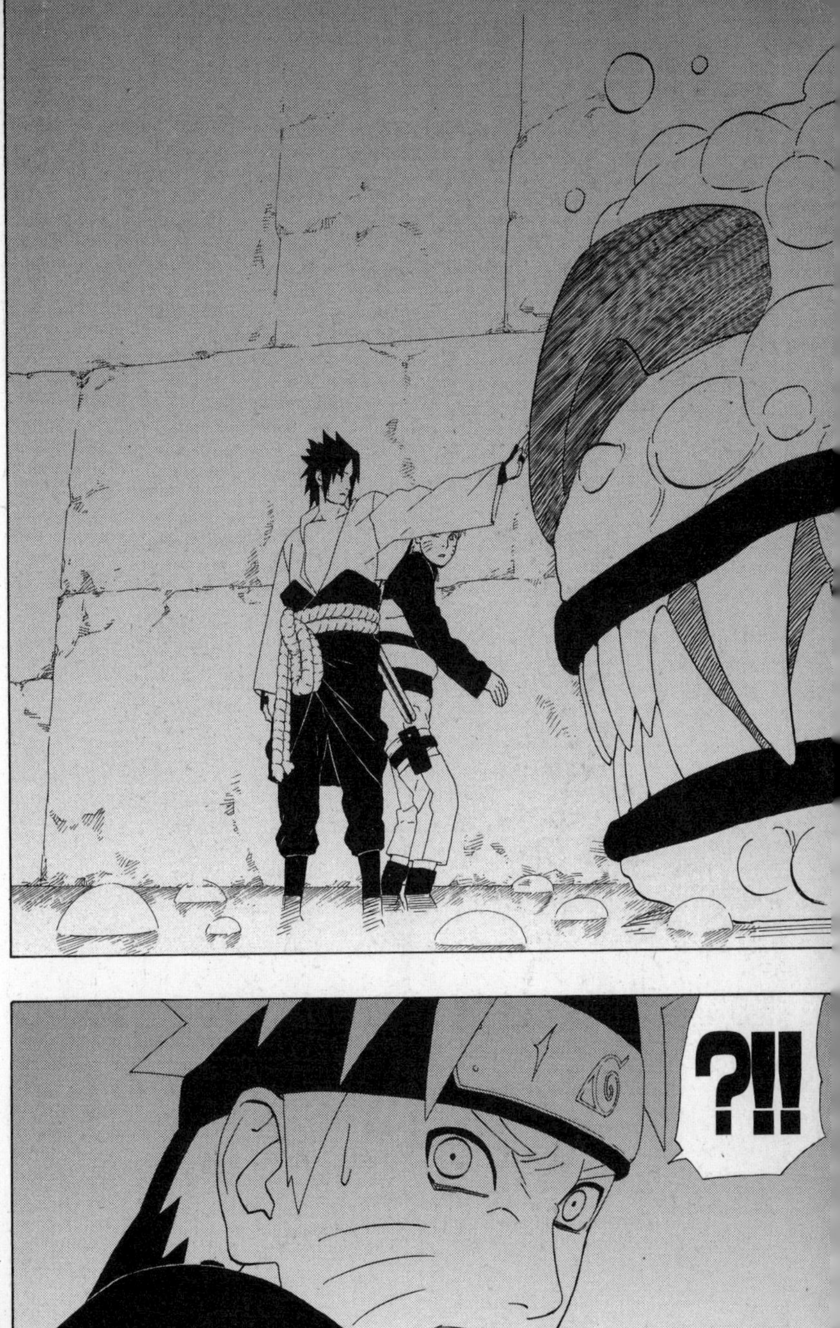
?!!

READ THIS WAY

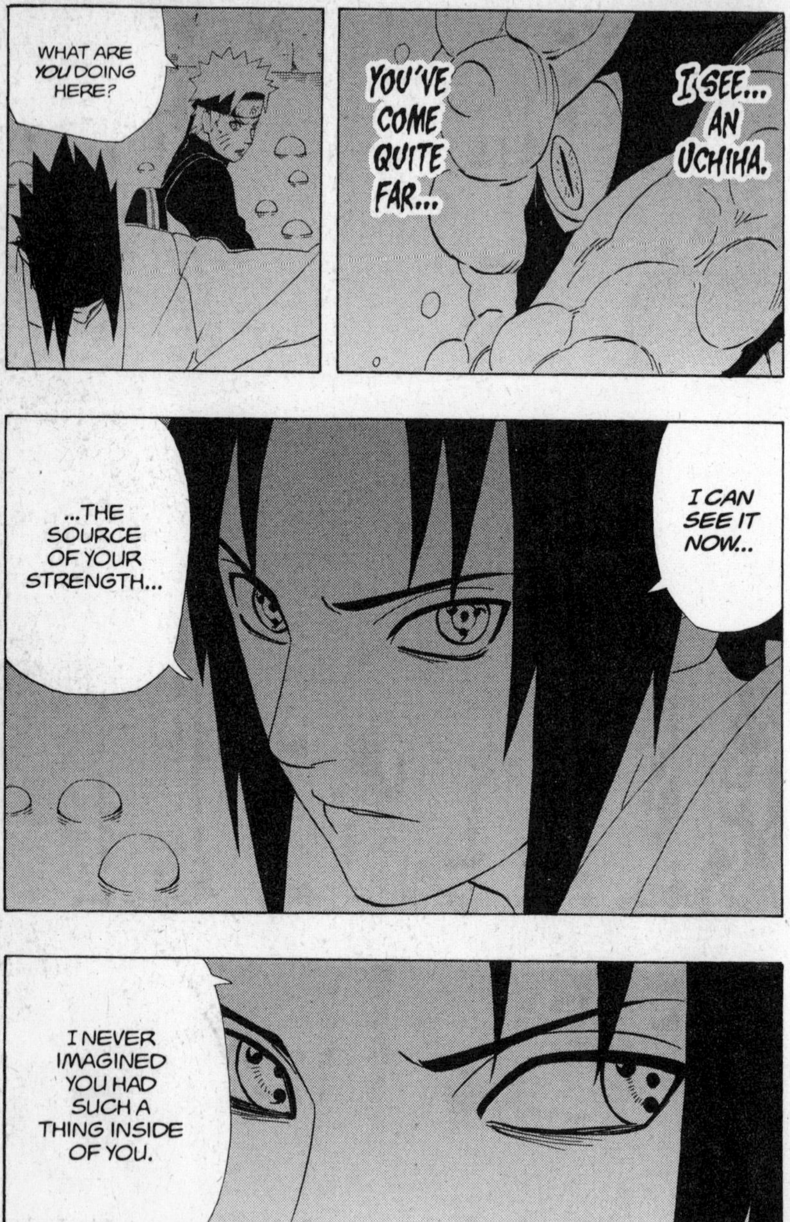
I SEE... AN UCHIHA.
YOU'VE COME QUITE FAR...
WHAT ARE *YOU* DOING HERE?
I CAN SEE IT NOW...
...THE SOURCE OF YOUR STRENGTH...
I NEVER IMAGINED YOU HAD SUCH A THING INSIDE OF YOU.

NARUTO

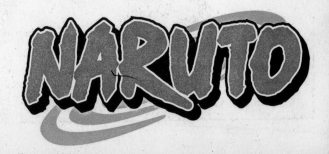

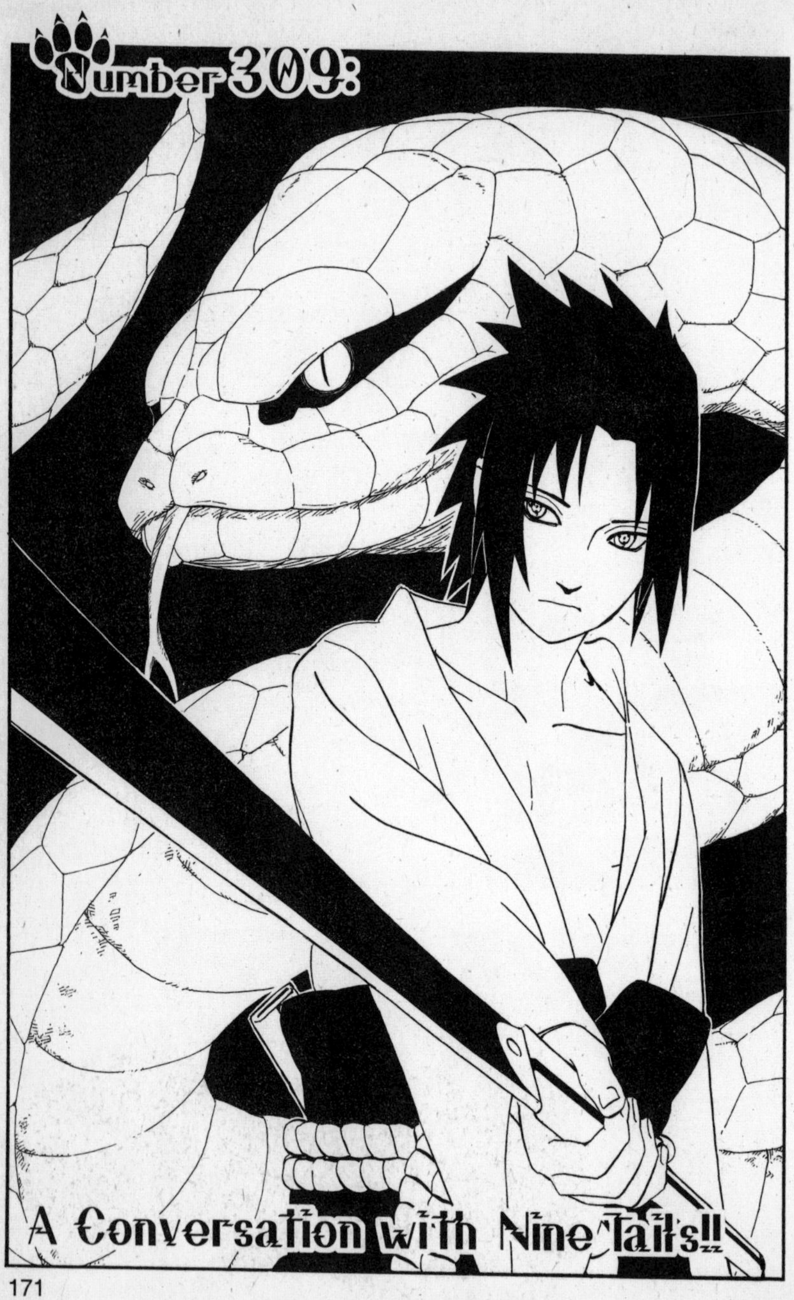
Number 309:
A Conversation with Nine Tails!!

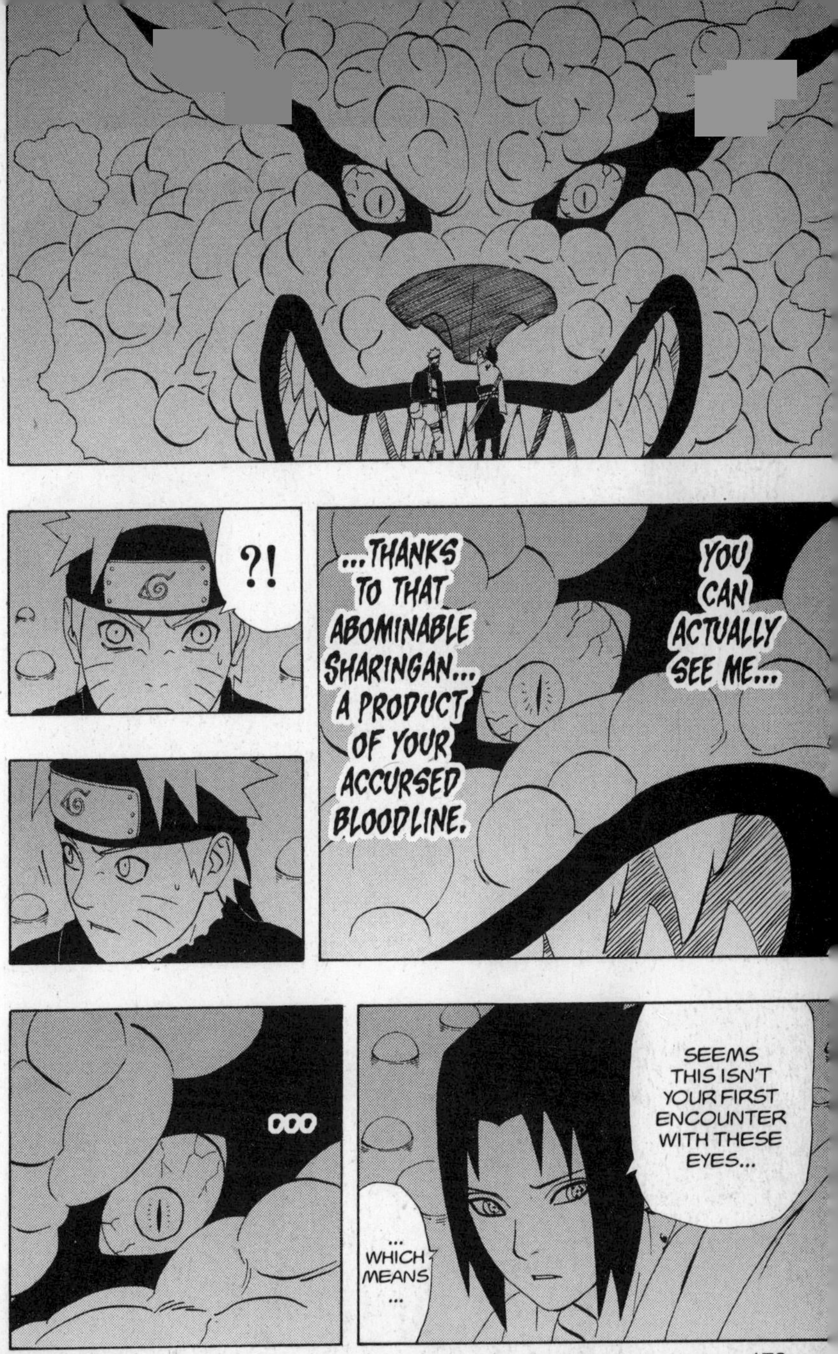
YOU CAN ACTUALLY SEE ME...
...THANKS TO THAT ABOMINABLE SHARINGAN... A PRODUCT OF YOUR ACCURSED BLOODLINE.
?!
SEEMS THIS ISN'T YOUR FIRST ENCOUNTER WITH THESE EYES...
...WHICH MEANS...
...

READ THIS WAY

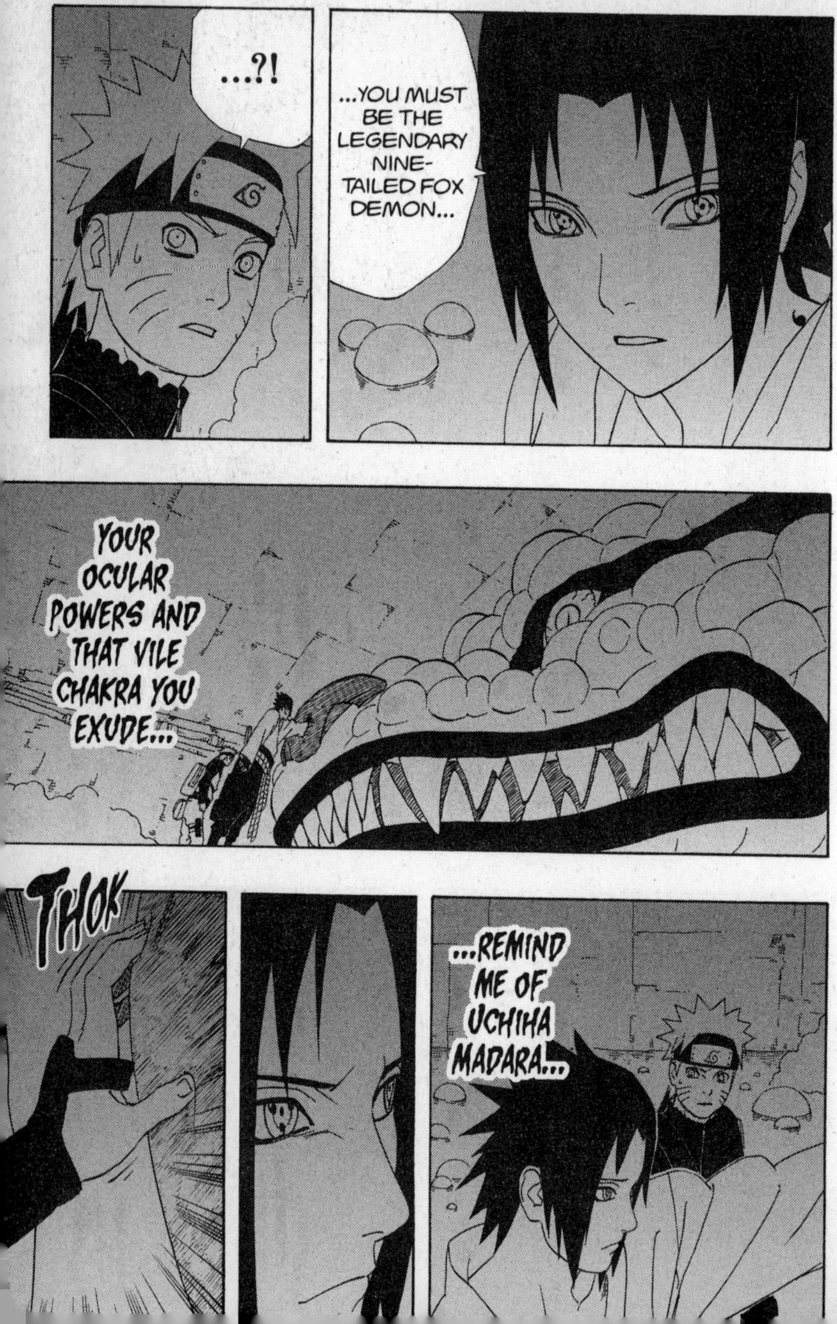
...YOU MUST BE THE LEGENDARY NINE-TAILED FOX DEMON...
...?!
YOUR OCULAR POWERS AND THAT VILE CHAKRA YOU EXUDE...
...REMIND ME OF UCHIHA MADARA...
THOK

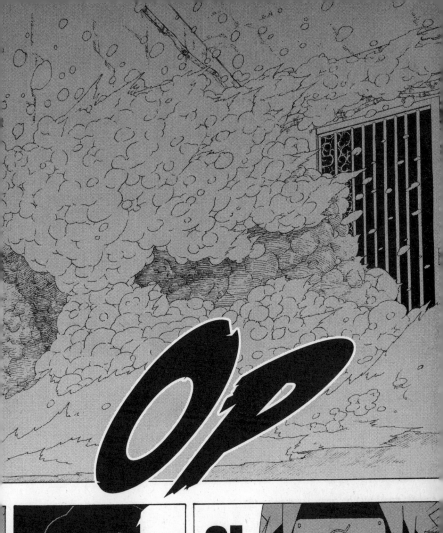

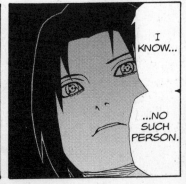

I KNOW...

...NO SUCH PERSON.

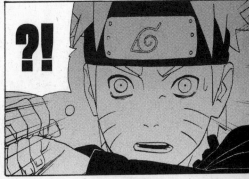

?!

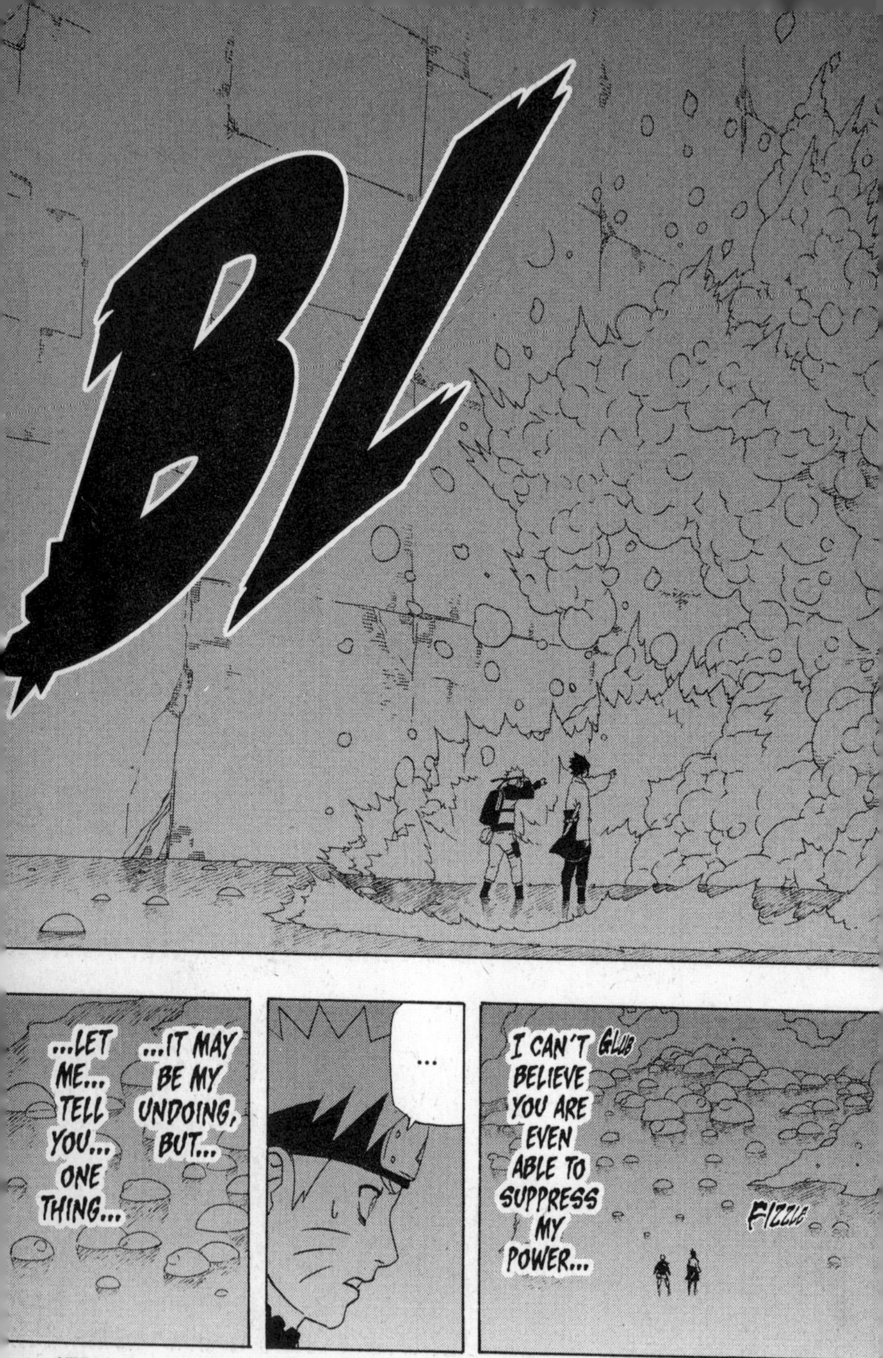
BL
I CAN'T GLUB BELIEVE YOU ARE EVEN ABLE TO SUPPRESS MY POWER...
FIZZLE
...
...IT MAY BE MY UNDOING, BUT...
...LET ME... TELL YOU... ONE THING...

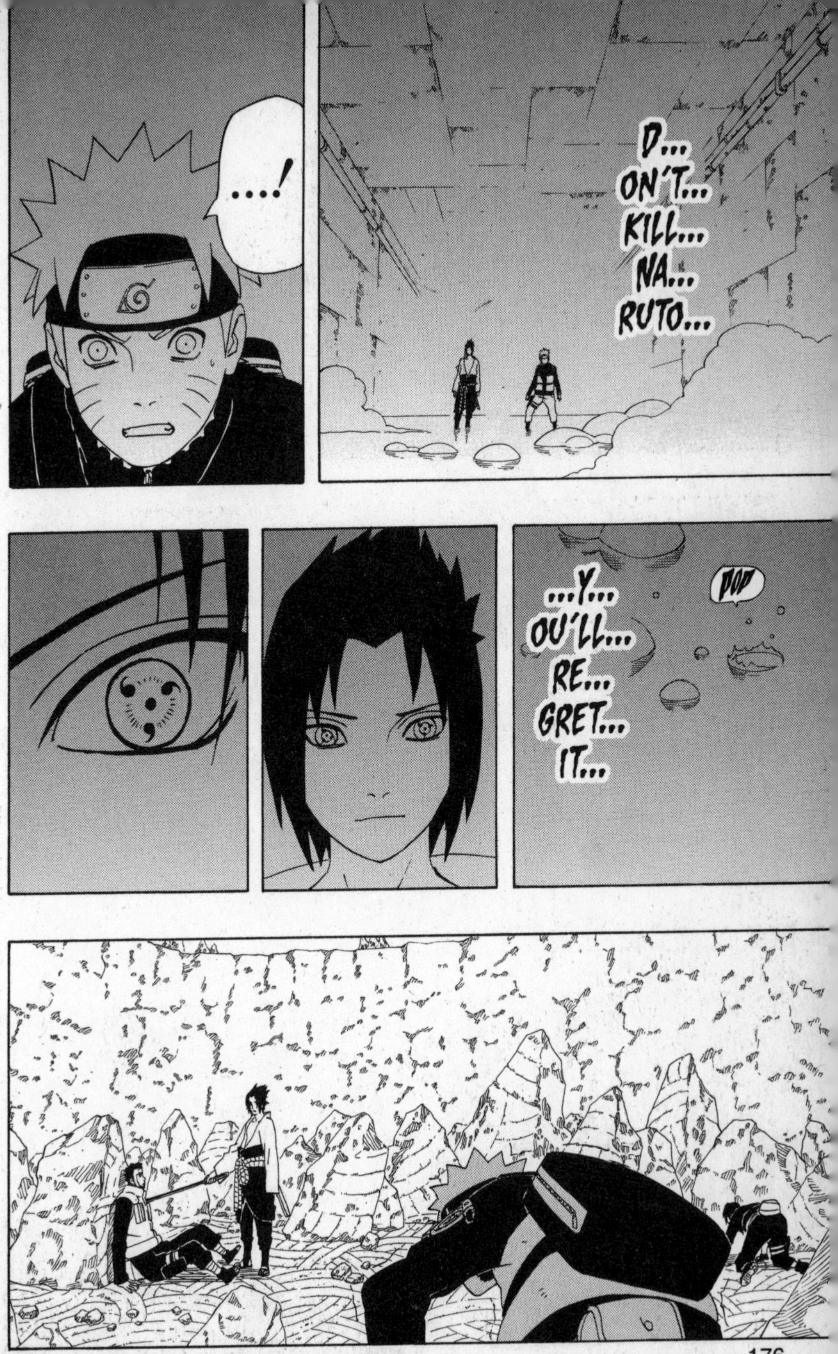
D... ON'T... KILL... NA... RUTO...
...!
...Y... OU'LL... RE... GRET... IT...
POP

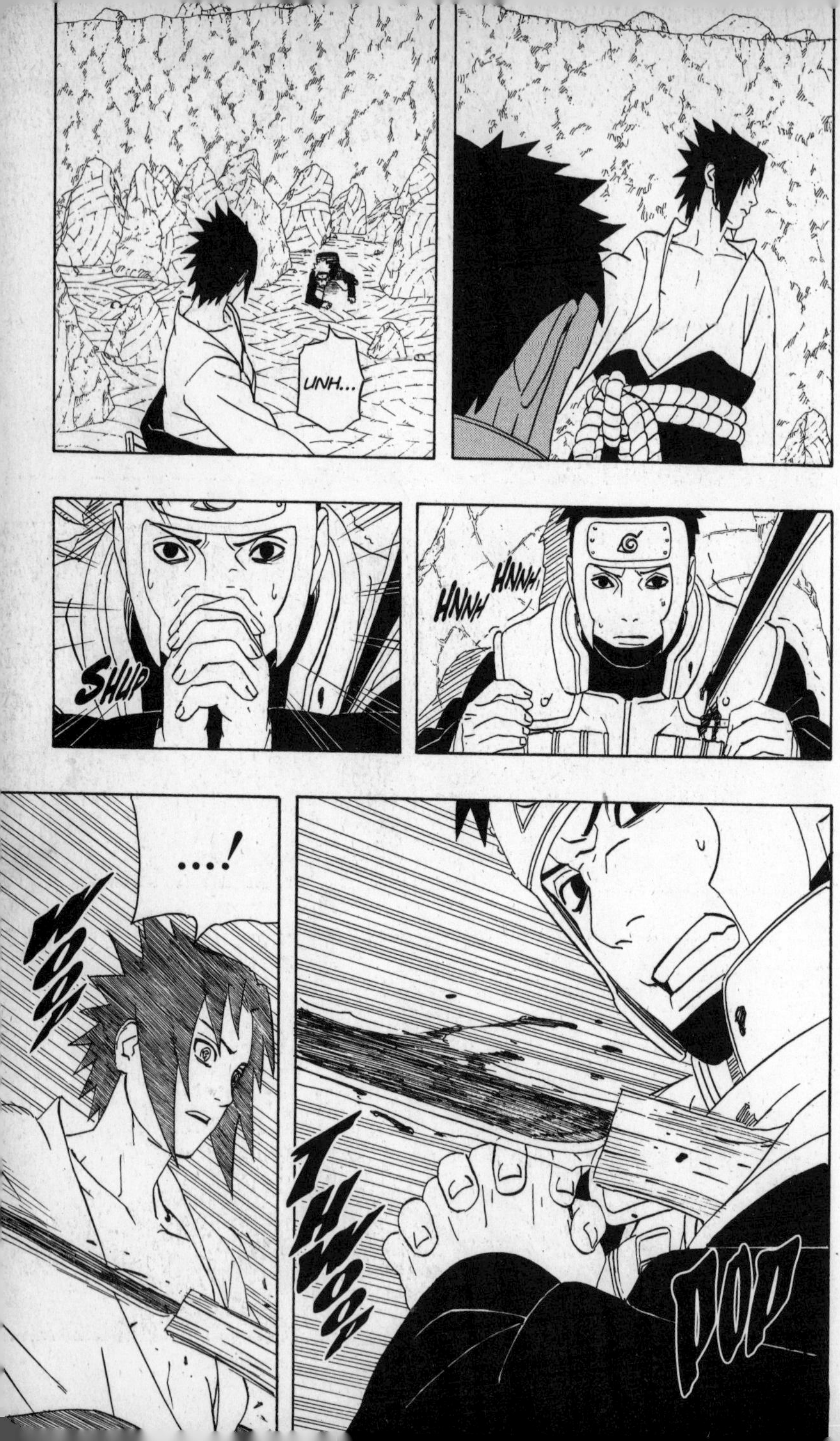
UNH...
HNNH, HNNH
SHUP
THWOOK
DOP
....!
WOOO

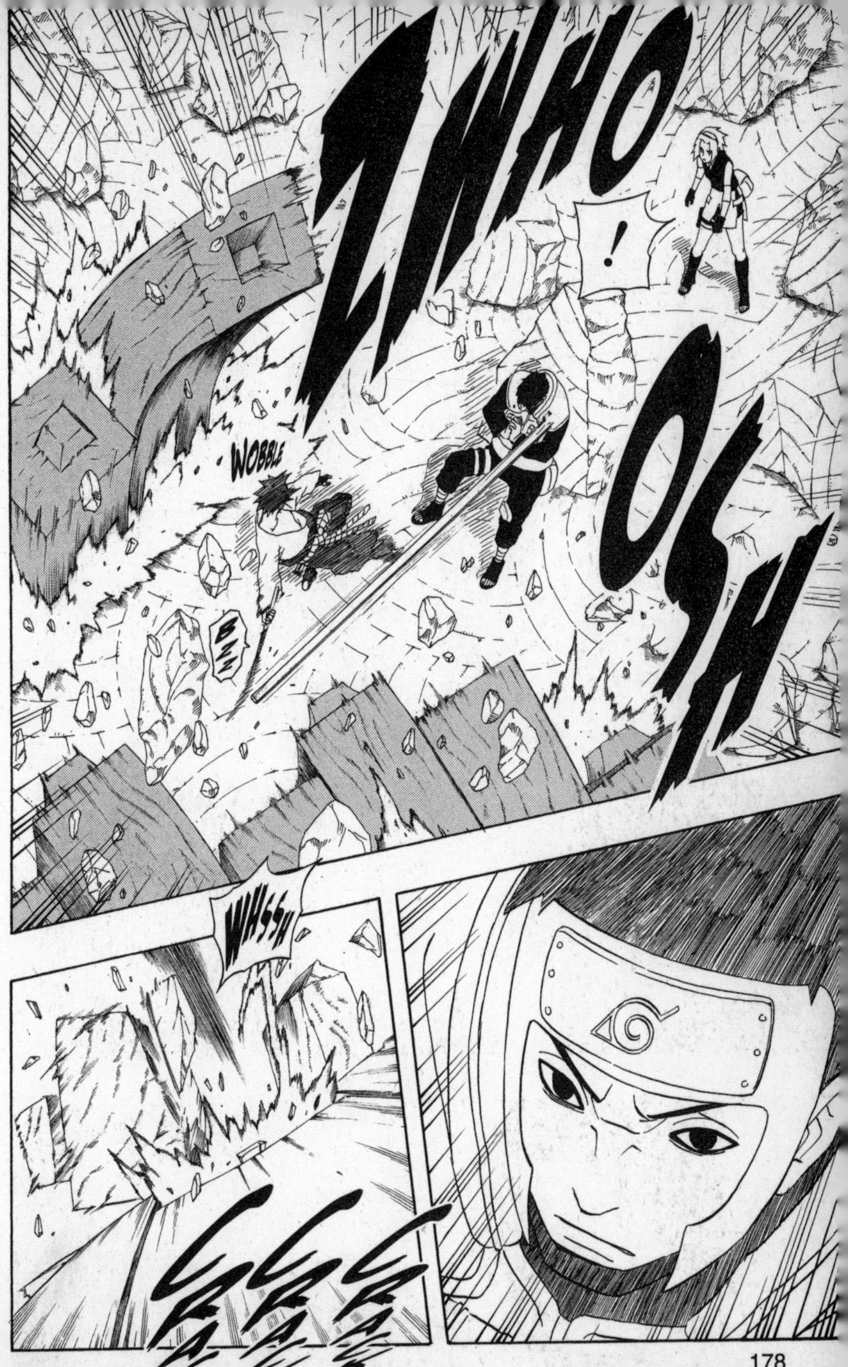
ZWHOOSH
!
WOBBLE
BZZZ
WHSSH
CRACK CRACK CRACK

READ THIS WAY

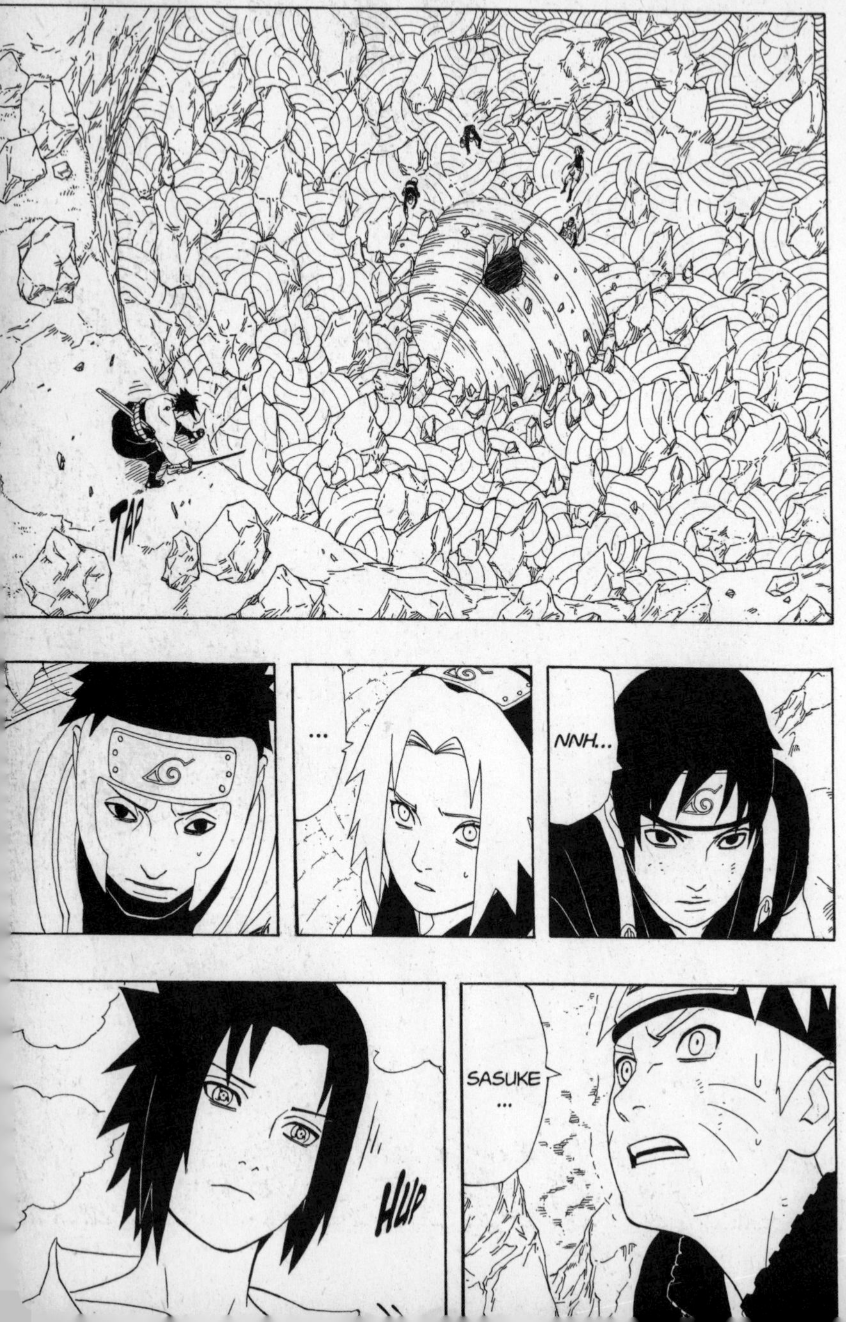
TAP
NNH...
...
SASUKE ...
HUP

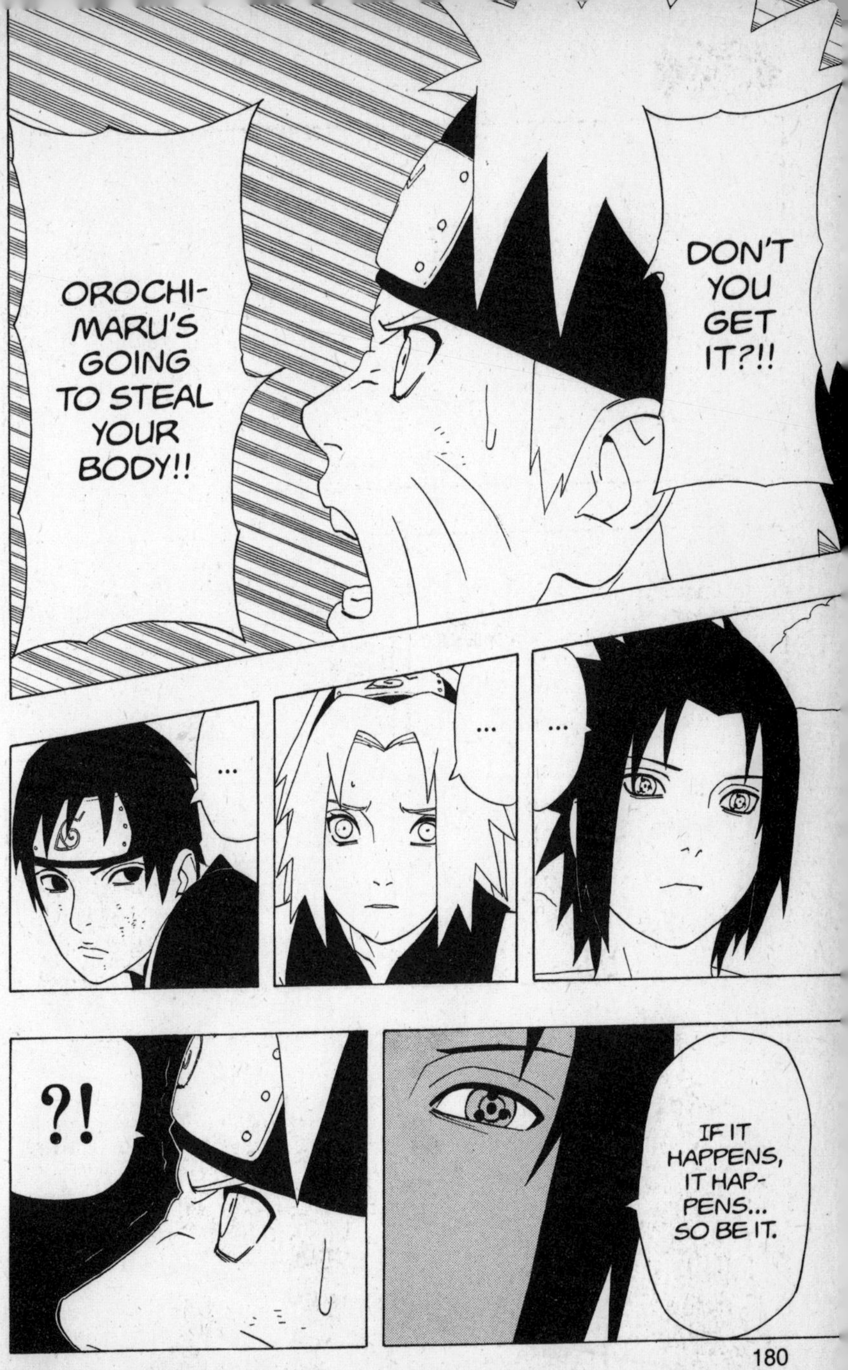
DON'T YOU GET IT?!!
OROCHI-MARU'S GOING TO STEAL YOUR BODY!!
...
...
...
IF IT HAPPENS, IT HAP-PENS... SO BE IT.
?!

READ THIS WAY

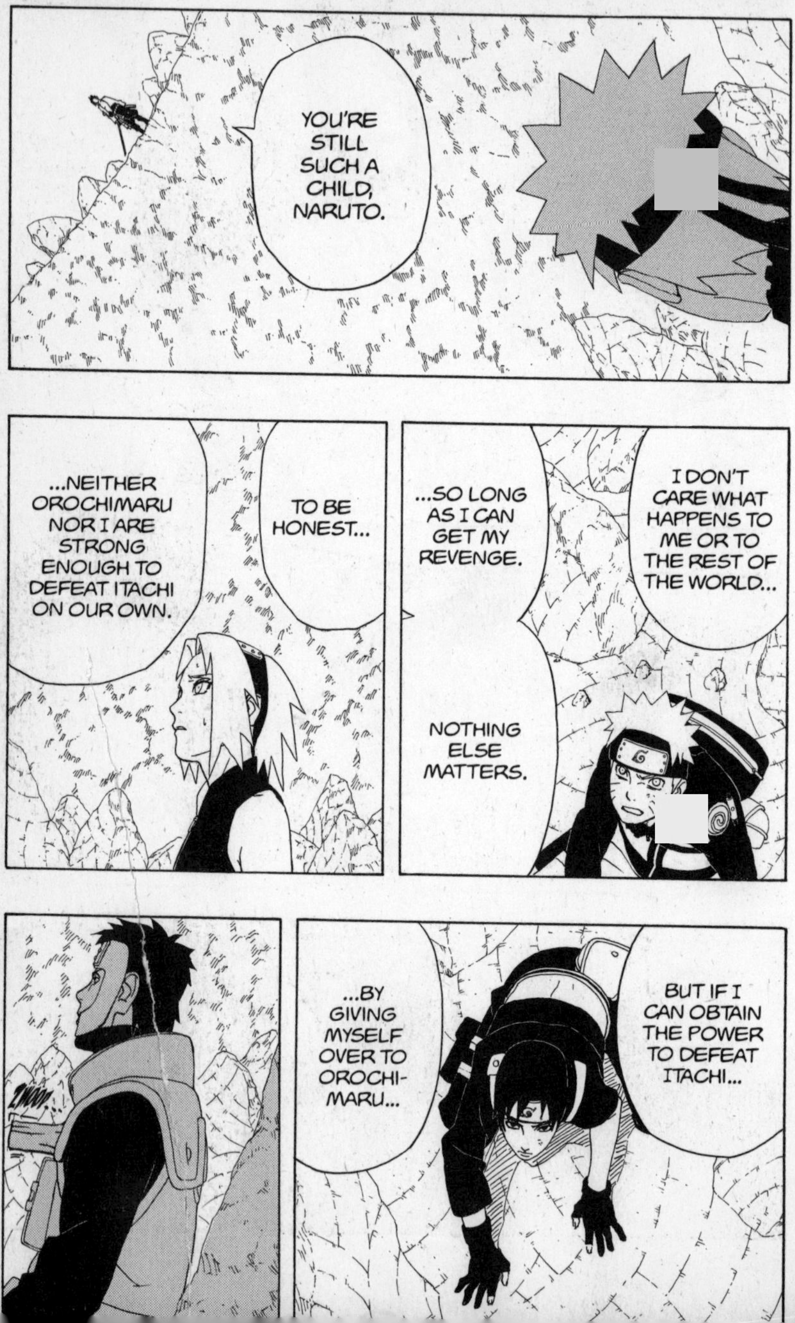
YOU'RE STILL SUCH A CHILD, NARUTO.
I DON'T CARE WHAT HAPPENS TO ME OR TO THE REST OF THE WORLD...
...SO LONG AS I CAN GET MY REVENGE.
NOTHING ELSE MATTERS.
TO BE HONEST...
...NEITHER OROCHIMARU NOR I ARE STRONG ENOUGH TO DEFEAT ITACHI ON OUR OWN.
BUT IF I CAN OBTAIN THE POWER TO DEFEAT ITACHI...
...BY GIVING MYSELF OVER TO OROCHI-MARU...

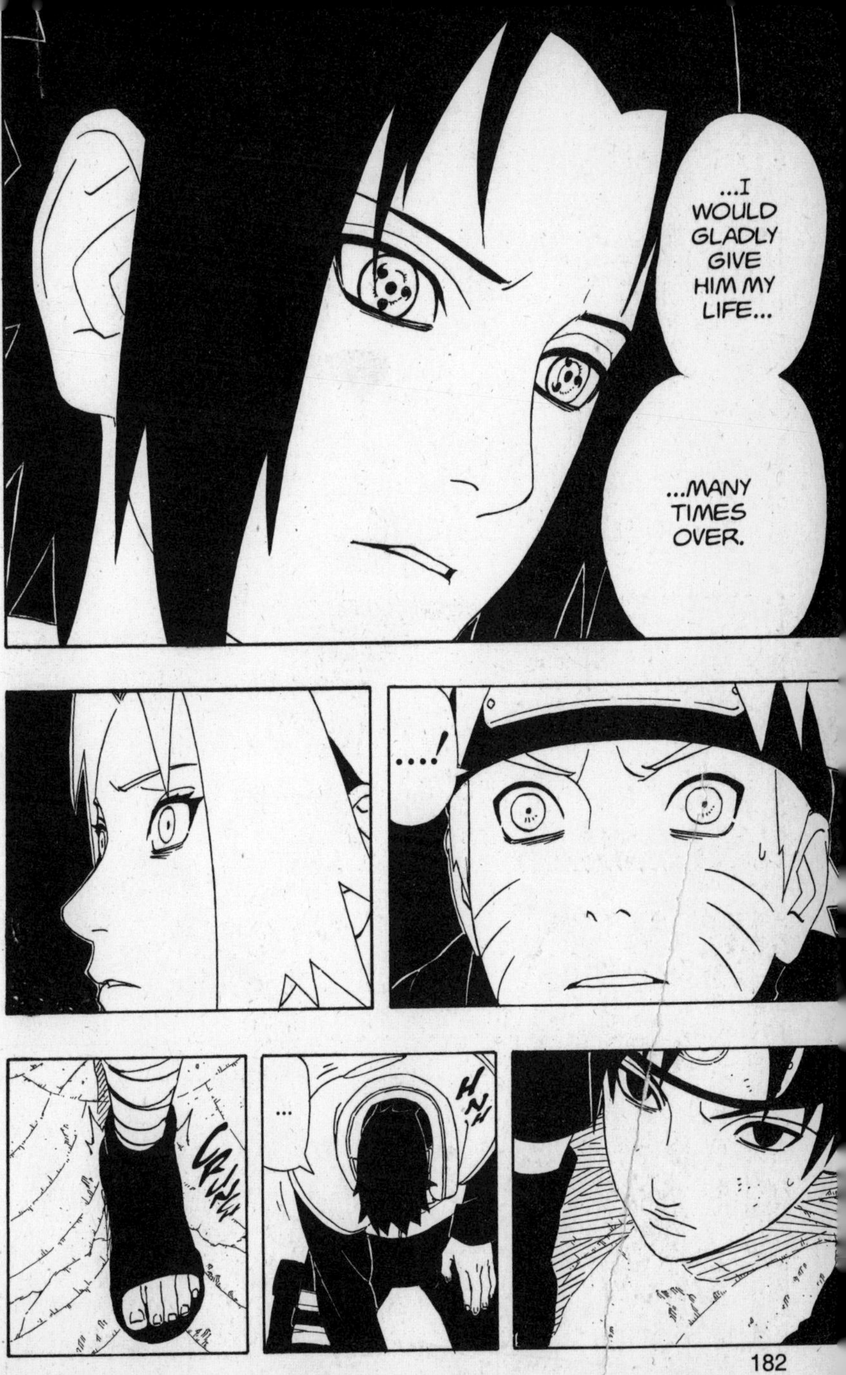
...I WOULD GLADLY GIVE HIM MY LIFE...
...MANY TIMES OVER.
....!
...
HNN

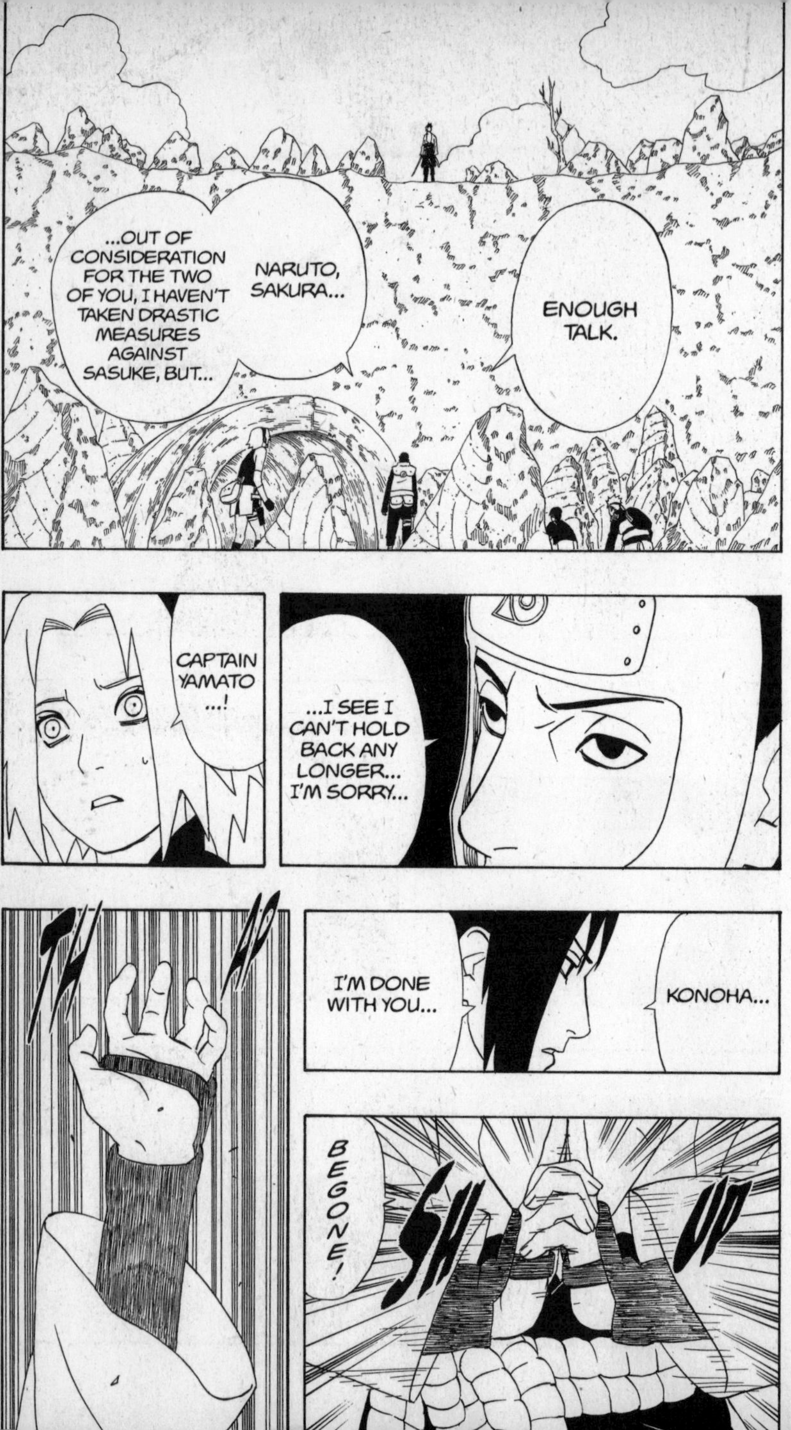
ENOUGH TALK.
NARUTO, SAKURA...
...OUT OF CONSIDERATION FOR THE TWO OF YOU, I HAVEN'T TAKEN DRASTIC MEASURES AGAINST SASUKE, BUT...
...I SEE I CAN'T HOLD BACK ANY LONGER... I'M SORRY...
CAPTAIN YAMATO ...!
KONOHA...
I'M DONE WITH YOU...
BEGONE!
SH
OOP
TH
AP

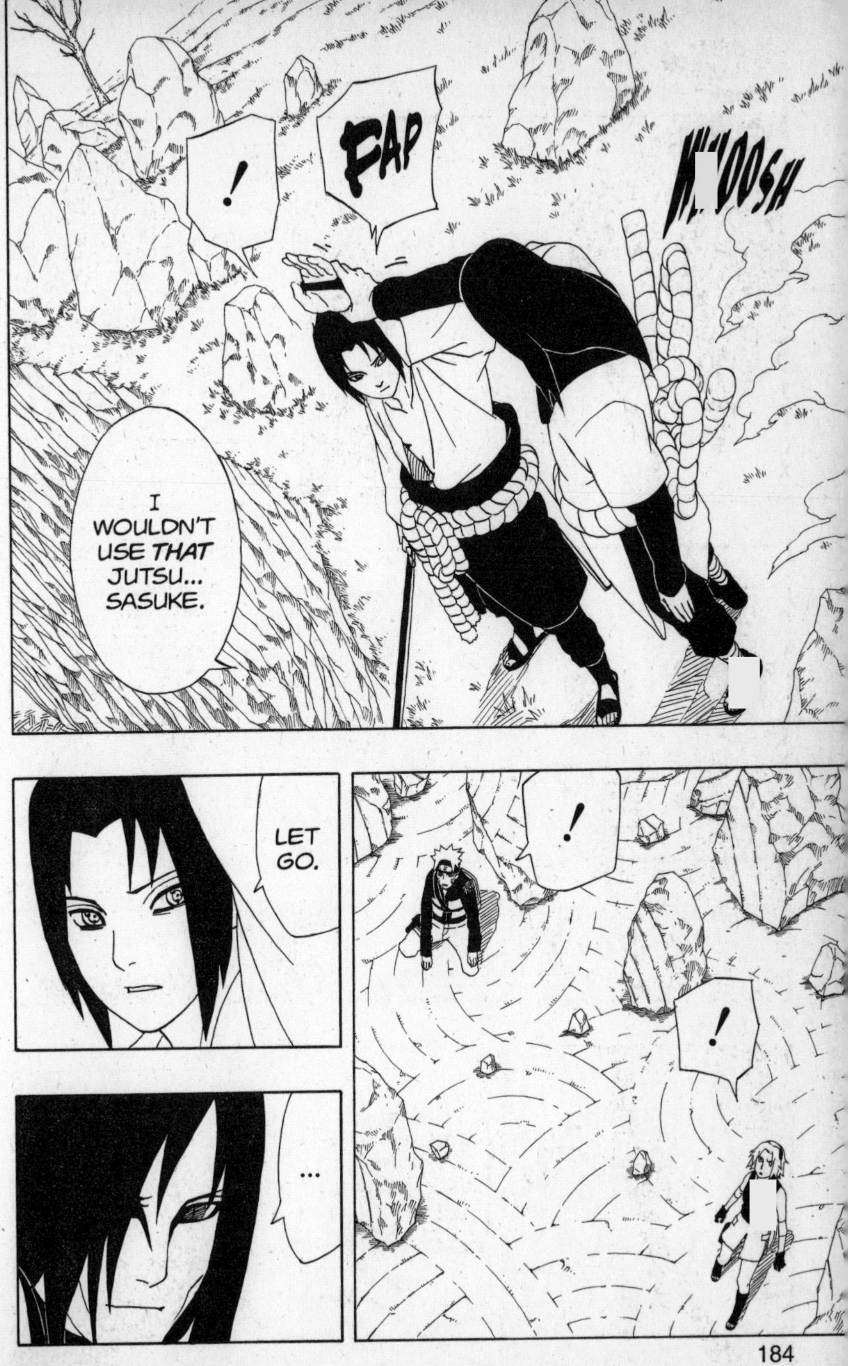
FAP
!
I WOULDN'T USE THAT JUTSU... SASUKE.
!
!
LET GO.
...

READ THIS WAY

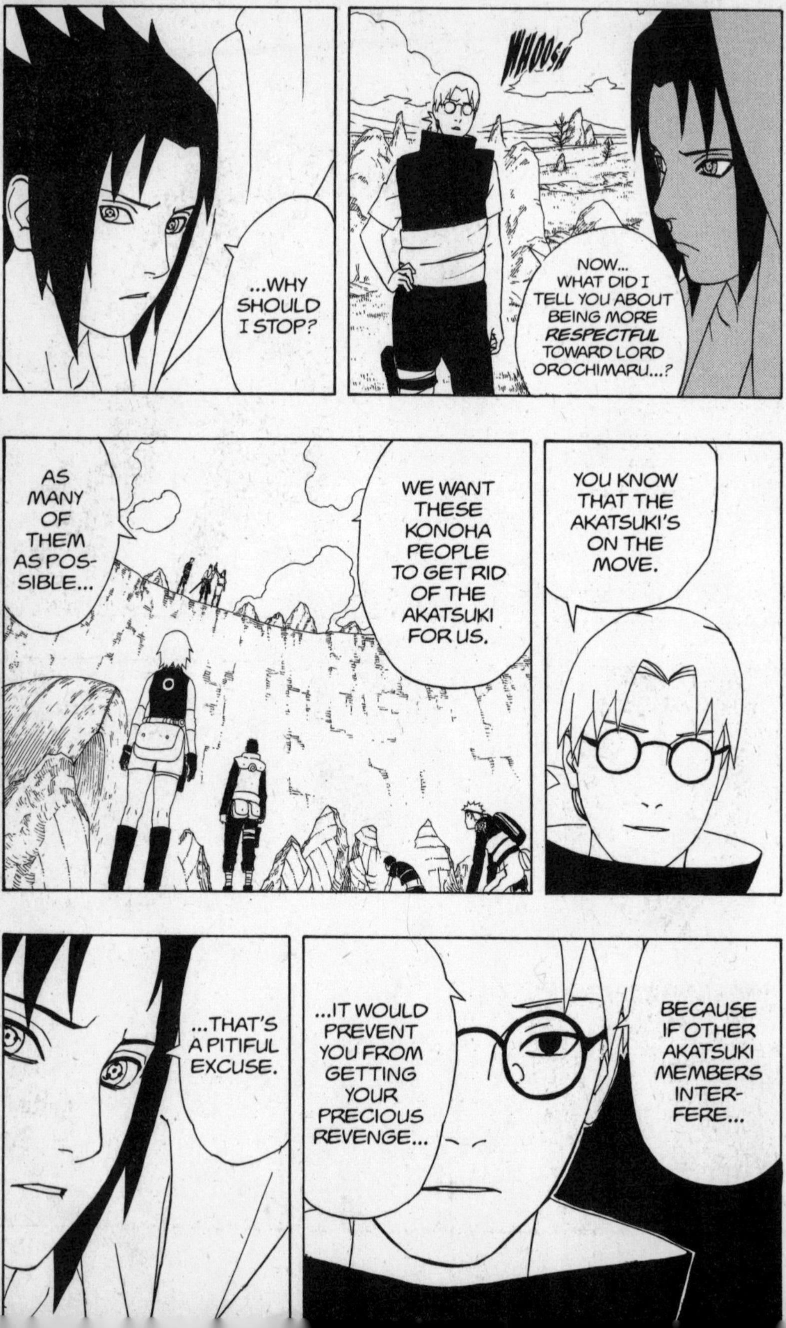
WHOOSH
NOW... WHAT DID I TELL YOU ABOUT BEING MORE ***RESPECTFUL*** TOWARD LORD OROCHIMARU...?
...WHY SHOULD I STOP?
YOU KNOW THAT THE AKATSUKI'S ON THE MOVE.
WE WANT THESE KONOHA PEOPLE TO GET RID OF THE AKATSUKI FOR US.
AS MANY OF THEM AS POS-SIBLE...
BECAUSE IF OTHER AKATSUKI MEMBERS INTER-FERE...
...IT WOULD PREVENT YOU FROM GETTING YOUR PRECIOUS REVENGE...
...THAT'S A PITIFUL EXCUSE.

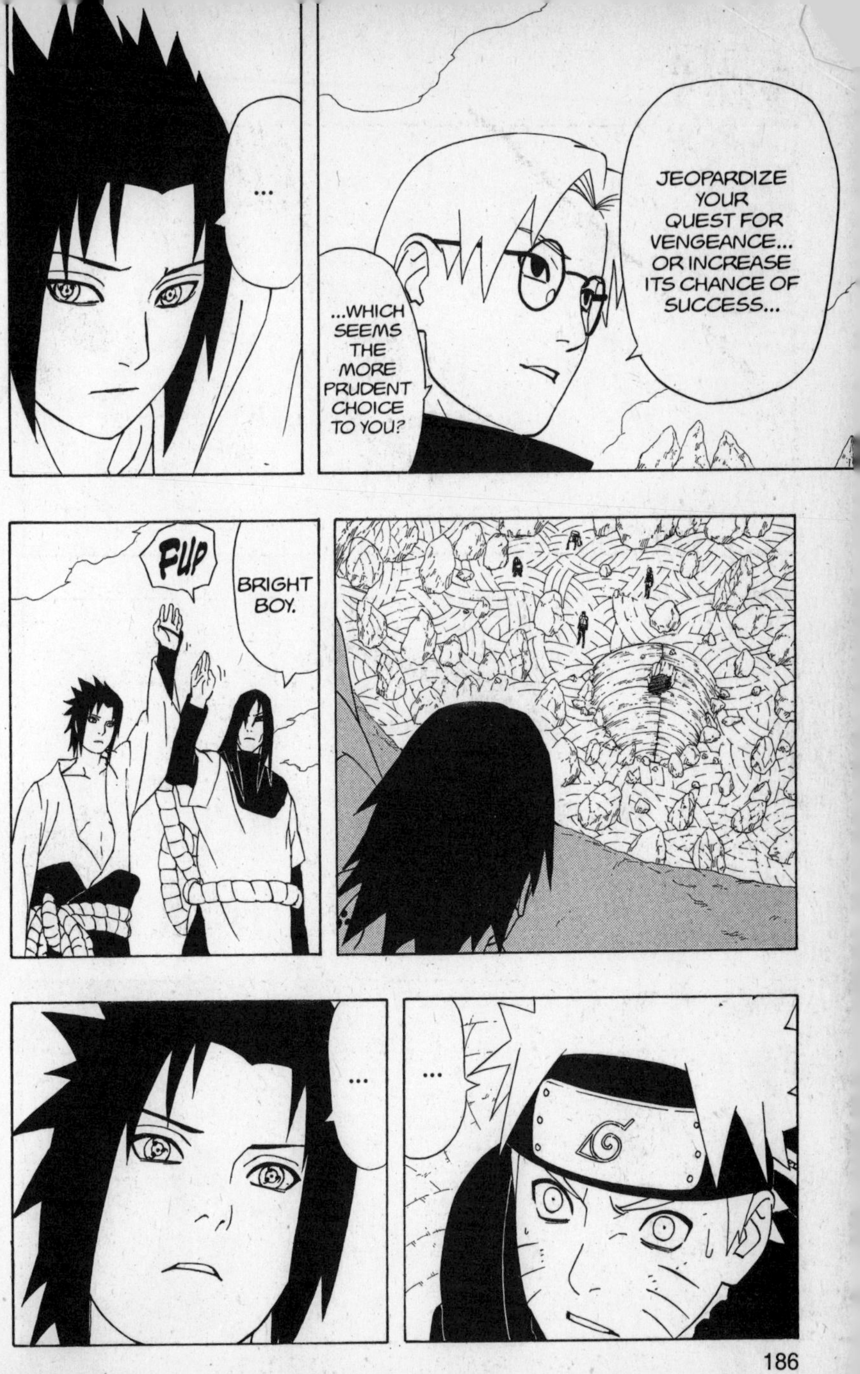
JEOPARDIZE YOUR QUEST FOR VENGEANCE... OR INCREASE ITS CHANCE OF SUCCESS...
...WHICH SEEMS THE MORE PRUDENT CHOICE TO YOU?
...
BRIGHT BOY.
FUP
...
...

READ THIS WAY

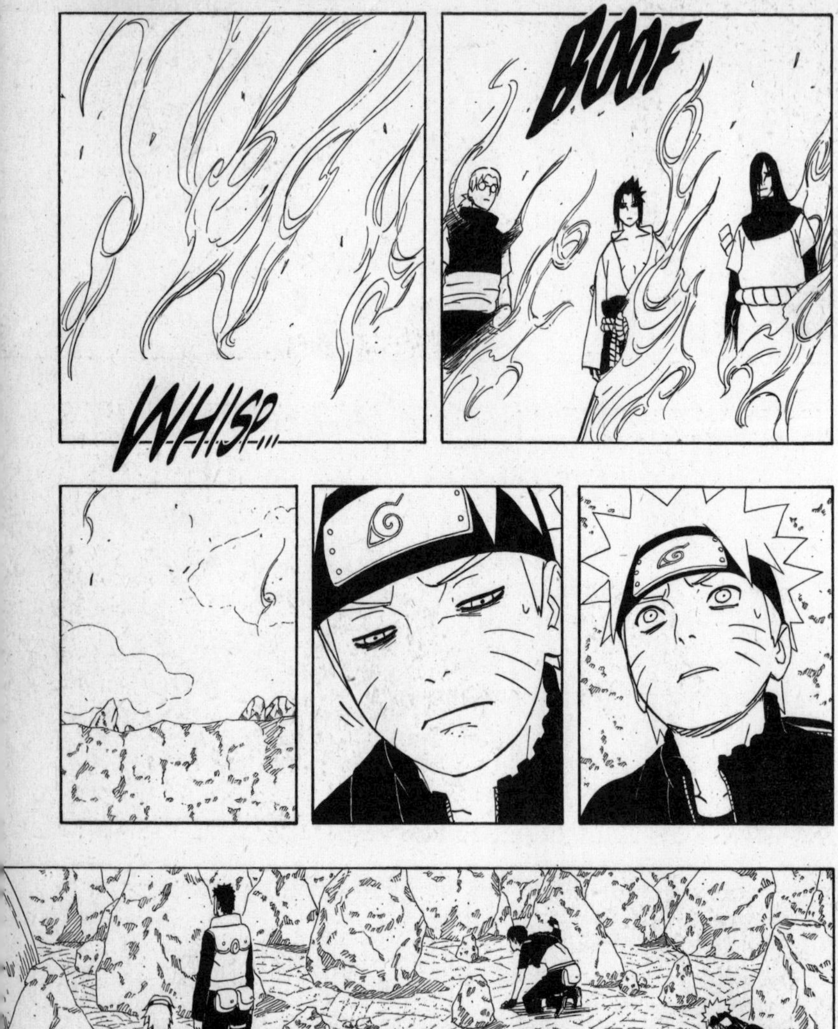
BOOF
WHISP...

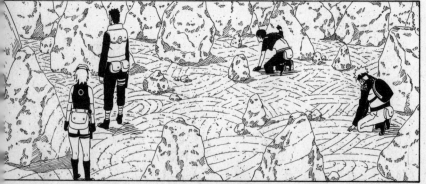

TO BE CONTINUED IN *NARUTO* VOL. 35!

ME? YOU'RE USUALLY THE DOER.

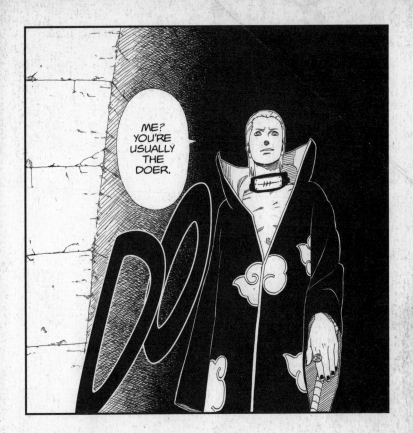

IN THE NEXT VOLUME...

THE NEW TWO

Naruto accelerates his training while the Akatsuki systematically continue their assault on those with the Tailed Beasts inside them. First on the list, Yukito, a ninja from the Land of Clouds believed to harbor the Two-Tailed Beast. Will yet another ninja fall to the evils of the Akatsuki?

AVAILABLE NOW!

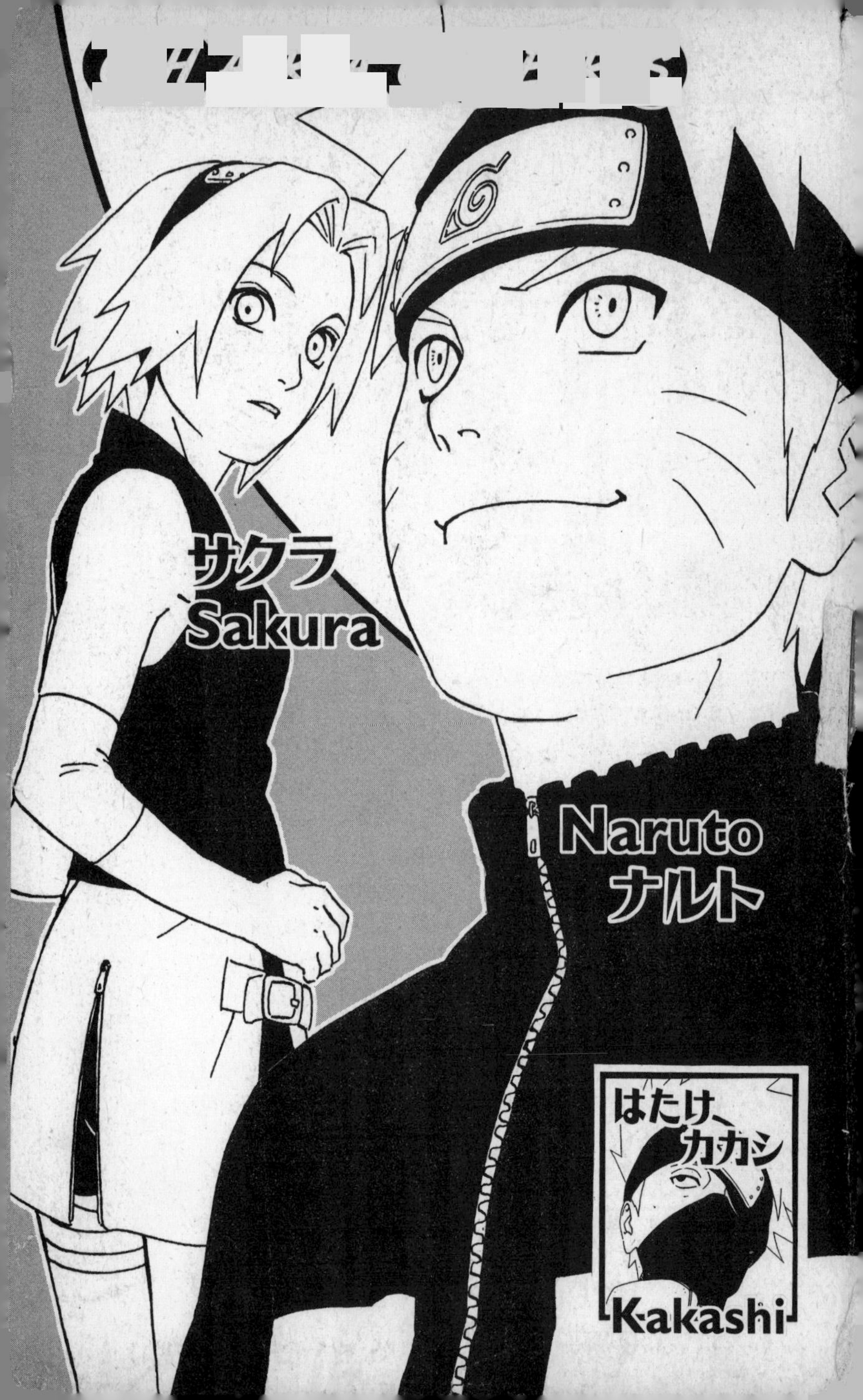
サクラ
Sakura
Naruto
ナルト
はたけカカシ
Kakashi

SHONEN JUMP MANGA EDITION

NARUTO

VOL. 34

THE REUNION

STORY AND ART BY

MASASHI KISHIMOTO

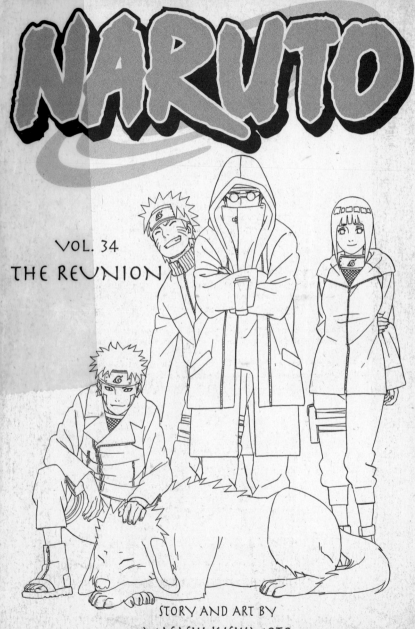

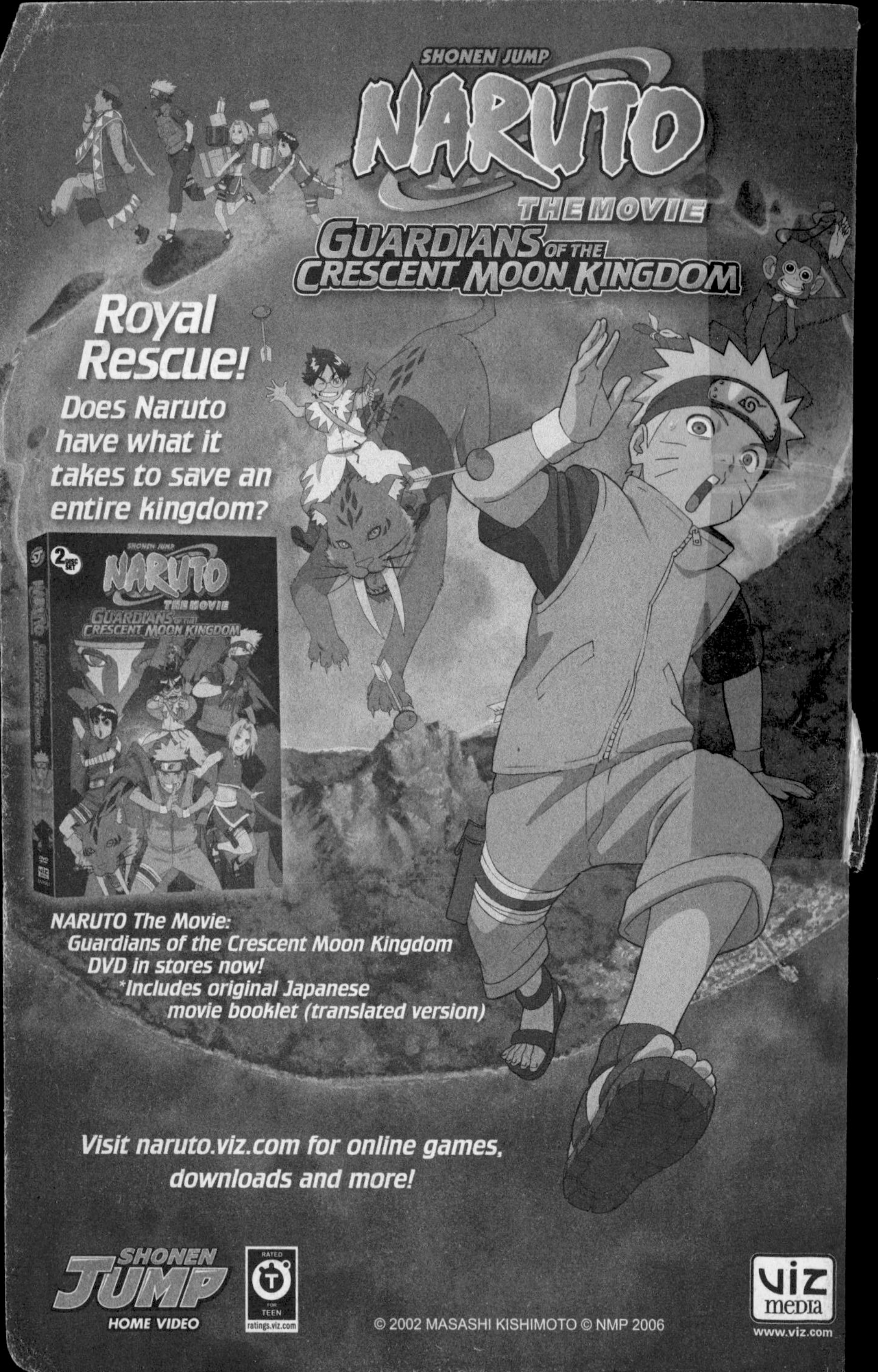
SHONEN JUMP
NARUTO
THE MOVIE
GUARDIANS OF THE CRESCENT MOON KINGDOM
Royal Rescue!
Does Naruto have what it takes to save an entire kingdom?
NARUTO The Movie: Guardians of the Crescent Moon Kingdom DVD in stores now!
*Includes original Japanese movie booklet (translated version)
Visit naruto.viz.com for online games, downloads and more!
SHONEN JUMP HOME VIDEO
RATED T FOR TEEN ratings.viz.com
© 2002 MASASHI KISHIMOTO © NMP 2006
viz media
www.viz.com

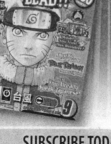
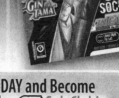

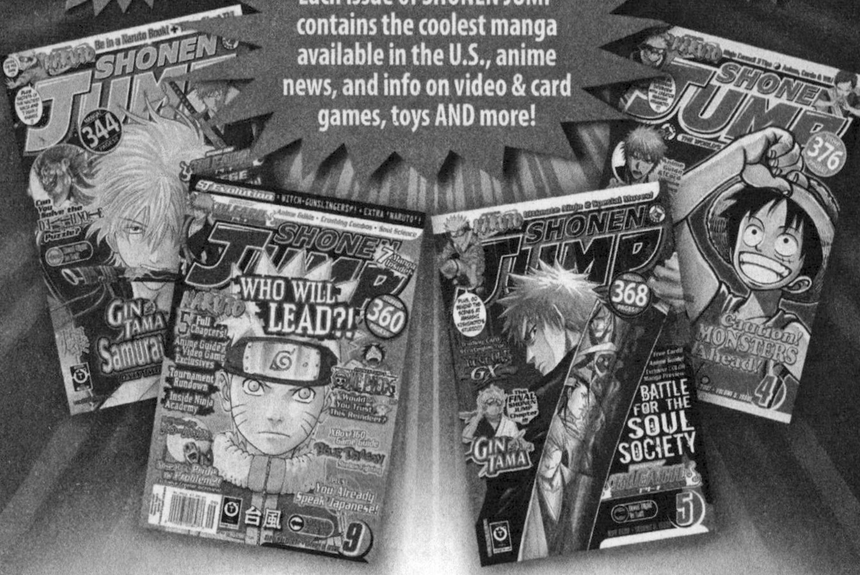

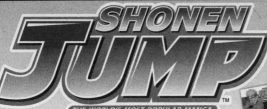

(stamped): CHASE BRANCH LIBRARY
17731 W. SEVEN MILE RD.
DETROIT, MI 48235
578-8002